LEGACIES OF ANCIENT GREECE IN CONTEMPORARY PERSPECTIVES

Edited by

Thomas M. F. Gerry
Laurentian University

Series in World History

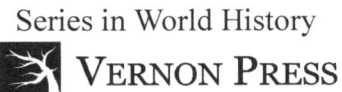

Copyright © 2023 by the authors.

All rights reserved. No part of this publication may be reproduced, stored in a retrieval system, or transmitted in any form or by any means, electronic, mechanical, photocopying, recording, or otherwise, without the prior permission of Vernon Art and Science Inc.
www.vernonpress.com

In the Americas:
Vernon Press
1000 N West Street, Suite 1200,
Wilmington, Delaware 19801
United States

In the rest of the world:
Vernon Press
C/Sancti Espiritu 17,
Malaga, 29006
Spain

Series in World History

Library of Congress Control Number: 2021947188

ISBN: 978-1-64889-554-8

Also available: 978-1-64889-111-3 [Hardback]; 978-1-64889-445-9 [PDF, E-Book]

Product and company names mentioned in this work are the trademarks of their respective owners. While every care has been taken in preparing this work, neither the authors nor Vernon Art and Science Inc. may be held responsible for any loss or damage caused or alleged to be caused directly or indirectly by the information contained in it.

Every effort has been made to trace all copyright holders, but if any have been inadvertently overlooked the publisher will be pleased to include any necessary credits in any subsequent reprint or edition.

Cover design by Vernon Press. Cover image by Senti Chanadiaki, used with permission.

To Senti Chaniadaki

Senti Chanadiaki, Paros, 2019

Table of Contents

List of Illustrations	vii
Acknowledgement	xi
List of Contributors	xiii
Editor's Introduction	xvii

Thomas M. F. Gerry

Chapter 1
Bearing Witness: Becoming Greek in the Diaspora   1

Helen Vatsikopoulos

University of Technology, Sydney, Australia

Chapter 2
Transatlantic Hellas: Archiving Eastern Mediterranean Collections and Materials in the Smithsonian Institution   23

Alexander Nagel

Fashion Institute of Technology, State University of New York; Smithsonian Institution, National Museum of Natural History

Chapter 3
The Greeks of Tarpon Springs in the Hollywood Imaginary   65

Velvet L. Yates

University of Florida

Chapter 4
Pedagogies and Possibilities of Crisis: Greek and Iranian Film   77

Sahar Siavashi

University of Lethbridge, Canada

William Ramp

University of Lethbridge, Canada

Chapter 5
**Decolonizing the Boundaries of Belonging and Citizenship:
Turning to Ancient Hellenic and Indigenous
Cosmopolitanisms during the Climate Crisis** 137
Cynthia J. Alexander
Acadia University, Canada

Chapter 6
**Common Divine Healing Themes in Ancient Greek and
Traditional Zulu Culture** 181
Stephen Edwards
University of Zululand, South Africa

Chapter 7
Athens is Burning: A Tragedy in Three Acts 197
Gabrielle Moyer
Stanford University, U.S.A.

Chapter 8
**The Inspirational Role of Greek Traditional Music in
the Composition of Modern and Postmodern Guitar
Repertoire** 235
Ioannis Andronoglou
University of Western Macedonia, Greece

Chapter 9
The Legacy of Talos: From Antiquity until Now 257
Hélène Jeannin
Orange Innovation, France

Ioannis Kostopoulos
Independent Researcher

Index 279

List of Illustrations

Figure 1.1.	Port Adelaide Greek school, 1973.	5
Figure 1.2.	Playing Northern Epirus in a Greek school play, 1975.	7
Figure 1.3.	Graffiti in Florina, Greece, 2016.	10
Figure 2.1.	Elisavet Contaxaki's "Classical Bouquet."	28
Figure 2.2.	Elisavet Contaxaki's "Classical Bouquet," interior detail.	29
Figure 2.3.	Elisavet Contaxaki's "Classical Bouquet," interior detail with pressed wild flowers from Athens in Greece.	29
Figure 2.4.	A plaque depicting the Parthenon, donated by George W. Samson in 1885 (NMNH A074624).	35
Figure 2.5.	Vase from the Collection of Thomas Wilson, National Museum of Natural History, Inv. No. A136415.	37
Figure 2.6.	Room in the east wing of the Smithsonian Institution building with a plaster copy of the Parthenon frieze. Unknown photographer, 1902.	38
Figure 2.7.	Immanuel Casanowicz (1853–1927).	39
Figure 2.8.	Model of the Athenian Acropolis. Prepared by G. P. Stevens, J. Travlos and C. Mammelis on display at *Western Civilization: Origins and Traditions*, which opened in 1978 in the National Museum of Natural History, Inv. no. AT13319.	43
Figure 2.9.	John Lawrence Angel (1915–86).	44
Figure 2.10.	Richard Hubbard Howland (1910–2006).	45
Figure 2.11.	R. H. Howland in traditional Greek costume.	46
Figure 2.12.	Award presented to J. L. Angel by John Koumaris, 1938.	48
Figure 2.13.	Amphora, National Museum of American History, Inv. No. 1979.0696.01. This amphora was used as a Model for the Sports Illustrated Sportsman of the Year Award.	50
Figure 3.1.	A sponge diver ready for action.	67
Figure 3.2.	Cocoris memorial plaque, Tarpon Springs.	68

Figure 3.3.	Tarpon Springs local newspaper headline for *16 Fathoms Under*: "Lon Chaney Plays Villain in Film He Once Starred in as the Hero."	70
Figure 3.4.	Sponge diver John Gonatos.	71
Figure 4.1.	Yanis Varoufakis speaking at the 6th Subversive Festival, "The Utopia of Democracy," Zagreb, May 14, 2013.	78
Figure 4.2.	Austerity protest, Syntagma Square, Athens, Greece, 2011.	94
Figure 4.3.	Ezzatollah Entezami as Masht Hasan in *The Cow*.	98
Figure 4.4.	Two Evzones (Greek Presidential Guards) crossing in front of the tomb of the Unknown Soldier, Athens, Greece.	105
Figure 4.5.	Still from Karimi's *Writing on the City*.	110
Figure 4.6.	Esmail with Ali's father on the streets of Tehran, from *The Cycle*.	122
Figure 5.1.	The Majority of the World's Population Lives in this Circle.	147
Figure 5.2.	Illustration of one of the stories of 'Naufraghi senza volto' about migrants who died in the Mediterranean.	155
Figure 5.3.	The IQ Adventure!	167
Figure 6.1.	The Delphi oracle.	186
Figure 6.2.	Zulu divination.	191
Figure 7.1.	The cover of Pascal Lamy's book *The Geneva Consensus: Making Trade Work for All* (2013).	224
Figure 8.1.	Dimitris Fampas, *Karaguna*, measures 1–8.	240
Figure 8.2.	Gerasimos Miliaresis, "Danza di Zalongo," measures 1–3.	241
Figure 8.3.	Yannis Papaioannou, *Sonatine for Flute and Guitar*, Allegretto con spirito, measures 1–2.	244
Figure 8.4.	Yannis Papaioannou, *Sonatine for Flute and Guitar*, Finale, measures 1–2.	244
Figure 8.5.	Dimitris Dragatakis, *Liz-Va*, Allegro molto, measures 1–6.	245
Figure 8.6.	Kiriakos Tzortzinakis, "Of the Valley," measures 1–2.	247
Figure 8.7.	Kiriakos Tzortzinakis, "Of the Mountain," measures 1–2.	248
Figure 8.8.	Kiriakos Tzortzinakis, "Of the Village," measures 1–2.	248
Figure 8.9.	I. Andronoglou, "Fantasia on a Thracian Folksong," measures 42–46.	249

List of Illustrations

Figure 9.1.	The giant Talos armed with a stone. Silver didrachm from Phaistos, Crete, c. 300 or 280–70 BCE, obverse.	261
Figure 9.2.	The death of Talos, depicted on the 5th-century BCE krater known as the Talos Vase. Collection of the Jatta National Archaeological Museum, Ruvo di Puglia, Italy.	262
Figure 9.3.	"Medeia and Talos." Illustration by Sybil Tawse (1886–1971), in Thomas Bulfinch, *Stories of Gods and Heroes* (Thomas Y. Crowell, c. 1919).	264

Acknowledgement

The authors and editor of this volume have benefited enormously from Gillian Watts's extraordinary copy editing and indexing skills, as well as her generous enthusiasm about sharing her expertise in our cooperative work.

List of Contributors

Cynthia Alexander is a Hellenophile who has studied and lived in Greece at different times throughout her life. She is a public policy analyst in the Department of Politics at Acadia University in Nova Scotia, Canada. She received her PhD from Queen's University in Kingston, Ontario, Canada. Cynthia co-authored *A Stake in the Future* (UBC Press, 1997), a book about multi-stakeholder, consensus-based decision-making. She co-edited *Digital Democracy* with Dr. Leslie Pal (Oxford University Press, 1998).

Ioannis Andronoglou holds a PhD in musicology from the National and Kapodistrian University of Athens, and he is a guitar soloist. His album, *Travelling*, recorded and released in 2010 on Legend Classics, was reissued by Aerakis Cretan Music Workshop and Seistron in 2014. His musical works *Mandilatos Impressions* and *Fantasia on a Thracian Folksong* were published in 2015, as well as his 2020 book *Greek Traditional Music as a Source of Inspiration in the Composition of Works for Guitar*, all published by Aerakis Cretan Music Workshop and Seistron.

Ioannis is a Teaching Fellow at the University of Western Macedonia in the School of Humanities and Social Sciences, where he has also completed postdoctoral research. As a guitar soloist, Ioannis has given numerous concerts in Greece and abroad. As a soloist-tutor, he has participated in international festivals such as the Guitar Foundation of America and the Volos International Guitar Festival. He has given lectures at conferences on the subject of guitar as well as at conferences of musicological, historical and pedagogical interest, including the Interdepartmental Musicological Conference/Greece, the Dublin Guitar Symposium and the 2019 Paros Symposium on the Greeks.

Senti (Stamatia) Chaniadaki held a bachelor's degree in pedagogical science from Athens University and bachelor's and master's degrees in painting from the Athens School of Fine Arts. She created illustrations for children's books and showed her work in exhibitions at galleries, institutions, biennales and various museums around Greece. The paintings and drawings that Senti shared at Paros for the 2019 Symposium on the Greeks, some of which are included in this volume, are based on the idea of how inspirational ancient Greek art can be for a contemporary artist.

Steve Edwards is currently an Emeritus Professor and Research Fellow at the University of Zululand. His qualifications include doctoral degrees in psychology and education and registration in South Africa and the United Kingdom as a clinical, educational, sport and exercise psychologist. Steve's research, teaching and professional activities are mainly concerned with health promotion. He has supervised many doctoral students, published much research, presented papers at many international conferences, and served on the boards of various national and international organizations. Academic and professional awards include a Fulbright Scholarship, South African National Research Foundation ratings, and the Psychological Society of South Africa Mentoring and Development Award. He is happily married with two children and four grandchildren. His research record is available at https://www.researchgate.net/profile/Stephen_Edwards11.

Thomas Gerry, editor of this volume, is Professor Emeritus, Laurentian University, where he taught in the English Department from 1988 to 2017. In 1983 Tom received his PhD from the University of Western Ontario, London, Canada. His thesis title is *David Willson (1778–1866): Canadian Visionary Writer and Hymnodist*. He has published more than 100 book reviews, 20 scholarly articles and the books *Contemporary Canadian and U.S. Women of Letters* (Garland, 1993) and *The Emblems of James Reaney* (Porcupine's Quill, 2013). For five years, Tom edited *Arachnē: An Interdisciplinary Journal of the Humanities*. He edited and helped translate from Spanish into English Mercedes Luanco's *Una experiencia sorprendente: Aprendiendo a Pintar / The Story of an Encounter: Painting My New Way* (Scrivener, 2013). Contributing to the organization of the 2019 Paros Symposium on the Greeks, participating in it and now editing this volume of essays are highlights of Tom's academic career.

Hélène Jeannin holds a master's degree in communication and a PhD in sociology of arts and media from the University of Paris III Sorbonne-Nouvelle. She is a sociologist in the Human and Social Sciences Research Department of Orange, a telecommunications company. Her work focuses on prospective and emerging topics related to technology, including surveillance, drones, augmented bodies, artificial intelligence and ethics. Her work takes a transdisciplinary approach crossing several angles of view, ranging from the concrete analysis of practices to discourses and representations. Her areas of expertise revolve around emerging digital and communication technologies and their repercussions on society. She is based near Paris, France.

Ioannis Kostopoulos is a researcher in Greek prehistory, focusing particularly on ancient Greek technologies.

Gabrielle Moyer teaches at Stanford University in the Program in Writing and Rhetoric. Her work attends to the stories we tell about ourselves and others—in the way aesthetics can form a response to philosophical doubts, and in the contingent relationship between ethics and epistemology. In the classroom and in her research, she asks how styles of reading and writing can help us countenance uncertainty and complexity: in others, in our choices and in our judgments. She is completing a book, *Suggestions for A New Magic*, which explores these questions in both modernist and contemporary fiction. She has published on modernist poetry, Samuel Beckett's letters, Joseph Conrad and Ford Madox Ford.

Alexander Nagel is Chair of the Art History and Museum Professions Program and Associate Professor at the State University of New York, Fashion Institute of Technology. He is a Research Associate in Residence at the Smithsonian Institution's National

Museum of Natural History in Washington, D.C. He received a PhD from the University of Michigan in 2010 and was Assistant Curator of Ancient Near East in the Smithsonian Institution's National Museum of Asian Art. Alex works on aspects of heritage preservation and legacies worldwide, on polychromies and materials from Persepolis and Susa in Iran, and on first millennium BCE materials from Aitoloakarnania in Greece. He has received grants and fellowships from the German Academic Exchange Service, the American Philosophical Society, the Smithsonian Institution, the Graham Foundation, State University of New York and other institutions and organizations. The volume *Cave and Worship in Ancient Greece: New Approaches to Landscape and Ritual*, which he co-edited with Stella Katsarou of the Hellenic Ministry of Culture, Ephorate of Palaeoanthropology-Speleology, was published by Routledge in 2020.

William Ramp is an Associate Professor at the University of Lethbridge, Alberta, Canada, where he teaches in the Department of Sociology and the graduate program in cultural, social and political thought. His publications include articles and book chapters on a range of subjects, including religion, identity, neo-Durkheimian social theory, and agrarian politics and culture. He is also a regular contributor to *Weekly Hubris* (https://weeklyhubris.com/), an online general-interest literary magazine, on a range of subjects including political, cultural and material history.

Sahar Siavashi was born in Iran and moved to Canada in 2015. Currently, she is a master's student in cultural, social and political thought at the University of Lethbridge. She specializes in film criticism and women's studies, with a special interest in Iranian and Middle Eastern politics. She has previous degrees (MSc, mathematics) from the Universities of Tehran and Lethbridge but has always been particularly interested in political and social studies. Her current master's thesis is about identity formation among Iranian immigrant women in Canada, exploring political and societal factors (neoliberalism, orientalism, patriarchy and despotism) that have shaped the identity of women in the Iranian diaspora.

Helen Vatsikopoulos is a Lecturer in Journalism at the University of Technology Sydney, Australia. Her research areas include journalism as a tool for discovering suppressed stories, hidden truths and histories as well as ways to counter the digital disinformation and misinformation filling the vacuum left by suppressed histories. She has worked for the Australian Broadcasting Corporation, the Australia Network and the Special Broadcasting Service in Australia. She has specialized in international reporting and has covered history-changing events such as the fall of the Berlin Wall, the collapse of communism, the Rwandan genocide, the HIV-AIDS crisis in West Papua, the Sri Lankan civil war, the assassination of Rajiv Gandhi, and the Bali bombings, among many others. Her reporting on the collapse of the USSR won her a coveted Walkley Award. She has also made three documentary films, *New World Borders* and the award-winning documentaries *Agatha's Curse* and *Getting Gehry*. Helen has a doctorate of creative arts awarded in 2018 for an exegetical investigation of identity and nationalism with an auto-ethnographical memoir on the Greek Civil War.

Velvet L. Yates is a Lecturer in Classics at the University of Florida, where she directs the Classics Graduate Distance Program. She received her PhD in classics, with a concentration in ancient philosophy, from Princeton University. Her main research interests are a feminist approach to Aristotle's *Politics* and ancient Greek stone-carving methods. She also enjoys visiting Tarpon Springs and scuba diving, so her topic for this volume was a natural.

Editor's Introduction

Thomas M. F. Gerry

A wonderful "Symposium on the Greeks" was held on the island of Paros from June 28 to 30, 2019. This volume includes nine essays that began as the authors' oral and visual presentations at the Symposium. How did the idea for the Symposium occur? Marianne Vardalos, Anas Karzai and I, colleagues at Laurentian University, had for some time been talking about our felt need for an expansive, intellectually engaged gathering to share ongoing research interests and develop areas for future studies. Marianne summarized our motivation this way: "We wanted to get back to the basics and thought, what better way to do that than to return to the Greeks? We lamented that professional development activities we were attending had become so formulaic. So boring. So uninspiring. We designed this symposium to put the passion back into professional development activities."

Starting from this dynamic of passion, we called on symposiasts from a variety of fields to reconsider aspects of Greek culture, particularly in terms of that culture's continuing influences. The richness of the responses to the call for presentations was extraordinary. Just as a block of marble can be transformed into a sculpture, the raw material of the Symposium emerged into a marvelous form on Paros.

Legacies of Ancient Greece in Contemporary Perspectives features artwork by the Athenian artist Senti (Stamatia) Chaniadaki, who also graciously exhibited and discussed her drawings and engravings during the Symposium. One of the symposiasts, Cynthia Alexander, commented that Senti "illuminated our gathering with her art and presence." Sadly, Senti died in 2021; she is deeply missed. Fortunately for us, though, Senti had agreed to our featuring her art in this volume. With her creations, Senti embodied the artistic spirit of ancient Greece in her own way. We are honored by the presence of her spirit in the pages of this volume.

Another major element of the richness of the Symposium, and now of this book, is the important work that all the contributors have done in order to get past the numerous clichés that abound in our notions of the Greeks. In her meditative essay "Bearing Witness: Becoming Greek in the Diaspora," Helen Vatsikopoulos unpacks the question "What is Greece?" Contemporary Greece, she says, is a product of 19th-century nation building, an "imagined community" in Benedict Anderson's phrase. A nation existentially requires unity, while actualities such as diverse populations within its borders be damned. A predominant tool for conceptualizing Greek unity—and, of course, for promoting tourism—is to connect with achievements in the ancient past as a way to construct status for the present nation. Vatsikopoulos writes that, as young Greeks in Australia, "we boasted that we were descendants of the cradle of Western civilization." Also examining the impacts of "commodities" from ancient Greece in a New World setting— Washington, D.C.—Alexander Nagel's essay "Transatlantic Hellas: Archiving Eastern Mediterranean Collections and Materials in the Smithsonian Institution" raises fascinating issues concerning recent political and social usages of ancient artifacts.

Velvet Yates's "The Greeks of Tarpon Springs in the Hollywood Imaginary" reflects on particular examples of the racist exploitation of Greek stereotypes in movies, insightfully rethinking the meanings of *Greece*. Sahar Siavashi and William Ramp also use film examples, in "Pedagogies and Possibilities of Crisis in Greek and Iranian Film." The authors contrast filmic depictions of the economic discipline of neoliberalism as it is imposed by "austerity regimes." In their essay, Siavashi and Ramp offer an intriguing overview of the "Symposium on the Greeks": "The present volume emerged from a symposium that gathered together a diverse group of artists, musicians, scholars and teachers. It generated a creative tension between two ways of understanding classical Greek culture: (1) as expressive of a harmonics of the human spirit or civilizational convergence, and (2) as particular, contingent, specific, variable, even contradictory."

Instances of the first way of understanding classical Greek culture include three essays in this volume that set out convergences in cultural contexts less expected than cinema. In "Decolonizing the Boundaries of Belonging and Citizenship: Turning to Ancient Hellenic and Indigenous Cosmopolitanisms during the Climate Crisis," Cynthia Alexander explores ideas of citizenship through the lenses of Hellenic cosmopolitanism and Inuit traditional knowledge, or Qaujimajatuqangit. With profound acumen based on research and personal witnessing, Stephen Edwards examines themes related to healing in both ancient Greek and contemporary Zulu cultures. In "Athens is Burning: A Tragedy in Three Acts," Gabrielle Moyer links Aristotelian ethics, modernist literature and neoliberalism in order to formulate possibilities for surviving neoliberalism. For readers, each of these sets of juxtapositions yields fresh perceptions.

In employing the critical potential of legacies of ancient Greece, two contributions stand out in emphasizing the "particular, contingent, specific, variable, even contradictory" aspects of classical Greek culture noted by Siavashi and Ramp. Guitarist, composer and scholar Ioannis Andronoglou, whose delightful presentation at the Symposium was partly verbal and partly musical, describes in his essay modern and contemporary Greek compositional strategies that engage Greek traditional music. In a similar way, Hélène Jeannin and Ioannis Kostopoulos focus on the world's first robot, Talos, constructed by the god Hephaestus. Jeannin and Kostopoulos explain Talos as a significant example of the technologies of antiquity and their impacts on today's culture.

For over two years, the authors and I have worked together to prepare *Legacies of Ancient Greece in Contemporary Perspectives*. Along with giving us opportunities to demonstrate scholarly patience and persistence, the time since the Symposium has allowed the authors to keep their contributions up to date.

This anthology of essays promises to challenge its readers, to fascinate them and to inspire them with the passion that the contributors have brought to their work.

Chapter 1

Bearing Witness:
Becoming Greek in the Diaspora

Helen Vatsikopoulos

University of Technology, Sydney, Australia

Abstract

The people came from all over Greece: Macedonia, Limnos, the Peloponnese, among other places with strong regional identities, escaping a war-ravaged country, political persecution and poverty. Peasants hoping for a better life. But it was in Australia that we, the children of migrants became Greek. The meanings of Bouboulina, Kolokotronis, Ohi Day and the 25th of March were all instilled in us in Saturday Greek schools. But hidden from us were the true stories of our parents– silence was the price they paid for a new start in the "lucky country." As an established journalist for Australia's two public broadcasters, telling other people's stories was my life's work. But the best story of all was hidden in my own family. Civil war, stolen children and a complex hybrid 'endopyia' identity. My family came from the border regions of north-western Greece in the wetlands region of Prespa. It remained obscure until the recent negotiation of the controversial Prespa Agreement. Through photographs, testimony and an exploration of identity theory, this chapter reflects on the toll of researching and writing an ethnographic memoir on place, memory and being the "Other."

Keywords: Macedonia, diaspora, multiculturalism, migration, ethnography, belonging.

***

They came from all over Greece, escaping a poverty-stricken, war-ravaged country. Some were fleeing political persecution. They were mostly peasants with strong ethnoregional identities—from Macedonia to Limnos to the Peloponnese. It was in Australia, however, that the children of migrants learned to identify as Greeks, during Saturday Greek schools run by Greek Orthodox Church communities. This tuition stressed a nationalist Greek narrative that began with the ancient Greeks and extended to the present. Absent from the narrative were the true stories of the country and the lives their parents left behind. Silence became the price that migrants paid for a fresh start in their new adopted homeland.

Greece has never publicly reconciled the traumatic events and polarization of the Greek Civil War (1946–49). This episode in its history is not taught critically in Greek schools, in either the diaspora or the homeland. Unencumbered, the second generation of the diaspora has been questioning these events and endeavoring to fill in gaps in the histories of their parents' homeland. Through the process of bearing witness to the past, this paper will examine the processes of identity formation in the diaspora and the awakening to tell suppressed and contested stories of the past.

Memoir, auto-ethnography and "writing from the heart"

I spent most of my early professional life as an international reporter. The journalist's role is to bear witness to tumultuous events that are the turning points of history. Denise Leith, who writes about the work of foreign correspondents and photojournalists, sees the journalistic craft as "the first cut of history" and my role as "part of the process of recording history."[1] After 27 years in the high-pressure, immersive field of international journalism, I moved on to academia, deciding that it was now time to give back and teach journalism. The change in career tempo also provided me with an opportunity to do some more reflective writing. I wanted to dig deep into my family history. It was my decision to find out more about where we came from and also to record stories from Greece that would contribute to the storytelling of migration and feed into larger narratives of Australia's multiculturalism. Bassot writes, "the process of writing forces us to slow down and to take time to reflect, which allows our knowledge and understandings to grow."[2] There was much I did not understand, and even less that I knew.

A different form of writing was needed, one that was rigorous, well researched and, most important, peer-reviewed, so I knew I was dealing with history and not myth. I chose to embark on a doctorate; the methodology was auto-ethnography. Journalists aspire to work without fear or favor as they encounter strangers in often conflicted lands, researching, observing, contextualizing and recording their stories. Their role is as eyewitnesses to history in the making. But this writing was also personal. I knew the people I was writing about. I was an outsider but also an insider. Could I write without fear of causing offence? Could I abstain from taking sides in a narrative that was so personal? Most important, was this a story I had the right to tell? The subjects were my mother and father, my aunts and uncles. Was it even possible?

Chang writes that the insertion of the self in auto-ethnography makes it work. "Self is an extension of a community rather than that it is an independent, self-sufficient being, because the possibility of cultural self-analysis rests on an understanding that self is part

---

1. Denise Leith, Bearing Witness: The Lives of War Correspondents and Photojournalists (Sydney: Random House, 2004), xv.
2. Barbara Bassot, *The Reflective Journal* (London: Palgrave, 2016), x.

of a cultural community."³ This cultural community was easy to write about in Australia, as were narratives of migration as part of the Hellenic diaspora. *Diaspora* is, after all, a Greek word: "Seeds are integral to the etymology of the word diaspora (the Greek *speirein* meant to sow or scatter)."⁴ The *diaspora* meaning of seeds taken from the mother plant and sown elsewhere also speaks of maintaining links to a homeland. Diasporas "were inside the *demos* but outside the *polis*: inside the nation but outside the state."⁵

When it came to the deeper reasons why some people left, in particular when those reasons were political, it became difficult to elicit answers. Silence was often the only response.

They came from all over Greece

I was born in the northern Greek town of Florina and spent the first five years of my life in the village of Lemos in Macedonia, western Greece. The village is 50 kilometers from Florina and 2 kilometers from the border with what was then known as the Republic of Macedonia in the Federal People's Republic of Yugoslavia. Lemos was only one of about 94 villages in the prefecture, also named Florina.⁶ In 1965 my father, mother and I migrated to Australia. We boarded a passenger ship, the *Patris*, which literally means "homeland." Between 1959 and 1975, the *Patris*, which accommodated up to 1,000 passengers, made about 91 voyages between the Greek harbor of Piraeus and Australia.⁷ Our final destination was the Port of Adelaide. Gidley writes that diasporic formations often occur along shipping routes: "port cities have often been the exemplary locations of diasporic and inter-diasporic cultures of translation."⁸ Why did so many Greeks decide to migrate? Roudometof writes that 1.3 million people left Greece during the years 1947

---

3. Heewon Chang, *Autoethnography as Method* (Walnut Creek, CA: Left Coast Press, 2008), 22.

4. Robin Cohen, "Seeds, Roots, Rhizomes and Epiphytes: Botany and Diaspora," in *Diasporas Reimagined: Spaces, Practices and Belonging*, eds. N. Sigona et al. (Oxford: Oxford Diasporas Programme, 2015), 2.

5. N. Sigona et al., eds., *Diasporas Reimagined: Spaces, Practices and Belonging* (Oxford: Oxford Diasporas Programme) 2015, xxii.

6. Riki Van Boeschoten, "When Difference Matters: Sociopolitical Dimensions of Ethnicity in the District of Florina," in *Macedonia: The Politics of Identity and Difference*, ed. J. K. Cowan (Sterling, VA: Pluto, 2000), 32.

7. John N. Yiannakis, Odysseus in the Golden West: Greek Migration, Settlement and Adaptation in Western Australia since 1947 (Waterford, WA: API Network, 2009), 43.

8. Ben Gidley, "Cultures of Translation: East London, Diaspora Space and an Imagined Cosmopolitan Tradition," in Sigona et al., *Diasporas Reimagined*, 37.

to 1977.[9] He attributes the migrations to two key events: the Second World War and the Greek Civil War.

People of the water

We moved to Adelaide, capital of the state of South Australia, specifically to the western suburban area known as Port Adelaide, 15 kilometers from the city. During the early decades, this modest fishing port had evolved into a major seaport. Its first Greek immigrant, 20-year-old George Tramountanas, arrived at Port Adelaide in 1842 from the island of Limnos. *Tramountána* is the lyrical name Greek sailors give to the northern winds, and George promptly anglicized his surname to North.[10] It was no surprise that Port Adelaide attracted migrants from the Greek Islands—mainly Limnos, Agios Efstratios, Rhodes and Cyprus. These islanders comprised 15% of the total number of migrants to Australia between 1947 and 1971.[11]

The migrant men and women found jobs easily because there was a demand for unskilled and semi-skilled workers. The western suburbs contained many factories, and there was always a shortage of unskilled laborers for the booming postwar industrial sector. In 1965 my father secured employment the day he arrived in Adelaide, at the James Hardies Industries Asbestos Company. Other men worked at General Motors Holden, the CSR Sugar factory and the Adelaide Brighton Cement Company, among many others. The women found work in factories assembling electrical and white goods or at fruit canneries. Once the Greeks secured employment, they began to seek new ways of belonging. The people of the water—the immigrant community of Port Adelaide that hailed from the Greek islands—soon found another group of recent immigrants from Macedonia who came from the inland mountain lake regions of Prespa and Kastoria. Soon others, who identified as "Pontians"—refugees who had fled to Greece from Asia Minor after Greece's catastrophic defeat in the Greco-Turkish war (1919–22)—also moved into the area. Initially, these groups retained their ethno-regional identities by socializing together informally and then establishing brotherhoods and associations named after their home villages or towns and gathering at picnics and social dances.

Strong bonds formed, which continue to this day. In 2019 the Port Adelaide Greek Orthodox Community celebrated its 60-year anniversary, and members, led by a former

---

9. Victor Roudometof, "From Greek Orthodox Diaspora to Transnational Hellenism: Greek Nationalism and the Identities of the Diaspora," in *The Call of the Homeland: Diaspora Nationalisms, Past and Present*, eds. A. S. Leoussi, A. Gal and A. D. Smith (Leiden: Brill, 2010), 153.

10. Penny Anagnostou, "Greeks in South Australia," in *The Australian People: An Encyclopedia of the Nation, Its People and Their Origins*, ed. J. Jupp (Cambridge: Cambridge University Press, 2001), 401.

11. Anastasios M. Tamis, *The Immigration and Settlement of Macedonian Greeks in Australia* (Bundoora, VIC: La Trobe University Press, 1994), xi.

Greek schoolteacher, Andreas Botsaris, wrote a history to mark the event. It is important to note that, in its introduction, the authors clearly stipulated that the manuscript would feature only the good news: "It has been decided that detailed reference to opinions which could possibly rekindle old divisions, complaints and bitterness of the 1970s, are not consistent with the aim of this effort. Therefore, they have either only been mentioned in passing or ignored completely."[12] Later in this chapter, I examine the reasons why there is a reluctance in this community and others to revisit turbulent or traumatic experiences, especially when they relate to ethno-regional issues of identity.

Figure 1.1. Port Adelaide Greek school, 1973.

Source: Author's personal collection.

Botsaris writes that, once the Greeks arrived and found common ground, it became necessary to seek new ways of belonging as Greeks: "For the Hellenism of the broader area of Port Adelaide the needs of that time were mainly religious, social and spiritual and having a place to gather where they could communicate in their own language and share happy and sad events."[13] The negotiation of a diasporic Hellenic identity required the establishment of a Greek community, a Greek Orthodox church and a school for the continuation of Greek language and culture among the second generation (including me). This coincided with the highly significant implementation of Australian government

---

12. Andreas Botsaris, [untitled] (unpublished manuscript, 2018), 1.
13. Botsaris, 4.

policies of multiculturalism, which embraced diversity as a basic tenet of nation building.[14] The first priest of this nascent community was Father Dimitrios Vivlios, who also worked at the Boral Cyclone Cable Company at Woodville North. The community hired a hall belonging to the Anglican parish of St. Paul's, where it began to hold religious services and perform the holy rites of baptisms, weddings and funerals.

For the second generation of migrants like me, there was a danger that we could lose the cultural signifiers of our parents' generation through our immersion in the Australian education system and the dominant Anglo culture. But with the establishment of Saturday-morning Greek schools, a Greek identity transplanted from the homeland began to take shape (see fig. 1.1). This enculturation of the second generation replaced the ethno-regional identities of the parents with a Greek homeland identity. In her study of the Greek schools of London, Aspasia Simpsi states that the aims and objectives of the schools were "designed according to three major aspects that reflect the homeland Greek Educational Policy: language, tradition and Orthodox Christianity."[15] My Greek school teacher was not a trained educator by profession but one of the most highly educated community members; he also worked with my father as a laborer at the asbestos factory. Apart from instructing us on language, grammar, reading and writing, he also supervised our performances of poems and plays on the occasions when we celebrated Greek national achievements. One of the main events was "Ohi (όχι) Day," October 28, which commemorated the day in 1940 when Greek prime minister Ioannis Metaxas rejected an ultimatum from Italy's Benito Mussolini, thereby plunging Greece into the Second World War. At no stage were we taught about how Metaxas was a totalitarian dictator who caused much hardship in Greece from 1936 to 1941, particularly for minorities and for those who disagreed with his politics. According to the official narrative, he was a hero.

The other main commemorative event was March 25, the day in 1821 when Greeks launched their successful War of Independence against the Ottoman Turks. Never were we taught that the Ottomans permitted the Greek Orthodox patriarchate to function relatively freely throughout the 400 years of occupation; instead, we were fed myths of secret nocturnal schools run by priests who risked execution. In our commemorative plays, students dressed as "Mother Greece" and "Freedom," often in the blue of the Greek flag and the Greek national costume. We were taught about the "Megali idea": the idea of a greater Greece incorporating territories that once formed part of Hellenic lands dating back to ancient times. In one of those plays, I was positioned in an embrace with "Mother Greece" and "Freedom," but I was dressed in black and bound in chains to represent

---

14. Anthony Moran, "Multiculturalism as Nation Building in Australia: Inclusive National Identity and the Embrace of Diversity," *Ethnic and Racial Studies* 34, no. 12 (2011): 2153.

15. Aspasia Simpsi, "'Do I Like the Queen Now?' Negotiating Ethno-cultural Identity Through National Celebration Theatre Performances: The Case of a Greek Community School in London" (PhD diss., University of Warwick, 2014), 262.

Northern Epirus, an unredeemed territory that did not join Greece after independence in 1913, but instead was contested and eventually ceded to Albania (see fig. 1.2).

Figure 1.2. Playing Northern Epirus in a Greek school play, 1975.

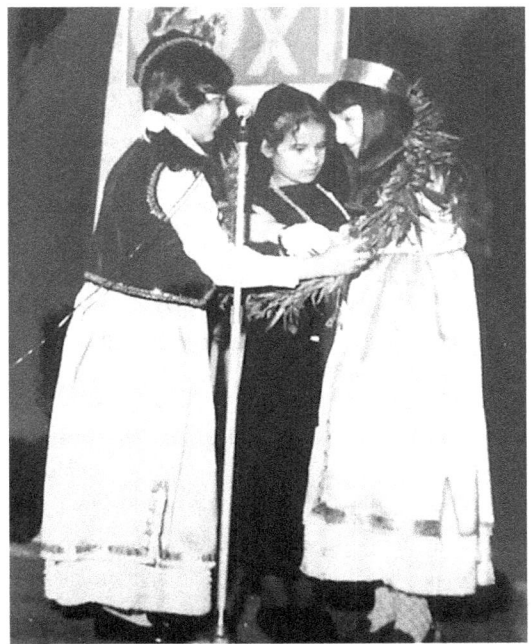

Source: Author's personal collection.

As Simpsi writes, these national commemorations were an essential part of fostering the community's collective memory and sense of belonging through embedded hegemonic ideologies:

> The students and the other members of the community negotiate aspects of their Greek ethnic identity while participating in these ritual national performances. It is mainly through the language and the history that they aim at creating a collective identity. This shared membership is often affirmed or re-affirmed with the occasion of national celebrations.[16]

So the Greek schools of the diaspora helped the second generation negotiate a Greek identity not unlike that of the homeland. Identity and motherland were one and the same, and sacrosanct.

---

16. Simpsi, 272.

What is Greece?

The Hellenic nation, according to Beaton, is a revival and re-identification constructed through names, language and landscapes: "The Hellenic nation, as constituted in the early 19th century, is a recent construct; its name and traditions to which it lays claim are ancient."[17] In our Australian homes, the migrants from the Greek islands and Greek Macedonia displayed framed prints and tapestries of the Acropolis and mass-produced statuettes of the goddess Athena and ancient Greek philosophers. Our mothers wore medallions of the Parthenon around their necks, and as we were inculcated, we boasted that we were descendants of the cradle of Western civilization. In Greek school, we were taught about the heroic independence figures Theodoros Kolokotronis and the philhellene Lord Byron and his "sacrifice" for the glory of Greece.

It was always the Greece of antiquity and its unbroken continuation to the present-day nation. This, according to Bakalaki, was exactly the discourse in Greece, where "students resort to clichés concerning the superiority of the Hellenic civilization and the continuities between Ancient and Modern Greece culture."[18] Ephe Avdela writes of the teaching of history in Greece that "the nation is understood to be a natural, unified, eternal, and unchanging entity, not a product of history. Analysis of history textbooks shows that this historical account is created through selective social memory, which conceals and omits all those crucial elements that might disturb the image of continuity and homogeneity."[19]

Richard Clogg attests to the power of education in homogenizing Greek identity: "Greece's educational system had proved to be an efficient mechanism for 'Hellenizing' populations of diverse ethnic and linguistic backgrounds as they were gradually incorporated into the Greek state."[20] Many scholars, including Eric Hobsbawm, Terence Ranger and John Gillis, have written about the invention of traditions by new states that selectively used memory and historical events as a way of constructing national identities.[21] Greece did the same and perpetuated the narrative through national days and commemorations that filtered through the education system and public museums. The homogenizing aspect of the Greek state was in direct opposition to the multicultural nature of the Australian state. Against that background, a historical event took place that caused me to question

---

17. Roderick Beaton, "Antique Nation? 'Hellenes' on the Eve of Greek Independence and in Twelfth-Century Byzantium," *Byzantine and Modern Greek Studies* 31, no. 1 (2007): 76.

18. Alexandra Bakalaki, "A Different Kind of Knowledge? Learning Anthropology in the Greek University System," *Journal of Modern Greek Studies* 24, no. 2 (2006): 264.

19. Ephe Avdela, "The Teaching of History in Greece," *Journal of Modern Greek Studies* 18, no. 2 (2000): 258.

20. Richard Clogg, Minorities in Greece: Aspects of a Plural Society (London: Hurst, 2002), xii.

21. See E. J. Hobsbawm and T. Ranger, *The Invention of Tradition* (London: Cambridge University Press, 1992).

not my Greek-Australian identity but my Greek-Macedonian one. The only way for me to process that questioning of identity was to endeavor to write about it.

The first cut of history

On September 8, 1991, the former Yugoslav Republic of Macedonia declared its independence. Other republics of the Socialist Federated Republic of Yugoslavia, of which they had all been part since 1945, did the same. Serbia, Croatia, Montenegro, Bosnia-Herzegovina and Slovenia all pulled away from the USSR-modeled Yugoslavia, which had been soldered together by socialist leader Marshall Josip Broz Tito's iron fist. Its neighbor, Bulgaria, immediately recognized the new state but not its nationality or language, because it believed that Macedonians were really regional Bulgarians who spoke a Bulgarian dialect. Macedonia's other neighbor, Greece, could not accept an independent state at all under that name. At the time, I was working as a foreign correspondent for the Special Broadcasting Service (SBS) on its international current affairs program, *Dateline*. Sent to cover the disintegration of Yugoslavia, I concentrated on the archrivals Croatia and Serbia.

Although Macedonia was not a key factor in the breakup, it became a key area of interest in the microcosm of my family. Very soon, Greeks in Greece and Macedonians in the new state were at loggerheads over Greece's refusal to recognize the new country as Macedonia, but only as the former Yugoslav Republic of Macedonia. This worsening dispute then spilled over into the diaspora. Greeks and Macedonians held angry protests in cities all over the world, including Australia. I began to take notice. Watching Greeks and Macedonians debating history and identity in television studios, I realized that they were debating the very essence of who I was. I knew myself as a Greek Macedonian. Now, this former communist state was asserting that it was the only legitimate Macedonian state, and a Slavic entity. But I was not a Slav—or at least I did not think I was. Television programs and newspapers pondered the question of what Macedonia was and who could claim to be a Macedonian. Some asserted that *Greek* and *Macedonian* were mutually exclusive terms. In Australia and other parts of the diaspora, families became divided over what the two terms really meant and to which group they belonged. Soon this opened up a new research field in academia.

In 2000 the American anthropologist Loring Danforth wrote his seminal essay "How Can One Woman Give Birth to One Greek and One Macedonian?" Danforth centered his research on the Greek Macedonian and Slavic Macedonian diasporic communities of Australia and Canada—that is, migrants who called themselves ethnic Macedonians but differed on what Macedonian ethnic identity really was. He believed it was possible to be both. There are two main theories of identity formation and nationalism: the primordialist or perennialist and the modern or constructivist. The first holds that a nation is immutable and you cannot choose to which nation you belong. It is born of DNA and bloodlines of belonging that can extend as far back as ancient times. This is what the

Greeks believe, and this is also why they claim an exclusivity of Hellenic ancestry dating back to the dynasty of Philip and Alexander (thus excluding the modern Macedonians). Constructivists believe that identity is fluid and emanates from self-ascription. So, according to Danforth, you can have two people born from the same womb with differing identities.

Figure 1.3. Graffiti in Florina, Greece, 2016.

Source: Author's personal collection.

It became clear to me that in Australia, the Greek diaspora had negotiated a Greek-Australian identity and instilled it in their children, while many of those people actually had a regional-ethnic identity and kept it from their children. Writing on the migration of Greek Macedonians in South Australia, Tamis states that, in the immediate post–Second World War era, Slavo-Macedonian associations existed without ethno-linguistic inclinations.

Later, however, they changed into either Greek Macedonian or Slavic Macedonian entities under the freedoms afforded them in a multicultural country such as Australia.[22] The disintegration of Yugoslavia brought the issue into prominence once more.

The Macedonias

"Macedonia [is] the most blood-soaked region of Greece," according to Greek-Australian academic Anastasios Tamis.[23] First, let me clarify. There are several Macedonias: ancient Macedonia; the province in northern Greece named Macedonia; the geographical Macedonia, which was once a mosaic of linguistic groups and today is split between Greece, Bulgaria and North Macedonia; and the Republic of North Macedonia. The last was officially recognized by Greece with the signing of the Prespa Agreement in June 2018. In the years following the 1991 declaration of independence until the 2018 agreement, Greece would refer to it only as "the Former Yugoslav Republic of Macedonia" (FYROM) or by its capital, "the Republic of Skopje," or just Skopje.

I have found many accounts of the blood-soaked history of this area, and most of the causes of the spilt blood have had to do with contested identity. In modern times, after the collapse of the Ottoman Empire, two Balkan wars were fought over Macedonia. What we did not learn in Greek school was that the hero of "Ohi Day," Prime Minister Ioannis Metaxas, outlawed the use of a Slavic language and persecuted those in Greece who spoke it. In his extensive research of archival sources in Western Macedonia, Greek historian Raymondos Alvanos discovered that, in the interwar years of 1922–40, there were concerted attempts to integrate the diverse ethnic groups into Greek society through parliamentary politics. Slavic speakers and those who came after the exchange of populations were divided over land acquisition, but they lobbied their local representatives and were listened to, and their needs were met by politicians.[24] This exemplified the theory that identity is not a fixed state and that it was a process requiring revision and negotiation. Alvanos lays the blame for the souring of relations to the Metaxas dictatorship, which came into effect on August 4, 1936. Metaxas withdrew power from local politicians and gave it to the military, the Slavic language was banned and the prosecution of those who would not forcibly assimilate became law.[25]

As part of her extensive fieldwork, in 1993, anthropologist Riki van Boeschoten was funded by the European Commission to visit the Florina area and analyze the use of

---

22. Tamis, 210.
23. Tamis, 354.
24. Raymondos Alvanos, "Parliamentary Politics as an Integration Mechanism: The Slavic-Speaking Inhabitants of Interwar (1922–1940) Western Greek Macedonia," *History and Anthropology* 30, no. 5 (2019): 603.
25. Alvanos, 615.

minority languages. While it was difficult to ascertain exact numbers because official figures were not kept and many people were still fearful of admitting to speaking the language, she estimated that 42% of the people in the area spoke the Slavic language.[26] The seeds of discontent were sown with the Metaxas dictatorship, and many of those people and their families chose to join the Greek Communist Party, which promised self-determination. The Greek Civil War (1946–49) has often been defined as the first "hot" war of the Cold War era, where the proxy forces of the democratic West and the Communist bloc faced off against each other. Beneath the faultlines between these political tectonic plates lay an equally dangerous fracture: the bitter divisions within communities and even families of Macedonia over Greek or Slavo-Macedonian identity.

When the communists lost the war, the persecution of the left—and therefore those with an ethno-Slavic identity—began. Migration was a form of escape. Of the quarter of a million Greeks who migrated to Australia after the Second World War and the Civil War, Macedonian Greeks were the largest group, comprising 35% of all Greek immigrants.[27] Danforth further clarifies that, of the 75,000 migrants from Macedonia, about 27,000 came from the Greek prefecture of Florina.[28] Danforth writes:

> These people are caught between mutually exclusive national identities. They are marginal participants in several national cultures and full participants in none, people who are struggling to construct a coherent sense of themselves from a complex, multi-layered set of identities—class, religious, regional, ethnic, and national. While these identities may coexist easily on some occasions, they conflict sharply on others, and this conflict often brings with it a great deal of uncertainty, alienation, and pain.[29]

During research into my family, I discovered that one of my grandmothers did not speak Greek and would be considered linguistically and culturally Slavo-Macedonian. She was born in 1903 in what was then the Ottoman Empire. In those years, girls were not sent to school, so even though Macedonia was ceded to Greece in 1912, her consciousness would have evolved into one that was considered Hellenic. At that time, Macedonia was still a complex patchwork of co-existing and competing ethnic and national identities, a world away from the monocultural identity projected by the modern Greek state. In the post-Ottoman Macedonia of 1912, it was even possible to be Slavo-Macedonian–speaking

---

26. Riki Van Boeschoten, "Usage des langues minoritaires dans les départements de Florina et d'Aridea (Macédoine) [Use of minority languages in the departments of Florina and Aridea (Macedonia)]," *Strates* 10 (2001), http://strates.revues.org/381.

27. Tamis, xi.

28. Loring M. Danforth, "How Can a Woman Give Birth to One Greek and One Macedonian? The Construction of National Identity among Immigrants to Australia from Northern Greece," in *Macedonia: The Politics of Identity and Difference*, ed. J. K. Cowan (London: Pluto, 2000), 94.

29. Danforth, 100.

and have a Greek identity. This subgroup was mockingly called "Grecomans" by a competing ethnic Slavic Bulgarian or self-identifying Slavic Macedonian community.

In the interwar years, the "Hellenization" process was difficult for my grandmother and other family members. During the Greek Civil War, the communists occupied our villages and, while my paternal uncle was conscripted into the Greek army, my father was conscripted by the communists. Being too small and weak to fight for the "liberation" of democratic Greece, he was packed off to Yugoslavia for secondary education and subsequent training as a tailor. It would take seven years and much lobbying to the authorities by my extended family, before he was permitted to return to Greece. When the shattered communist forces were retreating in defeat in 1949, their route took them through our village on their way to sanctuary in Albania and Yugoslavia, just a few hours' march away. My grandmother, along with her other two other sons (my uncles), who were then small boys, was also taken forcibly by the communists and eventually resettled in Poland. It would be nearly a decade before all were reunited at the family farm—all but one. My father's older sister (my aunt) had fought in the communist army, retreated and, along with many Greek true believers, was exiled by Stalin to Tashkent in the Soviet Union. She would never see Greece again. That side of my family was separated for almost a decade before being reunited.

This was a family narrative rich in history. I once asked my father if we were Greek or Macedonian. His response was severe: "Helen, we come from a country called Greece! Of course we are Greek." Yet there are members of our extended family who swear we are Macedonian.

Writing around silences

Greek-Australian historian Joy Damousi, whose family also hails from Florina, writes that the second generation receives the stories of their parents in ways that "position the child as a witness to unresolved family trauma."[30] When we begin to delve deeper into family narratives, they tend to be in direct opposition to the encultured narratives we were brought up on in the Greek schools. Damousi writes: "the essences of the meaning of being Greek is intertwined with—and heightened by—narratives of violence, trauma and war though indirect transmission of their parents' trauma."[31] Greek-American academic Irene Kacandes writes in her memoir *Daddy's War* that she was conscious of her father's difficult past despite not remembering ever being told about it. She claims that her father's past occupied her mind in vague vignettes of word associations such as "trapped-

---

30. Joy Damousi, *Memory and Migration: In the Shadow of War* (Cambridge: Cambridge University Press, 2015), 221.

31. Damousi, 221.

Greece-dictator" and "betrayed-relatives."[32] "When I was very young, I knew things about my father that had no plot, no narrator, no audience. I don't remember being told these things. They were just there, like unwelcome relatives installed for the long haul, sponging off my parents and preventing out family from living completely in the present."[33]

My attempts to bear witness—initially as a professional journalist and more recently in this case, engaged in academic research to write the stories of their battles with an authoritarian state and document the details of why they had to migrate—were often difficult. While I was able to interview my immediate family and record their stories, the more traumatic accounts of persecution and dislocation were not forthcoming. While the basic facts were communicated to me, the nuances and details were lacking. The reasons why they left Greece might have had much to do with poverty and living in a region that was still regarded with suspicion because it was the front line of the Greek Civil War, but the real reason was a new start and a future for me.

Silence on these issues was how my parents and many others coped with their past. Damousi explains that "for some individuals the need to forge to the future and to forget was imperative,"[34] and that a "wall of silence developed where parents do not tell and children do not ask."[35] There was not enough time between leaving the homeland and negotiating a Greek-Australian identity in a multicultural country for them to be psychologically ready to process the past and speak about it openly. I looked to other writers of a similar background.

Neni Panourgia writes on the "White Terror" of the Greek state against its left-wing citizens, and she too interviewed her father: "There are no clear interiorities and exteriorities here; at any given moment you are within and without; you are a comrade and you are not; you are a researcher and you are also the daughter who is called to make tea while the narrative is left hanging."[36] As in Panourgia's experience, I often found the narrative hanging inconclusively and then cut off with the phrase "*perasmena xehasmena*," accompanied by a lifting of the chin and followed by a *tsk*. "Past and forgotten" was often the answer to questions that had to be left unanswered. Panourgia was cautioned by her uncle, a prosecutor, "Since you are writing a book you should be

---

32. Irene Kacandes, *Daddy's War: Greek American Stories* (Lincoln: University of Nebraska, 2009), 2–3.
33. Kacandes, 1.
34. Damousi, 2.
35. Damousi, 199.
36. Neni Panourgia, *Dangerous Citizens: The Greek Left and the Terror of the State* (New York: Fordham University Press, 2009), 21.

very careful in what you write because, you know better than I do there are still a lot of people alive from that time."[37]

Andrea Cleland is another Greek-Australian whose family also emanates from the Florina region. Like me, she undertook a doctorate, and the outcome was almost exactly the same as mine—coming up against an inability to speak openly about the past. "The complexity and contested nature of even the meanings of the word 'Macedonia' and 'Macedonian' limited the ability for families to articulate a shared collective history that could be actively transmitted through the generations."[38] In more than 30 oral histories I conducted for my thesis, there were many times when I was told to turn off the recorder when the subject was revealing important information: "Please don't write about this." My own father on many occasions would revert from interview subject to dad, scolding his daughter, "No more! That is enough." Cleland found the same; her interviewees "urged that these things 'should not be written' and that 'it was better not talk about these things' due to its highly charged political nature."[39]

One of the women I interviewed, who came from Prespa and identified as Slavo-Macedonian, had been arrested and tortured by Greek police because her family had communist and therefore separatist ideas. She spoke only on guarantee of anonymity, "because I am afraid there may be repercussions and my sons will be prevented from visiting Greece in future."[40] This fear of publicly expressing themselves emanates from deep fear, even though, as Michael Radin explains, "Australian governments have responded positively to affirm the right to self-identification and absolute cultural rights within the parameters of Australia's democratic multiculturalism."[41]

Still, the ways of the homeland prevail. Cleland writes that she once asked her father if they were Greek or Macedonian. His response: "these things no longer mattered as we were in Australia."[42] So, what to make of the silences? Why the fear of reprisal for talking of events more than 70 years in the past? Trauma hung heavily over many interviews I conducted, and for a good reason. Historical accounts, eyewitnesses I have interviewed and photographs I have seen underscore the brutality, the barbarity of the 1946–49 Civil War years. In my family's region, there were mass executions of prisoners, bodies dumped in mass graves, beheadings with heads placed on stakes in town squares, and rape and torture of the civilian population. Betrayal of family, friends and neighbors,

---

37. Panourgia, 20.
38. Andrea Cleland, "The Pear Tree: Family Narratives of Greek Macedonian Migration to Australia" (PhD diss., University of Melbourne, 2018), 226.
39. Cleland, 142.
40. Helen Vatsikopoulos, "The Siren Songs: The Prespa Palimpsest" (PhD diss., University of Technology Sydney, 2019), 285.
41. Michael Radin, "Features of Settlement in Australia by Macedonians from the Aegean Region," in *Macedonian Agenda*, ed. V. Bivell (Marrickville, NSW: Pollitecon, 1995), 123.
42. Cleland, 224.

resulting in execution. A bleak barbarity. And once the fighting stopped, years of reprisals. Little wonder the survivors wanted to forget.

Writing taboos

There is a danger in unearthing Greek taboo subjects. In the early 1990s, Greek-American anthropologist Anastasia Karakasidou began to publish her research on the Slav minority of Greece. The Greek state still does not at all acknowledge that Greece has minorities; it only has slavophone Greeks in Macedonia and Turkish-speaking Greeks in Thrace. Dr. Karakasidou became persona non grata among nationalistic Greeks in both Greece and the diaspora. She published a journal article titled "Politicizing Culture: Negating Ethnic Identity in Greek Macedonia" in the *Journal of Modern Greek Studies* in 1993, examining the Hellenization of Slavic speakers in Greece during the assimilationist policies of the 1920s and '30s. She writes: "The efforts of the Greek intellectuals and politicians to construct a tradition of Greek heritage in Macedonia has led to a protracted campaign to denigrate or even deny the existence of a Slavo-Macedonian ethnic minority in Northern Greece."[43] She received death threats and threats of rape, and her address in Thessaloniki and car plates number were circulated.[44] Scholars around the world, PEN International, Amnesty International and Human Rights Watch urged the Greek government to protect her. *The Independent* reported details of threats from the right-wing Greek newspaper *Stohos* and from others based in the United States:

> She received a veiled death threat from a Greek-American newspaper in February, when it published an article describing a possible scenario for her death. It described an attack by a group of men, one of whom pushed a stick painted in the colours of the Greek flag into her heart, killing her as a traitor. It is thought that the veiled death threats were designed to frighten her away from academic research.[45]

When Karakasidou sought to publish her thesis, similar disturbing events took place. Cambridge University Press agreed to publish the book *Fields of Wheat, Hills of Blood: Passages to Nationhood in Greek Macedonia, 1870–1990*, but after receiving bomb

---

43. Anastasia Karakasidou, "Politicizing Culture: Negating Ethnic Identity in Greek Macedonia," *Journal of Modern Greek Studies* 11, no. 1 (1993): 9.
44. Leonard Doyle, "Writers Urge Athens to Shield Greek Scholar," *The Independent*, May 12, 1994, https://www.independent.co.uk/news/world/europe/writers-urge-athens-to-shield-greek-scholar-1435581.html.
45. Leonard Doyle, "Death Threats Haunt Greek Champion of Macedonians," *The Independent*, May 9, 1994, https://www.independent.co.uk/news/world/europe/death-threats-haunt-greek-champion-of-macedonians-in-the-first-of-two-articles-on-the-region-leonard-1434872.html.

threats, it sought the advice of the British embassy in Athens and then pulled the text.[46] Eventually, it was published by the University of Chicago Press in 1997.

Her experience haunts me. Panourgia was also warned that it could be dangerous to write about controversial subjects: "You'll get pummelled from every angle, my friends warned me about this project. Doubtless, but you need to understand and I need to explain what it means to be this generation of post-civil war Greeks."[47] I recall several times being told "Please be careful," or being warned "You're asking for trouble." While my thesis is finished, I am not in a hurry to get it published. As Bassot writes, "critically reflective practice means that we begin to engage with our emotional responses and to challenge some of the assumptions we might be making about people and situations."[48] It has been an emotional rollercoaster.

Conclusion

My generation, the second generation, inhabits a "culture of hybridity" and walks a fine line in negotiating identity in the diaspora. A second-generation writer faces challenges. Bearing witness is more than just a methodology of the journalist's craft. What Leith describes is more of a calling: "While journalists live with the horrors they witness and a commonly expressed sense of impotence, they all claim their job is a privilege and their work has given their life meaning."[49] If journalists were not there to document the first draft of history as eyewitnesses, they then have to find and tell suppressed stories to fill in the gaps. Bearing witness is not just the act of being there; it is the actual text that bears witness. As Frosh writes, "this text is a witnessing text, that the event described really happened and that the text was designed to report it."[50]

As I reflect on this, I am conflicted. As a journalist, I am saddened that stories have been suppressed. The traumatic experiences of the diasporic migrants who left their homeland for a new life will die with them, and we will all be the poorer. As a daughter, however, I am deeply grateful for their love as they tried to protect me from the unresolved issues in their past, not wanting me to carry that burden and seek retributive justice. As an academic, I am concerned that this information will not be available to fill gaps in the canon of historical knowledge. Cleland writes that the contested and complex

---

46. Fred Barbash, "Academics, Politics Clash in Cambridge," *Washington Post*, February 3, 1996, https://www.washingtonpost.com/archive/politics/1996/02/03/academics-politics-clash-in-cambridge/f72749a8-76c6-45cd-ba3a-4fce71dae398/?utm_term=.e9f9dbd7c01e.

47. Panourgia, 21.

48. Bassot, ix.

49. Leith, xx.

50. Paul Frosh, "Telling Presences: Witnessing, Mass Media and the Imagined Lives of Strangers," in *Media Witnessing: Testimony in the Age of Mass Communication*, eds. P. Frosh and A. Pinchevski (London: Palgrave Macmillan, 2011), 60.

nature of what the word *Macedonia* means has resulted in "a gap in our understanding of post-war family migration from Florina and hence intergenerational experiences of migration and Greek-Macedonian identity formation in the diaspora."[51] Damousi takes this further: "there is an absence in the Australian literature on the Greek second generation, whose sense of what it means to be Greek is influenced by the traumatic and war experiences of their parents."[52] It is a difficult task to bear witness and write about Greek history in diaspora, but someone has got to do it. Thankfully an emerging generation of young scholars is demonstrating a commitment to filling in the gaps, but the challenge is to do so before the first generation dies, taking its stories with it.

Bibliography

Alvanos, Raymondos. "Parliamentary Politics as an Integration Mechanism: The Slavic-Speaking Inhabitants of Interwar (1922–1940) Western Greek Macedonia." *History and Anthropology* 30, no. 5 (2019): 600–621.

Anagnostou, Penny. "Greeks in South Australia." In *The Australian People: An Encyclopedia of the Nation, Its People and Their Origins*, 401–5. Edited by J. Jupp. Cambridge: Cambridge University Press, 2001.

Avdela, Ephe. "The Teaching of History in Greece." *Journal of Modern Greek Studies* 18, no. 2 (2000): 239–53.

Bakalaki, Alexandra. "A Different Kind of Knowledge? Learning Anthropology in the Greek University System." *Journal of Modern Greek Studies* 24, no. 2 (2006): 257–83.

Barbash, Fred. "Academics, Politics Clash in Cambridge." *Washington Post*, February 3, 1996. https://www.washingtonpost.com/archive/politics/1996/02/03/academics-politics-clash-in-cambridge/f72749a8-76c6-45cd-ba3a-4fce71dae398/?utm_term=.e9f9dbd7c01e.

Bassot, Barbara. *The Reflective Journal*. London: Palgrave, 2016.

Beaton, Roderick. "Antique Nation? 'Hellenes' on the Eve of Greek Independence and in Twelfth-Century Byzantium." *Byzantine and Modern Greek Studies* 31, no. 1 (2007): 76–95.

Chang, Heewon. *Autoethnography as Method*. Walnut Creek, CA: Left Coast Press, 2008.

Cleland, Andrea. "The Pear Tree: Family Narratives of Greek Macedonian Migration to Australia." PhD diss., University of Melbourne, 2018.

Clogg, Richard. Minorities in Greece: Aspects of a Plural Society. London: Hurst, 2002.

Cohen, Robin. "Seeds, Roots, Rhizomes and Epiphytes: Botany and Diaspora." In Sigona et al., *Diasporas Reimagined*, 2–7.

Damousi, Joy. *Memory and Migration: In the Shadow of War*. Cambridge: Cambridge University Press, 2015.

Danforth, Loring M. "How Can a Woman Give Birth to One Greek and One Macedonian? The Construction of National Identity among Immigrants to Australia from Northern Greece." In *Macedonia: The Politics of Identity and Difference*, edited by J. K. Cowan, 85–103. London: Pluto, 2000.

---

51. Cleland, 226.
52. Damousi, 118–19.

Doyle, Leonard. "Death Threats Haunt Greek Champion of Macedonians." *The Independent*, May 9, 1994. https://www.independent.co.uk/news/world/europe/death-threats-haunt-greek-champion-of-macedonians-in-the-first-of-two-articles-on-the-region-leonard-1434872.html.

———. "Writers Urge Athens to Shield Greek Scholar." *The Independent*, May 12, 1994. https://www.independent.co.uk/news/world/europe/writers-urge-athens-to-shield-greek-scholar-1435581.html.

Frosh, Paul. "Telling Presences: Witnessing, Mass Media and the Imagined Lives of Strangers." In *Media Witnessing: Testimony in the Age of Mass Communication*, edited by P. Frosh and A. Pinchevski, 49–72. London: Palgrave Macmillan, 2011.

Gidley, Ben. "Cultures of Translation: East London, Diaspora Space and an Imagined Cosmopolitan Tradition." In Sigona et al., *Diasporas Reimagined*, 37-40.

Hobsbawm, E. J., and T. Ranger. *The Invention of Tradition*. London: Cambridge University Press, 1992.

Kacandes, Irene. *Daddy's War: Greek American Stories*. Lincoln: University of Nebraska, 2009.

Karakasidou, Anastasia. *Fields of Wheat, Hills of Blood*. Chicago: University of Chicago Press, 1997.

———. "Politicizing Culture: Negating Ethnic Identity in Greek Macedonia." *Journal of Modern Greek Studies* 11, no. 1 (1993): 1–28.

Leith, Denise. Bearing Witness: The Lives of War Correspondents and Photojournalists. Sydney: Random House, 2004.

Moran, Anthony. "Multiculturalism as Nation Building in Australia: Inclusive National Identity and the Embrace of Diversity." *Ethnic and Racial Studies* 34, no. 12 (2011): 2153–72.

Panourgia, Neni. *Dangerous Citizens: The Greek Left and the Terror of the State*. New York: Fordham University Press, 2009.

Radin, Michael. "Features of Settlement in Australia by Macedonians from the Aegean Region." In *Macedonian Agenda*, edited by V. Bivell, 113–31. Marrickville, NSW: Pollitecon, 1995.

Roudometof, Victor. "From Greek Orthodox Diaspora to Transnational Hellenism: Greek Nationalism and the Identities of the Diaspora." In *The Call of the Homeland: Diaspora Nationalisms, Past and Present*, edited by A. S. Leoussi, A. Gal and A. D. Smith, 138–68. Leiden: Brill, 2010.

Sigona, N., A. Gamlen, G. Liberatore and H. Neveu Kringelbach, eds. *Diasporas Reimagined: Spaces, Practices and Belonging*. Oxford: Oxford Diasporas Programme, 2015.

Simpsi, Aspasia. "'Do I Like the Queen Now?' Negotiating Ethno-cultural Identity Through National Celebration Theatre Performances: The Case of a Greek Community School in London." PhD diss., University of Warwick, 2014.

Tamis, Anastasios M. *The Immigration and Settlement of Macedonian Greeks in Australia*. Bundoora, VIC: La Trobe University Press, 1994.

Van Boeschoten, Riki. "Usage des langues minoritaires dans les départements de Florina et d'Aridea (Macédoine)" [Use of minority languages in the departments of Florina and Aridea (Macedonia)]. *Strates* 10 (2001). http://strates.revues.org/381.

———. "When Difference Matters: Sociopolitical Dimensions of Ethnicity in the District of Florina." In *Macedonia: The Politics of Identity and Difference*, edited by J. K. Cowan, 28–46. Sterling, VA: Pluto, 2000.

Vatsikopoulos, Helen. "The Siren Songs: The Prespa Palimpsest." PhD diss., University of Technology Sydney, 2019.

Yiannakis, John N. *Odysseus in the Golden West: Greek Migration, Settlement and Adaptation in Western Australia since 1947*. Waterford, WA: API Network, 2009.

Chapter 2

Transatlantic Hellas: Archiving Eastern Mediterranean Collections and Materials in the Smithsonian Institution

Alexander Nagel

Fashion Institute of Technology, State University of New York; Smithsonian Institution, National Museum of Natural History

Abstract

Since the mid-19th century, materials from Greece have found their way into public museums in Washington, D.C. At times donated by Greeks, at times gifted by antiquarians, diplomats and archaeologists, these materials and their histories have been the focus of new intensified research since 2015. This chapter will provide an introductory overview of a set of projects highlighting the history, development, individual personalities connected, as well as the roles the materials played in diplomatic exchange and exhibition cultures between Athens and Washington. Which roles did individuals connected with the Embassy of Greece play in the creation and dissemination of knowledge on ancient and modern Greece in Washington since the late 19th century? How were ancient Greek materials such as sculptures and vases displayed and how could these materials be better integrated into local, regional and international class-room education today? Highlights to be introduced include a new project on a beautiful book donated by the Greek Elizabeth Contaxaki; and a project highlighting Greek-American scientific exchange on excavations in Greece, introducing archival materials of Smithsonian Institution curators such as Lawrence Angel and Richard Howland.

Keywords: knowledge Transfer; Object Biographies; Anthropology; Museum Studies; Archives; Greece; Washington, D.C.

***

As a form of Old-World nostalgia, collecting world histories at the crossing between the Potomac and Anacostia Rivers, or "Town of Traders," as it was referred to then, did not begin with the early generations of European settlers who sought to make this place theirs. After and during the time when most of the Indigenous people were forcefully removed from the environs, after slaves enabled increased wealth for the new landowners in power, a new era of antiquarianism began.[1] Wealthy individuals embarked on a vision to create a new center of power away from, while at the same time often blatantly mirroring developments in, the Old World. After it was chosen as the young nation's capital in 1791 and the federal government moved to the grounds in December 1800, the status of the new federal seat of the United States grew fast. Today it must be considered an irony that, shortly after the burning of the first Capitol by British troops, the Columbian Institute for the Promotion of Arts and Sciences had been founded, with its goal to *reduce* the United States' dependence on a purely European cultural heritage. Although its first president, Edward Cutbush (1772–1843), had envisioned a large botanic garden for the Mall, and by an act of Congress the Columbian Institute was granted five acres in 1820, the institute was planned to be physically housed in an ancient temple–like building near the Capitol.[2] This physical institute remained a vision; the organization was dissolved in 1838 and absorbed in part by the National Institution for the Promotion of Science, founded by then Secretary of War (!) Joel Poinsett (1779–1851) in 1841.

This and the following are one way to introduce the beginnings of a long engagement with a potential to transplant European—in particular, Eastern Mediterranean—commodities and materials to the Potomac. In this chapter, I aim to offer a few more stories that illustrate and exemplify a longing for the Mediterranean in Washington, D.C. One could oppose the transfer and deposition of antiquities from the Mediterranean

---

1. A comparative approach to the caretaking of pasts by Indigenous nations and those who came late to the Potomac would be an interesting task; however, it is beyond the scope of this paper. See, for example, Peter Nabokov, *A Forest of Time: American Indian Ways of History* (Cambridge: Cambridge University Press, 2002) and papers in Junko Habu, Clare Fawcett, and John N. Matsunaga, eds., *Evaluating Multiple Narratives: Beyond Nationalist, Colonialist, Imperialist Archaeologies* (New York: Springer, 2008). On the concept of antiquarianism more recently, see Benjamin Anderson and Felipe Rojas, eds., *Antiquarianisms: Contact, Conflict, Comparison* (Oxford: Oxbow, 2017); on imperialism and decolonization, see Margarita Diaz-Andreu, "Archaeology and Imperialism: From Nineteenth-Century New Imperialism to Twentieth-Century Decolonization," in *Unmasking Ideology in Imperial and Colonial Archaeology: Vocabulary, Symbols, and Legacy*, eds. Bonnie Efros and Guolong Lai, 3–28 (Los Angeles: UCLA Cotsen Institute of Archaeology, 2018). For an earlier overview of the work of archaeology in the Potomac valleys, see, for example, Stephen Potter, *Commoners, Tribute, and Chiefs: The Development of Algonquian Culture in the Potomac Valley* (Charlottesville: University of Virginia Press, 1994). The preservation of past cultures in the Capital region is now largely administered through the National Park Service and the D.C. government's state archaeologist, Ruth Trocolli, and her team.

2. Pamela Scott, "'This Vast Empire': The Iconography of the Mall, 1791–1848," in *The Mall in Washington, 1791–1991*, ed. Richard Longstreth, 37–60 (Washington, DC: National Gallery of Art/New Haven, CT: Yale University Press, 2002). The Smithsonian Institution houses several archives related to the Columbian Institute for the Promotion of Arts and Sciences, many of which have been transcribed in recent years; see "The Correspondence of the Columbian Institute, 1816–1824," Smithsonian Institution, https://transcription.si.edu/project/7031. A watercolor of the temple structure can be found in a letter from June 1820; https://transcription.si.edu/project/7111.

against the efforts to document, map and narrate the histories of the Americas. One could take a gender-focused approach and write about the way in which women were involved, from the Cretan-born Elisavet Contaxaki, who never visited America, to passionate individuals and curators such as Diane Buitron-Oliver who were in many ways responsible for organizing the Washington exhibits *The Greek Miracle: Classical Sculpture from the Dawn of Democracy* (1992) and *The Birth of Democracy* (1993)—and now Ambassador Alexandra Papadopoulou.

One could contribute further, to write on the architects inspired by Classical architecture to create buildings such as Union Station, the Capitol or even the museums on the Mall itself.[3] Fred Wilson's groundbreaking *Mining the Museum* exhibition at the Maryland Historical Society in Baltimore in 1992 reminds us of a much-needed approach. Every new generation needs to be reminded that Washington, D.C., was considered part of America's South. The district's slave markets of the early 19th century have been described in contemporaneous correspondence; only through the Compromise Act of 1850 was slave trading in the district outlawed.[4]

Instead, the following is a snapshot of a relatively short engagement with and observations on archives, materials and diplomatic correspondence in Washington, D.C., that is not aiming to be comprehensive in any sense. The focus of this chapter is the Smithsonian Institution, physically in the heart of the district, on the Museum Mall, in an ideal spot to be observed through the looking glass.

---

3. Amy E. Burton, ed., *To Make Beautiful the Capitol: Rediscovering the Art of Constantino Brumidi* (Washington, DC: US Government Printing Office, 2014); Kirk Savage, *Monument Wars: Washington, D.C., the National Mall and the Transformation of the Memorial Landscape* (Berkeley: University of California Press, 2011).

4. Henry Celphane, "The Local Aspect of Slavery in the District of Columbia," *Records of the Columbia Historic Society* 3 (1900): 235–37; Mark Auslander, "Enslaved Labor and Building the Smithsonian," Southern Spaces, December 12, 2012, https://southernspaces.org/2012/enslaved-labor-and-building-smithsonian-reading-stones; Therese O'Malley, "'A Public Museum of Trees': Mid-Nineteenth Century Plans for the Mall," in Longstreth, 62. In 1848, "[f]or striking a white man, the slave's ears were 'to be cropt'"; Haynes Johnson, *Dusk at the Mountain: The Negro, the Nation, and the Capital; A Report on Problems and Progress* (New York: Doubleday, 1963), 20. See also Jeff Forret, "Early Republic and Antebellum United States," in *The Oxford Handbook of Slavery in the Americas*, eds. Mark M. Smith and Robert L. Paquette (Oxford: Oxford University Press, 2010); Jeff Forret and Christine E. Sears, eds., *New Directions in Slavery Studies: Commodification, Community, and Comparison* (Baton Rouge: Louisiana State University Press, 2015). For earlier periods, see Daniel C. Littlefield, "Colonial and Revolutionary United States," in Smith and Paquette, 201–26. For slavery's worship of pasts, see Christopher C. Fennell, *Crossroads and Cosmologies: Diasporas and Ethnogenesis in the New World* (Gainesville: University Press of Florida, 2007), 68–69; Theresa Singleton, "Archaeology and Slavery," in Smith and Paquette, 702–24.

Although the European born James Smithson (1765–1829) had provided in his will funds to establish an institution "for the increase and diffusion of knowledge among men" in 1826, and excitement grew around ideas of a national university, a museum and a great national library, the Smithsonian Institution was founded by an act of Congress only in 1846. Princeton University professor Joseph Henry (1797–1878) became the first secretary, and the Building Committee of the Board of Regents approved the plans of architect James Renwick Jr. (1818–95) for a permanent home west of the Capitol. The cornerstone for this building was laid in May 1847.[5] By then, Athens by the Piraeus had already been the capital of Greece for over a decade, and a ban to export antiquities became law.[6]

Since the middle of the 19th century, materials of Eastern Mediterranean origin have found their way into public museums and private collections in Washington, D.C. At times donated by ambitious consuls or diplomats—some born in the Eastern Mediterranean, some passionate philhellenes—these materials ("commodities") and their deep histories have been the focus of my research since 2010. How and why were Eastern Mediterranean materials collected and exhibited in Washington's major research institution? What do we know about the development and growth of the displays of such collections? What was the role of these materials and exhibits in diplomatic exchanges between the people from the Piraeus and those by the Potomac?

Among the first public lecturers in the new Smithsonian Institution was Adolph Ludvig Koeppen (1804–73). A Dane who had taught history in Athens, following the establishment of the Kingdom of Greece in 1832, Koeppen arrived in America in 1846.[7] In March 1849, he lectured for the Smithsonian Institution on "Attica and Athens," not on the Mall but, thanks to the connections of Henry and his colleagues, at Carusi's Saloon at 11th and Pennsylvania Avenues. First operated by the Italian immigrant Gaetano Carusi and his son Lewis, Carusi's Saloon was famous for attracting members of the district's high society. On Koeppen's lectures, Henry reports: "The lectures appear to have taken very

---

5. William Rhees, *The Smithsonian Institution: Documents Relative to Its Origin and History, 1835–1889* (Washington, DC: Government Publishing Office, 1901); reprinted as W. Rhees, *The Smithsonian Institution, 1835–1899* (New York: Arno Press, 1980). On Smithson see Nina Burleigh, *The Stranger and the Statesman: James Smithson, John Quincy Adams and the Making of America's Greatest Museum: The Smithsonian* (New York: Morrow, 2003). On the history of the owl motive see Walter Angst, *The Smithsonian Mace and Its Symbolism* (Washington, DC: Smithsonian Institution Press, 1984).

6. Recently; Maria Lagogianni-Georgakarakos, ed., *"These Are What We Fought For": Antiquities and the Greek War of Independence* (Athens: Archaeological Resources Fund, 2020).

7. Marc Rothenberg et al., eds., *The Papers of Joseph Henry*, vol. 7, *The Smithsonian Years: January 1847–December 1849* (Washington, DC: Smithsonian Institution Press, 1996), 495–96. On Koeppen's career and life between Europe and America see Harry Klein and Richard Altick, *Professor Koeppen: The Adventures of a Danish Scholar in Athens and America* (Lancaster, PA: Commercial Printing House, 1938).

well though they could not be more than half understood on account of the pronunciation of the speaker." Koeppen had been a close friend of Ludwig Ross and Christian Hansen, at that time presenting a pan-European interest in Greek heritage preservation, still trying to make amends with the growing independence from other Europeans who had recklessly pilfered the heritage of Athens, Bassae, Aigina and beyond in the preceding decades. Koeppen was briefly involved in excavating and restoring of monuments in Athens.[8]

Completed in 1855, the first building of the Smithsonian Institution (today referred to as "the Castle") soon became densely populated with scientists, their families and friends, volunteers and supporters. It also became home to a formidable collection of objects of Eastern Mediterranean origin, some of which had already been in Washington for years, either in the National Institute, established a few years earlier, or as gifts to the new government.[9] Among the early collections are plaster casts of monuments and sculptures found in Italy. These casts were used to advance crafting education among local Washingtonians. After a cast of the Apollo Belvedere arrived at the Smithsonian in 1858, for example, Joseph Henry's daughter Mary (1834–1903) herself displayed this and other then-canonic pieces of ancient Mediterranean art in a studio she owned on the Castle's second floor.[10] One of the early regents of the Smithsonian Institution was Harvard professor and president Cornelius Conway Felton (1807–62), who had studied Greek philology through German-inspired translations and became known early through a translation of Homer's *Iliad*.[11]

The Glory That Was Once: Elisavet Contaxaki's gift

Around the same time as Constantino Brumidi (1805–80) began his work of beautifying the Capitol with allegorical scenes of Mediterranean myths in an American context (see

---

8. On Koeppen as an archaeologist in Athens, see Klein and Altick, 8–9.

9. For example, Dinsmoor, 79; Wilcomb E. Washburn, "A Roman Sarcophagus in a Museum of Natural History," *Curator* 7, no. 4 (1964): 296–99.

10. Cynthia Field, Richard Stamm and Heather Ewing, *The Castle: An Illustrated History of the Smithsonian Building* (Washington, DC: Smithsonian Institution Press, 1993), 35–36, figs. 44 and 115. On reproductions of the Apollo from the Belvedere in the 19th century, see Francis Haskell and Nicholas Penny, *Taste and the Antique* (New Haven, CT: Yale University Press, 1981), 148–51. On early plaster cast collections in America, see Pamela Born, "The Canon Is Cast: Plaster Casts in American Museum and University Collections," *Art Documentation* 21, no. 2 (2002): 8–13; Stephen Dyson, "Cast Collecting in the United States," in *Plaster Casts: Making, Collecting and Displaying from Classical Antiquity to the Present*, eds. Rune Frederiksen and Eckart Marchant, 557–76 (Berlin: de Gruyter, 2010).

11. Dyson, *Ancient Marbles*, 21; David Wiesen, "Cornelius Felton and the Flowering of Classics in New England," *Classical Outlook* 59, no. 2 (1981–82): 44–48. The archives of Conway Felton at Harvard University might contain precious information about his influence on the secretary and the shaping of the Institution's early decades.

above), in 1857, a young Cretan woman named Elisavet Contaxaki (c. 1818–79) approached Carroll Spence (1818–96), a U.S. State Department envoy then residing in Constantinople. She had the idea of donating to the American people a 114-page volume of paintings and pressed flowers picked up at archaeological sites in Greece she had created earlier for the *Exposition Universelle* in Paris in 1855. Bound in blue velvet and embroidered with silver, this beautiful volume was kept in a wooden box carved with the names of famous Greek artists such as Apelles, Phidias and Zeuxis; it is preserved today in the Rare Book Division of the Smithsonian Institution's National Museum of Natural History (see figs. 2.1–2.3).[12]

Figure 2.1. Elisavet Contaxaki's "Classical Bouquet."

Photo by author.

---

12. I am grateful to Leslie Overstreet, Curator of the Rare Book Division in the National Museum of Natural History, who alerted me to the volume in 2013, for her continuing support. Following the rediscovery, I reached out to Polyvia Parara at the University of Maryland, who conducted new research on Contaxaki and the volume. In 2016 we held a colloquium on the volume at the University of Maryland, "The International Context of the Greek World in the 19th Century: Klassiki Anthodesmi, a 'Classical Bouquet,'" co-organized by L. Doherty, A. Nagel and P. Parara, April 2, 2016.

Figure 2.2. Elisavet Contaxaki's "Classical Bouquet," interior detail.

Photo by author.

Figure 2.3. Elisavet Contaxaki's "Classical Bouquet," interior detail with pressed wild flowers from Athens in Greece.

Photo by author.

Born in Chania in western Crete, Contaxaki had attended a high school in Athens founded by the American missionary Reverend John Henry Hill (1791–1882) and his wife, Frances (1799–1884), and must have learned about life in the New World from those who visited Athens then. Correspondence between the learned Contaxaki and the Hills, preserved at Georgetown University in Washington, D.C., proves Contaxaki's general dislike of contemporary Athenian politics.[13] Throughout the 1850s, she used her creative and organizational talent to engage a group of artists from the Greek mainland and the island of Tenos to produce the volume. In Spence's own words, Contaxaki appeared "ardent in her admiration of the United States and its institutions." He added that the illustrations included "a few from her native isle of Crete, not yet emancipated from the Moslem yoke."[14] The choice of sites, the emphasis on pre-Byzantine monuments, the ancient authors cited and some noted omissions in the narratives in the *Klassiki Anthodesmi* volume are worth investigating further. Among the drawings, the Aegina sculptures, then already in faraway Munich, are included, but not the pediment sculptures or the frieze from the Athenian Parthenon or other materials that had been earlier removed to London. Several drawings in the volume were inspired by photographs and postcards circulating at the time, rather than by actual visits of the artists to the site, at least for the illustrations from Athens.[15]

Contaxaki's passion and personality shine through in the sources we have. Being multilingual, she must have met not only Americans, French and Britons but also many more educated travelers and refugees from other parts of the Mediterranean after she arrived in Athens at a young age.[16] Contaxaki must have experienced the fundamental

---

13. Polyvia Parara, "The Journey of Elisavet Contaxaki's Classical Bouquet from Crete to Washington D.C.: Historical and Political Context," in *Proceedings of the 12th International Congress of Cretan Studies in Heraklion, Crete*, eds. C. Mitsotaki and L. Tzedaki-Apostolaki, 1–21 (ICCS, 2018), doi: https://12iccs.proceedings.gr/en/authors/271, 12.

14. Impressed by the volume's appearance, Spence continued that the "beauty of the finish and the faithfulness and accuracy of the quotations from Desiod [*sic*], Homer, Xenophon, Plato and others show that the present sons and daughters of the renowned ancient city of Minerva are not insensible of the glory that was once attached to her name, nor incapable of appreciating those monuments of art, science and literature which still survive." The correspondence is preserved along with the volume in the Rare Book Library Division of the National Museum of Natural History.

15. Alexander Nagel, "Greek Wild Flowers: Dialogues and Diplomats on the Parthenon and the Athenian Acropolis in the Nineteenth Century," *Unbound* (blog), Smithsonian Institution, March 18, 2016, doi: https://blog.library.si.edu/blog/2016/03/18/greek-wild-flowers/#.XmQn9qhKhPY. On the legacy of the Aegina monuments in Europe, see Louis Ruprecht, *Report on the Aeginetan Sculptures, with Historical Supplements* (Albany: State University of New York Press, 2018).

16. Crete experienced constant uprisings by Christian populations against the Ottoman rulers and Muslims, especially following the creation of the Greek state in 1830, and many Cretans wished for a union of their island with Greece. The Muslim presence was particularly strong in the large city centers such as Heraklion; in 1881 6,361 Christians lived alongside 14,597 Muslim inhabitants, and the Muslim

changes Athens went through after destructions caused by the Ottomans, and the impacts those changes in turn had on other parts of the Eastern Mediterranean for years to come.[17] Though she traveled between Crete, Athens, Constantinople and major European cities such as Paris, Contaxaki always remained close to her Cretan relatives and family.[18] As she carefully navigated among efforts and interests to renew a spiritual Hellenic past and engage with the Ottoman rulers still regulating life in Crete, Contaxaki's life and legacy offer a remarkable example of the great number of Greek intellectuals during those years, the philhellenes active in the past, and the developments in Greece at the time.[19] In her letters to America and the U.S. consulate in Constantinople (which are today preserved in Georgetown University's Booth Family Center for Special Collections), Contaxaki refers to antiquities that included ancient coins, which were already considered precious and valuable collector's tokens.

Lewis Cass (1782–1866), who was approached by Spence during the transaction, was not only Secretary of State but also on the board of the Smithsonian Institution in 1857, and he convinced Henry to accept Contaxaki's gift. The *Klassiki Anthodesmi* was deposited for many decades in the office of the Smithsonian Institution's secretary, in the Castle. It is unknown whether it was ever shown to wider audiences. In 1932 the volume entered the National Museum of Natural History Rare Book Division, where it remains to this day. The fate of Contaxaki, by contrast, remains unknown, though there is evidence that she spent much of her later life in Constantinople. Contaxaki, like Smithson, had never visited Washington, D.C.

In June 1854, the Greek statesman Pericles Argyropoulos (1809–61) had written to William Marcy (1786-1857), then U.S. Secretary of State, about the shipment of a marble block from the Parthenon for the new Washington Monument, then in the making. A year

---

population represented 26% of the entire population of Crete. It was not until the Pact of Chalepa in 1878 and the first Education Act of 1881 that high schools for girls began to operate on the island.

17. Sakis Gekas, "The Crisis of the Long 1850s and Regime Change in the Ionian State and the Kingdom of Greece," *Historical Review* 10 (2013): 57–84; Christos Aliprantis, "Political Refugees of the 1848–1849 Revolutions in the Kingdom of Greece: Migration, Nationalism, and State Formation in the Nineteenth-Century Mediterranean," *Journal of Modern Greek Studies* 37, no. 1 (2019): 1–33.

18. Correspondence from 1857 is preserved in the Carrol Spence Papers, Georgetown University Manuscripts.

19. Gonda Van Steen, *Liberating Hellenism from the Ottoman Empire: Comte de Marcellus and the Last of the Classics* (New York: Palgrave Macmillan, 2010); Peter Mackridge, *Language and National Identity in Greece, 1766–1976* (Oxford: Oxford University Press, 2010); William St. Clair, *That Greece Might Still Be Free: The Philhellenes in the War of Independence* (Oxford: Oxford University Press, 1972); Antonis Hadjikyriacou and Michalis Sotiropoulos, "Patris, Ethnos and Demos: Representation and Political Participation in the Greek World," in *Re-imagining Democracy in the Mediterranean, 1780-1860*, eds. Joanna Innes and Mark Philp, 99–124 (Oxford: Oxford University Press, 2018).

later, in 1855, the governor and community of the islands of Paros and Naxos offered a marble slab for the same project.[20]

Enthusiasts of knowledge and the Mediterranean: the formation of a collection

There was a drop in the acquisition of Old World–related materials by the Smithsonian Institution during and after the Civil War years, between 1861 and 1865. In 1867 Alexandros Rizos Rangavis (1809–92) arrived in Washington as the first official Greek ambassador to America. Writing from memory later in life, Rangavis describes his experiences and expresses particular sympathy with the situation of Native Americans.[21] Around the same time, the addition of a Parthenon fragment to the Washington Monument added further memorial connectivity with the Old World in Athens.

According to the important work by Yannis Galanakis, more than 50 antiquities dealers operated in Athens by the Piraeus in the second half of the 19th century alone, some of whom were registered and conducted their trade openly.[22] These individuals positioned themselves amid a growing group of scholars, diplomats and enthusiasts in a network that reached across all the major European capitals and America. At the same time, multiple efforts were being made in the Mediterranean to stem the pillaging of sites and monuments.[23] Compared to other major collections of ancient Eastern Mediterranean materials forming on the American east coast, only a modest number of original objects of Eastern Mediterranean origin entered the Smithsonian Institution in the late 19th century, however. This is in remarkable contrast to the large number of materials acquired for the institution from Italy (see below), and the large number of Eastern Mediterranean antiquities arriving in New York City during the same decades.

Collecting any Old world related materials in the Smithsonian Institution nearly ceased during the Civil War years. Following negotiations between Joseph Henry and the wealthy Washington banker William Wilson Corcoran (1798–1888) in 1874, casts of statues and engravings were transferred from the Smithsonian Institution to the Corcoran

---

20. John E. Ziolkowski, "The Parthenon Stone in the Washington Monument," *Our Heritage in Documents*, Winter 1993, 374–81; Judith M. Jacob, *The Washington Monument: A Technical History and Catalog of the Commemorative Stones* (Washington, DC: National Park Service, 2005); Lena Lambrinou, "The Parthenon from the Greek Revival to Modern Architecture," in *Hellenomania*, eds. Katherine Harloe, Nicoletta Momigliano and Alexandre Farnoux, 126–60 (London: Routledge, 2018).

21. Alexandros Rizos Rangavis, *The First Greek Ambassador to the American Federation, 1867–1868*, trans. Christine Gabrielides (Minneapolis: Nostos, 2019).

22. Yannis Galanakis, "Of Grave Hunters & Earth Contractors: A Look at the 'Private Archaeology' of Greece," *CHS Research Bulletin* blog, 2012, https://research-bulletin.chs.harvard.edu/2012/11/15/of-grave-hunters-earth-contractors-a-look-at-the-private-archaeology-of-greece/.

23. Voudouri, 78.

Gallery of Art.[24] In close proximity to the White House, Corcoran had established a museum for the capital's public and visitors that would become the place for art lovers and enthusiasts. The Smithsonian continued to accept gifts such as postcard illustrations and touristic souvenirs from Athens, as well as terracotta figurines, by then a characteristic portable object of attraction for tourists in Athens. Souvenirs included plaques depicting the Athenian Acropolis, which were donated by D.C.-based Columbian College professor George W. Samson (1819–96) in 1885 (fig. 2.4). It is unknown whether those plaques were ever displayed in the museum. When acquisitions for the Smithsonian were made during the final decade of the 19th century, they were few and limited to plaster casts of famous objects from major museum collections in Europe. These include sets made from the *Gipsformerei* of objects in the Royal Museums in Berlin and the British Museum in London.[25] Often those casts, including casts of the sculptures from the Parthenon of Athens in London, were traded through the Boston-based Caproni company.[26] Washingtonians interested in Old World art and inspiration would still primarily have visited the Corcoran Gallery.[27]

This changed with the arrival of a massive collection of Mediterranean materials accumulated under Thomas Wilson (1832–1902). Born in New Brighton, Pennsylvania, Wilson was originally interested in the history of Native Americans. He had learned early about the work of the Smithsonian Institution, especially scientist and curator Charles Rau (1826–87), himself an explorer of America's past. Wilson's excitement and interest

---

24. The transfer of "artworks" from the Smithsonian Institution to the Corcoran Gallery of Art remains one of the least studied periods in the history of the collections. Henry was as a trustee of the Corcoran Gallery, as was James C. McGuire (1812–88), a Washington-based auction and commission merchant. The National Archives preserve early journals of Corcoran Gallery curator William MacLeod (1811–92); https://www.archives.gov/nhprc/projects/catalog/william-macleod. The first catalogs of the displays do not contain much information about the transfers; William MacLeod, *Catalogue of the Paintings, Statuary, Casts, Bronzes, etc. of the Corcoran Gallery of Art* (Washington, DC: Gibson Brothers, 1883). According to MacLeod, the "Art of ancient Greece has been to succeeding ages the inspiring source of all excellence in Sculpture and Architecture" (p. 13). The archives of Corcoran in the Manuscript Division of the Library of Congress remain a valuable resource on Corcoran's business and philanthropic activities. See also Holly Tank, "Dedicated to Art: William Corcoran and the Founding of his Gallery," and "William Wilson Corcoran: Washington Philanthropist," *Washington History* 17, no.1 (Fall/Winter 2005), 26–65.

25. They include a cast of an "archaic" sepulchral banquet that was purchased in 1893 from the Royal Museum in Berlin, and a cast of the head of Apollo from the Zeus Temple at Olympia (accession no. 026942). These casts remain in storage at the National Museum of Natural History in Suitland, Maryland.

26. Born, 11; Dyson, "Cast Collecting," 572.

27. It is worthwhile to contrast the development of these cast collections with the formation of such collections in Greece during the same period. See Andromachi Gazi, "The Museum of Casts in Athens (1846–1874)," *Journal of the History of Collections* 10, no. 1 (1998): 87–91; Alexandra Alexandri, "'The Stamp of National Life': Plaster Casts and Their Uses in Greece at the End of the 19th Century," in Voutsaki and Cartledge, 130–47.

in the past and an appointment as U.S. consul to Ghent, Belgium, in 1881, and his subsequent transfers to Nantes and Nice in France (where he remained until his return to America in 1887), prepared him well to become appreciative of the Mediterranean past and the value and benefits of scientific research on such materials. Following negotiations between the State Department and Smithsonian officials, Wilson succeeded Rau as Curator of Prehistoric Archaeology in the National Museum in 1887.[28] As correspondence in the National Anthropological Archives of the Smithsonian Institution reveals, during his tenure as consul in Europe, he had already arranged for exchanges of collections between the Smithsonian and European research institutions and museums. A history of the formation of Wilson's collection of 14,000-plus objects, a great number of which he acquired in Italy between 1884 and 1886, remains to be written. Wilson was only one of a great number of consuls and diplomats who were involved in establishing major antiquities collections in the United States (and Europe) at the time, and one of several enthusiastic supporters of archaeological fieldwork in Italy. Studying Wilson's biography, we find interesting parallels with the biography of the Italian-born American consul Luigi Palma di Cesnola (1832–1904).[29]

Initially, the Wilson collection was only on loan to the National Museum. A great number of the objects shipped from Italy to Washington, D.C. in crates, came from tombs in Chiusi in ancient Tarquinia, Orvieto and Siena. Several pieces were singled out early. Signed with the name Duris, a kylix excavated at Orvieto went on display in the National Museum between 1887 and 1898. Together with another 10 objects, this kylix was then sold by Wilson to Frank Tarbell (1853–1920). Tarbell was an early director and secretary of the American School of Classical Studies at Athens; he had also taught as a professor at Yale University and the University of Chicago.

---

28. Otis Mason, "In Memoriam: Thomas Wilson," *American Anthropologist* 4, no. 2 (1902): 286–91.

29. Elizabeth McFadden, The Glitter and the Gold: A Spirited Account of the Metropolitan Museum of Art's First Director, the Audacious and High-Handed Luigi Palma di Cesnola (New York: Dial Press, 1971); Anna Marangou, The Consul Luigi di Cesnola, 1832–1904: Life and Deeds (Nicosia, 2000); Antoine Hermary and Joan Mertens, The Cesnola Collection of Cypriot Art: Stone Sculpture (New York: Metropolitan Museum of Art, 2014), 20–23; Elizabeth Bartman, "Archaeology versus Aesthetics: The Metropolitan Museum of Art's Classical Collection in Its Early Years," in Classical New York: Discovering Greece and Rome in Gotham, eds. Elizabeth Macaulay-Lewis and Matthew McGowan, 63–84 (New York: Fordham University Press, 2018); Katharine Baetjer and Joan Mertens, "The Founding Decades," in Making the Met, 1870–2020, eds. Andrea Bayer and Laura Corey, 34–47 (New York: Metropolitan Museum of Art, 2020). On American collectors in Italy during this period (with no reference to Wilson), see Richard de Puma, "Americans Collecting Antiquities in Italy, c. 1865–1920," in The Collection of Antiquities of the American Academy in Rome, eds. Larissa Bonfante and Helen Nagy, 3–12 (Ann Arbor: University of Michigan Press, 2015). On the role of consuls in the transfer of materials, see Zainab Bahrani, Zeynep Çelik and Edhem Eldem, eds., Scramble for the Past: A Story of Archaeology in the Ottoman Empire (Istanbul: Yalinari, 2011) and Michael Greenhalgh, Plundered Empire: Acquiring Antiquities from Ottoman Lands (Leiden: Brill, 2019).

Figure 2.4. A plaque depicting the Parthenon, donated by George W. Samson in 1885 (NMNH A074624).

Source: Smithsonian Institution, National Museum of Natural History.

Tarbell introduces us to the negotiations then being made in the offices of the Castle, as the National Museum was not interested in recommending a purchase.[30] Other contemporaneous correspondence reveals that visitors were unable to appreciate the Wilson collection, then on display in the National Museum. For Tarbell, an enthusiast who supported any increase in knowledge about ancient Eastern Mediterranean art, the transfer of objects to other collections was more lucrative: a vase signed with the name Duris had been excavated on the Athenian Acropolis only a few years earlier, providing a welcome new context for the kylix, which had been excavated in Italy.[31] Only after an

---

30. Frank Tarbell, "A Signed Cylix by Duris, in Boston," *American Journal of Archaeology* 4, no. 2 (1900): 183–91. Since 1900 the kylix has been owned by the Boston Museum of Fine Arts, where it is registered under accession number 00.499.

31. Detailed notes on the modern history of the Duris cup from the Wilson collection in Italy are preserved. "This vase was ... was found in 1886, between April 4 and 11, in the necropolis on the northwest slope of the rock on which Orvieto is situated. The discovery was made in the course of excavations conducted by Signor Riccardo Mancini, a well-known explorer of Orvieto, Dr. Wilson being himself present and assisting in the work"; Tarbell, "A Signed Cylix by Duris, in Boston," *American Journal of Archaeology* 4, no. 2 (1900): 183–84.

agreement between Smithsonian Institution official Otis Mason (1838–1908) and Wilson's son James Frank Wilson—who sold most of the objects to the Smithsonian on January 29, 1904—did the large reminder of the collection become the official property of the National Museum.[32] It is the single largest collection of ancient objects made to the Smithsonian in the early twentieth century. It would be interesting to learn more about the handling, mending and conservation of the corpus of ceramic fragments. Did Wilson entertain a laboratory at the premises on the Mall?

A growing interest in marking sites of importance for a new formation of Hellenic identity in the entanglement of archaeology, diplomacy, and power, becomes evident in another case. In 1893 Sophia Schliemann (1852–1932) donated to the Smithsonian Institution more than 177 artifacts from her husband's excavations at Troy. Heinrich Schliemann himself had schemed earlier to donate his entire Troy collection to the Smithsonian in exchange for a U.S. consulship to Greece. The story, recently described in a wonderful essay by Georgia Flouda, is also of interest in the context of politics, journalism and personal ambition in Washington, D.C. in the final decades of the nineteenth century.[33]

Thomas Wilson was also responsible for the acquisition of materials excavated by Flinders Petrie (1853–1942) in Egypt in 1898. Around the same time, the Baltimore-based German scholar Paul Haupt and his students Cyrus Adler and Immanuel Casanowicz began their careers in the Smithsonian Institution with the establishment of a new Department of Oriental Antiquities. The German archaeologist Adolf Furtwängler (1853–1907) describes the Smithsonian's collections of Old World artifacts on display around 1900 as a *buntes durcheinander* ("colorful mess").[34]

---

32. Accession no. 042207. Some of the Greek vases were published by classical archaeologist Shirley Schwarz, in "The Pattern Class Vases of the Gruppo di Orvieto in the US National Museum Collection, Smithsonian Institution," *Studi Etrusci* 47 (1979): 65–84; "Etruscan Black Figure Vases in the US National Museum," *Mitteilungen des Deutschen Archäologischen Instituts, Roemische Abteilung* 91 (1984): 47–77; *Greek Vases in the National Museum of Natural History: Smithsonian Institution, Washington, D.C.* (Rome: Erma di Bretschneider, 1996).The history of the Wilson collection in Washington's National Museum mirrors in some ways the earlier history of the Cypriot collections housed in the Metropolitan Museum in New York, which arrived in the city between 1873 and 1876 as the private property of Palma di Cesnola. Wilson's complex role in the removal of materials from Europe and his later advocacy for an antiquities bill in 1899 in the U.S. remains to be explored. The bill that led to the Antiquities Act, which aimed to protect American antiquities, laid the groundwork for modern legal protection.

33. Flouda.

34. Adolf Furtwängler, "Neue Denkmäler antiker Kunst: Antiken in den Museen von Amerika, Washington," Sitzungsberichte der philosophisch-philologischen und der historischen Klasse der Königlichen Bayerischen Akademie der Wissenschaften 5, no. 2 (1905): 250–51.

Figure 2.5. Vase from the Collection of Thomas Wilson, National Museum of Natural History, Inv. No. A136415.

Source: Smithsonian Institution, National Museum of Natural History, Anthropology Collections.

Figure 2.6. Room in the east wing of the Smithsonian Institution building with a plaster copy of the Parthenon frieze. Unknown photographer, 1902.

Source: Smithsonian Institution Archives, record unit 95, box 41, folder 20, negative no. 15882.

A photograph from 1902, from what is now the office of the Smithsonian's Undersecretary of History, on the second floor of the east wing of the Castle, shows prominently displayed casts of panels from the Parthenon's interior frieze in reduced size (fig. 2.6). The room was created under Samuel P. Langley (1834–1906), who had become the Smithsonian's third secretary in 1887. According to the Castle's curator, Richard Stamm, some 18 panels were added to an original group of three from the Parthenon frieze in the room in 1902. The panels had been acquired from the New York City–based "Louisa Castelvecchi, widow, L & Co. Statues" and "P. P. Caproni & Bro., Plaster Arts, Boston, USA."[35] Their creation and prominent display in the Castle can be contextualized within the framework of the creation of the "Hall of the Ancients" by Franklin Webster Smith (1826–1911) near the White House in 1899. Webster Smith had long complained about the lack of inspiring displays of ancient Mediterranean art on the Mall. In a pamphlet, he laments:

---

35. Richard Stamm, "The Mystery of the Art Room Frieze," *Smithsonian History* (blog), June 18, 2018; https://siarchives.si.edu/blog/mystery-art-room-frieze.

The collection ... reveals the utter poverty of the Smithsonian Institution of object lessons from the empires of antiquity ... While the Smithsonian has won position equal to any of the scientific organizations of the world, specimens, relics, models, effigies, casts, pictures etc. etc. that now fill the national museum, and others in storage, that demand its double capacity, almost exclusively relate to American Archaeology, ethnology, anthropology, etc. they throw *no* light on the history of modern civilization. *Religion, art, science, and literature have not descended to us through the Indian tribes of North America.*[36]

Figure 2.7. Immanuel Casanowicz (1853–1927).

Source: Smithsonian Institution, National Museum of Natural History, National Anthropological Archives.

---

36. Franklin Webster Smith, *National Galleries of History and Art: Descriptive Handbook of the Hall of the Ancients* (Washington, DC: Government Printing Office, 1900), 89 [emphasis added]. The Hall of the Ancients has been the focus of renewed research by the author since 2010.

The collections of Wilson and Schliemann were on display for several years in the National Museum, next to the Castle, before some were transferred to another display between 1910 and 1913, in the newly opened Anthropology halls on the second floor of the National Museum of Natural History. These new displays in these so-called Old-World Archaeology halls were curated by Johns Hopkins University–trained Immanuel Casanowicz (1853–1927) (fig. 2.7).[37] In 1922 Casanowicz published a comprehensive catalog of the Old World archaeology collections in the United States National Museum.[38]

Relevant for the history of Greece in the Smithsonian Institution are the depositions of collections assembled by Charles Lang Freer (1854–1919) and Alden Sampson (1853–1925) in the first decades of the 20th century. Sampson was friends with Harvard professor Charles Eliot Norton (1827–1908), between 1879 and 1890 the first president of the Archaeological Institute of America, and his son Richard Norton (1872–1918), who also became a director of the Archaeological Institute of America, as well as the young Edward W. Forbes (1873–1969).[39] In the late 19th century, Sampson had already

---

37. Casanowicz was a student of the German scholar Paul Haupt at Johns Hopkins University in Baltimore. Research into these early displays would be particularly useful from a museological point of view, as the work of Andromachi Gazi proves: "Archaeological Museums and Displays in Greece 1829–1909: A First Approach," *Museological Review* 1, no. 1 (1994): 50–69; "'Artfully Classified' and 'Appropriately Placed': Notes on the Display of Antiquities in Early Twentieth-Century Greece," in Damaskos and Plantzos, 67–82. At the Smithsonian, the divide between science and art persisted throughout those decades. Though it remains challenging to understand the developments, a few noteworthy collections related to Eastern Mediterranean landscapes and art were acquired during that time. Among them are drawings and paintings by Henry Bacon (1866–1924), who visited the Acropolis and other sites in Athens on several occasions in 1897. His paintings were displayed in the National Museum of Natural History in March and April 1931 and are today housed in the Smithsonian American Art Museum.

38. Immanuel Casanowicz, The Collections of Old World Archaeology in the United States National Museum (Washington, DC: Smithsonian Institution, 1922).

39. Sampson, Forbes and Norton also donated objects to other U.S. institutions, including a Palmyrene relief to Harvard University (1908.3). On objects donated to the American Academy in Rome, see Katherine Geffken, "The History of the Collection," in Bonfante and Nagy, 21–78. Charles Eliot Norton (1827–1908) has received a rather mixed modern reception, being once portrayed as a deluded "patrician aesthete and an ineffectual foe of democracy" and a "militant idealist"; Hugh Davis, review of *Charles Eliot Norton: The Art of Reform in Nineteenth Century America*, by Linda Dowling, *Journal of American History* 95, no. 2 (2008): 350. See also James Turner, *The Liberal Education of Charles Eliot Norton* (Baltimore, MD: Johns Hopkins University Press, 1999). Norton's wide-ranging interests brought him in contact with several members of the Smithsonian staff, including John Wesley Powell (1834–1902), who directed the institution's Bureau of Ethnology between 1879 and 1894 (Turner, 286). Norton was a key figure in the founding of the American School of Classical Studies at Athens in 1881 as "the AIA's first archaeological training school"; Caroline Winterer, "The American School of Classical Studies at Athens: Scholarship and High Culture in the Gilded Age," in *Excavating Our Past: Perspectives on the History of*

donated a study collection of ancient marbles to the American Academy in Rome.[40] Several sculptures and vases from the Sampson collection, "assembled in collaboration with Charles Eliot Norton,"[41] were on loan to the Smithsonian Institution from an unknown year until they were donated to Princeton University following an agreement signed in 1961.[42] The collections included marble fragments and heads such as Roman copies of portraits of Homer and Demosthenes. Next to nothing is known about the circumstances of their first arrival in America. Were they ever displayed in the National Museum of Natural History? Freer, though passionate about Asian art, owned a villa on Capri in Italy's Bay of Naples, where he collected a modest number of antiquities and enjoyed the luxurious life of a wealthy retired industrialist in gardens under the Mediterranean sun.[43]

In 1930, the Smithsonian Institution accepted a carved marble fragment from a molding "found in the Parthenon" on the Athenian Acropolis (A348943-0). The fragment belonged to American civil engineer Washington Roebling (1837–1926), who had visited Europe in the 1860s. It was inherited by his son John A. Roebling II. According to archival records, Washington Roebling had received the fragment from an artist named Loeher, who had picked it up on the site in Greece. The fragment seems not to have been among the 16,000 minerals John Roebling donated to the Smithsonian Institution following the death of his father earlier.

Some same materials and different display strategies

For many decades, curators in the National Museum of Natural History struggled to engage with updating the Old World displays; in the late 1950s, they decided to completely overhaul the by then very outdated Old World archaeology displays on the second floor. Scholarly initiatives related to Greece were thriving outside Washington, and the U.S. government reassessed foreign relations, including in the museum sector. In Athens, the American School of Classical Studies had opened a new museum in September 1956.[44]

---

the *Archaeological Institute of America*, ed. Susan Heuck Allen (Boston: AIA, 2002), 94; Elizabeth Lyding Will, "Charles Eliot Norton and the Archaeological Institute of America," in Heuck Allen, 49–61.

40. Geffken, 28.

41. Patrick Kelleher, "Interim News for a New Art Museum," *Princeton Alumni Weekly* 63 (November 1962): 9–10.

42. Brunilde Ridgway, ed., *Greek Sculpture in the Art Museum, Princeton University: Greek Originals, Roman Copies and Variants* (Princeton, NJ: Princeton University Press, 1994), 6.

43. Elaine Gazda, *In Pursuit of Antiquity: Thomas Spencer Jerome and the Bay of Naples (1899–1914)* (Ann Arbor, MI: Kelsey Museum of Archaeology, 1983).

44. Marlen Mouliou, "Museum Representations of the Classical Past in Post-war Greece: A Critical Analysis," in Damaskos and Plantzos, 90–91.

In February 1957, George Mylonas (1898–1988) lectured at the Smithsonian Institution on new research at the graves in Mycenae. Around the same time, Greece—since 1947 ruled by King Paul (1901–64)—offered through ambassadors and the Benaki Museum an exhibition on Greek costumes. *Greek Costumes and Embroideries* became the first official exhibition offered through the Smithsonian Institution Traveling Exhibition Service, organized by Annemarie Pope, in 1959.[45] Also in 1959, the Eisenhower administration donated to the Smithsonian Institution a small, eclectic group of materials that had been received as gifts from King Paul and Queen Frederica of Greece and Prime Minister Spyros Markezinis (1909–2000).[46]

In 1961, an earlier vision of a Center for Hellenic Studies in the U.S. capital became reality with its official inauguration on Whitehaven Street, while the Old World displays at the National Museum of Natural History closed permanently in 1960. The revamped Old World Archaeology halls in the NMNH were supposed to open in 1963, but *Western Civilization: Origins and Traditions* was an unusually long time in the making; it was curated by Gus Van Beek (1922–2012), then a curator of Old World archaeology at the museum. After its opening in June 1978, the exhibition, designed by Steven Makovenyi and featuring over 1,600 objects, remained on view until 2010.[47] Archival correspondence contains information about the ways in which Van Beek and his team tackled creating a narrative and display themes for the *Western Civilization* exhibit, which in early communications was referred to as the *Hall of Classical Archaeology*.

In early February 1961, Van Beek, on the advice of Richard Howland (see below), wrote to William K. Pritchett (1909–2007), a professor at the University of California, Berkeley, about a planned acquisition of a white model of the Parthenon, ordered from Petros Diamantides in California. In a letter related to the acquisition from February 20, 1961, Pritchett warns Van Beek "in advance that the ancient Greeks used bright colors which might seem garish to the modern eye. These colors need Mediterranean sunshine to be understood." The archives contain valuable information about the specifics of this planned acquisition. Delays in fabrication and other reasons led to an abrupt change of plans in 1964. Following internal communications among staff members in the National Museum of Natural History, in 1965, a new model of the entire Acropolis was ordered from Greece: again on the advice of Howland, Van Beek asked specifically for a replica

---

45. *Greek Costumes and Embroideries from the Benaki Museum* (Washington, DC: Smithsonian Institution, 1959). In 1959 the National Gallery of Art dedicated a small exhibition to contemporary Greek painting.

46. See, for example, accession no. 229785, presented during a "goodwill tour" in 1959 and accepted by the NMNH in 1960; Schwarz, *Greek Vases*, 34, no. 30. Markezinis's gifts to the U.S. government are being studied by Nassos Papalexandrou.

47. Gus Van Beek et al., Western Civilization: Origins and Traditions; An Exhibit at the National Museum of Natural History, Smithsonian Institution (Washington, DC: Elephant Press, 1979).

of a model of the Acropolis ("*no* tinting") originally prepared by Gorham Phillip Stevens (1876–1963).[48] Replicas of the Acropolis model had already been shared by Athens-based artists with museums in Toronto, Havana and New York. Correspondence between Van Beek, members of the American School of Classical Studies in Athens—including John Travlos (1908–85), Eugene Vanderpool (1906–89) and the model maker Christos Mammelis—relate to the arrival of the model in 1967 and slight damages that occurred in 1968. In 1976 Robert Evans, for a brief period an exhibit research archaeologist for Van Beek, asked Travlos about repairs on the model (fig. 2.8).

Figure 2.8. Model of the Athenian Acropolis. Prepared by G. P. Stevens, J. Travlos and C. Mammelis, on display at *Western Civilization: Origins and Traditions*, which opened in 1978 in the National Museum of Natural History, Inv. no. AT13319.

Source: Smithsonian Institution, National Museum of Natural History.

---

48. National Anthropological Archives, Gus van Beek Papers. Gus Van Beek, memorandum, May 21, 1964. In a note attached, Van Beek mentions that Howland asked that the model should be "stark white. … and that the Royal Ontario Museum model is overdone."

Prior to the opening of the exhibition, Van Beek, no expert in ancient Greek archaeology, was also involved in the acquisition of Greek vases and other materials from dealers such as the Jerome Eisenberg Gallery in New York City. A bequest of a group of antiquities from the art market that came with a collection of Joseph Hirshhorn (1899–1981)—who supported the institution throughout the 1960s and later—entered the National Museum of Natural History with the assistance of anthropologist Betty Meggers (1921–2012).

Richard Howland and John Lawrence Angel

Richard Hubbard Howland (1910–2006) and John Lawrence Angel (1915–86) deserve attention for several reasons (figs. 2.9–11). Both were involved in archaeological fieldwork conducted by the American School of Classical Studies at Athens. Both were trained at Harvard University. Both joined the Smithsonian Institution in the 1960s and remained active in the study and promotion of Greece from there throughout their careers. Only Howland's philhellenic orientation had some bearing on the evolving collections, however. The archives of Howland and Angel, which are shared today between institutions in Washington, D.C., the University of Maryland (Howland), and Athens, Greece, provide key information about the scientific exchanges between Athens, the Smithsonian Institution and the U.S. State Department.

Figure 2.9. John Lawrence Angel (1915–86).

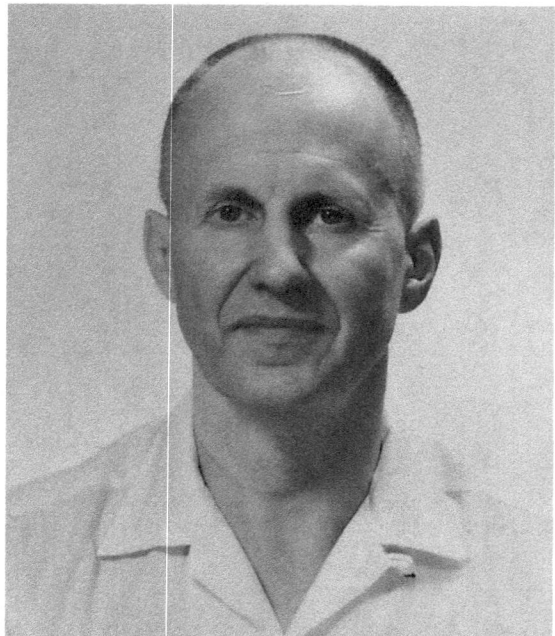

Source: Smithsonian Institution, National Museum of Natural History, National Anthropological Archives.

Figure 2.10. Richard Hubbard Howland (1910–2006).

Source: Smithsonian Institution, National Museum of Natural History, National Anthropological Archives.

Figure 2.11. R. H. Howland in traditional Greek costume.

Source: Smithsonian Institution, National Museum of Natural History, National Anthropological Archives.

Before officially joining the Smithsonian in 1962, Angel taught at the Universities of California, in Minnesota and at Jefferson Medical College in Philadelphia.[49] Before 1962, he had already conducted numerous cranio-morphological studies on skeletal human remains from excavations at Argos, Asine, Athens, Corinth, Eleusis, Mycenae, Lerna, Olynthus and elsewhere, work he continued while on staff at the Smithsonian.[50] **Throughout his time at the Smithsonian Institution, Angel kept up an avid** correspondence with Greek archaeologists and historians such as Spyridon Marinatos (1901–74), George Mylonas (1898–1988), Evangelia Protonotariou Deilaki, Nestor Constantoulis, John Melentis and Aris Poulianos (author of *The Origin of the Hellenes*), as well as John Caskey, Paul Clement, Theodore McCown, Alison Frantz, Virginia Grace, Benjamin D. Merrit, Theodore Leslie Shear, Lucy Shoe and Dorothy B. and Homer Thompson, all members of the ASCSA. There is also correspondence with Oscar Broneer (1894–1992), David Robinson (1880–1958) and others.[51]

In May 1938, Angel had received an award from University of Athens anthropologist John Koumaris (1879–1970). The document, created by Koumaris himself, is today

---

49. Born to a sculptor in London, Angel came to America when he was only 13 years old. Through his grandfather Thomas Day Seymour (1848–1907), who had taught classics at Yale University and had been chairman of the managing committee of the American School of Classical Studies at Athens between 1887 and 1901, and his mother, Elizabeth Day Seymour Angel (1876–1942), Angel had grown up with an education deeply grounded in the classics. His interest shifted early to the study of human remains, and today he is known as an early and ardent supporter of the development of a field of physical anthropology in Greece. Angel graduated from Harvard University with a doctorate in physical anthropology. See Thomas Jacobson and Tracey Cullen, "The Work of J. L. Angel in the Eastern Mediterranean," in *A Life in Science: Papers in Honor of J. Lawrence Angel*, ed. Jane Buikstra, 38–51 (Evanston, IL: Center for American Archeology, 1990); Jane Buikstra and Eleanna Prevedorou, "John Lawrence Angel (1915–1986)," in *The Global History of Paleopathology: Pioneers and Prospects*, eds. Jane Buikstra and Charlotte Roberts, 3–13 (Oxford: Oxford University Press, 2012). During the 1938–39 academic year, Angel was awarded a fellowship by the American Friends of Greece, a group of philhellenes then chaired by George H. Chase (1874–1952).

50. John Lawrence Angel, "Classical Olynthians," in *Excavations at Olynthus XI; Necrolynthia: A Study in Greek Burial Customs and Anthropology*, ed. David M. Robinson (Baltimore: Johns Hopkins University Press, 1942); "Skeletal Material from Attica," *Hesperia* 14 (1945): 279–363; "Skeletal Change in Ancient Greece," *American Journal of Physical Anthropology* 4 (1946): 69–97; "Classical Archaeology and the Anthropological Approach," in *Studies Presented to David Moore Robinson on His Seventieth Birthday*, eds. George Mylonas and Doris Raymond, 1224–31 (St. Louis: Washington University, 1953); *The People of Lerna: Analysis of a Prehistoric Aegean Population* (Princeton, NJ: American School of Classical Studies at Athens, 1971).

51. A few years following Angel's untimely death, the American School of Classical Studies in Athens awarded a fellowship for the study of human remains in the Wiener Laboratory in 1992. In 2008 the School received a leadership gift from the family toward an endowment, the J. Lawrence Angel Fellowship in Human Skeletal Studies at the Wiener Laboratory.

preserved among Angel's archives in the Smithsonian Institution (fig. 2.12). The drawing pays homage to iconic monuments excavated in Greece, including the Snake Goddess from Knossos, Minoan wall paintings, a Cycladic harp player, the gold masks from Mycenae and the Hermes of Praxiteles, all accepted as icons of Greek archaeology before the beginning of WWII.[52] While Angel was never involved in the actual presentation of Greek displays in the Smithsonian Institution, his knowledge network and familiarity with Greece made him a frequent lecturer and sought-after expert on the subject in Washington.

Figure 2.12. Award presented to J. L. Angel by John Koumaris, 1938.

Source: Smithsonian Institution, National Museum of Natural History, National Anthropological Archives.

Art historian Richard Hubbard Howland had finished a master's thesis on south Italian fish plates at Harvard University in 1933. He began a lifelong affiliation with the ASCSA soon thereafter. He became a student of the School in 1933–34. Howland's interest in lamps from fieldwork conducted at the Athenian Agora led to a dissertation that he

---

52. Today Koumaris's role and his legacy in the history of anthropology in Greece, as well as the contribution by foreign nationals to Greek anthropology during the 1930s and 1940s, is much better understood; Sevasti Trubeta, *Physical Anthropology, Race, and Eugenics in Greece (1880s–1970s)* (Boston: Brill, 2013), especially 57–78.

defended at Johns Hopkins University in Baltimore in 1946.[53] Howland, who also had a lifelong interest in the history of architecture and furniture, was first hired to work at the Smithsonian's newest museum, the Museum of History and Technology, in 1964 (since 1980 known as the National Museum of American History). Correspondence between Howland and Van Beek proves that the latter acknowledged Howland as the foremost expert on Greek art in Washington. Under Howland, the Institution's Office of the Special Assistant to the Secretary provided $1,000 in annual support to the ASCSA. Howland served on the board of trustees of the ASCSA for many years.[54] He was also a trustee member of the Society for the Preservation of the Greek Heritage (SPGH), originally founded in Washington in 1974. Well-publicized seminars, such as "Mycenaean Treasures of the Aegean Bronze Age Repatriated" and "The Destiny of the Parthenon Marbles," were held at the Smithsonian Institution's Ripley Center and at the Corcoran Gallery of Art.[55] To promote knowledge about Greece, through the Smithsonian Associates program, Howland also began leading regular tours for Americans, who would then visit major sites and excavations in Greece.[56] Today the Archaeological Institute of America's local Washington, D.C., society holds an annual lecture honoring his contributions to the field.[57] Howland's philhellenic legacy in the Smithsonian Institution is manifested by a collection of lamps from Greece, amassed over his career, and his role in the acquisition of materials throughout the institution. New gifts included an amphora that was given by the American ambassador to Italy Clare Boothe Luce

---

53. Richard Howland, *Greek Lamps and Their Survivals* (Princeton, NJ: American School of Classical Studies at Athens, 1958). The early excavations in Athens and Corinth in which Howland participated have now been critically examined; see, for example, Kostas Kourelis, "Byzantium and the Avantgarde: Excavations at Corinth, 1920s to 1930s," *Hesperia* 76, no. 2 (2007): 391–442; Yannis Hamilakis, "Double Colonization: The Story of the Excavations of the Athenian Agora (1924–1931)," in Davis and Vogeikoff, 153–77.

54. Lucy Shoe Meritt, *History of the American School of Classical Studies at Athens, 1939–1980* (Princeton, NJ: American School of Classical Studies 1984), 97–120.

55. Richard Howland, ed., *Mycenaean Treasures of the Aegean Bronze Age Repatriated* (Washington, DC: Society for the Preservation of Greek Heritage, 1996); *The Destiny of the Parthenon Marbles* (Washington, DC: Society for the Preservation of Greek Heritage, 2000).

56. Angel and Howland are only two of many more individuals who were active in research in Greece during the twentieth century. In 1968 Richard Grant (1927–94), a curator in the Smithsonian Institution's Natural History Museum Paleobiology Division, began studying aspects of the formation of the islands of Hydra and Chios, which he continued between 1974 and 1979, though he never published his research. George E. Watson (born 1931), a former ornithologist employed at the National Museum of Natural History.

57. Howland has become of interest again with the archival blog of Natalia Vogeikoff, archivist of the ASCSA. See, for example, "Greece 1935–1938: Involuntary Testimonies," *From the Archivist's Notebook* (blog), May 2, 2017, https://nataliavogeikoff.com/2017/05/02/greece-1935-1938-involuntary-testimonies/.

(1903–87) before 1954. Today the amphora is in storage at the National Museum of American History (fig. 2.13).[58]

Figure 2.13. Amphora, National Museum of American History, Inv. No. 1979.0696.01. This amphora was used as a Model for the Sports Illustrated Sportsman of the Year Award.

Source: Smithsonian Institution, National Museum of American History

---

58. National Museum of American History, acquisition no. 1979.0696.

Among the secretaries who had a major impact on Old World representation in the Smithsonian Institution, Dillon Ripley (1913–2001) is notable. Ripley started a tradition that every new secretary following him would receive a badge with a golden owl, a characteristic feature of Athenian economic power in the ancient world. In his rhetoric, Ripley often compared the Smithsonian Institution to notable Old World institutions.[59]

Following a generation of Europeans who had immigrated and begun teaching ancient art, the archeologist Stephen Dyson noted a "re-Europeanization of American classical archaeology."[60] During the 1960s, when Ripley, Van Beek, Angel and Howland were involved in research, display and promotion of Greece, Greek politics in Athens had obviously changed dramatically, in part because of U.S. interventions following the Second World War. These shifting politics had an impact on Greece in Washington, D.C., too. On September 11, 1967, Melina Mercouri (1920–94) was among a large crowd of protestors near the White House, only a few blocks away from the Smithsonian Institution as President Johnson had luncheon with King Constantine.[61] A Greek far-right military junta had ruled Greece from 1967 to 1974. It is of interest that nothing in the archives of Angel or Howland refers to the changes in the political landscape in Athens. Almost indifferent to the changes, it seems, their fascination with Greece remained strong as other institutions such as the Center for Hellenic Studies or Dumbarton Oaks promoted other classical pasts of Greece in Washington, D.C.

Circulating images and ideas of Greece in the United States, then and now

A full history of the formation, development and display of Eastern Mediterranean collections in the U.S. capital remains to be written. It is not offered here. Scholars have reevaluated ways of looking at and studying heritage in Greece, as there never was a "singular antiquity." The material worlds of the Eastern Mediterranean do indeed matter in Washington today. Following protocols established with other governments in the world—in particular, the case of Cyprus since 2002—a memorandum of understanding (MoU) was signed by Stavros Lambrinidis, Hellenic Republic of Greece minister of foreign affairs, and Hillary Rodham Clinton, U.S. secretary of state, in the Acropolis Museum in Athens in 2011, to ensure mutual help in preserving the cultures and fighting an illicit trade in antiquities that had flourished for much of the 20th and early 21st centuries. It is a challenging task. Up for review every five years, such MoUs aim to reduce the looting and trafficking of illicitly excavated. Greece has a long legacy of

---

59. "The Smithsonian Institution at Washington is to Americans somewhat as the Museum at Alexandria was to the Greek world in antiquity. But how much finer and vaster!" stated Ripley during a ceremony in Cambridge, England, in 1974; "Secretary Ripley Receives Degree from Cambridge," *The Torch*, July/August 1974, 3.

60. Stephen Dyson, *Ancient Marbles to American Shores: Classical Archaeology in the United States* (Philadelphia: University of Pennsylvania Press, 1998), 223.

61. Melina Mercouri, *I Was Born Greek* (New York: Doubleday 1971), 220 and 115, fig. 25.

preserving its monuments and sites in effective ways, since the 19th century. The impact and legacy of Eastern Mediterranean materials in America is a topic of great interest for American scholars. The MoU was renewed for another five years in September 2021.

Against this background, a deep history of materials of Eastern Mediterranean origin and their displays in the Smithsonian Institution is particularly relevant. It offers an opportunity to look through the lens of development of a particular popular institution known to the average American. To many Americans who move to the U.S. capital, many of whom want to make America great (again), the Roman Empire has always been an attractive legacy. The presence, however, of materials from Greece in the Smithsonian Institution seems in retrospect to appear as an "innocent" and uncontested chapter in transatlantic relationships. Is that really the case? Can we argue, that the "Classical" legacy was fertile ground for the events that happened in January 2021?[62]

As scholars begin to address and question the role and validity of the term *classics* in America, as well as aspects of identity formation in Greece throughout the 20th and 21st centuries,[63] we should also consider allowing for alternative readings of the role of scientists, collections and exhibitions as a diplomatic tool between Athens and the Potomac people. Only a few aspects have been introduced here, but there is more. There are the thousands of coins of Eastern Mediterranean origin housed in the Smithsonian Institution's National Museum of American History.[64] When and why were those collected and displayed? Why are casts from the frieze of the Parthenon displayed in such

---

62. Johann Chapoutot, *Greeks, Romans, Germans: How the Nazis Usurped Europe's Classical Past* (Berkeley: University of California Press, 2016); originally published in French as *Le nazisme et l'Antiquité* (Paris: Presses universitaires de France, 2008).

63. See, for example, Argyro Loukaki, *Living Ruins, Value Conflicts* (Aldershot, UK: Ashgate, 2008); Despina Lalaki, "On the Social Construction of Hellenism: Cold War Narratives of Modernity, Development and Democracy for Greece," *Journal of Historical Sociology* 25, no. 4 (2012): 552–77; Salvatore Settis, *The Future of the Classical* (Cambridge: Polity, 2006); Dimitris Tziovas, ed., *Re-imagining the Past: Antiquity and Modern Greek Culture* (Oxford: Oxford University Press, 2014); Yannis Hamilakis, *The Nation and Its Ruins; Antiquity, Archaeology and National Imagination in Greece* (Oxford: University Press, 2007); Stathis Gourgouris, *Dream Nation: Enlightenment, Colonization and the Institution of Modern Greece* (Stanford, CA: Stanford University Press, 1996); Dimitris Plantzos, "The Glory That Was Not: Embodying the Classical in Contemporary Greece," *Interactions* 3 no. 2 (2012): 147–71; Dimitris Plantzos, *Recent Futures: Classical Antiquity and Modern Greek Biopolitics* (Athens: Nefeli, 2016) [in Greek]; Johanna Hanink, *The Classical Debt: Antiquity in the Era of Austerity* (Cambridge, MA: Harvard University Press, 2017; Maria Malamud, *African Americans and the Classics: Antiquity, Abolition and Activism* (London: I. B. Tauris, 2016).

64. Elvira Clain-Stefanelli, "Donors and Donations: The Smithsonian's National Numismatic Collection," in *Perspectives in Numismatics,* ed. Saul B. Needleman, 251–68 (Chicago: Ares, 1986).

an important office in the Smithsonian Institution?[65] Why did Secretary Dillon Ripley so prominently that presented to every new secretary a badge with a golden owl? We may look at other early ways of disseminating knowledge about Greece in America: plates from the Underwood and Underwood collections that are now housed in the National Museum of American History once formed part of the successful volume *Greece Through the Stereoscope*, the accompanying text of which was written by Rufus B. Richardson (1845–1914), another former director of the American School of Classical Studies in Athens. Members of the Smithsonian Institution surely helped disseminate these images throughout high schools in Washington, D.C., in the early 20th century.[66]

Combined, the archives and collections reflect an ongoing enthusiasm for Greek cultures and may offer a tool in developing future relationships between the people in Washington, D.C., Athens and beyond. Understanding the motives behind the donations and exchanges, we may ask: what role did Eastern Mediterranean–themed displays and exhibitions in the U.S. capital play in the formation and development of diplomatic relationships and museum displays in general?[67]

In November 1992, the exhibition *The Greek Miracle: Classical Sculpture from the Dawn of Democracy, the Fifth Century B.C.* opened at the National Gallery of Art.[68]

---

65. See, for example, Dimitris Philippides, "The Parthenon as Appreciated by Greek Society," in *The Parthenon and Its Impact in Modern Times*, ed. Panayiotis Tournikiotis, 278–309 (Athens: Melissa, 1996); Elena Yalouri, *The Acropolis: Global Fame, Local Claim* (Oxford: Berg, 2001).

66. Rufus Richardson, *Greece Through the Stereoscope* (New York: Underwood and Underwood, 1907); Kostas Ioannidis and Eleni Mouzakitis, "Greece Through the Stereoscope: Constituting Spectatorship Through Text and Images," in *Camera Graeca: Photographs, Narratives, Materialities*, eds. Philip Carabott, Yannis Hamilakis and Eleni Papargyriou, 159–68 (Farnham, UK: Ashgate, 2015); Nikos Panayotopoulos, "On Greek Photography. Eurocentrism, Cultural Colonialism and the Construction of Mythic Classical Greece," *Third Text* 23, no. 2, (2009): 181–94.

67. Diana Buitron-Oliver, *The Greek Miracle: Classical Sculpture from the Dawn of Democracy, the Fifth Century B.C.* (Washington, DC: National Gallery of Art, 1993); Charles Hedrick and Josiah Ober, eds., *The Birth of Democracy: Catalogue of an Exhibition held at the National Archives in Washington, D.C.* (Princeton, NJ: American School of Classical Studies at Athens, 1993); Johannes Siapkas and Lena Sjogren, *Displaying the Ideals of Antiquity: The Petrified Gaze* (New York: Routledge, 2014); Beth Cohen, "Displaying in Modern Museums," in *The Oxford Handbook of Greek and Roman Art and Architecture*, ed. Clemente Marconi, 473–98 (Oxford: Oxford University Press, 2015).

68. Buitron-Oliver; Gary Wills, "Athena's Magic," *New York Review of Books*, December 17, 1992, 47–51, https://www.nybooks.com/articles/1992/12/17/athenas-magic/; Yalouri, 67; Marlen Mouliou, "Ancient Greece, Its Classical Heritage and the Modern Greeks: Aspects of Nationalism in Museum Exhibitions," in *Nationalism and Archaeology*, eds. John Atkinson, Iain Banks and Jerry O'Sullivan (Glasgow: Cruithne Press, 1996), 191–94. Buitron-Oliver had already curated a first exhibition on ancient Greek art at the National Gallery of Art; Alan Boegehold et al., *The Human Figure in Early Greek Art*

Among the objects included were a fragment from the Parthenon frieze, objects from Aegina, Eleusis, Olympia and elsewhere, only a few minutes away from *Western Civilization: Origins and Traditions*. The exhibition catalog featured a statement by the staff office of the White House under President George Bush, under whom the first Gulf War had started only a few months earlier. According to the White House "these sculptures ... might well be viewed as symbols of the longstanding ties that exist between the United States and Greece. ... The ideas of Solon, Plato and other Greek philosophers and statesmen greatly influenced our Nation's Founders."[69] The exhibition was supported by the cigarette-manufacturing company Philip Morris.

Only a few months later, in June 1993, the ASCSA and the National Archives featured a second exhibition; *The Birth of Democracy* celebrated the 2,500-year anniversary of democracy in Greece, again near the Museum Mall. While the catalog was edited by the historians Josiah Ober and Charles Hedrick, the exhibition of objects was curated by Diane Buitron-Oliver, who had already overseen *The Greek Miracle*, and archaeologist John McK. Camp II. The exhibition was accompanied by a panel on democracy organized by Ober and Hedrick at Georgetown University, which was published in 1996 under the title *Demokratia: A Conversation on Democracies, Ancient and Modern*.[70]

Back then, Greece was already in the news again in Washington, as a highly controversial case made its way to the courts in the same year. An illicitly traded set of gold jewelry from Aidonia, in the Peloponnese, was offered for sale at a gallery in New York. The settlement included a payment to the Washington-based Society for the Preservation of Greek Heritage, which had emerged as a negotiator between Greece and the United States. Well-publicized seminars followed, such as "Mycenaean Treasures of the Aegean Bronze Age Repatriated" and "The Destiny of the Parthenon Marbles," which were held at the Smithsonian Institution's Ripley Center and at the Corcoran Gallery of Art.[71]

In June 2003, the Smithsonian Institution partnered with other D.C. institutions, including the American University's main campus, to hold the fifth World Archaeology Congress. Following the illegal invasion of Iraq under George Bush's son George W. Bush a few weeks earlier, in April 2003, the organizers of the congress had become

---

(Athens: Ministry of Culture/Washington, DC: National Gallery of Art, 1988). Boegehold (1927–2015) was a close friend of Richard Howland. See also Siapkas and Sjogren; Cohen.

69. Buitron-Oliver, 7.

70. Josiah Ober and Charles Hedrick, eds., *Demokratia: A Conversation on Democracies, Ancient and Modern* (Princeton, NJ: Princeton University Press, 1996).

71. Richard Howland, ed., *Mycenaean Treasures of the Aegean Bronze Age Repatriated* (Washington, DC: Society for the Preservation of Greek Heritage, 1996); Richard Howland and Anna Lea, eds., *The Destiny of the Parthenon Marbles* (Washington, DC: Society for the Preservation of Greek Heritage, 2000). On the settlement related to the Aidonia treasure, see Emily Ehl, "The Settlement of *Greece v. Ward*: Who Loses," *Boston University Law Review* 78 (1998), 661–90.

deeply concerned. A few archaeologists, including the Greek Yannis Hamilakis, lamented how deeply the toxic relationship between archaeology and the politics of a very particular situation had manifested itself.[72] Some 20 years later, new exhibitions and displays in D.C. again presented the idea of Greece as the origin of Western cultures, just as new U.S. military bases were being established in that country. It remains to be seen how Hellenic-American relationships continue to unfold and how even the eclectic collections from Greece in the Smithsonian Institution, those connecting the people from Piraeus and from the Potomac, and future exhibitions will be used in the theater of operations when once again on display.[73]

Acknowledgments

I am grateful to Thomas Gerry for his efforts to make possible this publication of the proceedings of the Symposium on the Greeks held on the beautiful island of Paros in 2019. I am grateful to Marianne Vardalos for the invitation to present at the conference and to all involved in the stimulating discussions. I thank the many students at the University of Maryland, New York University and the State University of New York who participated in seminars held at the National Museum of Natural History and in the storerooms of the Smithsonian Institution. For responses to an earlier draft of this chapter, I send my sincere thanks to the anonymous reviewers who helped sharpen arguments and approaches to the materials presented here. I also remain indebted to the work of many archivists and colleagues in Greece and in the United States, who inspire my research and thinking.

Bibliography

Note: Information on the Smithsonian Institution's collections is available online at www.collections.si.edu.

Alexandri, Alexandra. "'The Stamp of National Life': Plaster Casts and Their Uses in Greece at the End of the 19th Century." In Voutsaki and Cartledge, 130–47.

Aliprantis, Christos. "Political Refugees of the 1848–1849 Revolutions in the Kingdom of Greece: Migration, Nationalism, and State Formation in the Nineteenth-Century Mediterranean." *Journal of Modern Greek Studies* 37, no. 1 (2019): 1–33.

Anderson, Benjamin, and Felipe Rojas, eds. *Antiquarianisms: Contact, Conflict, Comparison*. Oxford: Oxbow, 2017.

Andreadaki-Vlazaki, Maria, and Anastasia Balaska, eds. *The Greeks: Agamemnon to Alexander the Great*. Athens: Kapon, 2014.

Angel, John Lawrence. "Classical Archaeology and the Anthropological Approach." In *Studies Presented to David Moore Robinson on His Seventieth Birthday*, edited by

---

72. On the context of the Iraq invasions and the WAC conference in 2003, see Hamilakis, "War on Terror."

73. For a recent exhibition on Greece in Washington, D.C., see Maria Andreadaki-Vlazaki and Anastasia Balaska, eds., *The Greeks: Agamemnon to Alexander the Great* (Athens: Kapon, 2014).

George Mylonas and Doris Raymond, 1224–31. St. Louis: Washington University, 1953.

———. "Classical Olynthians." In *Excavations at Olynthus XI; Necrolynthia: A Study in Greek Burial Customs and Anthropology*, edited by David M. Robinson. Baltimore: Johns Hopkins University Press, 1942.

———. *The People of Lerna: Analysis of a Prehistoric Aegean Population*. Princeton, NJ: American School of Classical Studies at Athens, 1971.

———. "Skeletal Change in Ancient Greece." *American Journal of Physical Anthropology* 4 (1946): 69–97.

———. "Skeletal Material from Attica." *Hesperia* 14 (1945): 279–363.

Auslander, Mark. "Enslaved Labor and Building the Smithsonian." *Southern Spaces*, December 12, 2012. https://southernspaces.org/2012/enslaved-labor-and-building-smithsonian-reading-stones.

Baetjer, Katharine, and Joan Mertens. "The Founding Decades." In *Making the Met, 1870–2020*, edited by Andrea Bayer and Laura Corey, 34–47. New York: Metropolitan Museum of Art, 2020.

Bahrani, Zainab, Zeynep Çelik and Edhem Eldem, eds. *Scramble for the Past: A Story of Archaeology in the Ottoman Empire, 1753–1914*. Istanbul: Yalinari, 2011.

Bartman, Elizabeth. "Archaeology versus Aesthetics: The Metropolitan Museum of Art's Classical Collection in Its Early Years." In *Classical New York: Discovering Greece and Rome in Gotham*, edited by Elizabeth Macaulay-Lewis and Matthew McGowan, 63–84. New York: Fordham University Press, 2018.

Boegehold, Alan, et al. *The Human Figure in Early Greek Art*. Athens: Ministry of Culture/Washington, DC: National Gallery of Art, 1988.

Bonfante, Larissa, and Helen Nagy, eds. *The Collection of Antiquities of the American Academy in Rome*. Ann Arbor: University of Michigan Press, 2015.

Born, Pamela. "The Canon Is Cast: Plaster Casts in American Museum and University Collections." *Art Documentation* 21, no. 2 (2002): 8–13.

Buikstra, Jane, and Eleanna Prevedorou. "John Lawrence Angel (1915–1986)." In *The Global History of Paleopathology: Pioneers and Prospects*, edited by Jane Buikstra and Charlotte Roberts, 3–13. Oxford: Oxford University Press, 2012.

Buitron-Oliver, Diana. *The Greek Miracle: Classical Sculpture from the Dawn of Democracy, the Fifth Century B.C.* Washington, DC: National Gallery of Art, 1993.

Burton, Amy E., ed. *To Make Beautiful the Capitol: Rediscovering the Art of Constantino Brumidi*. Washington, DC: US Government Printing Office, 2014.

Casanowicz, Immanuel. The Collections of Old World Archaeology in the United States National Museum. Washington, DC: Smithsonian Institution, 1922.

Celphane, Henry. "The Local Aspect of Slavery in the District of Columbia." *Records of the Columbia Historic Society* 3 (1900): 235–37.

Chapoutot, Johann. *Greeks, Romans, Germans: How the Nazis Usurped Europe's Classical Past*. Berkeley: University of California Press, 2016.

Choulia-Kapeloni, Suzanne, ed. *3rd International Conference of Experts on the Return of Cultural Property: Athens and Ancient Olympia, October 23–6, 2013*. Athens: Archaeological Receipts Fund, 2014.

Clain Stefanelli, Elvira. "Donors and Donations: The Smithsonian's National Numismatic Collection." In *Perspectives in Numismatics,* edited by Saul B. Needleman, 251–68. Chicago: Ares, 1986.

Cohen, Beth. "Displaying in Modern Museums." In *The Oxford Handbook of Greek and Roman Art and Architecture,* edited by Clemente Marconi, 473–98. Oxford: Oxford University Press, 2015.

Damaskos, Dimitris, and Dimitris Plantzos, eds. *A Singular Antiquity: Archaeology and Hellenic Identity in Twentieth Century Greece.* Athens: Mouseio Benaki, 2008.

Davis, Hugh. Review of *Charles Eliot Norton: The Art of Reform in Nineteenth Century America,* by Linda Dowling. *Journal of American History* 95, no. 2 (2008): 350–51.

Davis, Jack, and Natalia Vogeikoff, eds. *Philhellenism, Philanthropy, or Political Convenience: American Archaeology in Greece.* Princeton, NJ: American School of Classical Studies at Athens, 2013.

de Puma, Richard. "Americans Collecting Antiquities in Italy, c. 1865–1920." In Bonfante and Nagy, 3–12.

Diaz-Andreu, Margarita. "Archaeology and Imperialism: From Nineteenth-Century New Imperialism to Twentieth-Century Decolonization." In *Unmasking Ideology in Imperial and Colonial Archaeology: Vocabulary, Symbols, and Legacy,* edited by Bonnie Efros and Guolong Lai, 3–28. Los Angeles: UCLA Cotsen Institute of Archaeology, 2018.

Dinsmoor, William. "Early American Studies of Mediterranean Archaeology." *Proceedings of the American Philosophical Society* 87, no. 1 (1943): 70–104.

Dyson, Stephen. *Ancient Marbles to American Shores: Classical Archaeology in the United States.* Philadelphia: University of Pennsylvania Press, 1998.

———. "Cast Collecting in the United States." In *Plaster Casts: Making, Collecting and Displaying from Classical Antiquity to the Present,* edited by Rune Frederiksen and Eckart Marchant, 557–76. Berlin: de Gruyter, 2010.

———. *In Pursuit of Ancient Pasts: A History of Classical Archaeology in the Nineteenth and Twentieth Centuries.* New Haven, CT: Yale University Press, 2006.

Ehl, Emily. "The Settlement of *Greece v. Ward*: Who Loses." *Boston University Law Review* 78 (1998): 661–90.

Fennell, Christopher C. *Crossroads and Cosmologies: Diasporas and Ethnogenesis in the New World.* Gainesville: University Press of Florida, 2007.

Field, Cynthia, Richard Stamm and Heather Ewing. *The Castle: An Illustrated History of the Smithsonian Building.* Washington, DC: Smithsonian Institution Press, 1993.

Flouda, Georgia. "Figures of Modernity: Heinrich Schliemann, Kate Field and a Smithsonian Collection." *CLARA* 4 (2019). doi: 10.5617/clara.v4i0.4373.

Forret, Jeff. "Early Republic and Antebellum United States." In Smith and Paquette, 227–51.

Forret, Jeff, and Christine E. Sears, eds., *New Directions in Slavery Studies: Commodification, Community, and Comparison.* Baton Rouge: Louisiana State University Press, 2015.

Furtwängler, Adolf. "Neue Denkmäler antiker Kunst: Antiken in den Museen von Amerika, Washington." *Sitzungsberichte der philosophisch-philologischen und der historischen Klasse der Königlichen Bayerischen Akademie der Wissenschaften* 5, no. 2 (1905): 250–51. https://libmma.contentdm.oclc.org/digital/collection/p16028coll4/id/5043.

Galanakis, Yannis. "Of Grave Hunters & Earth Contractors: A Look at the 'Private Archaeology' of Greece." *CHS Research Bulletin* blog, 2012. https://research-bulletin.chs.

harvard.edu/2012/11/15/of-grave-hunters-earth-contractors-a-look-at-the-private-archaeology-of-greece/.

Gazda, Elaine. *In Pursuit of Antiquity: Thomas Spencer Jerome and the Bay of Naples (1899–1914)*. Ann Arbor, MI: Kelsey Museum of Archaeology, 1983.

Gazi, Andromachi. "Archaeological Museums and Displays in Greece, 1829–1909: A First Approach." *Museological Review* 1, no. 1 (1994): 50–69.

———. "'Artfully Classified' and 'Appropriately Placed': Notes on the Display of Antiquities in Early Twentieth-Century Greece." In Damaskos and Plantzos, 67–82.

———. "The Museum of Casts in Athens (1846–1874)." *Journal of the History of Collections* 10, no. 1 (1998): 87–91.

Geffken, Katherine. "The History of the Collection." In Bonfante and Nagy, 21–78.

Gekas, Sakis. "The Crisis of the Long 1850s and Regime Change in the Ionian State and the Kingdom of Greece." *Historical Review* 10 (2013): 57–84.

Gourgouris, Stathis. *Dream Nation: Enlightenment, Colonization and the Institution of Modern Greece*. Stanford, CA: Stanford University Press, 1996.

Greek Costumes and Embroideries from the Benaki Museum. Washington, DC: Smithsonian Institution, 1959.

Greenhalgh, Michael. *Plundered Empire: Acquiring Antiquities from Ottoman Lands*. Leiden: Brill, 2019.

Habu, Junko, Clare Fawcett and John N. Matsunaga, eds. *Evaluating Multiple Narratives: Beyond Nationalist, Colonialist, Imperialist Archaeologies*. New York: Springer, 2008.

Hadjikyriacou, Antonis, and Michalis Sotiropoulos. "Patris, Ethnos and Demos: Representation and Political Participation in the Greek World." In *Re-imagining Democracy in the Mediterranean, 1780–1860,* edited by Joanna Innes and Mark Philp, 99–124. Oxford: Oxford University Press, 2018.

Hamilakis, Yannis. "Double Colonization: The Story of the Excavations of the Athenian Agora (1924–1931)." In Davis and Vogeikoff, 153–77.

———. *The Nation and Its Ruins: Antiquity, Archaeology and National Imagination in Greece*. Oxford: University Press, 2007.

———. "'The War on Terror' and the Military-Archaeology Complex: Iraq, Ethics and Neo-Colonialism," *Archaeologies* 5, no. 1 (2009): 39–65.

Hanink, Johanna. *The Classical Debt: Antiquity in the Era of Austerity*. Cambridge, MA: Harvard University Press, 2017.

Haskell, Francis, and Nicholas Penny. *Taste and the Antique*. New Haven, CT: Yale University Press, 1981.

Hedrick, Charles, and Josiah Ober, eds. *The Birth of Democracy: Catalogue of an Exhibition held at the National Archives in Washington D.C.* Princeton, NJ: American School of Classical Studies at Athens, 1993.

Hermary, Antoine, and Joan Mertens. *The Cesnola Collection of Cypriot Art: Stone Sculpture*. New York: Metropolitan Museum of Art, 2014.

Heuck Allen, Susan, ed. *Excavating Our Past: Perspectives on the History of the Archaeological Institute of America*. Boston: AIA, 2002.

Howland, Richard, ed. *The Destiny of the Parthenon Marbles*. Washington, DC: Society for the Preservation of Greek Heritage, 2000.

———. *Greek Lamps and Their Survivals*. Princeton, NJ: American School of Classical Studies at Athens, 1958.

―――. ed. *Mycenaean Treasures of the Aegean Bronze Age Repatriated.* Washington, DC: Society for the Preservation of Greek Heritage, 1996.

Ioannidis, Kostas, and Eleni Mouzakitis. "Greece Through the Stereoscope: Constituting Spectatorship Through Text and Images." In *Camera Graeca: Photographs, Narratives, Materialities,* edited by Philip Carabott, Yannis Hamilakis and Eleni Papargyriou, 159–68. Farnham, UK: Ashgate, 2015.

Jacob, Judith M. *The Washington Monument: A Technical History and Catalog of the Commemorative Stones.* Washington, DC: National Park Service, 2005.

Jacobson, Thomas, and Tracey Cullen. "The Work of J. L. Angel in the Eastern Mediterranean." In *A Life in Science: Papers Honor of J. Lawrence Angel,* edited by Jane Buikstra, 38–51. Evanston, IL: Center for American Archaeology, 1990.

Johnson, Haynes. *Dusk at the Mountain: The Negro, the Nation, and the Capital; A Report on Problems and Progress.* New York: Doubleday, 1963.

Klein, Harry, and Richard Altick. *Professor Koeppen: The Adventures of a Danish Scholar in Athens and America.* Lancaster, PA: Commercial Printing House, 1938.

Kourelis, Kostas. "Byzantium and the Avantgarde: Excavations at Corinth, 1920s to 1930s." *Hesperia* 76, no. 2 (2007): 391–442.

Kouroupas, Maria. "The 1970 UNESCO Convention U.S. Experience." In Choulia-Kapeloni, 209–15.

Lagogianni-Georgakarakos, Maria, ed. *"These Are What We Fought For": Antiquities and the Greek War of Independence.* Athens: Archaeological Resources Fund, 2020.

Lalaki, Despina. "On the Social Construction of Hellenism: Cold War Narratives of Modernity, Development and Democracy for Greece." *Journal of Historical Sociology* 25, no. 4 (2012): 552–77.

―――. "Soldiers of Science–Agents of Culture: American Archaeologists in the Office of Strategic Services–OSS." In Davis and Vogeikoff, 179–202.

Lambrinou, Lena. "The Parthenon from the Greek Revival to Modern Architecture." In *Hellenomania,* edited by Katherine Harloe, Nicoletta Momigliano and Alexandre Farnoux, 126–60. London: Routledge, 2018.

Lekakis, Stelios. "The Cultural Property Debate." In Smith and Plantzos, 683–97.

Littlefield, Daniel C. "Colonial and Revolutionary United States," in Smith and Paquette, 201–26.

Longstreth, Richard, ed. *The Mall in Washington, 1791–1991.* Washington, DC: National Gallery of Art; New Haven, CT: Yale University Press, 2002.

Loukaki, Argyro. *Living Ruins, Value Conflicts.* Aldershot, UK: Ashgate, 2008.

Luke, Christina, and Morag Kersel. *U.S. Cultural Diplomacy and Archaeology.* London: Routledge, 2013.

Macaulay-Lewis, Elizabeth, and Matthew McGowan, eds. *Classical New York: Discovering Greece and Rome in Gotham.* New York: Fordham University Press, 2018.

Mackridge, Peter. *Language and National Identity in Greece, 1766–1976.* Oxford: Oxford University Press, 2010.

Macleod, William. *Catalogue of the Paintings, Statuary, Casts, Bronzes, etc. of the Corcoran Gallery of Art.* Washington, DC: Gibson Brothers, 1883.

Malamud, Maria. *African Americans and the Classics: Antiquity, Abolition and Activism.* London: I. B. Tauris, 2016.

―――. *Ancient Rome and Modern America.* Hoboken, NJ: Wiley-Blackwell, 2009.

Marangou, Anna. *The Consul Luigi di Cesnola, 1832–1904: Life and Deeds.* Nicosia, 2000.

Mason, Otis. "In Memoriam: Thomas Wilson." *American Anthropologist* 4, no. 2 (1902): 286–91.

McFadden, Elizabeth. *The Glitter and the Gold: A Spirited account of the Metropolitan of Art's First Director, the Audacious and High-Handed Luigi Palma di Cesnola.* New York: Dial Press, 1971.

Mercouri, Melina. *I Was Born Greek.* New York: Doubleday 1971.

Meritt, Lucy Shoe. *History of the American School of Classical Studies at Athens, 1939–1980.* Princeton, NJ: American School of Classical Studies 1984.

Moskos, Charles. *Greek Americans: Struggle and Success.* New Brunswick, NJ: Transaction, 1989.

Mouliou, Marlen. "Ancient Greece, Its Classical Heritage and the Modern Greeks: Aspects of Nationalism in Museum Exhibitions." In *Nationalism and Archaeology*, edited by John Atkinson, Iain Banks and Jerry O'Sullivan, 174–99. Glasgow: Cruithne Press, 1996.

———. "Museum Representations of the Classical Past in Post-war Greece: A Critical Analysis." in Damaskos and Plantzos, 83–109.

Nabokov, Peter. *A Forest of Time: American Indian Ways of History.* Cambridge: Cambridge University Press, 2002.

Nagel, Alexander. "Greek Wild Flowers: Dialogues and Diplomats on the Parthenon and the Athenian Acropolis in the Nineteenth Century." *Unbound* (blog). Smithsonian Institution, March 18, 2016. doi: https://blog.library.si.edu/blog/2016/03/18/greek-wild-flowers/#.XmQn9qhKhPY.

———. "Stories We Tell: On the Athenian Acropolis in Washington, D.C." Paper presented at "The International Context of the Greek World in the 19th Century: Klassiki Anthodesmi, a 'Classical Bouquet,'" University of Maryland, April 2, 2016.

Ober, Josiah, and Charles Hedrick, eds. *Demokratia: A Conversation on Democracies, Ancient and Modern.* Princeton, NJ: Princeton University Press, 1996.

O'Malley, Therese. "'A Public Museum of Trees': Mid-nineteenth Century Plans for the Mall." In Longstreth, 60–76.

Panayotopoulos, Nikos. "On Greek Photography: Eurocentrism, Cultural Colonialism and the Construction of Mythic Classical Greece." *Third Text* 23, no. 2 (2009): 181–94.

Parara, Polyvia. "The Journey of Elisavet Contaxaki's Classical Bouquet from Crete to Washington D.C.: Historical and Political Context." In *Proceedings of the 12th International Congress of Cretan Studies in Herakleion, Crete*, edited by C. Mitsotaki and L. Tzedaki-Apostolaki, 1–21. ICCS: 2018. doi: https://12iccs.proceedings.gr/en/authors/271.

Philippides, Dimitris. "The Parthenon as Appreciated by Greek Society." In *The Parthenon and Its Impact in Modern Times,* edited by Panayiotis Tournikiotis, 278–309. Athens: Melissa, 1996.

Pilides, Despo. "Repatriating Antiquities: The Case of Cyprus." In Choulia-Kapeloni, 117–28.

Plantzos, Dimitris. "The Glory That Was Not: Embodying the Classical in Contemporary Greece." *Interactions: Studies in Communication and Culture* 3, no. 2 (2012): 147–71.

———. *Recent Futures: Classical Antiquity and Modern Greek Biopolitics.* Athens: Nefeli, 2016 [in Greek].

Potter, Stephen. *Commoners, Tribute, and Chiefs: The Development of Algonquian Culture in the Potomac Valley.* Charlottesville: University of Virginia Press, 1994.

Rakopoulos, Theodoros. "The Poetics of Diaspora: Greek US Voices." *Journal of Modern Greek Studies* 34, no. 1 (2016): 161–67.

Rangavis, Alexandros Rizos. *The First Greek Ambassador to the American Federation, 1867–1868*. Translated by Christine Gabrielides. Minneapolis: Nostos, 2019.

Rhees, William. *The Smithsonian Institution: Documents Relative to Its Origin and History, 1835–1889*. Washington, DC: Government Publishing Office, 1901. Reprinted as W. Rhees. *The Smithsonian Institution, 1835–1899*. New York: Arno Press, 1980.

Richard, Carl. *The Golden Age of the Classics in America*. Cambridge, MA: Harvard University Press, 2009.

———. *Greeks and Romans Bearing Gifts: How the Ancients Inspired the Founding Fathers*. Lanham, MD: Rowman and Littlefield, 2008.

Richardson, Rufus. *Greece Through the Stereoscope*. New York: Underwood and Underwood, 1907.

Ridgway, Brunilde, ed. *Greek Sculpture in the Art Museum, Princeton University: Greek Originals, Roman Copies and Variants*. Princeton, NJ: Princeton University Press, 1994.

Rothenberg, Marc, Paul H. Theerman, Kathleen W. Dorman, John C. Rumm and Deborah Y. Jeffries, eds. *The Papers of Joseph Henry*. Vol. 7, *The Smithsonian Years: January 1847–December 1849*. Washington, DC: Smithsonian Institution Press, 1996.

Ruprecht, Louis. *Report on the Aeginetan Sculptures, with Historical Supplements*. Albany: State University of New York Press, 2018.

St. Clair, William. *That Greece Might Still Be Free: Philhellenes in the War of Independence*. Oxford: Oxford University Press, 1972.

Savage, Kirk. *Monument Wars: Washington, D.C., the National Mall and the Transformation of the Memorial Landscape*. Berkeley: University of California Press, 2011.

Schwarz, Shirley. "Etruscan Black Figure Vases in the US National Museum." *Mitteilungen des Deutschen Archaeologischen Instituts, Roemische Abteilung* 91 (1984): 47–77.

———. *Greek Vases in the National Museum of Natural History: Smithsonian Institution, Washington, D.C*. Rome: Erma di Bretschneider, 1996.

———. "The Pattern Class Vases of the Gruppo di Orvieto in the US National Museum Collection, Smithsonian Institution." *Studi Etrusci* 47 (1979): 65–84.

Scott, Pamela. "'This Vast Empire': The Iconography of the Mall, 1791–1848." In Longstreth, 37–60.

"Secretary Ripley Receives Degree from Cambridge." *The Torch*, July-August 1974, 3.

Settis, Salvatore. *The Future of the Classical*. Cambridge: Polity, 2006.

Siapkas, Johannes, and Lena Sjogren. *Displaying the Ideals of Antiquity: The Petrified Gaze*. New York: Routledge, 2014.

Singleton, Theresa. "Archaeology and Slavery." In Smith and Paquette, 702–24.

Smith, Franklin Webster. *National Galleries of History and Art: Descriptive Handbook of the Hall of the Ancients*. Washington: Government Printing Office, 1900.

Smith, Tyler Jo, and Dimitris Plantzos, eds. *Companion to Greek Art*. Hoboken, NJ: Wiley-Blackwell, 2012.

Squire, Michael. "The Legacy of Greek Sculpture." In *Handbook of Ancient Greek Sculpture*, edited by Olga Palagia, 727–67. Berlin: de Gruyter, 2019.

Stamm, Richard. "The Mystery of the Art Room Frieze." *Smithsonian History* (blog), June 18, 2018. https://siarchives.si.edu/blog/mystery-art-room-frieze.

Tank, Holly. "Dedicated to Art: William Corcoran and the Founding of his Gallery." *Washington History* 17, no. 1 (Fall/Winter 2005): 26–51.

———. "William Wilson Corcoran: Washington Philanthropist." *Washington History* 17, no. 1 (Fall/Winter 2005): 52–65.

Tarbell, Frank. "A Signed Cylix by Duris, in Boston." *American Journal of Archaeology* 4, no. 2 (1900): 183–91.

Trubeta, Sevasti. *Physical Anthropology, Race, and Eugenics in Greece (1880s–1970s)*. Boston: Brill, 2013.

Turner, James. *The Liberal Education of Charles Eliot Norton*. Baltimore: Johns Hopkins University Press, 1999.

Tziovas, Dimitris, ed. *Re-imagining the Past: Antiquity and Modern Greek Culture*. Oxford: Oxford University Press, 2014.

Tzortzaki, Delia. "Myth and the Ideal in 20th century Exhibitions of Classical Art." In Smith and Plantzos, 667–682.

Van Beek, Gus, et al. *Western Civilization: Origins and Traditions; An Exhibit at the National Museum of Natural History, Smithsonian Institution*. Washington, DC: Elephant Press, 1979.

Van Steen, Gonda. *Liberating Hellenism from the Ottoman Empire: Comte de Marcellus and the Last of the Classics*. New York: Palgrave Macmillan, 2010.

Vogli, Elpida. "The Making of Greece Abroad: Continuity and Change in the Modern Diaspora Politics of a 'Historical' Irredentist Homeland." In *Diaspora and Citizenship*, edited by Elena Barabantseva and Claire Sutherland, 14–34. London: Routledge, 2012.

Voudouri, Daphne. "The Legal Protection of Antiquities in Greece and National Identity." In Voutsaki and Cartledge, 77–94.

Voutsaki, Sophia, and Paul Cartledge, eds. *Ancient Monuments and Modern Identities: A Critical History of Archaeology in 19th and 20th Century Greece*. London: Routledge, 2017.

Washburn, Wilcomb E. "A Roman Sarcophagus in a Museum of Natural History." *Curator* 7, no. 4 (1964): 296–99.

Wiesen, David. "Cornelius Felton and the Flowering of Classics in New England." *Classical Outlook* 59, no. 2 (1981–82): 44–48.

Will, Elizabeth Lyding. "Charles Eliot Norton and the Archaeological Institute of America." In Heuck Allen, 49–61.

Wills, Gary. "Athena's Magic." *New York Review of Books*, December 17, 1992, 47–51. https://www.nybooks.com/articles/1992/12/17/athenas-magic/

Winterer, Caroline. "The American School of Classical Studies at Athens: Scholarship and High Culture in the Gilded Age." In Heuck Allen, 93–104.

———. *The Culture of Classicism: Ancient Greece and Rome in American Intellectual Life, 1780–1910*. Baltimore: Johns Hopkins University Press, 2002.

Wong, Amelia. "When an Amphora Is Not Just an Amphora: Greek Antiquities as Presidential Gifts; An Interview with Nassos Papalexandrou." Blog of the J. Paul Getty Trust, February 15, 2016. https://blogs.getty.edu/iris/when-an-amphora-is-not-just-an-amphora-greek-antiquities-as-presidential-gifts/.

Yalouri, Elena. *The Acropolis: Global Fame, Local Claim*. Oxford: Berg, 2001.

Ziolkowski, John E. "The Parthenon Stone in the Washington Monument." *Our Heritage in Documents*, Winter 1993, 374–81.

Chapter 3

The Greeks of Tarpon Springs in the Hollywood Imaginary

Velvet L. Yates

University of Florida

Abstract

Tarpon Springs, Florida, is home to the largest concentration of Greek-Americans in the United States. Until the 1950s, sponge diving was a major industry, and the sponge divers were Greeks. Hollywood was attracted to these sponge divers. I will argue that the Greek characters in these films and TV shows, spanning 1932 to 1961, were as imaginary, exotic, and dangerous as the underwater monsters and geography. Greeks, rarely played by actual Greeks, were stereotyped as boastful, passionate, religious, and violent. Likewise, the geography is exotic but hazy: Greece is just "The Old Country" in one film; in another, Tarpon Springs is a short sail from Key West. The sea monsters, including a giant clam, were even more unlikely. The locations for the "undersea" sequences were often freshwater Florida springs. Nothing is what it seems: a rare coelacanth swimming 150 feet deep off the coast of Madagascar is really a bowfin, a common Springs fish, swimming 10 feet deep in Silver Springs. The actors playing Greeks in these shows are bowfins pretending to be coelacanths, populating a wrongly imagined "Tarpon Springs" in the Hollywood dreamscape.

Keywords: Greeks in America, Tarpon Springs, Greeks in American popular culture, Greeks in American movies and TV, Greek sponge divers.

***

The Greek-American sponge divers of Tarpon Springs, Florida, were represented in mass media as vaguely "ethnic" types—swarthy and passionate foils to WASPish leading men. This chapter will examine representations of Tarpon Springs Greek-Americans in Hollywood films and television shows produced between 1934 and 1961. I will argue that they are portrayed as exotic and dangerous creatures, like the sea monsters they battle, and just as erroneously.[1]

Before recounting a brief history of the Greeks in Tarpon Springs, I would first like to mention the most famous "Greek" in Hollywood history: Zorba. The role of Zorba in *Zorba the Greek* (1964) was played by Anthony Quinn, who was born Antonio Rodolfo Quinn Oaxaca in Chihuahua, Mexico.[2] He had already played a Greek character in *The Guns of Navarone* (1961). Quinn represents the most conspicuous case of a Mexican-American, Italian-American or Greek-American actor pigeonholed into interchangeably "ethnic" roles; in addition to playing Greeks and Mexicans, he also played a Bedouin sheikh in *Lawrence of Arabia* (1962) and the prophet Mohammed's uncle in *The Message* (1976). Casting a Mexican-American as Zorba is but one example of how Hollywood saw little difference between "white ethnic" Greeks or Greek-Americans and "nonwhite" racial minorities.[3]

Even Tarpon Springs was sometimes played by non–Tarpon Springs locations. The city is located on the Gulf of Mexico side of Florida, about 20 miles north of Tampa Bay. In 1886 John Cheyney established the sponge industry there and in 1897 hired John Cocoris, a sponge buyer and technical expert from Leonidion, an Arcadian village on the eastern coast of the Peloponnese. Cocoris brought over his family from Greece and established the use of the diving helmet and suit. Until then, sponges (which are living sea animals) were spotted by men in small boats using glass-bottomed buckets, who then harvested them with long hooks.[4] A plaque honoring Cocoris is still displayed on the main thoroughfare of Tarpon Springs, Dodecanese Boulevard (see figure 3.2).

In 1905, 500 Greek sponge divers, mostly from the Dodecanese (especially Kalymnos), arrived in Tarpon Springs. The immigrants built Greek-style boats for sponging (see figure 3.1). The community prospered and grew for several decades, until a red tide outbreak in 1947 ground the sponge industry to a virtual halt. By the time the sponges had recovered from the outbreak, many Greeks had moved on to other occupations, and there was also new competition from the synthetic sponges developed in the 1940s and '50s.

---

1. I would like to thank the organizers of the Symposium on the Greeks, the University of Florida Department of Classics and the Center for Greek Studies for making my attendance possible; the Tarpon Springs Area Historical Society for their kind assistance; and the anonymous reader of the first draft of this paper for very helpful suggestions.

2. Wikipedia, s.v. "Anthony Quinn," https://en.wikipedia.org/wiki/Anthony_Quinn.

3. I am using the terms developed by Yiorgos Anagnostou, *Contours of White Ethnicity: Popular Ethnography and the Making of Usable Pasts in Greek America* (Athens: Ohio University Press, 2009), 13–14.

4. Jeff Moates, "What Happened to All Those Boats? A Sketch of Maritime Heritage," in *Celebrating Community; Tarpon Springs: Reflections on 125 Years*, eds. Genevieve Crosby et al. (Tarpon Springs, FL: City of Tarpon Springs, 2013), 18.

Figure 3.1. A sponge diver ready for action.

Source: State Archives of Florida, Florida Memory. Accessed April 3, 2021. https://www.floridamemory.com/items/show/26525.

Today tourism is the main industry of Tarpon Springs. The central Sponge Exchange, incorporated in 1908, where boat crews used to auction off their sponges to the highest bidders, is now called the Sponge Exchange Shopping Village. It displays an authentic Greek fishing boat built in 1935, alongside a giant plaster shark with which tourists can pose for pictures. Even so, Tarpon Springs offers an authentic glimpse of Greece, as it has the highest concentration of Greek-Americans in the United States. The visitor can hear locals speaking Greek while sipping a frappé or sampling Greek delicacies from the shops and restaurants lining Dodecanese Boulevard. The Greek Orthodox Church has a strong presence, especially in its famous Epiphany celebration every January, when hopeful young men dive into the spring to retrieve a cross thrown by the priest. The 2020 celebration, the 114th, was attended by Greek prime minister Kyriakos Mitsotakis.[5] The pageantry and excitement of the Epiphany celebration was a natural draw for Hollywood, as will be seen in a couple of the films to be examined.

Figure 3.2. Cocoris memorial plaque, Tarpon Springs.

IN MEMORY OF
JOHN M. COCORIS
FROM
LEONIDION, GREECE
THE FOUNDER OF
SPONGE DIVING INDUSTRY IN 1905
BY CITY OF TARPON SPRINGS

Photo by the author.

The perceived dangers and excitement of hardhat diving lured Hollywood to Tarpon Springs in the 1930s, the halcyon days of sponge diving in the area. The first film, *16 Fathoms Deep* (1934), is barely recognizable as a film about the Greeks of Tarpon Springs, however. The unnamed harbor town fronts dry, arid hills that clearly belong to southern California, not South Florida. The atmosphere, like the actors, is vaguely ethnic; the townspeople speak only of "the Old Country."[6] The local tavern features the checkered tablecloths of a cheesy faux-Italian restaurant, and the hero's (Greek?)

---

5. For local coverage of the event, see "Tarpon Springs Native Grabs the Cross at 114th Epiphany Celebration," 10News WTSP, January 6, 2020, YouTube video, 1:55 min., https://youtu.be/a8-giPfLJWs.

6. This ethnic pastiche seems to assimilate the "white ethnic" groups described by Anagnostou (14–15), though each with each other rather than with "white" America. Anagnostou also notes that "groups such as Armenian Americans, Greek Americans, Jewish Americans, Irish Americans, Italian Americans, and Polish Americans are recognized as distinctly ethnic, claiming unique cultures, histories, and religions. The Americanization of these populations, on the other hand, has entailed a specific kind of assimilation, their eventual incorporation into whiteness"; Anagnostou, 14.

sweetheart, played by Sally O'Neill, is named Rosita and flaunts a frilly off-the-shoulder "señorita" top. Still, there are a couple of Greek references to be gleaned from the plot. The (Greek?) hero, sponge diver Joe Bethel (a very young Lon Chaney Jr., credited under his real name, Creighton Chaney), wants to buy a fishing boat named *Athena* from a Mr. Papadopoulos. (Joe promptly renames the boat *Rosita Darling*.) The wealthy villain, Theo Savanis, played by George Regas, is a rare instance of a Greek actor playing a Greek character.[7] Theo loans the money for the boat to Joe, but then plants a saboteur on Joe's sponging expedition. The stakes are high because the expedition must be successful so that Joe is able to pay off the loan and marry Rosita. The saboteur repents when Joe is nearly killed in a diving accident; Rosita uses her feminine wiles on Theo to steal his racing boat and warn Joe of the danger; just in time, Joe makes it back to the sponge exchange to auction off his huge haul, thereby saving the day.

The only explicitly Greek character is the villain Savanis, driven by lust for Rosita and hatred for his rival Joe. The other marginally Greek characters are likewise awash in their passions: Rosita is unafraid to manipulate Theo through sex appeal, and Joe is a young man storming through life who simply must have his own sponge boat and simply must have Rosita. The "Greek" townspeople are also awash in religious superstition; in an early scene, a grizzled fisherman throws a brash young lad overboard for questioning the divine assistance of "Santa Margarita." The fisherman lets the boy back onboard only when he recants his blasphemy and kisses the saint's image. This "baptism" scene may be a deliberate echo of the boys of Tarpon Springs diving for the cross on Epiphany.

In *16 Fathoms Deep*, the Greeks are barely Greeks, really just vaguely ethnic stereotypes driven by passionate emotions and religious fervor. In the later examples to be considered, the Greek characters are explicitly identified as Greek but are even more subject to ethnic stereotyping. Hollywood denied Greek-Americans the "contextual self-manipulability of identity"[8] that was part of being considered a "white ethnic" group. An actual Greek-American could "self-identify as a Greek in one context and as a white American in another,"[9] but Hollywood Greek characters, denied this flexibility, are always depicted as decidedly *not* white Americans.

Other details would sharpen in later treatments as well. In *16 Fathoms Deep* Tarpon Springs is a vague location in southern California, but it plays itself in the remake of the film. The sea monsters are vague, perhaps because of the technical limitations of underwater filming, but gain (a little) in frightening reality in subsequent treatments. There are a few dim underwater sequences obviously shot through the glass of a large

---

7. It should be noted, however, that Regas's "Mediterranean complexion allowed him to play a wide variety of nationalities" in film. See Wikipedia, s.v. "George Regas," https://en.wikipedia.org/wiki/George_Regas.

8. Anagnostou, 25.

9. Anagnostou, 25.

aquarium; the biggest undersea threat is a rock that crushes a diver's air hose. These details changed in the 1948 remake of *16 Fathoms Deep*, now called *16 Fathoms Under*.

Figure 3.3. Tarpon Springs local newspaper headline for *16 Fathoms Under*: "Lon Chaney Plays Villain in Film He Once Starred in as the Hero."

Source: Tarpon Springs Area Historical Society. Photo by author.

As the Tarpon Springs area newspaper trumpeted, "Lon Chaney Plays Villain in Film He Once Starred in as the Hero." Sixteen years after the first film, Chaney now plays Mr. Demitri, as the Theo Savanis character is now named. This remake proudly states at the beginning: "All Scenes in This Motion Picture Were Filmed in TARPON SPRINGS, FLORIDA," claiming in addition that "The Underwater Sequences Were Filmed in RAINBOW SPRINGS, FLORIDA and MARINELAND STUDIOS, ST. AUGUSTINE, FLORIDA."

Figure 3.4. Sponge diver John Gonatos.

Source: State Archives of Florida, Florida Memory. Accessed April 3, 2021. https://www.floridamemory.com/items/show/245076.

The 1948 on-location remake features not only the "baptism" of a young skeptic (this time for doubting the assistance of Saint Catherine), but also an actual Epiphany dive. The young hero, Alex, retrieves the cross (even though he's not nearly young enough; the cut-off age for Epiphany divers being 18). The WASPish narrator, Ray Douglas, intones over the scene of a triumphant Alex kneeling before the priest: "They had faith down here. They believed." This scene is perhaps an acknowledgment of the singular power of the Greek Orthodox Church in shaping Greek-American identity,[10] but it sounds more in keeping with Caesar's account of the Druids.[11] In both cases, the observer's admiration for the importance of religion in the half-civilized target culture serves mostly as an indictment of his own dominant yet morally backsliding civilization, be it late republican Rome or mid-century white America.

Ray Douglas is a new character, our fair-haired guide into the exotic world of the Greeks of Tarpon Springs (see figure 3.4). An ex-Navy diver looking for a job, he is played by Lloyd Bridges, who would play exactly the same role as Mike Nelson in the TV series *Sea Hunt*. Douglas tells us about the sponge divers: "Their grandfathers and great-grandfathers were Greek." Most of the roles are not played by Greeks, though, but by actors who usually played "ethnic" roles: Eric Feldary (a Hungarian) is Alex, the hero; Tanis Chandler (born in France) is Simi, his sweetheart; and, of course, Chaney himself plays Mr. Demitri.[12]

A notable exception is the supporting role of Johnny, a sponge diver played by real-life sponge diver John Gonatos. His grandfather, Michael Gonatos, was a sponge diver who came to Tarpon Springs from Kalymnos in 1903. The Gonatos Building, with its large tile plaques proclaiming "M. GONATOS" and "1927," still stands on Dodecanese Boulevard; it serves as a prominent backdrop in both this film and the next one to be considered (*Beneath the 12 Mile Reef*). John Gonatos was a colorful local legend who tried his hand at boxing and acting, even directing his own documentary film, *Story of the Sponge*.

Matching the exotic Greek characters topside are equally exotic creatures below the sea. Ray Douglas grimly lists the monsters awaiting the sponge divers: sharks, turtles, grouper, the vicious moray eel, the deadly manta ray. It should be noted that none of these animals pose a threat to the average diver, even sharks, and especially not turtles or grouper, a large fish. In one scene, obviously filmed through an observation window at Marineland, a diver desperately tries to make a sea turtle look vicious. The "deadly manta ray" is very rare in Florida and is played in the film by the much smaller and equally harmless spotted eagle ray.

A luckless young crewman on Alex's boat manages to get killed by a vicious sea creature, however—a giant (and very fake-looking) clam. Yes, a giant clam, which is not found in the Atlantic Ocean and is decidedly not vicious. This wildly imaginative approach to the denizens of the deep counters the film's attempt to provide an authentic

---

10. Widely acknowledged, as Anagnostou observes, 78–79.

11. Caius Julius Caesar, *The Gallic War*, 6.13.

12. It is worth pointing out that Chaney's most famous role was the Wolfman, and in fact he was the only actor to play all of the "Big Three" movie monsters, Dracula, Frankenstein and the Wolfman. So Chaney's roles ranged well beyond the "ethnic" and into the literally monstrous.

atmosphere by filming on location. The filmmakers take advantage of the audience's ignorance of the ocean to luridly portray an exotic world full of danger. The same may be said about Tarpon Springs in the film: Ray Douglas guides the audience safely through an exotic world of dangerous Greek characters spurred on by extremes of passion and religious excitement.

The final film to be considered before moving on to the TV series *Sea Hunt* is 1953's *Beneath the 12-Mile Reef*. This is the best-known of the Tarpon Springs films, and the most lavish, being in Technicolor and also one of the first Cinemascope films. It features a Romeo-and-Juliet tale of sweethearts from rival sponge-diving families based in Tarpon Springs (the Greeks) and Key West (the "Englishmen" or "Conchs"). This Tarpon Springs vs. Key West rivalry was real, as the Greek diver Philip Fatolitis affirmed in 2007.[13]

The Greeks and the sea monsters, however, are just as unreal as ever. The young hero, Adonis (Tony) Petrakis, is played by Robert Wagner (whose later roles included starring in *Hart to Hart* on TV) sporting a curly perm (presumably to make him look more "ethnic"). Peter Graves (whose later roles included starring in the *Mission: Impossible* TV series) plays Arnold Dix, Tony's blond, blue-eyed Conch rival for Conch girl Gwyneth Rhys, played by Terry Moore. Tony's sponge-diving father is played by Gilbert Roland, who was born Luis Antonio Dámaso de Alonso in Chihuahua, Mexico. His character is a swaggering stereotype of ethnic machismo—smoking cigars, threatening to get into fights—yet piously religious.

Young Tony is brash, reckless and continually boasting, not only about what a great sponge diver he is, but also about his appearance: "My name is Adonis! My mother named me after a god! I'm a very beautiful young man!" Only slightly joking, he declares this twice in the film. Like Alex in the 1948 remake of *16 Fathoms*, Tony retrieves the Epiphany cross (he makes a far more convincing 18-year-old). Some of the scenes were filmed at Tarpon Springs; for instance, the sponge auction is staged in the actual Sponge Exchange. The Epiphany dive was filmed at Tarpon Springs but in the wrong location (the river instead of the spring basin), for reasons known only to the filmmakers.

The underwater filming is much more sophisticated than in the previous films. While not specified in the credits, some scenes were obviously filmed in the open ocean and others in freshwater springs, such as the Rainbow River location used in the 1948 version of *16 Fathoms*. However, the climactic battle between Tony and a giant octopus seems to have been filmed in an aquarium location as artificial as the octopus. Again the monster is fake, not only physically in its huge, rubbery glory, but also in terms of marine biology. The giant Pacific octopus is clearly not found in the Atlantic and is actually not very giant; adults usually weigh around 33 pounds.[14] They have never been known to attack humans.

---

13. Lester R. Dailey, "Former Sponge Diver Recalls Tarpon Springs' Glory Days," Tampa Bay Newspapers, January 10, 2007, https://www.tbnweekly.com/pinellas_county/article_792db565-89b1-54ed-ace5-e071ccd6c2a8.html.

14. Wikipedia, s.v. "giant Pacific octopus," https://en.wikipedia.org/wiki/Giant_Pacific_octopus.

Beneath the 12-Mile Reef relies heavily on clumsy stereotypes for both the "sea monster" and the Greeks depicted. The "Greeks" provide an exotic contrast to the WASPish Conchs, being visibly swarthier and demonstrably more religious and passionate (as when Tony literally dances off with Arnold's girl). These stereotypes are perpetuated in the final set of examples to be considered, from the TV series *Sea Hunt*. In this show, the guide is once again, as in 1948's *16 Fathoms* remake, a fair-haired ex-Navy diver played by Lloyd Bridges.

Sea Hunt, which aired from 1958 to 1961, was a tremendously popular TV show that features the adventures of freelance ex-Navy diver Mike Nelson (played by Bridges). Almost all the underwater sequences for the show were filmed at Silver Springs, Florida, even though Nelson is based in California.[15] Fakery is built into the show, with Silver Springs filling in for exotic locations around the world. In one episode, for example, an exceedingly rare coelacanth, spotted at a depth of 200 feet off the coast of Madagascar, is in reality, a bowfin (a fairly common freshwater springs fish) cruising through the eelgrass of Silver Springs at a depth of about 15 feet.

It is not terribly surprising that such fakery would extend to the human characters as well, especially since more than 20 hour-long episodes were being pumped out per season. Actors and locations would often be filmed "in batch" for use in several episodes within a season. In season 1, for example, Larry Hagman (later of *I Dream of Jeanie* and *Dallas* fame) plays a Greek character in two separate episodes. The first is "The Sponge Divers," set (of course) in Tarpon Springs. Hagman plays Johnny Greco (!), a young Greek sponge diver whose jealousy is aroused when his girlfriend, Elena (Regina Gleason), makes brazen overtures to Mike. Armed with a knife, Johnny ambushes Mike, who shames him into dropping the knife and fighting with his fists. Mike promptly knocks out Johnny with one blow.

Having established his alpha male status, Mike now mentors Johnny to face up to Elena's father, Tom Londos. Mike has already rescued Londos underwater, in spite of the latter's boast, "Londos is the best diver in the world!" Johnny wants to go into business with him and marry his daughter, but Londos is a bully who also claims to be the "best fighter in Tarpon Springs!" Mike tutors Johnny in both scuba diving and boxing, so that by the end of the episode, Johnny beats Londos in a fight, forces him to take a business deal and insists that Elena come to the church to marry him *right now*. Elena, overwhelmed by Johnny's display of machismo, suddenly switches her attitude from disdain to compliant adoration.

The previously discussed "ethnic" stereotypes provide shortcuts for the TV audience. Once identified as Greek, the characters can be assumed to exhibit passionate emotions, religious excitement and machismo, with the women being flirtatiously sexy and somewhat

---

15. Silver Springs still hosts periodic Sea Hunt Days, with divers in vintage gear recreating iconic fight scenes with rubber knives and other props.

conniving. With a few broad strokes, the "Greeks" are portrayed as being as exotic and dangerous as their occupation.

While the religious excitement and superstition supposedly characterizing the Greeks is not so prominent in the first episode, it certainly is in the second one featuring Larry Hagman, "The Legend of the Mermaid." Hagman is again paired with Regina Gleason; they play a Greek couple hosting Mike in dives off the west coast of Florida near Tarpon Springs. There is a cave where the superstitious Greeks believe a mermaid lures divers to their deaths, but Mike solves the mystery with a rational explanation.

In the season 2 "Hermes" episode of *Sea Hunt*, Mike ventures to the Mother Country itself, Greece; as was almost always the case, the actual locations are southern California for the land and water-surface shots and Silver Springs for the underwater shots. Two Greek divers, played by Anthony George and Lisa Gaye, attempt to illegally retrieve an ancient statue they have found underwater, and are afraid that Mike will notify the authorities of the find. They plot to get rid of Mike, but the woman ends up callously killing her boyfriend and nearly succeeds in killing Mike as well. The very worst "ethnic" stereotypes are at play in this episode: the Greek man is jealous and violent; the Greek woman is flirtatious, treacherous and downright murderous.

In summary, the Greeks of Tarpon Springs, as portrayed by Hollywood in films and TV shows, were often as wildly imaginary as the depictions of sea monsters and locations. In contrast to the fluid self-identity available to actual Greek-Americans as an "ethnic white" group, Hollywood Greeks were profoundly nonwhite. In their appearance, character and culture they often acted as foils to WASPish main characters. The physical environs were just as illusory: Tarpon Springs was often not Tarpon Springs, and harmless sea creatures were depicted as vicious monsters, some that did not even belong in the Atlantic Ocean. The underwater ocean scenes were usually filmed in aquariums or freshwater springs, and the Greeks, of course, were not Greeks, being portrayed as exotic and dangerous, through a clumsy collection of "ethnic" stereotypes, by non-Greek character actors.

Bibliography

Anagnostou, Yiorgos. *Contours of White Ethnicity: Popular Ethnography and the Making of Usable Pasts in Greek America*. Athens: Ohio University Press, 2009.

Dailey, Lester R. "Former Sponge Diver Recalls Tarpon Springs' Glory Days." Tampa Bay Newspapers, January 10, 2007. https://www.tbnweekly.com/pinellas_county/article_792db565-89b1-54ed-ace5-e071ccd6c2a8.html.

Moates, Jeff. "What Happened to All Those Boats? A Sketch of Maritime Heritage." In *Celebrating Community; Tarpon Springs: Reflections on 125 Years*, edited by Genevieve Crosby, Phyllis Kolianos, Kathleen Monahan and Cynthia Tarapani, 14–21. Tarpon Springs, FL: City of Tarpon Springs, 2013.

"Tarpon Springs Native Grabs the Cross at 114th Epiphany Celebration." 10News WTSP, January 6, 2020. YouTube video. 1:55 min. https://youtu.be/a8-giPfLJWs.

Chapter 4

Pedagogies and Possibilities of Crisis: Greek and Iranian Film

Sahar Siavashi

University of Lethbridge, Canada

William Ramp

University of Lethbridge, Canada

Abstract

This chapter discusses how Greek and Iranian films reflect and respond to crises of everyday life and nationhood under austerity. How are the same imperatives imposed and reproduced differently in national, local, even intimate contexts? We link film to political theory and collective psychology via three propositions about austerity regimes derived from Yanis Varoufakis and Adam Kotsko: (1) the imposition of austerity isn't "neoliberal" in the classic sense of minimalist government and free markets; it re-purposes government to expand commodification, protect cronies and police economic discipline; (2) a primary mechanism of this discipline is debt; and (3) neoliberalism works as a political theology of subject-formation, demonizing those under economic discipline as contractually responsible for their own disadvantage. These propositions delineate an austerity meta-narrative that lends itself to cinematic representation. Iranian and Greek films illustrate different instances in which economic discipline is mobilized to de-mobilize: to block resistance; divert agency into fatalism or opportunism; normalize exploitation or disruption. Its successes and failures shape personal fates and national histories.

Keywords: austerity, Cinema, Crisis, Debt, Diaspora, Family, Film, Gender, Greece, Iran, Neoliberalism, Narrative, Nationhood, Patriarchy, Pedagogy, Personhood, Political Theology, Representation, Resistance, Revenge, Ritual Condensation, Subjectivity, Urban, Agency, Capitalism, Cities, Class, Discourse, Film studies, Individualism, Memory and history, Narrative analysis, Politics of the family, Reception theory, State, Subject-formation.

***

Introduction

This chapter arose from a shared interest in the way political and personal crises intersect in circumstances of austerity, and how neoliberal imperatives have been woven into interpersonal lives and anxieties in recent periods of economic uncertainty. These intersections also feature in cinematic narratives that intertwine different dimensions of the human condition, from the intimate to the national and international, locating or disrupting shared history and memory. For 18 months, under the shadow of continuing economic and political instability, the authors committed to a weekly regime of film-watching, largely focused on Iranian and Greek film: Iranian because of the nationality and interests of one, and Greek because the other had fallen under the directorial spell of Theodor (Theo) Angelopoulos. Concurrently, we also read and listened to books, articles, speeches and interviews by former Greek finance minister Yanis Varoufakis, trying to understand the exigencies of our post-2008 worlds. Varoufakis convinced us that the austerity politics that followed the Greek financial crisis had international resonance, and that the policies of the Iranian theocratic state and democratic governments in North America were in some important ways analogous to those imposed on Greece, despite differences in severity and sociopolitical context.

Figure 4.1. Yanis Varoufakis speaking at the 6th Subversive Festival, "The Utopia of Democracy," Zagreb, May 14, 2013.

Source: Wikimedia Commons, https://commons.wikimedia.org/wiki/File:Yanis_Varoufakis_on_Subversive_Festival. jpg#mw-jump-to-license. Photo courtesy of Robert Crc.

Yanis Varoufakis (see fig. 4.1) is a fascinating figure whose career recalls a term from classical Greek literature and theatre: *hubris* (ύβρις, or *hybris*). There it meant, among other things, "insolence" or "presumption toward the gods."[1] A former economics professor, Varoufakis catapulted into power as finance minister in the first Syriza government, responsible for negotiating a bailout package with the European Union (EU). He subsequently resigned and spilled the beans on the process in numerous popular articles, speeches and books. His critics claimed he failed to recognize political or economic realities, was in over his head, and engaged beyond his capabilities. Refusing to be a political has-been, he has since leveraged an inveterate online presence into a new role as international pedagogue and consciousness-raiser about international finance and the dismantling and commodification of the social fabric. An opportunist to some, a noble failure to others, Varoufakis is a theatrical personage who recast his resignation as public drama and told its backstory as tragicomedy. There is a bit of the chancer about him: he is an aleatory figure (from the Latin *aleator*, "dice player")[2] attuned to the contingency of the dramatic moment—play and counterplay, risk and dice throws. Unafraid to gamble on new roles or to pivot in a different direction, he turned a lack of Eurocratic credentials into advantage, and political crisis into pedagogical opportunity.

Our approach

Our effort reflects something of Varoufakis's example. We gambled on a symposium topic that seemed fertile, little aware at the time of its magnitude and complexity; hence our discussion of it may remain somewhat amateurish. But an amateur is a lover, if not a professional one, prone to neophyte hubris like those ancient Greeks who stepped out of ordinary lives to try their prowess in the first olympiads. On such enthusiasms are authorial reputations risked.

Film narrative can convey powerfully, in sonic, image-centric and condensed symbolism, the reach, dimensionality and isomorphisms of existential and social crisis and of human responses to adversity: resistance, paralysis, fatalism, opportunism. We hope to persuade the reader that a conversation about and between Greek and Iranian film can illuminate—both within and beyond these national contexts—how austerity is imposed under the sign of crisis; how that imposition re-engineers both economies and subjectivities; and how resistance to it can persist both in and through personal and national damage. Perhaps this reflects something distanced or diasporic in both film traditions: not only that they play to extraterritorial viewers or reflect the legacies of exiled directors, but that something about being Greek or Iranian, creative and politically aware can encourage both engagement and a sort of internal exile.

---

1. *Online Etymology Dictionary*, s.v. "hubris," https://www.etymonline.com/word/hubris.
2. *Online Etymology Dictionary*, s.v. "aleatory," https://www.etymonline.com/word/aleatory.

Our approach to film analysis here is eclectic but anchored in attention to three aspects of filmic representation. We should specify right at the start that we focus here mainly on representational film: film that purports to represent things and ideas in imagery linked, however magically or critically, to experiences of actuality. First, we treat film as a medium through which discourse is produced, disseminated, modified and limited.[3] That is, the film does not simply reflect or represent realities; it *creates* them as effects of making and connecting visual and auditory statements—via imagery, linguistic coding, sound, color and so on—about what is, what was, what will be and what ought to be. Discourse analysis applied to film can easily slip into a hermeneutics of a director's, writer's or producer's intent, but it is important to bear in mind that, as with all discourse, neither film-making nor what a film "says" is ever the simple outcome of what a director or auteur wants;[4] the final product is always shaped by a web of cultural, economic, technical, organizational, technological and political considerations.

Second, we have chosen to discuss films with narrative structure and content, and thus borrow from narrative analysis[5] to understand how they construct a story arc, how that arc unfolds, what imagery it relies upon, what cultural tropes and structures of myth it adopts or adapts, and what genres it links to or plays with. Understanding narrative

---

3. Recent literature on film as discourse includes John A. Bateman, "Critical Discourse Analysis and Film," in *The Routledge Handbook of Critical Discourse Studies*, eds. John Flowerdew and John E. Richardson, 612–25 (London: Routledge, 2018); Janina Wildfeuer, *Film Discourse Interpretation: Towards a New Paradigm for Multimodal Film Analysis* (London: Routledge, 2014); Jannis Androutsopoulos, "Introduction: Language and Society in Cinematic Discourse," *Multilingua* 31, no. 2/3 (2016): 139–54; Stephen Prince, "The Discourse of Pictures: Iconicity and Film Studies," *Film Quarterly* 47, no. 1 (1993): 16–28; B. Afshin and A. Gholamreza, "Critical Discourse Analysis of Iranian Political Cinema with Fairclough Approach," *Journal of Political Sciences and Public Affairs* 5, no. 1 (2017): 1–5, https://www.longdom.org/open-access/critical-discourse-analysis-of-iranian-political-cinema-with-faircloughapproach-2332-0761-1000233.pdf; and Mohammad Reza Amirian, Ali Rahimi and Gholamreza Sami, "A Critical Discourse Analysis of the Images of Iranians in Western Movies: The Case of *Iranium*," *International Journal of Applied Linguistics and English Literature* 1, no. 5 (2012): 1–13.

4. Michel Foucault, "What Is an Author?" in *Language, Counter-memory, Practice: Selected Essays and Interviews by Michel Foucault*, ed. D. F. Bouchard (Ithaca NY: Cornell University Press, 1980), 113–38.

5. See Helen Fulton et al., eds., *Narrative and Media* (Cambridge: Cambridge University Press, 2005); also Lothar Mikos, "Analysis of Film," in *The SAGE Handbook of Qualitative Data Analysis*, ed. Uwe Flick, 409–23 (Thousand Oaks, CA: SAGE, 2014); Paul Cobley, "Narrative," in *Oxford Bibliographies in Communication*, ed. P. Moy, Oxford Bibliographies Online (Oxford: Oxford University Press, 2016), https://eprints.mdx.ac.uk/20006/1/Pre-print%20Narrative%20Oxford%20Bibliographies.pdf; Janis Teruggi Page, "Towards a Theory of Visual Narrative Analysis" (PhD diss., University of Missouri–Columbia, 2005), ProQuest 45-6845-68; and David Bordwell, "ApProppriations and ImProprieties: Problems in the Morphology of Film Narrative," *Cinema Journal* 27, no. 3 (1988): 5–20, doi: https://doi.org/10.2307/1225288.

construction involves paying attention to metaphor, symbolism and imagery, and to the cultural mechanism that Fiske and Hartley term "ritual condensation": "projecting abstract ideas ... on to the external world" (in this instance, the world as represented) as concrete images. The film thereby has the capacity to perform what Fiske and Hartley called a bardic function, representing to viewers elements of what could be their own lives in terms of a common culture.[6] Like bards of old, film can also play this role critically, weaving ambiguously in and out of affirmation and dissent, transposing the familiar and the *unheimlich*. Like television, film is a product of intersecting popular and cultural economies[7] and (as Fiske asserts of television) can refract the struggles of ordinary persons caught up in those economies[8] "to assert aspects of their own needs and desires through their relationship with mass-produced culture": a culture in which old and new forms of media now converge.[9] Most of the films we discuss here flirt with the popular economy of the film business and the cultural economy of acceptability that governs its social and representational codes. Most of them also attempt to subvert or undo some of these codes, for example, by displaying how they are produced, and how that production is then forgotten or denied.

Third, we bring to our analysis a sense of ourselves less as experts than as people caught up in dilemmas, situations and struggles analogous to those depicted in the films we have chosen to discuss. We did not watch these films as an audience for a Hollywood thriller might: as a diversion or an affirmation of some hegemonic nostrum. But, like any film audience, we brought our lives, hopes, dreads, successes and failures to our watching and discussion. We tried to keep in sight how we represented a third moment in which films are "made" as discourse and as narrative representation: through their reception[10] and in

---

6. John Fiske and John Hartley, *Reading Television* (London: Routledge, 2004), 68–70.

7. John Fiske, *Understanding Popular Culture* (London: Routledge, 2011), 21–26, 35–39; see also John Fiske, *Television Culture* (London: Methuen, 1987), 309–26.

8. See Lauren Berlant, *Cruel Optimism* (Durham, NC: Duke University Press, 2011), 23–51, 95–222.

9. Henry Jenkins, "John Fiske: Now and the Future," *Confessions of an ACA-Fan* (blog), June 16, 2010, http://henryjenkins.org/blog/2010/06/john_fiske_now_and_the_future.html. See also Henry Jenkins and David Thorburn, eds., *Democracy and New Media: Media in Transition* (Cambridge, MA: MIT Press, 2003); Henry Jenkins and Nico Carpentier, "Theorizing Participatory Intensities: A Conversation about Participation and Politics," *Convergence* 19, no. 3 (2013): 265–86; James Hay and Nick Couldry, "Rethinking Convergence/Culture: An Introduction," *Cultural Studies* 25, no. 4/5 (2011): 473–86; Henry Jenkins, "The Cultural Logic of Media Convergence," *International Journal of Cultural Studies* 7, no. 1 (2004): 33–43; Henry Jenkins, *Convergence Culture: Where Old and New Media Collide* (New York: New York University Press, 2006); and Henry Jenkins, "Rethinking 'Rethinking Convergence/Culture,'" *Cultural Studies* 28, no. 2 (2014): 267–97.

10. Fiske urged students of film not to forget this moment. See Shaun Moores, "Texts, Readers and Contexts of Reading: Developments in the Study of Media Audiences," *Media, Culture and Society* 12, no. 1 (1990), 9–29; G. J. Oud, A. Weijers and F. Wester, *Narrative and Culture; The WOW Method: An*

terms of the horizons of expectation governing that reception in a given place, time and sociocultural context.[11]

The present volume emerged from a symposium that gathered together a diverse group of artists, musicians, scholars and teachers. It generated a creative tension between two ways of understanding classical Greek culture: (1) as expressive of a harmonics of the human spirit or civilizational convergence, and (2) as particular, contingent, specific, variable, even contradictory. This chapter reflects both tendencies. We were attracted to Varoufakis's globalized pedagogy (the Greek crisis as a lesson for the world) but were faced with and here acknowledge the manifold challenges of taking a synthetic approach to different modes, genres and nationalities of cinematic representation and reception, let alone of capitalism or neoliberalism. We hope to have given a fair account of both interpretive possibilities, and to have wrung a measure of wisdom from the challenge.

Central questions and initial comparisons

We do not claim that Greek and Iranian film uniquely link everyday and national life in terms of national traditions; our catchment of examples is insufficient in either case. Nor

---

Approach to Textual Analysis of Television Drama (Nijmegen: Instituut voor Masscommunicatie, Katholieke Universiteit Nijmegen, 1997), 1–19; Daniel Biltereyst and Philippe Meers, "Film, Cinema and Reception Studies : Revisiting Research on Audiences' Filmic and Cinematic Experiences," in *Reception Studies and Audiovisual Translation*, eds. E. Di Giovanni and Y. Gambier (Amsterdam: John Benjamins, 2018), 21–42; William Ramp, "Heads and Tales: Story in An Age of (Dis)information," *Weekly Hubris*, February 3, 2017, https://weeklyhubris.com/heads-tales-story-in-an-age-of-disinformation/; and William Ramp, "Heroes, Archetypes and Politics," *Weekly Hubris*, March 1, 2017, https://weekly hubris.com/heroes-archetypes-politics/. See also Marzieh Akhavan and Asghar Fahimifar, "Analyzing 'Ambiguity' in Realistic Iranian Movies: Using Reception Aesthetics Theory of Iser and Jauss (Case Study: *About Elly* by Asghar Farhadi)" (presentation to First National Conference on Fundamental Researches in Language and Literature Studies, Tehran, Iran, December 2018), 1–14, https://www.researchgate.net/publication/329990548_Analyzing_Ambiguity_in_Realistic_Iranian_Movies_Using_Reception_Aesthetics_Theory_of_Iser_and_Jauss_Case_Study_About_Elly_by_Asghar_Farhadi?enrich Id=rgreq-5dee2ad34b9bf86622337feaff09e1f6-XXX&enrichSource=Y292ZXJQYWdlOzMyOTk5MD U0ODtBUzo3MDkyMzY3MzY2Nzk5MzZAMTU0NjEwNjYyMzU1MA%3D%3D&el=1_x_3& _esc=publicationCoverPdf; and Gordana Tkalec, Iva Rosanda Žigo and Žarka Dolinara, "Film Reception by Means of New Media, or How the Film Escaped from the Cinema," *European Journal of Interdisciplinary Studies* 3, no. 2 (2017): 105–11.

11. See Hans Robert Jauss and Elizabeth Benzinger, "Literary History as a Challenge to Literary Theory," *New Literary History* 2, no. 1 (1970): 7–37; Alice Healy, "Altering Horizons: An Aesthetic of Reception and Reproduction in *Oscar and Lucinda*," in *Australian Literary Studies in the 21st Century: Proceedings of the 2000 ASAL Conference*, ed. P. Mead (Hobart, Australia: AASL, 2000): 145–50, https://openjournals.library.sydney.edu.au/index.php/JASAL/article/view/9601; and Hans Robert Jauss, *Toward an Aesthetic of Reception*, trans. T. Bahti (Minneapolis: University of Minnesota Press, 1982).

do we claim that film reflects social crisis transparently. It responds to and refracts it diversely, depending on political and economic conditions, location (indigenous or diasporic), technology, intended audience, genre and school. Rather than asserting typicalities, this chapter responds to three questions:

1. How do cinematic narratives of personal crisis refer to, condense and complicate wider social issues?
2. In what ways can film take up time, history and memory (personal, familial or national) to address the circumstances and consequences of austerity?
3. How might films that make such links fuel transnational comparison and conversation?

To prefigure the third of these questions, we begin with a brief schematic outline of some characteristics of the two countries whose cinema is our focus.

Both Greece and Iran are burdened by disputed national narratives rooted in both distant and recent history. Both have entertained geopolitical aspirations and have geopolitical rivals. Both have been sanctioned for economic or political choices made by their governments. Both are faced with refugee influxes. Both have significant international diasporas. In both, the political right promotes national pride and historical grievance. Both have endured and are enduring severe bouts of austerity, driven in Greece by loan repayments and in Iran by sanctions. Both are beset by institutionalized corruption and crony capitalism, and by divisions between disadvantaged regions and cosmopolitan metropoles. Both have experienced border changes and population shifts that left ethnic Greeks and Persians outside national boundaries or brought other populations within. These have heightened and politicized consciousness of borders, particularly in Greece (see Angelopoulos's *The Suspended Step of the Stork*[12]).

In both countries, ancient civilizational pasts inflect present political and aesthetic cultures. Their legacy is problematic in post-revolutionary Iran (the shah promoted it). Greece is made by two such legacies in tension, classical and Byzantine.[13] In both countries, a dominant religion is implicated (diversely) in nationalist narratives. Both Iranian and Greek politics are divided and inflected by enduring left and right political cultures; in both, strong postwar communist movements were fiercely but incompletely repressed (in Greece, through a civil war). Movements for democracy and autonomy have marked both nations since the 19th century, interrupted by parliamentary crises, monarchies, dictatorships and (in Iran) a theocracy. In both, a sharpening gender politics

---

12. Theo Angelopoulos, *The Suspended Step of the Stork*, Theo Angelopoulos Collection, vol. 2 (London: Curzon Artificial Eye, December 1991), DVD, 143 min.
13. Alexander Billinis, "The Eagle Has Two Faces: Journeys Through Byzantine Europe," *Byzantine Blog*, September 30, 2011, https://mybyzantine.wordpress.com/tag/alexander-billinis/.

inflects the vitality and relevance of the left and a repressive politics of the family is mobilized on the right (in Iran it is enshrined in the regime's legal foundations). In both countries, the arts have been subject to periodic repression.

The filmography of both nations addresses unrealized destinies and failed promises of modernization that inhibited the organic development of autonomous Greek[14] and Iranian[15] film industries but opened both to international influence and attention (especially in the case of Iran's directorial diaspora). Both Greek and Iranian film are cosmopolitan in stylistic reference (*cinéma vérité*, magic realism, Italian neorealism, postmodernism), and both articulate domestic political and social issues in ways that appeal to international audiences.

In Greece, relaxation of censorship in the early 1970s led to a politically engaged film revival in which Angelopoulos,[16] Alexis Damianos, Pantelis Voulgaris and others featured

---

14. For discussions of recent Greek film, see especially Alex Lykidis, "Crisis of Sovereignty in Recent Greek Cinema," *Journal of Greek Media and Culture* 1, no. 1 (2015): 9–27, doi: 10.1386/jgmc.1.1.9_1.9-27; also L. Papadimitriou and Y. Tzioumakis, eds., *Greek Cinema: Texts, Histories, Identities* (Bristol: Intellect, 2012); Lydia Papadimitriou, "Greek Film Studies Today: In Search of Identity," *Kambos: Cambridge Papers in Modern Greek* 17 (2009): 49–78, https://www.academia.edu/1272469/Greek_Film_Studies_Today_In_Search_of_Identity; Dan Georgakas, "Greek Cinema For Beginners: A Thumbnail History," *Film Criticism* 27, no. 2. (2002–03): 2–8; Vrasidas Karalis, *A History of Greek Cinema* (London: Bloomsbury, 2012); Marios Psaras, "Weirdly/Queerly Ethical: Contemporary Greek Cinema and the Crisis of Meaning," E-International Relations, February 14, 2018: 1–5, https://www.e-ir.info/pdf/72752; Andrew Horton, "Theodor Angelopoulos and the New Greek Cinema," *Film Criticism* 11, no. 1/2 (Fall/Winter 1986–87): 84–94; Rodney Uhler "'The Lobster,' 'Chevalier,' and the Importance of New Greek Cinema," IndieWire, October 19, 2015, https://www.indiewire.com/2015/10/the-lobster-chevalier-and-the-importance-of-new-greek-cinema-129248/; and Steve Rose, "*Attenberg, Dogtooth* and the Weird Wave of Greek Cinema," *The Guardian*, August 37, 2011, https://www.theguardian.com/film/2011/aug/27/attenberg-dogtooth-greece-cinema. On the attraction of Greek filmmakers (such as Angelopoulos) to issues of identity, borders and migrations, see Philip E. Phillis, *Greek Cinema and Migration, 1991–2016* (Edinburgh: Edinburgh University Press, 2020).

15. For Iranian cinema and its history, see Saeed Zeydabadi-Nejad, *The Politics of Iranian Cinema: Film and Society in the Islamic Republic* (London: Routledge, 2010); Hamid Naficy, *An Accented Cinema: Exilic and Diasporic Filmmaking* (Princeton NJ: Princeton University Press, 2001); Hamid Naficy, "Making Films with an Accent: Iranian Émigré Cinema," *Framework* 43 no. 2 (Fall 2002): 15–41; Hamid Naficy, *A Social History of Iranian Cinema*, vol 1, *The Artisanal Era, 1897–1941* (Durham, NC: Duke University Press, 2011; Hamid Dabashi, "How Did Iranian Cinema Go Global?" Al Jazeera, March 21, 2018, https://www.aljazeera.com/indepth/opinion/iranian-cinema-global-180321085138324.html; and Maryam Ghorbankarimi, "Redefining the Filmic Genres of Iranian Cinema: The Generic Qualities of New Iranian Cinema," Association for Iranian Studies, accessed May 14, 2019, https://associationforiranianstudies.org/node/124.

16. See Eleftheria Rania Kosmidou, "Theo Angelopoulos's *O Thiasos/The Travelling Players* (1975) and *Oi Kynigoi/The Hunters* (1977) and How They Affect the Brechtian Project," *Journal of Modern*

prominently. Despite claims that Greek cinema had retreated into aesthetic and narrative refinement, a second Greek new wave in the 2000s embraced critical politics, for example, *Miss Violence* (2013), *Lines* (2016) and *Cloud* (2019). In such films, parallels are drawn from personal and existential crises to crises of national sovereignty.[17] In Iran, socially critical film remains under severe if variable official constraint. The exodus of Iranian directors and other personnel since 1979 acutely raises the question of what to consider as "Iranian" cinema: does it include the work of diaspora directors who address Iranian issues either directly or indirectly? Here we answer in the affirmative, but that answer raises further questions.

Finally, we claim that the film industries, cultures and social orders of both nations have been beset, if differently to a degree, by conditions we call neoliberalism and austerity. Our first task is to explain what we mean by calling these "conditions" rather than policies or ideologies.

On a neoliberalism that does and does not exist

Yanis Varoufakis argues that the Greek economic crisis, and the privatization and austerity terms imposed by the European bailout deal, exemplify developments in global financial capitalism that are at once displayed and obscured. But he asserts that to treat the Greek bailout as an example of neoliberalism is like explaining the economics of the latter-day USSR in terms of the writings of Marx.[18] While he uses the term *neoliberal* frequently, he challenges its definitional status in a way that begs a Socratic test. Let's imagine him encountering Socrates, time-transported to Syntagma Square, sometime in the previous or present decade.

> *Socrates*: Ah, Yanis! You have argued, in the building behind us, that neoliberalism does not inhabit our present troubles.
>
> *Varoufakis*: Indeed, Socrates, that could be said.
>
> *Socrates*: Yet you continue to use the term. Here, sit down; let us explore this assertion or refusal to assert. Tell us how you define this non-present thing you insist on referring to? How is it not present? Is it an appearance of some non-apparent actuality? Or the converse?

Greek Studies 35, no. 2 (October 2017): 513–38; also Angelos Koutsourakis and Mark Steven, eds., *The Cinema of Theo Angelopoulos* (Edinburgh: Edinburgh University Press, 2015), chap. 4, 6 and 7.

17. Lykidis.

18. Yanis Varoufakis, interview by Bruce Livesey, "Is Neoliberalism Destroying the World?" *Ideas*, CBC Radio, August 29, 2019, https://www.cbc.ca/radio/ideas/is-neoliberalism-destroying-the-world-1.4839399.

Hearers, Chorus: Indeed, Yanis, will have trouble answering! Is it not obvious what misery neoliberalism has wrought? Was not Yanis himself powerless against its force? Is its presence not evident in our suffering?

Socrates: See how your skepticism excites our hearers! But let us hear from you. Tell us how such a name, in the absence of the thing, has purchase on our hearers.

Varoufakis: Ah, Socrates, what complications arise, like a thousand ghosts, from your questions!

Socrates: Ghosts? Well, then, what is the ghost in this instance?

Varoufakis: The ghosts, in this instance, we can call appearances.

Socrates: And are these appearances not actualities, not present?

Varoufakis: Indeed they *are* actual. They flicker in front of us on the walls of the cave of which your student Plato speaks; we see them. Their causes, however, lie in another set of actualities: the actions of powerful men. But causes are not reflections.

Socrates: Ah, then we have two modes of actuality to consider: those that we see, which you say are not present, and those which are present, which you say we do not see.

To cut to a conclusion, Varoufakis argues that the real actions of powerful Eurocrats and cowed politicians imposed a disciplinary regime called austerity on Greece. Those actions are said to emanate from a philosophy and a set of policies called "neoliberalism" that advocate minimal government, free markets, entrepreneurship, self-reliance and individual responsibility. But for Varoufakis, this confuses effect with cause. The terms of the Greek bailout were communicated through a loose and contradictory mix of narrative tropes and applied ad hoc for momentary political and economic leverage.[19] They produced "socialism for the banks,"[20] not free-market capitalism, and did not dismantle the Greek state but repurposed it to oversee sell-offs of public assets, cuts to public benefits and a disciplining of the national population to accept the results. There was no strict compliance with a creed delivered whole from Chicago or Mont Pèlerin. Greece's fiscal penitence was cobbled together in haggling, inertia, blindness, reactivity and arrogance. *Neoliberalism* was applied to this mess of contingencies as a convenient

---

19. Yanis Varoufakis, "The Deep State Part 5: From Goebbels to Donald Trump's Campaign Against the Deep State," Soundcloud, 2019, https://soundcloud.com/yanisv/the-deep-state-part-5-from-goebbels-to-donald-trumps-campaign-against-the-deep-state.

20. Iain MacWhirter, "How to Survive the Recession," *New Statesman*, August 21, 2008, accessed May 27, 2018, https://www.newstatesman.com/economy/2008/08/government-credit-banks.

shorthand for global newsrooms. The term remains useful to Varoufakis only to name a sort of moralized meta-drama invoked post hoc by politicians and pundits.

Adam Kotsko agrees that neoliberalism has less philosophical rigor than is often claimed for it.[21] While it may have its core theorists (e.g., Hayek, Friedman) and venues,[22] it resembles more an assemblage of formulae variously combined, depending on circumstances and agents.[23] We concur partially but argue that it does still name something coherent, and that *what* it names reaches into our souls, our intimate relations and our civic identities, and is thereby *made for film*.

Neoliberal history and demonology: austerity as moral ontology

If neoliberal ideas were skimmed selectively from a turbulent stream of economic and political pedagogy and plunged back into it in variable if patterned ways, certain of them are repeatedly cited and linked to each other. These ideas include, for example,[24]

- various iterations of possessive individualism, serving as a connective tissue linking freedom, responsibility and private property rights;[25]
- proposals for minimalist government (state intervention being taken to distort the efficient signaling of economic and even social information by market prices);
- encouragement of competition as an optimal matrix for human flourishing.

The ideas combine into a general moral regime in which legitimate wealth-generating agency lies with individuals, families and corporations, who purchase capital or personal goods and services, who work or direct work, and who innovate, using market and technical information. Its central regulative agents are the market and the family, legitimated by contract and nature respectively.[26] State regulation beyond a strictly necessary minimum threatens both forms of legitimation and descends into rent-seeking. Tenets such as these are

---

21. Adam Kotsko, *Neoliberalism's Demons: On the Political Theology of Late Capital* (Redwood City, CA: Stanford University Press, 2018), 13, 16.
22. See Philip Mirowski and Dieter Plehwe, eds., *The Road from Mont Pèlerin: The Making of the Neoliberal Thought Collective* (Cambridge, MA: Harvard University Press, 2015).
23. Kotsko, especially 22, 35–38, 53, 64–65, 76, 89–90, 94–95.
24. Philip Mirowski gives a summation in "Is Neoliberalism Destroying the World?" Interview by Bruce Livesey, *Ideas*, CBC Radio, August 29, 2019, https://www.cbc.ca/radio/ideas/is-neoliberalism-destroying-the-world-1.4839399. See also Kotsko, 6, 9–16, 35–37, 89–90, and Mark Fisher, *Capitalist Realism: Is There No Alternative?* (Ropley, UK: Zer0 Books, 2008), 39–53.
25. Charles Brough Macpherson, *The Political Theory of Possessive Individualism: Hobbes to Locke* (1962; repr., Oxford: Oxford University Press, 2010).
26. Kotsko, 71, 111–13, argues that neoliberalism addresses economic and political life as one: families and other social institutions are to be incorporated into capital accumulation and the market, rather than reserved from them.

commonly taken to inform "neoliberal policy," but they are teleologically *anti*-policy, inasmuch as their aim is a largely self-regulating atemporal state.

While actual policy applications may lip-serve these general formulae,[27] they must address diverse and changing historical conditions that have introduced a skepticism about pure market regulation into what has become a neoliberal moral discourse. Some such conditions were specific to national, regional or even local contexts; others have become more generalized, such as an unprecedented marketizing of human beings as self-contractors, branding vectors and informational commodities, and a massive expansion of chronic debt. Debt has always served and disciplined capital accumulation, but today marketized debt and its derivatives fuel economic stimuli enabled by financialization, a loosening of monetary and other regulation since the 1960s[28] that shifted capital accumulation from production to speculation, expanded the ubiquity of debt, and proliferated its instruments.

Now central to personal, corporate and state budgets, debt is "serviced" in the interests of organizations "too big to fail" and policed against the weakest at all three levels. The moral hegemony of capital now acts through a systematic disciplinary subjection of individual and public debtors. As Leitner and colleagues note,

> Neo-liberal governmental technologies are indirect: setting targets and monitoring outcomes; transforming the ethos of governance from bureaucracy to business; giving agencies autonomy to act as long as they are accountable; and creating calculable spaces to monitor outcomes (relying heavily on auditing, targets, and rankings). Governance remains rather unidirectional, however: Institutions, agencies, and individual citizens are expected to make their activities visible to centers of calculation, but these centers are less often required (much less enticed or persuaded) to make their activities transparent to neoliberal subjects. Governmental technologies help construct neoliberal subjectivity. Under neoliberalism, individual freedom is redefined as the capacity for self-realization and freedom from bureaucracy rather than freedom from want, with human behavior reconceptualized along economic lines. Individuals are empowered to actively make self-interested choices and are made responsible for acting in this way to advance both their well-being and that of society. Employees are redefined as entrepreneurs with an *obligation* to work, to better themselves and society, rather than having a right to work. They are *responsible* for their own education and retraining, to build human capital, and for their own well-being and risk management by behaving prudently,

---

27. Kotsko, 95; also 4, 89–90.

28. Yanis Varoufakis, *And the Weak Suffer What They Must? Europe's Crisis and America's Economic Future* (New York: Nation, 2016), 73–83, 212–15, 219–21. See also Kotsko, 13, 40.

instead of relying on the state. Personal and social responsibility are equated with self-esteem.[29]

Driven by fears of individual dependency and state overreach, the moral policing of debt reflects a vision of human nature that seeks to guard against certain of its alleged tendencies. Adam Smith hoped that shared moral sentiments might counterbalance self-interest. Neoliberalism represents collective self-interest as a road to serfdom.[30] If the light of the neoliberal ideal type cast shadows on its Platonic cave walls, that which blocked the light had also entered the cave.

For Adam Kotsko, neoliberalism is best described as a practical political theology: an ontological structure of legitimation and destiny, a theodicy of moral justification, an explanation of evil or failure and a mode of subject-formation[31] that is reproduced in discursive, institutional and interpersonal practices, often in combination with austerity messaging. Political theologies are "how political, social, religious and economic orders maintain explanatory power and justify the loyalty of their adherents," informing everyday consent to modes of authority.[32] Neoliberal moralism is flexible enough to suit a variety of regimes and national societies, but in all of them, it characteristically demonizes failed economic agents by situating them in narratives of free will, choice, competitive justification and reproach.[33] It links the macro and micro worlds of capitalism in a form of recruitment tying families and households to the wider accumulative process, linking institutional and self-policing, and instituting parallels between national, familial and personal character.

In short, neoliberalism is a rhetorical and practical combination of motivational, consensual and retributive representations that, where it is hegemonic, shapes our sense of possibility and accountability,[34] diverting attention from power to responsibility. It depersonalizes subjection by treating debt, credit and property as formal instruments rather

---

29. Helga Leitner et al., "Contesting Urban Futures: Decentering Neoliberalism," in *Contesting Neoliberalism: Urban Frontiers*, eds. H. Leitner, J. Peck and E. S. Sheppard, 1–25 (New York: Guilford, 2007) [emphasis added].

30. For example, Friedrich A. Hayek, *The Road to Serfdom: Text and Documents; The Definitive Edition*, ed. Bruce Caldwell (Chicago: University of Chicago Press, 2007).

31. "A neoliberal subjectivity has also emerged which normalizes the logics of individualism and entrepreneurialism, equating individual freedom with self-interested choices, making individuals responsible for their own well-being, and redefining citizens as consumers and clients. Margaret Thatcher's notorious 'there is no alternative' seems to be a self-fulfilling prophecy." Leitner et al., "Contesting Urban Futures," 1. See also Carl Schmitt, *Political Theology: Four Chapters on the Concept of Sovereignty* (1922), trans. G. Schwab (Chicago: University of Chicago Press, 2005).

32. Kotsko, 6–10, 30–32.

33. Kotsko, 2, 35–38, 79–81, 85–95, 103, 105–6, 121–22.

34. Kotsko, 103, 105, 111.

than concrete relations, and thereby also fetishizes them.[35] But it also radically *personalizes* individual and collective will, though in an equally fetishized and moralistic manner, by representing economic agency as context-free choice and economic failure as freely willed irresponsibility, costly and sinful. The conditions of such failure are immaterial. Choices that impose unwarranted "costs" on others are deemed willfully inimical (as when those on social assistance are called takers of others' "hard-earned tax dollars"). Thus are the terms of debt capitalism legitimated:[36] those with "the barest sliver" of "constrained agency" in choice-making are treated as abstract equals to the healthiest and most privileged, and thus as targets of punitive "responsibilization,"[37] dispossessed of assets and agency by their own bad choices.

Neoliberal moralism thereby promotes a model of human nature and seeks to form subjectivity through a totalizing moral pedagogy. It represents as "unimaginable" that the conditions of this morality could be otherwise, and as "obvious" that the market is provident and that our success depends on the merits of our choices.[38] But it teaches different expressions of this to differently positioned populations. For the disadvantaged, "the assumption of rational choice in the absence of meaningful agency can generate blameworthiness," in which judgment shifts from choices to inner worth. It can also generate self-justifying assertions of one's victimization by demonized "takers." For example, Trumpian rhetoric asserts that in conditions of freedom I would win; if I do not, others must be cheating me. Sometimes these others are identified as "elites," more often as public employees, the poor, the exploited, the racialized or the displaced. In short, punitive demonization works in both directions to reinforce affect-laden regimes of social and existential (un)worthiness.[39] It poses a double bind that both counsels and delegitimates despair:

> A human being has only so much in them, and yet you must learn through experience, until you finally reach the maddening conclusion that the world wrote you off a long time ago, or accept the prison sentence that *your crime is your existence*. And the world keeps turning as if nothing has happened. The forced smiles of the lucky ones say it all: It's either this, or getting stabbed in the chest with a bayonet, getting raped, dragging yourself onto the highway overpass,

---

35. Our argument here draws in part on Derek Sayer, *Capitalism and Modernity: An Excursus on Marx and Weber* (London: Routledge, 1991), 36–58.

36. Kotsko, 81, 95, 99, 109, 121–22.

37. Mark Fisher, "Good for Nothing," *Occupied Times*, March 19, 2014, https://theoccupiedtimes.org/?p=12841; also Kotsko, 121–22.

38. Kotsko, 111, 79–96. See also Philippe Steiner, *Durkheim and the Birth of Economic Sociology*, trans. K. Tribe (Princeton, NJ: Princeton University Press, 2011) on economic subject formation, especially chapters 2, 5, 6 and 7.

39. Kotsko, 89–90, 96, 99, 105–6, 110, 112.

or checking into a mental institution. No one will ever know about your tragedy, and the world eluded its responsibility ages ago. All that you know is that you've been crucified for something, and you're going to spend the rest of your life feeling like no one and nothing will help you, and that you're in it alone.[40]

Among the privileged, this attitude bends toward callousness of the sort embodied in Hoche and Binding's famous phrases "life unworthy of life" and "useless eaters."[41] Chronic debt thus becomes a "temporal colonialism," a subjection that forecloses futures.[42]

This is neoliberal austerity as subject-formation. But the conditions that produce it are historical, not eternal. Like Marx, Varoufakis describes capitalism as ever generative of new social formations and new systemic social crises.[43] Neoliberalism arose partly in response to a crisis of regulation following the de-legitimation of Fordism,[44] and it has accompanied a wave of global economic deregulation:

> [N]eoliberalism's geography differs from preceding promarket initiatives. It is a global project, accepted by elites and mainstream political parties in varying forms almost everywhere around the world, and implemented at scales ranging from municipal to supranational authorities. Previous attempts were implemented in a small group of countries or forced on other dependent nation-states and localities. It has become easy to implement neoliberal policies via fast policy transfer and to monitor it, and harder to find space for pursuing alternative imaginaries and practices.[45]

The resultant system is globally integrated but uneven and contradictory, expansive but needing periodic rescue, deregulated but regulative. It seeks to overpower alternatives but shapeshifts constantly in response to resistance. As Leitner and colleagues note, contestation "was critical to the emergence of neoliberal regimes, and remains closely articulated with neoliberalism"; thus, its present hegemony "cannot be mistaken for

---

40. Qiu Miaojin, *Notes of a Crocodile*, trans. B. Huie (New York: New York Review of Books, 2017), quoted in Lilith, "A Response to the Meritocratic Revolution," *Queen Mob's Teahouse*, May 28, 2020, https://queenmobs.com/2020/05/a-response-to-the-meritocratic-revolution/?fbclid=IwA R0ZRC8hiAK9-JJgHb-r91arvYthV8z7ko2lOv2oj_krjn8K0KONRLXk5-g [emphasis added].

41. Karl Binding and Alfred Hoche, *Allowing the Destruction of Life Unworthy of Life: Its Measure and Form*, trans. C. Modak (Greenwood, WI: Policy Intersections Research Center/Suzeteo Enterprises, 2012–15).

42. Kotsko, 99, 122–23.

43. See Yanis Varoufakis, *Talking to My Daughter about the Economy: A Brief History of Capitalism* (London: Bodley Head, 2018), chap. 2 and 3; also Kotsko, 5, 12, 74–76.

44. Leitner et al., "Contesting Urban Futures," 5–6.

45. Leitner et al., "Contesting Urban Futures," 3.

everlasting life."⁴⁶ Above all, neoliberal directives are dependent on the state's steering and enforcement of changing conditions of accumulation. Friedman himself argued that the neoliberal state "cultivates and maintains the conditions necessary for vigorous market competition," that periodic tightening and easing of the terms of debt and market discipline, and even financial bailouts, are a crisis-aversion duty of the state as "ultimate guarantor of market structures."⁴⁷ Even deregulation is a state function⁴⁸ integrated with national and international governance. Accumulation now relies on sovereign states servicing their own debt by transferring public assets to private interests. The Greek crisis resulted not from an out-of-control state sector but from unregulated international lending unable to avoid the consequences of unemployed international capital.

The resulting "bankruptocracy" burst unsustainable economic bubbles,⁴⁹ leaving finance ministries, state and private banks and investment funds too exposed to each other's debt in order to stabilize the conditions of speculative lending, facing the Scylla of "quantitative easing" or the Charybdis of punishing state debtors. Greece got both: a requirement to cash out public assets and drastic public spending cuts as the price of a float⁵⁰ sufficient to ensure payment over a (now chronic) longer term. The European banking system was saved for another day by a massive transfer of value from the Greek people to the Greek state's lenders.⁵¹ Ironically, this entailed both massive market distortion and the necessity of the Greek state's (in Syriza's unhappy hands) acting as austerity's executor and enforcer, restricting the power of unions and popular organizations, undermining local business and widening the monetization of natural and human life as assets or costs—all in the collective interests of finance-capital lobbyists engaged in a collusive asset-stripping exercise.

For Varoufakis, the crises sparked in 2008 remain very much at the center of our present. The same crisis is taking different shapes in different places, migrating from continent to continent, from country to country. It morphs from an unemployment generator to a deflation machine, to another banking crisis, to a maximizer of trade and capital global imbalances. It depletes middle-class savings in Germany and Holland, suppresses wages

---

46. Leitner, et al., "Contesting Urban Futures," 4–7. Contestation can also reshape resistance to neoliberalism in complex ways; see pp. 9–13.
47. Kotsko, 12–13, 21, 65.
48. Kotsko, 35, 38, 40.
49. Yanis Varoufakis, "Bankruptocracy: How Bankrupt Banks Rule the Economy Today; Explained by Yanis Varoufakis," acTVism Munich, n.d., YouTube video, 0:3:42, https://www.youtube.com/watch?v=jl W9DCRQeiE. Varoufakis asserts that a bankruptcy of thinking was also manifest at the highest levels of European finance. There was no secret conspiracy, only systemic blindness and illogic serving one central mandate: to protect capital accumulation at all costs.
50. Varoufakis, *And the Weak Suffer*, 202–3, 221–30.
51. Varoufakis, *And the Weak Suffer*, 120–97.

across the West, causes credit bubbles in China, and keeps Greece and Europe's periphery in a permanent Great Depression; it fuels Brexit and discontent in middle America, in Europe. Last but not least, it jeopardizes the life prospects of millions of people across the so-called emerging countries.[52]

In these conditions, neoliberal moral pessimism has become central to the political governance of austerity. "Economic discipline" invokes a claim that human nature entails the "harsh medicine" of adversity, fear or shame to curb fiscal "irresponsibility." The Greek state and the entire Greece workforce were represented as irresponsibly unproductive.[53] The moralized policing of the economy[54] also includes predatory lending and collection agencies, loan consolidation and renegotiation services, and credit counseling, which maintain on life support debtors' ability and felt obligation to pay, recruiting them into a generalized moral economy of responsibility extending from individuals to states.[55]

Actualities, imaginaries, destinies: social and cinematic force fields

But again, the actual spread and application of such austerity and policing measures is uneven and variable. While "neoliberalism has become a hegemonic signifier for 'best-practice' governance,"[56] its practices are typically not imposed holus-bolus on a fatalistic populace. Some have been popularly welcomed in certain circumstances.[57] They pervade and are tailored to different national economies, nation-states, societies, cultures and

---

52. Yanis Varoufakis, "2008 and the International New Deal We Need for the Post-2018 World: OECD Keynote, 14 Sep 2018," Yanis Varoufakis (website), September 18, 2018, https://www.yanisvaroufakis.eu/2018/09/18/2008-and-the-international-new-deal-we-need-for-the-post-2018-world-oecd-keynote-14-sep-2018/?fbclid=IwAR0gOBYjLSrft6jZvoBfnFE2-I9yNqZnlYpFA7Aou4fVafAonminJ8rSBqo.

53. See, for example, Doug Bandow, "Into the Economic Abyss: Foolish Europeans Give Irresponsible Greeks Third Bailout," *Forbes*, July 22, 2015, https://www.forbes.com/sites/dougbandow/2015/07/22/into-the-economic-abyss-foolish-europeans-give-irresponsible-greeks-third-bailout/?sh=3e417b3d7094. Varoufakis counters that Greek workers were and are in fact among the world's most productive.

54. Varoufakis, *Talking to My Daughter*; see especially his analysis of Marlowe's *Doctor Faustus* and Goethe's *Faust* in chapter 3. See also Kotsko, *Neoliberalism's Demons*, 38, 86, 90–94, 111.

55. Samuel Chambers, *There's No Such Thing as "the Economy": Essays on Capitalist Value* (Goleta, CA: Punctum, 2018). Chambers argues that the economy is less an impersonal mechanism for the production and exchange of value than a social assemblage that reproduces qualitative values in specific political circumstances, defining and judging agents and objects.

56. Leitner et al., "Contesting Urban Futures," 1.

57. Helga Leitner, Jamie Peck and Eric S. Sheppard, "Squaring up to Neoliberalism," in Leitner et al., *Contesting Neoliberalism*, 311–27. See also Wendy Larmer and Maria Butler, "The Places, People, and Politics of Partnership: After Neoliberalism in Aotearoa, New Zealand," in the same volume, 71–89.

localities, whether deftly[58] or not, as Brenner and Theodore note: "Neoliberal programs of capitalist restructuring are rarely, if ever, imposed in a pure form, for they are always introduced within politico-institutional contexts that have been molded significantly by earlier regulatory arrangements, institutionalized practices, and political compromises."[59]

Figure 4.2. Austerity protest, Syntagma Square, Athens, Greece, 2011.

Source: Wikimedia Commons,
https://commons.wikimedia.org/wiki/File:2011_Greece_Uprising.jpg.
Photo courtesy of Kotsolis at English Wikipedia.

Neoliberal austerity policies also apply differently in urban and rural settings. Major cities and metropolitan areas are key targets for (and heavily impacted by) measures such as fiscal devolution, privatization, deregulation and the "responsibilizing" of welfare and other social services.[60] This targeting has given rise to a so-called neoliberal urbanism,

---

58. See Larner and Butler, "Places, People, and Politics."
59. Neil Brenner and Nik Theodore, "Cities and the Geographies of 'Actually Existing' Neoliberalism," in *Spaces of Neoliberalism: Urban Restructuring in North America and Western Europe* (Oxford: Blackwell, 2012), 2–32.
60. "Geographic rescaling after Fordism has emphasized the supra- and subnational scales: 'hollowing out' the nation-state and making cities increasingly responsible for realizing international competitiveness. Cities remain crucibles for new ideas, are where most people live and/or work, and are characterized as the scale at which state policies and practices are particularly sensitive to democratic pressure and local agendas. For all these reasons, successful implementation of neoliberal urban policy agendas has been key to neoliberalization." Leitner et al., "Contesting Urban Futures," 1. See also Jamie Peck and Adam Tickell,

its model the "entrepreneurial city" dedicated to "economic success in competition with other cities for investments, innovations, and 'creative classes'"—a city in which municipal social services "are progressively replaced by professionalized quasi-public agencies empowered and responsible for promoting economic development, privatizing urban services, and catalyzing competition among public agencies." This is a city organized in terms of "cost-benefit calculations" whose citizens are "expected to behave responsibly, entrepreneurially, and prudently" and are "made responsible for their own successes and failures."[61]

But such measures are redirected, blunted and reshaped, both locally and nationally, by various forms of urban resistance (see fig. 4.2).[62] Cities generate a variety of "social and spatial imaginaries"[63] that inform both specific application of neoliberal measures and specific resistances to them. Such resistance need not even be directly anti-neoliberal to have an impact; it may incorporate some aims associated with neoliberalism,[64] such as calls for more "accountability" of public institutions, a perennial feature of Greek urban protest. Resistance may be driven by different social imaginaries, may develop out of long-established civil society and other organizations or new ones,[65] or may "pop up" in spontaneous "flash" movements. Some forms of resistance may be localized to particular areas of a city, for example, that of older labor organizations in working-class districts of Athens, or a bifurcation of resistive forms between the middle-class north of Tehran (home to several early anti-hijab and cultural protests against theocratic measures) and the working-class and refugee-populated southern half of the city, where lack of services, women's vulnerability to policing, lack of employment rights, repression of union activity and wage theft loom large.

In the abstract, neoliberalism presents as markedly ahistorical; history is its unconscious. But in practice, it pervades and responds to history, meeting victory and defeat, dividing itself, conjoining diverse political forms, orienting their agents and objects toward various narrative destinies, locating events in complex maps of meaning and memory, and linking accumulation to different personal, familial or national missions. It mixes with populism

---

"Neoliberalizing Space," in *Spaces of Neoliberalism: Urban Restructuring in North America and Western Europe* (Oxford: Blackwell, 2012), 33–57.

61. Leitner et al., "Contesting Urban Futures," 4.

62. See Margit Mayer, "Contesting the Neoliberalization of Urban Governance" (90–115); Jamie Peck and Adam Tickell, "Conceptualizing Neoliberalism, Thinking Thatcherism" (26–50); and William Sites, "Contesting the Neoliberal City? Theories of Neoliberalism and Urban Strategies of Contention" (116–37), all in Leitner et al., *Contesting Neoliberalism*. Also see also the several case studies in the same volume.

63. Leitner et al., "Contesting Urban Futures," 19.

64. Leitner et al., "Contesting Urban Futures," 9.

65. Leitner et al., "Contesting Urban Futures," 16.

and nationalism, co-producing a variegated roster of angels, demons and horrors.[66] It makes national and international politics a stew of promise inflation, resentment management, crisis patriotism and states of exception,[67] generating a wealth of epic,[68] intimate, immersive or deconstructive tropes for potential cinematic elaboration. It represents "the family" ideally as an honorable institution of moral formation, a vehicle of intergenerational accumulation and an allegorical mediator between personal and national economies and their associated moral imaginaries. But the competitive individualism of the gig economy and the slashing of public services erode family bonds, aspirations and values. Families and households serve as precarious and affect-laden absorbent pads for the everyday shocks of precarity and austerity, and as sites for disciplining and managing the contradictions of reproductive, sexual and economic agency—all of which is food for film narrative: dramatic, tragic, and even comic.

Neoliberalism in practice, then, is a contingent and social ordering of family, sexuality, racial hierarchy and subordination[69] that can consume its own dramatically when it fails. Cinematic works by Avranas, Lanthimos, Voulgaris, Beyzai, Persson Sarvestani and Shahid-Saless unfold these complex and temporal dynamics against the grain of neoliberal common sense. Film can condense individual and national fates without collapsing them; can make things immediate or measure critical distance; can configure everyday resistance, complicity or defeat; can dramatize the complex formation and deformation of individual and collective subjects; and can trace the interlinked destinies of nations and intimate relations. In Greek cinema, austerity's moral economy lends itself to both tragedy and farce, to a scenography of chimeric legitimation and actual consequences.

It does so too in Iran, which has suffered successive economic crises since 2000, though international sanctions, theocracy, a militarized parallel economy and repression of the critical arts complicate narrative possibilities there. Still, there are familiar features and outcomes. Funding for the revolution's early social and health initiatives has been eroded; botched privatizations and wage theft[70] are common, as is victim-blaming of

---

66. See Kotsko, 101–24. Neoliberalism valorizes the free movement of capital; populist nationalism problematizes the free movement of peoples, with selective exceptions.
67. See Giorgio Agamben, *State of Exception*, trans. K. Attell (Chicago: University of Chicago Press, 2005) and Achille Mbembe, "Necropolitics," trans. L. Meintjes, *Public Culture* 15, no. 1 (Winter 2003): 11–40.
68. Pantelis Voulgaris's *Little England* (Riegelsville, PA: Corinth Films, 2013), DVD, 132 min., http://corinthfilms.com/films/little-england/, and the brooding oeuvre of Theo Angelopoulos are cases in point.
69. Kotsko, 94.
70. See, for example, "Haft Tappeh Workers Urge International Labor Organization to Investigate Suppression of Labor Protests," Center for Human Rights in Iran, June 7, 2019, https://iranhuman

those least in control of their economic fates—addicts, beggars, immigrant workers, women-out-of-place.[71] Workers are pressured to relinquish labor rights while privatization commodifies and delivers public assets (including the legacy labor and past tax revenue they embody) to crony capitalists. The Iranian state gives such activities a veil of legitimacy, suppressing resistance to them harshly, if arbitrarily. Repression is also visited on indigenous filmmakers who cross variable lines that define what may be alluded to and what allusions are permitted.

Macrocosms in microcosm: *The Cow* and *Four Wives – One Man*

The Cow (Dariush Mehrjui, 1969) falls outside our temporal and thematic criteria, but it is a landmark in critical Iranian "New Wave" film[72] because, as Sara Saljoughi notes, its politics "can be understood as an allegory of competing domestic visions of nationhood"[73] during the Pahlavi-era "white revolution," which was focused on urban construction and rural land reform.

Karl Polanyi claims that the European transition to modern capitalism was propelled by a land-tenure revolution: dispossessed agriculturalists populated the first industrial workforces and commercial agricultural surpluses underwrote industry and liberal democracy.[74] But in Iran, it all went wrong. The Pahlavi government relied on oil rather than agriculture for revenue. Top-down and corrupted land reform did not turn peasants into profitable farmers; it made some wealthy but emptied villages. Those without experience in a monetized economy migrated to ballooning urban slums, forming a low-skilled, precarious labor force sporadically employed on state-financed construction projects. While Iranian land reform produced neither modern economic individuals nor

---

rights.org/2019/06/haft-tappeh-workers-urge-international-labor-organization-to-investigate-suppression-of-labor-protests/. This is a case of corrupted privatization.

71. See Human Rights Watch, "Iran: Targeting of Dual Citizens, Foreigners, Prolonged Detention, Absence of Due Process," press release, September 26, 2018, https://www.hrw.org/news/2018/09/26/iran-targeting-dual-citizens-foreigners; Sima Shakhsari, *Politics of Rightful Killing: Civil Society, Gender, and Sexuality in Weblogistan* (Durham, NC: Duke University Press, 2020); and Homa Nategh, "Women: The Damned of the Iranian Revolution," in *Caught Up in Conflict*, eds. Rosemary Ridd and Helen Callaway, 45–60 (London: Macmillan, 1986).

72. Richard Gabri, "Recognizing the Unrecognizable in Dariush Mehrjui's 'Gav,'" *Cinema Journal* 54, no. 2 (Winter 2015): 49–71; see also Dariush Mehrjui, *The Cow* (*Gaav*) (1969; Toronto: Knightscove-Ellis International, 2004), DVD, 105 min; *The Cow* (*Gaav*), "1979: Revolution of the Images," Iranian Film Festival, 2019, https://www.1979ir.de/en/filme/the-cow-gaav/.

73. Sara Saljoughi, "The Boundaries of Community: Sara Saljoughi on Dariush Mehrjui's *The Cow*," *Crosscuts*, Walker Art Gallery, July 17, 2017, https://walkerart.org/magazine/sara-saljoughi-dariush-mehrjui-the-cow. See also Ghorbankarimi. The film is adapted from a short story by Gholam-Hossein Sa'edi.

74. See Karl Polanyi, The Great Transformation: The Political and Economic Origins of Our Time (Boston: Beacon 2001).

modern citizens, in a prefiguration of neoliberal moralism, its victims were often blamed for their own relapse into poverty.

Figure 4.3. Ezzatollah Entezami as Masht Hasan in *The Cow*.

Source: BBC Persian.com, November, 11, 2005, http://www.bbc.co.uk/persian/arts/story/2005/11/051123_pm-pa-saedi.shtml. Posted to Wikimedia Commons, January 13, 2013, https://commons.wikimedia.org/wiki/File:Gaav_movie.jpg#mw-jump-to-license.

In *The Cow*, the fears of rural villagers facing arbitrary and baffling modernization are personified in the form of the Bolouris, enigmatic figures who appear on the horizon and seem to threaten the village's tenuous hold on its goods and property. Masht Hasan, a prominent villager, is the custodian of a beloved cow that provides his livelihood and the evening milk ration for his fellow villagers. He also owns a wheelbarrow and periodically goes to a nearby city; he's a bit of an entrepreneur, unlike his peers. But in his absence on such a trip, the cow dies. The impact of that death (symbolic of a crisis of village production posed by land reform) begins a collapse of truth. Fearing the effect on its owner, Hasan's neighbors bury the cow and concoct a story that the Boulouris stole it. Hassan gradually descends into madness (see fig. 4.3). Too late, his neighbors try to set him straight on the real story. He dies as they finally act to take him for medical treatment to the city he has so often visited.

The fictional village in *The Cow* is hyperreal in Baudrillard's sense;[75] as fiction, it displays reality better than the reality. With the death of the cow, a symbol of what self-sufficiency the village has, everyone looks for culprits, finding them in imagined demons. "Bolouriha" show up whenever they have something to protect, and Bolouriha cause everything to go wrong. They are nowhere and everywhere, and they foreshadow fears stoked by a neoliberal demonology.

Four Wives – One Man (Nahid Persson Sarvestani, 2007), a very different film from *The Cow*, also probes village dynamics in a time of change.[76] Both examine microcosms (a village, a family) that encapsulate or hyper-realize a national macrocosm. They share a certain fatalism: in *The Cow*, the inevitable defeat of Hasan, his fellow villagers and sanity; here, a transgenerational resistive resignation of women parsing the different futures of their children under the domination of their shared husband. *Four Wives – One Man* documents a real family but is also about delusion: the delusions of a husband about his identity and role, the delusions of vulnerable women taken in by his dynastic ambitions, disguised as the blandishments of love.

The film opens with a wealthy and economically predatory village farmer scheming to take a fifth (technically illegal) wife,[77] and is structured around interviews with him, his other four wives and his mother. The first wife is an informal custodian of the husband's history. The second is obedient but discontented. The third is precariously idealistic, antagonistic to the second wife, threatened by the presence of the fourth and the prospect of a fifth, helplessly hopeful of her place and his love. The mother has a series of cameos as a hilariously blunt but hardened truth-teller; her age and status allow her a particular frankness.

The husband is almost a caricature of the savvy peasant farmer who would have done well out of the Pahlavi land reforms four decades earlier. He wheedles strategic land deals out of fatalistic and perhaps naive smallholders and knows how to make vulnerable women think he loves them (despite their recurring doubts) and that they made a free choice in marrying him. Throughout the film, he asserts himself as boss by entreaty and by threat, dividing the women against one another as he plots new acquisitions. At the same time, he carries a burden and propagandizes it incessantly. His wives complain all the time. He doesn't have enough money for their endless wants. He must persuade (or threaten) them constantly to accept domestic austerity. He also claims, paradoxically but

---

75. Jean Baudrillard, "Simulacra and Simulations," in *Jean Baudrillard: Selected Writings*, ed. Mark Poster (Stanford, CA: Stanford University Press, 1988), 166–84, https://web.stanford.edu/class/history 34q/readings/Baudrillard/Baudrillard_Simulacra.html. See the section "Hyperreal and Imaginary."

76. Nahid Persson Sarvestani, *Four Wives – One Man* (New York: Women Make Movies, 2007), DVD, 76 min., https://www.wmm.com/catalog/film/four-wives-one-man/.

77. Najwa Adra, "Four Wives – One Man Directed by Nahid Persson," *Visual Anthropology Review*, AnthroSource, May 5, 2009, https://anthrosource.onlinelibrary.wiley.com/doi/full/10.1111/j.1548-7458.2009.01034.x.

compulsively, that they all love him and that this is the main reason they do not leave him. In this domestic analog of a national society, the women are less citizens than complainants who burden the man's governance with costs on his purse and energies. Their roles in his production of agricultural and village political capital go unmentioned. His governance represents care as an extra, and the women themselves as responsible for their own dependency. They made choices and now, he sighs, they don't want to stick to them.

A north Tehran urbanite might sigh, "Oh, villages. So backward, so remote, not representative," particularizing the subject-matter to counter its critical, allegorical thrust. But this small patriarchate reproduces mechanisms common to forms of neoliberal governance and populism that, on a larger scale, disadvantage and take advantage of the labor and reproductive power of women, cloaking that exploitation in valorization of the private family as a vehicle of class pride and intergenerational accumulation.

Microcosms and macrocosms: family, brothel, nation

Utopia (Sohrab Shahid-Saless, 1983), directed by a member of the Iranian diaspora, is set in Germany without explicit reference to Iran.[78] But its tale of gender subordination and resistance forbidden in Iran uncovers a kind of violence that Iranian officialdom often countenances but doesn't admit. It takes place in a brothel with class pretensions, run by a man who emanates a controlled violence that overspills into Hitlerian shouting and coldly ruthless beatings. Like Hitler, he is marked by father problems, by an inability to connect with women as equals, and by violent misogyny. He employs women of different backgrounds who are trying to make money for various reasons (autonomy, a child, glamour). All are apparently dependent on him, though one denies it. He throws that dependence in their faces and divides them against one another. As in *Four Wives – One Man*, one woman has been entangled with him the longest and knows his history. Another fantasizes that she can work for a while for the money and choose her moment to leave. A third is new and afraid. A fourth is desperate to do anything for her semi-estranged children and tries to deflect abuse by adapting uncomplainingly to the situation. Except for the first, they are not aware that the money they earn won't be returned to them.

The brothel boss is roused from a menacing quiet by any questioning of his authority, whether implicit or explicit. He directs degrading slurs their way, beats them viciously at key moments in the film, and makes it clear that they disgust him, despite (actually, because of) the fact that he needs them for his income and his occasional sexual satisfaction. They are his means of economic and status production, but he must hide this fact, appearing to them as utterly self-sufficient, throwing their dependence in their faces. The key to his engineering of their dependence is that he makes it out to be their choice.

---

78. Sohrab Shahid-Saless, *Utopia* (Hamburg: Multimedia Gesellschaft für audiovisuelle Information, May 1983), film, 198 min., https://www.filmportal.de/video/utopia-1983 [trailer].

They didn't have to become whores for him, but now that they are, where else are they going to go? Who else will take them? One woman leaves for a time but returns to his punishment.

In short, the brothel is a miniature dystopia masquerading as a utopia of neoliberal morality. Everyone is there, it seems, as a consequence of "choices," but the pimp represents his own choices as exemplary of rational autonomy. Nothing that happens to the women, by contrast, is anything but their own fault. They demand too much; he demands that they own the shame of their dependency. Like the village farmer in *Four Wives – One Man*, he does things for them and is burdened and angered by their "demands." He motivates them to comply in their own exploitation by a combination of shame and fear and by turning them against each other. They in turn talk about him among themselves, fail to make an alliance and fail (except temporarily) to take opportunities to break free of him. They suffer a kind of voluble paralysis, as if life outside the brothel (like life outside capitalism) is impossible for them to conceive. This is reinforced by visits from police and other inspecting officials who avail themselves of the women's services as perks of their official status. Thatcher's "There is no alternative" haunts this film; it "posits prostitution as the truth of the then-nascent service economy ... the women are trapped inside a claustrophobic tomb of eternally recurring humiliations—a thinly veiled microcosm of German society, just after chancellor Kohl had announced his neoliberal agenda of 'spiritual-moral renewal.'"[79]

But the pimp, like a neoliberal politician, has a secret. He is *not* autonomous; he is controlled by and owes money to a syndicate that inflicts its own violence on him to make him pay up. Badly injured, he tries to murder his way out of his predicament. In the process, his secret weakness becomes visible to the women in a way that his denigration and violence can no longer erase. That, and their desperation as he comes unglued, finally unites them. The woman who knows his history leads a plot to murder him. As the film ends, they return to work under her direction. Having taken collective responsibility for murdering and disposing of their master, they make the brothel (temporarily) a new kind of utopia; they have seized autonomy over the process of selling themselves. The viewer is left with a foreboding sense that new "creditors" will soon be pushing the door buzzer.

As in *Four Wives – One Man*, the women in this film are the means of economic and status production for a beneficiary who represents them, in the face of their pleas or complaints, as his burdens and costs, deluded about their agency, place, capacities and prospects. As they produce his revenue, they experience his threats and his fading interest in each of them; they sense his exploitation of them. But they and their "places" in *Utopia* are under threat, not only from the man but also from their own potential betrayal of each

---

79. Close-Up Film Centre, "*Utopia*," film programmes, November 18, 2017, https://www.closeupfilmcentre.com/film_programmes/2017/sohrab-shahid-saless/utopia/.

other in his interests. They are both dependent and complicit within a disciplinary regime engineered from fear and contempt.

Both *Utopia* and *Four Wives – One Man* use domestic or quasi-domestic situations to draw a parallel between the situation of vulnerable women in domestic and in national life, treated less as citizens than as (disavowed) exploitable labor and as costs. Those who govern them claim to provide for their care but treat them as burdensome and unproductive. In the patriarchal cultures that so often inflect neoliberal politics, women occupy a naturalized place of domestic subordination and exploitation, while women out-of-place are made individually responsible, *by their own choice*, for any disadvantages they suffer. In both films, this disciplinary governance both forms and deforms subjects in the interests of complicity and resignation. In *Utopia* its reliance on the administration and inculcation of fear and shame is laid bare. The humanity of women is sacrificed to a dark moral vision; they stand symbolically for a weakness and dependence that belie the neoliberal utopia of autonomous individualism, a weakness that paragons of neoliberal morality must deny in themselves, externalize and demonize. Those who pretend to mastery of their own fate (and that of their competitors) must tell themselves they depend on no one, neither those who do their bidding nor those whom they owe. They see the weak or vulnerable as pitiable, but the pity cloaks hate.

In these films, the women sense their exploitation but are trapped by concern for their individual situations or those of their children. They are encouraged to see other women as competitors, and to read male threats of abandonment or violence as consequent on their own action or inaction, or as the fault of some other woman or women. They are encouraged to reproduce the semantic politics imposed on them. A political marriage of neoliberalism and patriarchy, as portrayed in *Four Wives – One Man* marks Iranian society even if polygyny is an outlier in it, but it is not unique to Iran. The setting of *Utopia* in Germany militates against exceptionalism.

Miss Violence (Alexandros Avranas, 2013), set in Athens, opens with an apparently model family celebrating a birthday.[80] Here again is a patriarch who represents himself as the soul of caring, surrounded by his wife, their daughter, Eleni, and granddaughters. But the image is shattered when the young adolescent Angeliki disrupts the party tableau by leaping out a window to her death. The grandfather is eventually revealed as an amateur pimp, an abuser of his daughter and granddaughters and an enforcer of the family secret. But, like the brothel boss of *Utopia*, his autonomy is impaired. He draws benefits and attention from government because he is officially unemployed, and he fends off perfunctory attempts by officials to probe small cracks in his self-presentation. The family façade imaged here is, as in a neoliberal utopia, above reproach, an honorable institution. But this family, headed by a state-dependent, is precarious, and problematized

---

80. Alexandros Avranas, *Miss Violence* (New York: EFF/Vimeo, September 2013), film, 99 min., https://player.vimeo.com/video/91461803 [trailer].

in the eyes of an authority that has a reach beyond the grandfather. The effects of everyday austerity are evident in the meagre dole he brings in, the paltry jobs he is offered, and the threat that these, and his age, pose to his domestic power. The context inscribes the image of a government going through the motions of care while complicit in selling its own dependents—the national workforce—to international capital.

Behind the family façade, the politics of use and abuse, reproach and shame, threat and denigration that we have seen in *Four Wives – One Man* and *Utopia* are reproduced under the auspices of kinship and "love," which work to depoliticize domestic power. The day following the suicide, one of the (grand)daughters (there is intentional ambiguity over who is a daughter or a granddaughter) challenges the circumstances of the party. The grandfather deflects her insolence with a series of reproaches. Did she not want the family to gather? Where was she? Later, in a simulacrum of the employment office functionary, he doles out a tranquilizer to Eleni, who signals both complicity and discontent, asking him why he let "them" talk like that to her. But the secret is set to unravel. Angeliki's suicide (represented to authorities as an accident) opens the doors of perception on the family, destroying the image of the stricken paterfamilias. He himself produced the crisis. He made the family decisions: when to "have fun," when to punish, when to medicate and when to shut them up, exactly as might the government of a crisis-stricken country, complicit in its difficulties but continuing to legislate "on behalf of" its citizens and to intervene in their lives, using the revenue and infrastructure they produce.

Miss Violence and other films produced in the same period and with similar styles (*Dogtooth, Attenberg, Alps*[81]) have sometimes been represented as contrived, their revelations too brutal, too sudden.[82] But this weirdness is arguably a response in kind to the brutality of the social crisis visited on a Greece sandwiched temporally between the regime of the Colonels and that of Eurozone bankers and their enforcers.

Dogtooth (Yorgos Lanthimos, 2009) is a darker comedy than *Miss Violence* but again presents a sinister controlling father figure.[83] He is a wealthy manufacturer who, with the complicity of his wife, has constructed a fenced-in private universe corralling his adult children, refusing them knowledge of the wider world and fabricating an alternative reality for them instead. The children get stickers for good behavior and violence for bad. They are taught a distorted language, disabling them from outside social participation: "highway" is a strong wind; "shotgun" is a bird. They develop a shared fantasy life, believing they have a brother "outside" to whom they throw things over the fence. When they ask about going beyond the compound, they are told they can when their dogtooth

---

81. Yorgos Lanthimos, *Alps* (New York: Kino Video, December 2012), DVD, 123 min.
82. Peter Bradshaw, "*Miss Violence* Review: Macabre Tale of Evil and Greek Anguish," *The Guardian*, June 19, 2014, https://www.theguardian.com/film/2014/jun/19/miss-violence-review-evil-and-greek-anguish.
83. Yorgos Lanthimos, *Dogtooth* (New York: Kino Entertainment, May 2009), DVD, 97 min.

comes out, and then only by car; the only car, of course, is the father's Mercedes. The father knows something about the world in which he makes his money; a moral pessimist, he fears its corrupting influence on his children. He wants to keep his capital and his moral fears tightly corralled within the family.

Sensing his power slipping as the children become older and more inquisitive, the father orchestrates a bloody fake drama in which the imaginary outside brother is supposedly murdered by a cat; he enjoins the children to fear cats and to get down on all fours and bark like dogs to banish the threat they pose. He also provides a concessionary outlet, setting up a paid sexual encounter for his son with an attractive outsider, a security guard at his factory. This event inadvertently generates the involvement of first one and then both daughters. The outsider is banished, a daughter is beaten and then the sexual services of both daughters are offered by the father to the son. Eventually, the younger daughter knocks a tooth out of her mouth, hides in the back of the father's car and escapes to the outside, using the Freudian fruits of her repression (fantasy, creativity) to escape. Perhaps she has learned in the end that there was never any dogtooth and she is not a docile domestic animal. In escaping the compound, she has a chance to escape what it made of her, to accept and live once-unrecognizable possibilities. Will she do so by forging new social connections or as an individual, using social amenities without an ability to develop new and different social loyalties?

The motif of the paranoid compound in *Dogtooth* reflects actual analogs such as the case of the Austrian Josef Fritzl, noted by *The Guardian*'s reviewer. He takes the analogy further, but then pulls the punch of his argument:

> I don't think, however, that Lanthimos is ... saying anything as simplistic as that Fritzl is some sort of Everyman. What the movie does suggest is that for good or ill, and rarely properly examined, there is lurking in all societies a desire at every level to control what young people believe and understand. And this extends from apparently innocent practices like expecting presents from Santa Claus and teaching them childish euphemisms for physical functions, to the inculcation of religious beliefs, social practices and taboos intended to last a lifetime.[84]

The generalization "in all societies" unfortunately diverts questions about a "desire at every level to control" into pan-human speculation and away from politics. What if we were to situate *Dogtooth* in light of Greek history specifically? Both the 1967 Colonels' coup and the post-2008 financial crisis added escapees to the international Greek diaspora. The junta sought to fence in Greece, at least in matters of politics, culture and morality. The crisis of 2009 sparked a legitimation collapse of old-line politics, haunted

---

84. Philip French, "Dogtooth" [review], *The Guardian*, April 25, 2010, https://www.theguardian.com/film/2010/apr/25/dogtooth-film-review.

Pedagogies and Possibilities of Crisis 105

by ghosts of the Colonels in the rise of Golden Dawn.[85] In response, Greek filmmakers began to reconsider formerly taken-for-granted elements of national identity and authority as alien, fossilized effects of a weird and crumbling pedagogy. They resituated national impotence in microcosms of personal estrangement and disintegrating familial and professional hierarchies.

Figure 4.4. Two Evzones (Greek Presidential Guards) crossing in front of the tomb of the Unknown Soldier, Athens, Greece.

Source: Wikimedia Commons,
https://commons.wikimedia.org/wiki/File:Crossing_Evzones_Tomb_Unknown_Soldier_Athens-2.jpg#mw-jump-to-license. Photo courtesy of Jebulon.

---

85. Varoufakis, *And the Weak Suffer*, 204–11.

Athina Rachel Tsangari's *Attenberg* (2011) is a case in point.[86] Marina, the protagonist, lives with her father in voluntary but resigned social isolation. She watches nature documentaries as if she might find in them some clue to the responses of humans outside her bubble, and perhaps also to her own nascent sociality. Her friend Bella tries to teach her about "normal" sexual and social relations, which she finds strange and repugnant. One telling shot ties this personal alienation to a national context. Marina and Bella practice a strange walk, striding down a path side by side, hiking up their already short skirts and taking giant, exaggerated steps in unison as if they were birds in a slow-motion mating dance. That scene is baffling unless one knows the visual and seismic impact of the short-skirted, hobnail-booted Presidential Guard slow-stepping along the top of Syntagma Square in Athens (see fig. 4.4), guarding the parliamentary theatre of a national politics flailing in the Eurozone net. Marina's father, a dying architect, refers to both his career and Greek history with chagrin and distance. Greece, he says, has progressed from shepherds to bulldozers to mines, and finally to "petty bourgeois hysteria"—a hyper-dramatic stasis. He describes his own career as one of ineffectual bourgeois arrogance, "designing ruins with mathematical precision," constructing an "industrial colony on top of sheep pens—and we thought we were making a revolution, a small revolution." Whether or not Tsangari himself intended the allusion, this self-summative moment recalls to knowing viewers the constricting atmosphere and historical burden conveyed in Angelopoulos's historical epics.[87]

Constriction and confinement are not exclusive to Greek historical tragedy. The revolutionary regime in Iran sought to inscribe a politically limited language on its people, especially women, to insulate them from Western "corruption." As that moral/linguistic pedagogy began to fray, the Iranian state lurched clumsily between controlled "reform" and violent repression, eventually trying to cut off the entire population from the outside world by shutting down the internet during a political crisis in 2019. The motif of the paranoid compound speaks both to the neoliberal ideal of keeping things within the accumulative family and to the suspicious policing of household and national cultures and their borders, to complex frictions between movements of capital and those of people.

The entrepreneurial city: political portal, palimpsest, theatre of walls

Families and households are not the only symbolic intermediaries between persons and nations. Cities have long stood for civilizational ideals and served as mirrors of the human scale. Athens, it is said, gave us democracy, philosophy and the citizen. Jerusalem

---

86. Athina Rachel Tsangari, *Attenberg* (London: Curzon Artificial Eye, 2010), DVD, 97 min., https://www.curzonartificialeye.com/attenberg/.

87. See Koutsourakis and Steven, chap. 11, 14, 15 and 17.

was the site of revelation, the city of God. European philosophy from Augustine to Leo Strauss stood in tension between these bipolar cities on hills.[88] Islamic civilization also knew these urban icons: Jerusalem stands third in its sacred geography, and our knowledge of the literary and philosophical legacies of Athens owes much to their preservation by Islamic scholars.

Is there a coherent discourse of the city that accompanies neoliberal urbanism? Neoliberal and neoconservative scholars (e.g., Strauss) have written on the city, but the urban/rural distinction is not strongly linked to neoliberal ideal types. Historically the commonwealth political tradition and yeoman ideals did have an impact on the English Revolution, Lockean liberalism and Jacksonian democracy, but liberalism has largely forsaken its rural roots without fully embracing an urban ideal. If any city were inspirational for neoliberalism, it would be Carl Sandburg's Chicago:

Stormy, husky, brawling,

City of the Big Shoulders: ...

Come and show me another city with lifted head singing so proud to be alive and coarse and strong and cunning.

Flinging magnetic curses amid the toil of piling job on job, here is a tall bold slugger set vivid against the little soft cities ...

Bareheaded,

Shoveling,

Wrecking,

Planning,

Building, breaking, rebuilding,

Under the smoke, dust all over his mouth, laughing with white teeth,

Under the terrible burden of destiny laughing as a young man laughs,

Laughing even as an ignorant fighter laughs who has never lost a battle,

Bragging and laughing that under his wrist is the pulse, and under his ribs the heart of the people,

Laughing!

Laughing the stormy, husky, brawling laughter of Youth, half-naked, sweating, proud to be Hog Butcher, Tool Maker, Stacker of Wheat, Player with Railroads and Freight Handler to the Nation.[89]

---

88. See Kotsko, 59; also Pierre Manent, "Between Athens and Jerusalem," *First Things*, February 2012, https://www.firstthings.com/article/2012/02/between-athens-and-jerusalem.

89. Carl Sandburg, "Chicago," *Poetry* 3, no. 6 (March 1914): 191–92.

Chicago has been the agora of commodity trading, the Parthenon of supply, the temple of transportation and the metropolis of mail-order. Property, markets and movement animated it more than reason or revelation. Sandburg's ode resonates with Nietzsche's glad willing of plastic fate or, more ambiguously, with Walter Benjamin's destructive character.[90] But Chicago is less a model of neoliberalism than an environment in which its thinkers flourished for a time.

As Chicago dominated the Midwest, so Athens and Tehran today dominate the national personalities of Greece and Iran and the scenography of their national cinema. Angelopoulos's films are marked by figures who explore the neglected borders and hinterlands of Greece, but many of them must leave or return to Athens to do so. Athens is a world-scale symbolic center, drawing tourists to the Parthenon and delivering them inexorably downhill on its oldest streets, which are laid out in a processional and devotional itinerary, to the remains of the temple of Olympian Zeus, and now to boutique shops and Athens' homeless. The Agora and its *stoai*, venues of democratic debate, free inquiry and peer commerce, inspire a sacred history of democracy and a more local counter-history of underclasses. Their clash and interplay lend to cinematic treatments of the city's destroyed and rebuilt modern periphery, its alienated suburbs, its industrial areas and the port of Piraeus; its spatialization and juxtaposition of wealth, middle-class precarity and destitution; its refugees and organized or petty criminals. Michael Demetrius's short film *Cloud* takes up troubled and indefinite urban intimacies to hold a mirror to this troubled, complicated, neoliberal and resistive Athens, city of austerity and deferred revolution.[91]

Even more than Athens is to Greece,[92] Tehran is Iran's central city and its vortex, drawing in a constant stream of migrants from the provinces along with Afghan and other refugees.[93] It has no significant urban rivals. Its aggregate population of over 15 million more than quadruples that of greater Athens. Mashhad, a literary, artistic and religious center, is less than a fifth of Tehran's size; Isfahan is smaller still, despite a glorious past; Karaj is now a Tehran satellite. But Tehran was long overshadowed by the neighboring city of Rhages; in the 9th century CE it was still a village. Though chosen as capital of the Qajar kings in 1786, it numbered only 80,000 people as late as the 1830s. Modern Tehran dates tentatively from redevelopment plans of 1855 and 1878, but definitively from Reza Shah's demolition and rebuilding of the city in the 1920s and '30s. His son

---

90. Walter Benjamin, "The Destructive Character," in *Reflections: Essays, Aphorisms, Autobiographical Writings*, trans. E. F. N. Jephcott and P. Demetz (New York: Harcourt, Brace Jovanovich, 1978), 301–03.

91. Michael Demetrius, *Cloud* (Athens: Michael Demetrius, 2019), film, 20 min., https://vimeo.com/339640786 [trailer].

92. Athens at least has a storied if significantly smaller urban rival in Thessaloniki.

93. For summary descriptions of Athens and Tehran and their histories, see Wikipedia, s.v. "Athens," "agora," "Parthenon" and "Tehran."

continued a tradition of monumental modernist megaprojects until overthrown in 1979, and the city is populated by monuments of several recent eras.

Today Tehran has a somewhat different place in the Iranian consciousness than does Athens for Greeks. It is the magnetic center of Iranian commerce, education, industry and culture and the seat of many government functions, despite plans to relocate the capital to a seismically safer and less polluted region. Though Pahlavi redevelopment sought to make it a high-modernist metropolis, it remains divided between a self-consciously cosmopolitan north and a poorer south, its planning process overwhelmed by chaotic growth. It is a city of dreams and ruin, hustle and graft, division and assemblage, repression and resistance. Tehran and its symbols dominate national commentary and much of domestic Iranian film, but the city itself does not embody a set of ancient ideals. Its northern half dreams of being a "world city" in neoliberal terms, attracting capital through culture by leveraging its boutiques and venues, its intellectual workforce and its artistic entrepreneurs while denying its dependency on the exploited labor of its southern counterpart.

Nonetheless, both Athens and Tehran harbor a variegated politics of outsized national impact. Both Greek and Iranian national politics tend to be urban-centric and suspicious of regions, especially so in Iran. The economic and demographic power of Tehran and Athens means that city politics—even at the level of city planning, city government, or neighborhoods—can have a disproportionate effect on the national society and culture. Social and spatial processes of segmentation and inequality within major cities mark national politics, as does urban resistance to national governance.[94]

Tehran Has No More Pomegranates (Massoud Bakhshi, 2006) gives viewers Tehran as Potemkin city, satirically examining its staging as a new urban utopia.[95] The film's fictive pretense is that it is a failed historical documentary. It opens with a mock cover letter to the Ministry of Culture and Islamic Guidance, returning the incomplete footage. It gradually becomes clear that the failure lies elsewhere. The mockumentary cuts back and forth between historical clips showing the pomp and glory of Qajar and Pahlavi-era officialdom and present-day "interviews" with residents repeating that Tehran is a wonderful place. One man only, in successive cameos, reiterates the same thing: It is bad here, I am leaving, I *have* to leave (but he doesn't leave). Other scenes highlight the north/south divisions of the city through the voices of Afghan workers from south Tehran who build apartments (more and more of them) and of "Sweetie" Babak, a wealthy northsider who flips apartments on speculation.

Tehran Has No More Pomegranates both benefits from and satirizes Iranian reformism, which has periodically promised to open the nation to the rest of the world and to

---

94. See Neil Brenner and Nik Theodore, eds., *Spaces of Neoliberalism: Urban Restructuring in North America and Western Europe* (Oxford: Blackwell, 2012) and Leitner et al., *Contesting Neoliberalism.*
95. Massoud [*sic*] Bakhshi, *Tehran Has No More Pomegranates* (Prague: DA Films, 2006), DVD, 58 min.

"modernize" Iranian society through democratic reform, economic development and the elimination of corruption. It has repeatedly failed those promises, generating its own culture of corruption. It produced a façade of democracy that allowed women modest freedoms but also delivered them to the economy as cheap labor. Critical but light-hearted, the film's satire accords with the brief flowering of a reformist "openness" strategy, and its popularity opened doors for similar documentary efforts. But its depiction turns Tehran inside out, showing how the city on display was made and staged, and by whom: on one hand, exploited construction workers fearing for their jobs, and on the other, speculators and officials buying, selling and granting permissions, not in response to social need but in terms of who one knows and how to skim side money from the process.

Figure 4.5. Still from Karimi's *Writing on the City*.

Source: Wikimedia Commons,
https://commons.wikimedia.org/wiki/File:Writing_on_the_city_picture_scene_5.jpg
#mw-jump-to-license.

Keywan Karimi's *Writing on the City* exchanges satire for a more critical and documentary approach.[96] Karimi was arrested in 2013 and sentenced in 2015 to six years' imprisonment and 223 lashes for "propagating against the Islamic Republic" and "insulting religious sanctities." *Writing on the City* is a political history of Tehran graffiti as a record of conflict between official and unofficial realities, using the city's walls as a canvas: along streets and in subways and even sewers. Walls shut people out (or in),

---

96. Keywan Karimi, *Writing on the City* (Iran, 2015), film, 60 min., https://www.youtube.com/watch?v=3laaKrp5ebE [trailer].

enclose property and make prisons of urban spaces, but they are reclaimed as surfaces of expression in a proxy war between city workers (who remove tags on behalf of officialdom) and graffiti artists channeling popular *zeitgeists*. Official reality appears on walls too, in giant fading revolutionary murals glorifying martyrs and wars against the enemy (Iraq, imperialism), in later messages praising commerce and, later still, in "think-washing" images intended to divert tensions generated by social disruption and inequality into bland appreciation of "nature" or village nostalgia. The most recent official images eerily echo Western analogs, vaguely signifying aspiration, success, access ("access to what?" one might ask; one striking image depicts a stairway leading into nowhere, neither earth nor sky).

Countering these official images is a plethora of furtively spray-painted graffiti criticizing the manipulation of martyr culture, drawing attention to ties between environmental pollution and corruption, noting who does and does not "succeed." In the regime's version of neoliberal fantasy, everyone has social and economic "access." In reality, middle-class men corner the fringes of the market while cronies sit at its center. But under cover of darkness, walls are always available, their messages free for the seeing. After the flooding that devastated Iran in 2019, an official mural portrayed the country as one big family working together to save the stranded, sandbag buildings and repair damage. Aesthetically and ideologically, it echoed the "big society" motifs of British politics in the late 1990s and early 2000s, which justified public service cutbacks by promoting a naturalized but abstract *atopia* of private initiatives and family or community self-help. Ironically, the Iranian mural showed women doing the actual helping while men directed the work; the fantasy it projected was belied by reality. During the floods, many inundated families and communities were left to drown. Like *Tehran Has No More Pomegranates*, this film turns the city inside out, offering a perspective "through the mirror," as Raoul Vaneigem, a Belgian Situationist philosopher, wrote after seeing the film:

> ... The wall is a mirror
> A mirror of the house, of the city, of the world
> Reflections of every shape and form stream by it as clouds do in the sky
> We have learned to go through the mirror so what was closed will open up. ...
> Under the clothing of creeds and of ideas, what is lived is always bare
> Then nothing more conceals a human being from himself
> Someday the walls will have the transparency of our desires.[97]

If cities do not figure in models of neoliberalism, the urban implementation of neoliberal imaginaries has marked cityscapes and the striving of their inhabitants through two governmental technologies. One is austerity; the other, by contrast, is *selective*

---

97. Raoul Vaneigem, "The Wall Is a Mirror," Punto de Vista, December 2, 2015, https://www.puntodevistafestival.com/en/noticias.asp?IdNoticia=399.

permission. Privatization and deregulation agendas, justified post hoc in principled terms, lend themselves easily to one-sided implementation. Unions, public services and public education are aggressively and punitively regulated by accountability regimes under the whip of "performance-based" funding, while regulation of private business, especially of larger corporations, is eased, as are urban zoning regulations. Measures taken in the name of neoliberal "freedoms" allow blue-sky ideas floated in urban boardrooms to emerge as vanity megaprojects, transforming city spaces through massive destruction and reconstruction under the rubric of development. On the other side of society, those pressed too far by punitive accountability regimes or displacement periodically challenge the investment in urban spaces by private capital with bodily counter-occupations, popular actions and street art.

However, the whipsaw of austerity and selective permission also feeds an everyday reworking of hegemonic entrepreneurialism into creative work-arounds, eventually producing a semi-illicit but still recognizably neoliberal terrain of everyday corruption, façade construction and shadow play. This is the terrain of an intimate "austerity city" built on a micropolitics of small personal opportunities, loyalties and betrayals; of interpersonal responsibilization, power and blame; of interpersonal violence, symbolic or physical; of personal subordination and protection; of individual or familial complicity, connivance and avoidance. This micropolitics plays out cinematically in a kaleidoscopic mêlée of depicted spaces and locations that are minor, heterotopic[98] and "empty to the extent that they are void of visual markers associated with the events that they document."[99] These include generic and claustrophobic apartments, workplaces and business premises (legal and illegal); nondescript bars and clubs; gangster digs, jail cells, hospital corridors and basements; grubby streets, alleys and corners; subway and train stations; abandoned or half-built buildings; empty lots, graveyards and industrial sites; fenced-off storage compounds and transshipment facilities; car interiors and the seats of mopeds. Demetrius's *The Cloud*, though filmed as a short drama, shows a documentarian sensibility in its penetrating, almost ethnographic insight into an off-label intimate urbanism in which relative deprivation and diverging class and gender worlds feed after-hours sexual competition and hunger for a chance at something acquisitive or connective. Mehrjui's *The Cycle* (discussed below) opens on a street-level Tehran demimonde of interpersonal loyalties and everyday betrayals; their consequences and punishments are in the open yet hidden, as much by sheer mundanity as by subterfuge.

---

98. Michel Foucault, "Of Other Spaces: Utopias and Heterotopias," translated by J. Miskowiec, *Architecture/movement/continuité* 5 (1984): 46–49, https://web.mit.edu/allanmc/www/foucault1.pdf.

99. Kimberly Mair, *Guerilla Aesthetics: Art, Memory, and the West German Urban Guerilla* (Montreal: McGill-Queen's University Press, 2016), 271.

Retribution, repetition, revolution: on vengeance and the human

Varoufakis defines capitalist modernization as a transition from societies-with-markets to market societies, in which spreading commodification accompanied the systematic incorporation of debt into the production cycle.[100] In this new dispensation, access to loan capital enabled the production of commodities and speculation on their value. Initial expenses were paid out of loans, and the loans out of eventual revenue. A surplus against future activity indicated success. Those unable to access or repay debt fell into wage slavery, to the social margins or outside the law. What was their recourse? The historical record gives us highwaymen, Luddites, Chartists; peasant revolts, unions, co-operatives; reform and revolution; theft and revenge.

The ideal type model of neoliberalism valorizes agency and choice, but, like deregulation, these are promoted selectively in practice. The agency of collectives is suspect. The agency of the deprived is circumscribed. If one is in debt, however unjustly, that is a consequence of prior choice and one has the remaining choice to pay up. Agency is legitimate if it respects property (and its factual distribution under the law) and reflects individual responsibility. Agency against the property system itself, against legal but unequal distribution or against legally permitted exploitation (e.g., the sale of labor power) is condemned as a collective disorder or individual pathology. The only revolution neoliberalism admits is the revolutionary institution of private property in place of traditional or state property regimes. What forms, then, do dreams of forbidden release or revolution take under conditions of austerity and responsibilization? How do they enter film and affect its agency? What distinguishes revolution from revenge, and is that distinction political?

In *The Genealogy of Morals* Nietzsche claims that retaliation lies at the core of the human; we are the only creatures that seek revenge. Competition, war and exploitation are mediated expressions of the impulse to avenge. Catherine Malabou notes that, for Nietzsche, "revenge is essentially another name for repetition,"[101] and it finds its source in the temporality of human existence, in awareness of (the impossibility of) immortality. The past imposes forms, but those too pass on. Whether or not we repeat the forms that shape us, we and our works are transient, and we know it. Thus our hatred of temporality:

> The human is the only being for whom time is a spiritual injury. If there is only one thing the human seeks revenge for, it is the passage of time, and thus, of course, finitude. Having to die is the utmost injury. Time is the utmost offense. In this regard, Nietzsche, through Zarathustra, says: "This, yes, this alone is revenge itself: the will's ill will toward time and its 'It was.'" ... Revenge is the will's ill will toward time, toward passing away, toward transiency. Transiency is

---

100. Varoufakis, *Talking to My Daughter*, 27–64.
101. Catherine Malabou, "Superhumanity," *Repetition, Revenge, Plasticity*, e-flux Architecture, February 21, 2018, https://www.e-flux.com/architecture/superhumanity/179166/repetition-revenge-plasticity/.

that against which the will can take no further steps, that against which it constantly collides. There is nothing we can do against time. Finitude is the unpassable obstacle. Life is short, what is done is done. This engenders resentment. We repeat what we cannot change. We repeat because we cannot change. The essence of humanity is to repeat its anger and dispossession; it is always too late. For a god, it is always early. For an animal, time is always now. But for the human, time is a repetition of instants that each say "nevermore."[102]

This inescapability incites attempts to escape into difference, transcendence or futurity. Nietzsche argued that justice originates in attempts to escape repetitive vengeance by turning revenge against itself and into legislation. The "low" in human relations is sacrificed on the altar of the "high," retribution exchanged for justice, morality and religion. Motivated by *ressentiment*, these devolve into a hatred of life itself. For Nietzsche, forgiveness is no better; it evacuates the space in which violator and violated might face each other directly and allows the rule of past over present. Acts become subsequent to type. To know to act differently is still repetition—a repetition of repetition.

In the pre-revolutionary mise-en-scène in which Brecht would say we are caught, repetition means choosing (or not choosing, for that matter) from available options. Disempowerment repeats both us and itself with minor variations. Conversely, revolution promises to break old matrices, to pour in new forms impossible at present to imagine. But past revolutions always had their own infernal accountancy, carrying forward past sums. History repeats, Marx said, first as tragedy, then as farce. Alexander the Great imagined and carried to the far shore of the sea a revolutionary vision of empire as infinite expansion. Theo Angelopoulos reimagined this revolutionary Alexander repeated as a peasant leader consumed—in an act of *theophagia*, as if a god (a failed god)—by history and spat into the next century to "enter the cities."[103] To every revolution its repetitive unconscious.

However, Malabou writes, Nietzsche saw possibility in desiring repetition anew:

> Zarathustra teaches his soul to treat time in a non-vengeful way by reforming its relationship with repetition itself: instead of thinking of repetition as the return of the same—that "most abysmal thought"—he learns to recognize the space for difference it opens. That is, he learns to *affirm what is repeated, thus transforming repetition itself.* Instead of passively bearing what happens, *one can desire it, plastically.*[104]

---

102. Malabou.
103. Theo Angelopoulos, *Alexander the Great*, Theo Angelopoulos Collection, vol. 2 (London: Curzon Artificial Eye, July 1980), DVD, 210 min.
104. Malabou [emphasis added].

Malabou represents this Nietzschean "plasticity" as encompassing an active acceptance of and alternatively a remolding of forms. It may involve destruction, but not destruction bound to vengeful *ressentiment*. To know what is being repeated but nonetheless willingly choose to repeat it anew (or not) is affirmation. Could that affirmation be an event, an act in-the-now[105] opening on new life, repetition out of repetition, plastic and generating revolutionary "space for difference"?

Today, says Malabou, repetition is demanded incessantly in both negative and positive forms: in calls to bring oppressors to account and in gestures of reconciliation. These may promise the new, but they may also chain it to a hundred pasts. Even technological immortalization may only repeat human revenge against time: "Are we, the superhumans to come, different from post-humans in being able to open ourselves to the future without developing hatred against time, without trying to crucify transiency and passage?"[106] It is likely no accident that the moment in which the neoliberal state's crisis of sovereignty manifests as terminal—impending end and moment of revolutionary anticipation—also marks the emergence of a cultural fascination with haunting.[107] What haunts is not only the burden of the past but also alternative temporalities and the boundaries of the known. Instead of a revolution taking place in future time, might a contest of futurities[108] revolutionize time itself? This would be to re-vision revolution (aesthetic or political) as contingent and involving unexpected juxtapositions—like those in which Greek and Iranian directors Yorgos Lanthimos and Rouzbeh Rashidi both went to make new work in, of all haunted places, Ireland.[109]

The challenge to embrace repetition freely, to "repeat plastically," also confronts this chapter. We describe neoliberal moral pessimism as repetitive: it repeatedly posits a radical voluntarism of choice and continually reiterates what it demonizes. Does our use of a term like *neoliberalism* also risk repetitive invocation of demons?[110] Re-descriptions of present-day social traps, on the page or in film, may express desire for difference but risk locking in repetition—another instance of "the will's ill will toward time," in this instance as utopian vengeance. Malabou says that to "develop out of oneself" and "recreate broken molds" implies openness to events that explode the routine of time. But,

---

105. *Jetztzeit*, as used by Walter Benjamin, "On the Concept of History" (1940), trans. D. Redmond, Marxists Internet Archive, 2005, https://www.marxists.org/reference/archive/benjamin/1940/history.htm.
106. Malabou.
107. See Mark Fisher, "What Is Hauntology?" *Film Quarterly* 66, no. 1 (2012): 16–24.
108. Avery F. Gordon, "Some Thoughts on Haunting and Futurity," *Borderlands* 10, no. 2 (2011): 1–21.
109. See Hilary M. V. Leathem, "Ghostly Excesses: Ethnography and Experimental Cinema," Society for Cultural Anthropology, December 30, 2019, https://culanth.org/fieldsights/everything-is-full-of-ghosts-experimental-cinema-and-ethnography.
110. One of us recalls (ruefully) a student response to a course evaluation question, "What is one important thing you learned from this course?" The response was "Because, capitalism."

she asks, "do we really wish for the other to come?" Perhaps this was Angelopoulos's central question. His films are criticized for evacuating revolutionary possibility, using slow, circular pans to emphasize cyclical temporality, a return of the same. Was he instead challenging a revolutionary tendency to avenge history, erasing the past out of a wish to make something both new and permanent? Angelopoulos began his career in the twilight of the Colonels. An urge to wipe clean their legacy would be understandable. Was he warning that erasure serves repetition?[111]

Unlike gods, humans cannot simply delete the scenes that they are given and set off on a particular course.[112] Repetition may be obedient and reproductive, playing upon subordinates the same game in which one is played. Or (as in *Utopia*) one may kill the boss and find oneself in a new but possibly still recursive game. On the other hand, how we avenge ourselves within or against a set scene may project us into situations in which we (re)find ourselves and others as new kinds of agents: hapless, relapsing or even (despite ourselves) revolutionary. Only those who come after may be able to see clearly the potential for repetition or difference we had. Christopher Pavsek's film *To Those Born After* uses a Brecht poem to imagine members of a future *habitus* looking back on us:[113]

> We who wanted to prepare the ground for friendship
> Could not ourselves be friendly.
> But you, when the time comes at last
> When man is helper to man
> Think of us
> With forbearance.[114]

In today's "cities in a time of disorder,"[115] films about vengeance tend to be popular, a consequence of audience wishes for something possible beyond repetitive resignation. Anger demands agency. Forced repeatedly to face "necessity" in an economy gamed by the powerful, we respond to narratives that seize and expose the game. Films such as

---

111. Andrew Russell characterizes so-called "slow film" as a retreat from a "fast-paced world" in "Slow Cinema: What It Is and Why It's on a Fast Track to the Mainstream in a Frenetic World," The Conversation, April 29, 2019, https://theconversation.com/slow-cinema-what-it-is-and-why-its-on-a-fast-track-to-the-mainstream-in-a-frenetic-world-114769. It's possible to interpret Angelopoulos's oeuvre selectively as "slow" (or even nostalgic) in this sense, but that would be a rather tendentious reading.

112. This is the conceit of the context-free individual will that neoliberal ideals champion. Yet does not even this imagined will persist in expressing a hunger for something beyond repetition and ressentiment? Neoliberalism, after all, clothes itself in the aspirational language of freedom.

113. Christopher Pavsek, *To Those Born After* (Vancouver, BC: Christopher Pavsek, November 2005), film, 28 mins., http://www.sfu.ca/~cpavsek/.

114. Bertolt Brecht, "To Those Born Later," in *Bertolt Brecht: Poems, 1913–1956*, eds. J. Willett and R. Manheim (London: Methuen, 1987), 318–20.

115. Brecht.

Tangsir (Amir Naderi, 1973) and the oeuvre of Masoud Kimiayi speak to this wish, as does *The Killing of a Sacred Deer* (Yorgos Lanthimos, 2017) and *Killing Mad Dogs* (Bahram Beyzai, 2001). Both the latter allusively refuse to separate revenge, justice-seeking and something like revolutionary anger in the face of class (*The Killing of a Sacred Deer*) or the intersection of economic power and gender (*Killing Mad Dogs*). Both hint at a vengeance that is a sort of individualized justice-seeking, refusing to smooth over its disturbance or to depoliticize its individuality. Both feature wronged subjects who change the game set for them, but in both, vengeance brings other consequences that both protagonists and audiences must confront.

Killing Mad Dogs, made during a reformist period in Iranian politics, is the story of a woman played by her husband in a way that endangers her life.[116] His name, Nasser Moasser (ironically meaning "triumphant in the contemporary era"), positions him as a personification of reformist politics.[117] His wife, Golrokh Kamali, is a banned writer who is effectively being paid not to publish. She returns to Tehran from a long trip to discover that her husband, who has been unfaithful to her, is enmeshed in illegal economic activity. He owes money with which a partner has absconded and he is about to be jailed for bankruptcy. After having played with Golrokh's feelings and rejected her, Moasser tries to gaslight her into believing that her loss of trust in him is her own fault. He constructs a vision of a promising future but repeats his using of her, this time to pay his debts. Golrokh resolves to help him by selling his bad promissory notes back to his creditors at a discount and for a promise not to prosecute him. In her quest to do this, she confronts misogyny, corruption and violence at seemingly every turn but engages in graphic counterviolence, refusing to back down even when it seems to make no sense to continue.

Repetition is key to this narrative. Golrokh is called on to help a husband stuck in men's games and gets a rough initiation. In the end, she finds that Moasser has played her again. But his revelation of that fact parallels another, different revelation. The vengeance she visits on Moasser's creditors exposes them—and him—for what they are. Her actions seem to have morphed into something new, as if in retrospect, they have become her revenge, both on him and on the larger game he joined. The wider implication is clear: as one comment on the film puts it, "Was it Iran [*sic*] really like this? No, but did it feel like this? Absolutely."[118]

---

116. Bahram Beyzai, *Sag Koshi* [*Killing Mad Dogs*] (Aukland, NZ: Farsiland, February 2001), film. 135 min., https://farsiland.com/movies/killing-mad-dogs/. Constructed as a thriller, *Killing Mad Dogs* was a commercial success in Iran. See Jonathan Rosenbaum, "The World Is Watching," Chicago Reader, March 8, 2001, https://chicagoreader.com/film/the-world-is-watching/.

117. Official reformism represented itself as peace-loving and willing to engage in global dialogue, but under the guise of modernization it engaged in a neoliberal dismantling of state buffers against national and international capital accumulation.

118. Sardinman, November 5, 2019, review of *Killing Mad Dogs*, Letterboxd, https://letterboxd.com/film/killing-mad-dogs/reviews/by/added/page/2/.

However, consider the consequences Golrokh would have faced as a woman in Iran had she fully owned her vengeance. Her agency on behalf of her husband and his debts may involve illegal means, but it is understandable in patriarchal terms. Those terms define her agency as derivative, through her husband. For her to avenge her own situation would have placed her objectively in opposition to her society, as a rebel or a revolutionary, whether she herself was motivated by personal vengeance or by social change. Likewise, for her to own her anger would also have placed her outside the patriarchal coding. It would have brought down on her both punishment and a pathologizing of her choice, her agency and her feelings as symptomatic of some personal deviance. Again we see how the neoliberal ideal of free agency and others like it are selectively constricted. Moasser doesn't need to claim individual agency; he already has it, and he is free to claim or dispense with the agency of the woman to whom he is married. Her actions, if understood as driven by her own anger, would place her outside the codes, in a new situation, making her a new agent in a new time. But exactly in that sense, anger—even if it originates within a patriarchal coding of rescue or vengeance—can become revolutionary.

In *The Killing of a Sacred Deer* (2017), Yorgos Lanthimos updates Euripides' *Iphigenia in Aulis* as the story of a son whose identity is forged in betrayal and revenge after he loses his father to surgery performed by a drunk doctor.[119] His vengeance is "driven by an inflexible moral imperative,"[120] but in a way that demonstrates how repetition inhabits both revenge and justice. Nothing will satisfy the son but to see one of the doctor's family members die in return for and in addition to his father's death.

Steven Murphy, the surgeon, lives a materially wealthy but empty life and is obsessed with control of his family (it is worth noting here that obsession is a kind of repetition). He encounters Martin, the son of the man who died under his hands, and takes an interest in him, which Martin exploits. Gradually entanglements develop among Martin, his mother and Steven's family. Then Steven's son, Bob, develops paralysis, and Martin reveals to Steven who he is—that he has caused Bob's paralysis and that the rest of the family will sicken and die unless Steven becomes the agent of Martin's revenge and kills a member of his own family. This, says Martin, is "the only thing ... that's close to justice."[121] Steven's wife discovers the truth about the operation her husband performed, at the price of sexually servicing her informant. In desperation, Steven kidnaps and beats Martin, who remains unmoved. The family argues over who should die and Steven's daughter and son engage in a futile confessional exercise. Finally, Steven, in a bizarre version of Russian roulette, blindfolds himself, loads a rifle, spins around and fires,

---

119. Yorgos Lanthimos, *The Killing of a Sacred Deer* (Toronto: Elevation Pictures, 2017), DVD, 121 mins.

120. Mark Kermode, *"The Killing of a Sacred Deer* Review: Uneasy about a Boy," *The Guardian*, November 5, 2017, https://www.theguardian.com/film/2017/nov/05/killing-of-sacred-deer-review-yorgos-lanthimos-colin-farrell-nicole-kidman.

121. Quoted in Wikipedia, *"The Killing of a Sacred Deer,"* last modified November 15, 2021, https://en.wikipedia.org/wiki/The_Killing_of_a_Sacred_Deer.

Pedagogies and Possibilities of Crisis 119

killing his son on the third shot. Later the remaining family members encounter Martin at the diner where he first met Steven; he stares at them and they briefly return his gaze.

The revenge Martin exacts is not only the death of Bob. It includes the self-punishment undergone by members of the family after their justifications and pleas run out. But who is Martin? Reviewer Mark Kermode notes that we are left tantalizingly uncertain as to whether this intense young man is the architect or the messenger of forces beyond our ken. When awful truths are revealed, they are recited like cursed verse, conjuring a fable-like sense of fate, out of step with contemporary concepts of choice.[122] Martin is an enigma. Is he driven by vengeance or has he chosen it freely? In the end, is he satisfied?

Now let's shift focus and position. A fascination with Martin results from taking the subject position of Steven, that is, of privilege. Is it significant that Martin's revenge includes inflicting paralysis on the surgeon's family? In ordinary circumstances—the ordinary circumstances of privilege, inequality and the ideology of individualism—Steven's social class and occupational status give him an agency denied to Martin. When they first meet, Steven's interest in Martin fits the mold of philanthropy: a person of privilege exercises his option to select a disadvantaged individual or group for special treatment, as an object of improvement, perhaps to set them on the "right path." Martin refuses that status and uses Steven's agency against him. Technically, Martin had other options; he could have sued Steven—if he had enough money for a good lawyer and a long trial, or influential friends. But Martin chooses differently, outside the lines drawn by money, property and status, and acts on that different choice. We don't have access to his psyche to know if he is driven by resentment or exercising a Nietzschean freedom to "affirm what is repeated." In the abstract, he is simply a free individual making a free choice. But the film concretely pits a disadvantaged boy against an advantaged family, leaving open the question of whether the payment he extracts fulfills justice or restores a status quo ante, albeit a damaged one.

Two things are certain. First, Martin finds a way to hold an advantage, despite his inferior social position. Second, he succeeds in avenging himself on the family but fails to avenge the past. Does his revelatory wounding of this privileged family accomplish anything else? The answer is yes. He tears away its legitimating veil, dispenses with its secrets, destroys its sovereignty. On a larger scale, unmasking is arguably an initial step toward revolution. Is Martin angry? And is his anger revolutionary or reactionary? The film leaves that question open, suggesting that in a sense it doesn't matter. What does matter is whether you approach the enigma of Martin from the standpoint of privilege and individualism, in which case his inner motivations become central to figuring out what is "wrong" with him. If instead you see Martin through the eyes of his own cohort, his social stratum, perhaps you might see his actions as speaking from a larger context,

---

122. Kermode.

and out of an anger that is impersonal, despite the personal nature of its target—an anger that seeks to expose something rather than to obtain something or to restore a status quo.

On May 20, 1887, 21-year-old Aleksandr Ilyich Ulyanov was hanged in the small town of Schlisselburg, Russia, for conspiring against the life of Tsar Alexander III. Thirty years and a few months later, his younger brother seized the power of the Tsar in the name of Russian workers and the Bolshevik Party, and under his own, new and impersonal name: Lenin. Like Martin, Lenin has been described as implacable, enigmatic, observant. He was not a personality like Trotsky and didn't care to be; he would have dismissed questions about his personal psychology.

> The inhuman (the historical problem of evil), the nonhuman (animal or machine), or more recently, the transhuman and the post-human are all different versions of the same idea, that the human might contain its own alterity. We can therefore say that the human is that which repeats itself beyond, and perhaps even in spite of, all attempts to challenge or deconstruct its essence. The "properly" human relationship to repetition is thus always at the same time a debasement of any "proper" essence of the human.[123]

Perhaps the freedom offered both by revenge and by justice hides the seeds of tyranny. Perhaps revolution "in the name of" does not bestow freedom. Perhaps, though, the act that places one *outside one's time and place* produces its own unexpected revelation, and freedom. Perhaps revolution lies, prior to naming, in that initial unmasking, opening vertiginously on all possibility, or none. In contemporary Iran, revenge films form a popular genre, *Tangsir* being a classic and politically charged, if veiled, example.[124] But even when such films are formally apolitical and consumed as entertainment, the genre itself embodies a politics for ordinary people consigned to play bit parts in a struggle for economic survival defined by the games of the powerful.

Concluding remarks: filming the soul under late capitalism

Lauren Berlant[125] does a phenomenological reading of the affective lives of those marginalized in contemporary capitalism through two 1990s Dardenne brothers films, *La Promesse* and *Rosetta*.[126] She argues that those lives embody desire and aspiration, particularly an aspiration to somehow *become real* through relations that provide proxies of "success" in the form of access or proximity to others with resources or possibilities—

---

123. Malabou.
124. Amir Naderi, *Tangsir* (Iran, 1973), film, 118 min., https://www.youtube.com/watch?v=RwxICKH07wA.
125. Berlant.
126. Luc Dardenne and Jean-Pierre Dardenne, *La Promesse* (New York: Criterion Collection, 1996), DVD, 94 min.; Luc Dardenne and Jean-Pierre Dardenne, *Rosetta* (New York: Criterion Collection, 1999), DVD, 93 min.

economic resources or affective promise: the possibility of being considered, being treated as human. The "proximation" necessary to this hope entails taking chances that may or may not pan out. This sounds entrepreneurial, but whereas neoliberal moralism hallows contract, taking chances at the social margins involves no margin for error and a survival imperative to escape rather than face possible consequences. On the streets, consequences are more personal and more directly brutal than the abstractions of bankruptcy court. The neoliberal moralism of official austerity means both more and less to those who are the first to be cut from state programs or social consideration, or most likely to feel the sharp end of selective policing of the move-on or roundup sort.

Proximation is aleatory, gambling on contingent and momentary chances: for money to get through the day or the week; for a job or a task or an "angle" that might offer some income; for protection; for a place to sleep or stay a while; for documentation, real or adequately forged; for affection, some simulacrum of love or loyalty or the feel of skin on skin; for minor affirmations. Or for niches in time or space to engage in what Berlant calls "spreading out" or "lateral agency"—time-outs from survival to share fast food, take a break and a breath, have a smoke, be unfocused, do something unproductive or useless, play, nap. We see this at particular moments in *Utopia*, when the women gather at the bar for a drink, always under threat of a beating for drinking too much, being too slow to answer the doorbell or saying the wrong thing. We see it in fleeting moments when the woman with the longest history in the brothel expresses, tentatively and unsuccessfully, not only appeasement but a wish for some fleeting affection from her violent boss. We see it in the chances taken by the women of *Four Wives – One Man* to gain some recognition and protection for themselves and some leverage for their children, though their marriages are rigged to the husband's advantage and for their own denigration. In short, life at the margins is about both taking chances in the moment and hedging against chance for a moment beyond the moment.

Shelter, safety, protection and connection are at once necessities and contingencies. But their pursuit is driven by a desire to live a day longer; by yearning for attachment, for hope; by a wish for *relief*. These are measured and cut by fates that grant and legitimate relief selectively, to fit budgetary constraints and moral judgments, favoring those who are owed favors, those who are demonstrably successful at appropriative accumulation, legal or illegal. But even the favored are favored contingently. Wrong bets on markets, employment, sectors of the economy or state favoritism are always possible. The factory executive father in *Dogtooth* rightly senses this and wrongly fantasizes that he can fence off his children from such contingency, not realizing that he has imported contingency to behind the compound walls he has constructed.

Societies subordinated by their states to the austerity requirements of loan capital, to emergencies of various kinds or to the vanity projects of shahs, presidents, prime ministers or charismatic billionaires are societies that are gamed. They are societies in which, as Lykidis argues, sovereignty enters chronic crisis, which seeps down within its hierarchies and out through the cracks and connections between public and private, impersonal and intimate.[127] *The Cycle* (Dariush Mehrjui, 1975) chronicles such crisis in the final years of Iran's last Pahlavi sovereign, in ways that anticipate the world of Golrokh Kamali in *Killing Mad Dogs* a quarter-century and one revolutionary dispensation later.[128] The film opens with a truck full of men seemingly off to a day of temporary labor, but instead diverted to a clinic to give blood; the clinic is run by an entrepreneur who will sell the blood to a Tehran hospital for which he has finagled favored-supplier status. A subplot involves a doctor at the hospital who points out that the supply is likely to be tainted and argues for an in-house blood donation clinic with proper screening. His pleas fall on politely deaf ears, and he may end up being framed by the street entrepreneur whose business he threatens.

Figure 4.6. Esmail with Ali's father on the streets of Tehran, from *The Cycle*.

Source: Wikimedia Commons,
https://commons.wikimedia.org/wiki/File:Dayereh_mina01.jpg#mw-jump-to-license.

The main plot concerns Ali, a young man who takes his ill father to the city in search of treatment. Ali quickly figures out that medical access comes at a price, and that meeting the price means working angles that involve graft. The hospital itself provides

---

127. Lykidis, 11–12.
128. Dariush Mehrjui, *The Cycle* (London: IMVBox, April 1975), film, 101 min., https://www.imvbox.com/watch-persian-movie-iranian-movies/the-cycle-dayereh-mina. Like Mehruji's earlier *The Cow*, *The Cycle* is adapted from a story by Gholam-Hossein Sa'edi.

those in abundance. Esmail, a hospital supplies staffer, recruits Ali to divert hospital food for sale to people on the street and sets up Ali's father in a street-side tea business (using liberated hospital food-service equipment). Because Ali has also become a subcontractor to the corrupt blood business, their impoverished, diseased, drug-addicted clientele provide donors. While Ali initially pursues these semi-criminal opportunities to get care for his father, his frenetic involvement in them takes his attention away from the latter, who dies.

Ali's is the aleatory life embodied; he is a classic entrepreneurial chancer. His subcontracting enterprises are illegal and damaging to the very medical care he seeks, but he is otherwise a self-starter in classic neoliberal mode. He doesn't beg; he finds markets, inserts himself between them and supplies both, skimming off a cut for himself, just as do the more powerful figures with whom he negotiates. He is a model of neoliberal entrepreneurialism on the margins of a corrupted neoliberal moral order in a time of corrupted modernization. Yet there is something more than aleatory in his actions. At the end of the film, he is set to forget, to move on from his humiliation at his father's burial to new opportunities and chances. But his inconsistent loyalty to his father has plucked at him throughout, as does a connection to a nurse that threatens to turn into an attachment neither can risk. He is willing to exploit others but does so in the service of longings that extend, at least for a while, beyond exploitation and accumulation.

Like *The Cow* but more explicitly, *The Cycle* presents an isomorphism between everyday life—in this case, life on the streets—and national politics. But it is more neorealist than magical realist, enabling its audiences to connect these different levels in more than an allegorical sense, to recognize parallels between small- and large-scale graft but also to see how they feed each other in a single vast system of entrepreneurial wealth-skimming. That said, *The Cycle* is neither epic nor tragedy; it includes moments of comedy and has more affinity to the narrative styles of Lanthimos and Tsangari than to those of Angelopoulos and Voulgaris. Nonetheless, it addresses the same kind of linkage between social systems and personal life that Raymond Williams draws on in connecting tragic drama to tragic history.[129] The death of Ali's father because of impoverishment and medical neglect is tragic in Williams's sense, as is the fate of the double-crossed ethical doctor and the hospital's mission to heal, both betrayed by its blood supply. In Williams's analysis, as in *The Cycle* and in the work of Angelopoulos, tragedy links to repetition or (in Marxist terms) to reproduction of the relations of corrupt accumulation. Ali's frenetic entrepreneurialism is not without echoes in Angelopoulos's films—for example, the ever hopeful violinist-impresario of *The Weeping Meadow* (2004) and the film director on a

---

129. Raymond Williams, *Modern Tragedy*, ed. P. McCallum (Peterborough, ON: Broadview, 2006).

quest for lost footage in *Ulysses' Gaze* (1995)—and in the rising sea captain/shipowner of Voulgaris's *Little England* (2013).[130]

Neoliberalism and austerity as a moral/theological combinatory lead, in ideal speech, to repetition of the same nostrums of individual responsibility, the same visions of private accumulation. In practice, they lead to repetitive corruption, social division, blame and despair—to tragedy. For every New Zealand, there is a Greece or Iran or an impoverished shadow America. Granted, corruption and hopelessness have as many hues as an oil slick—but an oil slick feeds only bacteria. Granted also, the seeds of revolution may sprout in seemingly impossible cracks. But something must crumble to form soil for equity and democracy. People must be able to visualize and to seize realistic possibilities, however marginal, to gather in common, to engage in diverse works of resistance and creation, to discuss or open themselves to some other, perhaps unexpected imaginary— an imaginary that does not aestheticize or philosophize power into air; encourage neglect, blame and cruelty; or incite unbounded but obsessively repetitive accumulation at the other's expense. Surprisingly little will suffice to provide life enough to maintain this ability. Athenian democracy and Socratic inquiry were seeded, sprouted and persisted in the arid, rocky substrate of political division and chronic warfare that accompanied the rise and fall of city-states. The question that remains is how film will continue to shake loose some soil from today's monoliths, illuminate the unlikely cracks in which it might lodge, and sow aleatory seeds of new life.

Postscript: politics and/of representation

Alea and lateral agency; desire and frustration; hope and despair; attachment and exploitation; risk, revenge, relief: such are the tropes that inform the cinematic narratives we have considered here. In conclusion, we want briefly to emphasize that we have privileged narrative and depiction in this venture into the politics of film, but that that is not the only form such a venture can take. Our approach privileges the representational element of film, and thus also realism (if that term includes magical realism, neorealism, film that marks realism as its *point de départ*, and Brechtian distancing). This raises questions about non-representational and anti-representational films that reflect back on narrative representation. Does representation bear an inherent politics that could be made apparent by foregrounding in film the representational technologies and social apparatuses of film itself? Do narrative and representation need to be blasted (to use Walter Benjamin's term) from the matrix they occupied long before film became technologically possible, perhaps by some post-narrative Brecht shaking loose viewers and film-makers not just from

---

130. Theo Angelopoulos, *Trilogy: The Weeping Meadow*, Theo Angelopoulos Collection, vol. 3 (London: Curzon Artificial Eye, 2004), DVD, 169 min.; Theo Angelopoulos, *Ulysses' Gaze*, Theo Angelopoulos Collection, vol. 3 (London: Curzon Artificial Eye, 1995), DVD, 176 min.; Voulgaris.

particular narratives but from narrative expectation itself?[131] Perhaps we will know anew the politics of the narrative form only with the passing of the mode of information,[132] when half-sensed possibilities given in the present are realized in diverging futures: consumer immersion in sensate virtual experience; dissolution of the division between making and viewing, new filmographies of gesture, stop-motion, juxtaposition, montage, collage. Perhaps the futures of film lie less in making films about politics than in making the making of film and other media central political issues. Perhaps McLuhan's prophecies or those of Situationism, even a half-century since *The Society of the Spectacle*,[133] are not yet exhausted of possibility.

Giorgio Agamben raises similar questions, starting from a claim that Western bourgeois culture has entertained a progressive fragmentation of gesture and its loss from social life, leading to frantic efforts "to recover or record what has been lost."[134] Film attempts to evoke gesture in the process of its loss and in the production of images. Whereas Deleuze defined cinematic images as movement images, Agamben, as Benjamin Noys notes, breaks the unity of the image into gestures:

> The image is a kind of force field that holds together two opposing forces ... the image reifies and obliterates the gesture, fixing it into the static ... [but] the image also preserves the dynamic force of the gesture, linking the gesture to a whole. What we need to do is to liberate this dynamic force from the static spell of the image. ... In a sense the film still is the image that obliterates the gesture—but as, precisely, a still, it relates the image back to the whole and to gesture. The power of cinema is that, in Agamben's words, it "leads images back to the homeland of gestures." If cinema leads us back to gestures, then it also leads us back to ethics and politics, but not to aesthetics. According to Agamben, the gesture is a particular type of action—it is neither about acting or making, producing or action, but instead about enduring and supporting. It is neither a means in view

---

131. In relation to this point, see Bargu on Althusser's Brechtian moment and his later development of an "aleatory materialism"; Banu Bargu, "In the Theater of Politics: Althusser's Aleatory Materialism and Aesthetics," *Diacritics* 40, no. 3 (September 2012): 86–111.

132. See Mark Poster, *The Mode of Information: Poststructuralism and Social Context*, Chicago: University of Chicago Press, 1990); also Ramp, "Heads and Tales."

133. Guy Debord, *The Society of the Spectacle*, trans. D. Nicholson-Smith (New York: Zone Books, 1995).

134. See Giorgio Agamben, "Notes on Gesture," in *Means Without End: Notes on Politics*, trans. V. Binetti and C. Casarino (Minneapolis: University of Minnesota Press, 2000), 49–62; also Giorgio Agamben, "Difference and Repetition: On Guy Debord's Films," in *Guy Debord and the Situationist International: Texts and Documents*, ed. T. McDonough (Cambridge, MA: MIT Press, 2002), 313–19.

of an end, nor an end without a means, it is means as such. ... What the gesture opens is our own being-in-a-medium, our own ethical and political dimension.[135]

Agamben draws on the cinematic practice of Guy Debord to reveal "the image in movement by revealing the conditions of cinematic montage."

> In doing so Debord reveals that cinematic montage works through two conditions: repetition and stoppage. Once this is revealed cinema starts to work on itself, dissolving the boundary between genres and working on its own images. [Debord] repeats images to free the gestures fixed within them and stops images to allow us to think the image as such. ... In Agamben's terms, Debord's cinematic practice dismantles the image to reveal the gesture. The task of cinema is to create but also to decreate, to decreate what exists to create something new.[136]

Repetition and stoppage "reveal the medium" and disallow the image from "disappearing into what makes it visible."[137] As Noys points out, rather than an image merely serving as a conveyance for something else—a mood, a moment in a narrative—it can open "our connection to the gesture and to the image as the gesture of connection ... the exhibiting of the gesture as our medium, the pure means of our being-in-the-world."[138] The films we have discussed here take a narrative form, but all are densely populated by images—entrapment, tricks, jokes, connection, disconnection, abandonment, risk, renunciation, revenge—that haunt viewers because they repeat to us what we have done, not done, wished or feared, and stop us in the moment of recognition, not to admire the image but to face the ethical and political questions raised by that recognition. Do we watch *The Killing of the Sacred Deer* from Steven's point of view, from that of his wife or daughter, or from Martin's? How does our watching implicate us in creating a point of view in which some images resonate and others don't, in which we catch our breath at one gesture and not another? How are we enabled (or not) to de-create that point of view? How does the weaving of image and gesture into plot that we must do reveal our reception of the film as both political act and political effect, part of a web of intimate and institutional practices that produce or resist powers? Noys concludes: "Whether we have lost our gestures or not, Agamben redeems cinema as a site of the messianic promise contained in the image. Every image is, as he paraphrases Walter Benjamin, 'charged with history because it is the door through which the Messiah enters.'"[139]

---

135. Benjamin Noys, "Gestural Cinema? On Two Texts by Giorgio Agamben, 'Notes on Gesture' (1992) and 'Difference and Repetition: On Guy Debord's Films' (1995)," *Film-Philosophy* 8, no. 2 (2004), https://www.euppublishing.com/doi/full/10.3366/film.2004.0012.

136. Noys.

137. Agamben, "Difference and Repetition," 315.

138. Noys.

139. Agamben, "Difference and Repetition," 315.

We can only indicate, not address, such possibilities, save to note that they might also link to an interrogation of aesthetic judgment, the commodity form, and distinctions between popular and art-house film. Ghosts of past and future artistic ideals, political hopes and economic aspirations still haunt the art house and the Cineplex even as the "house" crumbles before YouTube and the mobile phone. How will virtual reality, gamification and video podcasting shape the future of political film? What forms of political or pedagogical communion are emerging, and with what consequences? Will film be frozen into images and imaginaries that lead repetitively elsewhere or *before*, or will it be de-created and reconfigured in entirely new modes of communicative and critical engagement? Such definitional questions are important. What we have suggested about cinema as political pedagogy will be worthless if film itself becomes critically and politically irrelevant; if politics is now post-film; if film no longer has purchase on the moral, social and communicative regimes we reproduce and resist, or on whatever will follow them.

Bibliography

Adra, Najwa. "Four Wives–One Man Directed by Nahid Persson." *Visual Anthropology Review*, 5 May 2009. AnthroSource. https://anthrosource.onlinelibrary.wiley.com/doi/full/10.1111/j.1548-7458.2009.01034.x.

Afshin, B., and A. Gholamreza, "Critical Discourse Analysis of Iranian Political Cinema with Fairclough Approach." *Journal of Political Sciences and Public Affairs* 5, no. 1 (2017): 1–5. doi: 10.4172/2332-0761.1000233. https://www.longdom.org/open-access/critical-discourse-analysis-of-iranian-political-cinema-with-faircloughapproach-2332-0761-100023 3.pdf.

Agamben, Giorgio. "Difference and Repetition: On Guy Debord's Films." In *Guy Debord and the Situationist International: Texts and Documents*, edited by T. McDonough, 313–19. Cambridge, MA: MIT Press, 2002.

———. "Notes on Gesture." In *Means Without End: Notes on Politics*, 49–62. Translated by V. Binetti and C. Casarino. Minneapolis: University of Minnesota Press, 2000.

———. *State of Exception*. Translated by K. Attell. Chicago: University of Chicago Press, 2005.

Akhavan, Marzieh, and Asghar Fahimifar. "Analyzing 'Ambiguity' in Realistic Iranian Movies: Using Reception Aesthetics Theory of Iser and Jauss (Case Study: *About Elly* by Asghar Farhadi)." Presentation at First National Conference on Fundamental Researches in Language and Literature Studies. Tehran, Iran, December 2018. https://www.researchgate.net/publication/329990548_Analyzing_Ambiguity_in_Realistic_Iranian_Mo vies_Using_Reception_Aesthetics_Theory_of_Iser_and_Jauss_Case_Study_About_Elly_by_Asghar_Farhadi?enrichId=rgreq-5dee2ad34b9bf86622337feaff09e1f6-XXX&enrich Source=Y292ZXJQYWdlOzMyOTk5MDU0ODtBUzo3MDkyMzY3MzY2Nzk5MzZA MTU0NjEwNjYyMzU1MA%3D%3D&el=1_x_3&_esc=publicationCoverPdf.

Amirian, Mohammad Reza, Ali Rahimi and Gholamreza Sami. "A Critical Discourse Analysis of the Images of Iranians in Western Movies: The Case of *Iranium*." *International Journal of Applied Linguistics and English Literature* 1, no. 5 (2012): 1–13.

Androutsopoulos, Jannis. "Introduction: Language and Society in Cinematic Discourse." *Multilingua*. 31, no. 2/3 (2016): 139–54.

Angelopoulos, Theo., dir. and prod. *Alexander the Great*. Theo Angelopoulos Collection. Vol. 2. London: Curzon Artificial Eye, 1980. DVD. 210 min.

———. *The Suspended Step of the Stork*. Theo Angelopoulos Collection. Vol. 2. London: Curzon Artificial Eye, 1991. DVD. 143 min.

———. *Trilogy: The Weeping Meadow*. Theo Angelopoulos Collection. Vol. 3. London: Curzon Artificial Eye, 2004. DVD. 169 min.

———. *Ulysses' Gaze*. Theo Angelopoulos Collection. Vol. 3. London: Curzon Artificial Eye, 1995. DVD. 176 min.

Avranas, Alexandros, dir. *Miss Violence*. New York: EFF/Vimeo, 2013. Film. 99 min. https://player.vimeo.com/video/91461803 [trailer].

Bakhshi, Massoud [sic], dir. *Tehran Has No More Pomegranates*. Prague: DA Films, 2006. DVD. 58 min.

Bandow, Doug. "Into the Economic Abyss: Foolish Europeans Give Irresponsible Greeks Third Bailout." *Forbes*, July 22, 2015. https://www.forbes.com/sites/dougbandow/2015/07/22/into-the-economic-abyss-foolish-europeans-give-irresponsible-greeks-third-bailout/?sh=1dd98f847094.

Bargu, Banu. "In the Theater of Politics: Althusser's Aleatory Materialism and Aesthetics." *Diacritics* 40, no. 3 (September 2012): 86–111.

Bateman, John A. "Critical Discourse Analysis and Film." *The Routledge Handbook of Critical Discourse Studies*, edited by John Flowerdew and John E. Richardson, 612–25. London: Routledge, 2018.

Baudrillard, Jean. "Simulacra and Simulations." In *Jean Baudrillard: Selected Writings*, 166–84. Edited by Mark Poster. Stanford, CA: Stanford University Press, 1988. https://web.stanford.edu/class/history34q/readings/Baudrillard/Baudrillard_Simulacra.html.

Benjamin, Walter. "The Destructive Character." In *Reflections: Essays, Aphorisms, Autobiographical Writings*, 301–3. Translated by E. F. N. Jephcott and P. Demetz. New York: Harcourt, Brace Jovanovich, 1978.

———. "On the Concept of History" (1940). Translated by D. Redmond. Marxists Internet Archive, 2005. https://www.marxists.org/reference/archive/benjamin/1940/history.htm.

Berlant, Lauren. *Cruel Optimism*. Durham, NC: Duke University Press, 2011.

Beyzai, Bahram, dir. *Sag Koshi* [*Killing Mad Dogs*]. Aukland, NZ: Farsiland, 2001. Film. 135 min. https://farsiland.com/movies/killing-mad-dogs/.

Billinis, Alexander. "The Eagle Has Two Faces: Journeys Through Byzantine Europe." *Byzantine Blog*, September 30, 2011. https://mybyzantine.wordpress.com/tag/alexander-billinis/.

Biltereyst, Daniel, and Philippe Meers. "Film, Cinema and Reception Studies: Revisiting Research on Audience's Filmic and Cinematic Experiences." In *Reception Studies and Audiovisual Translation*, edited by E. Di Giovanni and Y. Gambier, 21–42. Amsterdam: John Benjamins, 2018.

Binding, Karl, and Alfred Hoche. *Allowing the Destruction of Life Unworthy of Life: Its Measure and Form*. Translated by C. Modak. Greenwood, WI: Policy Intersections Research Center/Suzeteo Enterprises, 2012–15.

Bordwell, David. "ApProppriations and ImProprieties: Problems in the Morphology of Film Narrative." *Cinema Journal* 27, no. 3 (1988): 5–20. doi: https://doi.org/10.2307/1225288.

Bradshaw, Peter. "*Miss Violence* Review: Macabre Tale of Evil and Greek Anguish." *The Guardian*, 19 June 2014. https://www.theguardian.com/film/2014/jun/19/miss-violence-review-evil-and-greek-anguish.

Brecht, Bertolt. "To Those Born Later." In *Bertolt Brecht: Poems, 1913–1956*, 318–20. Edited by J. Willett and R. Manheim. London: Methuen, 1987.

Brenner, Neil, and Nik Theodore, eds. Spaces of Neoliberalism: Urban Restructuring in North America and Western Europe. Oxford: Blackwell, 2012.

Brenner, Neil, and Nik Theodore, "Cities and the Geographies of 'Actually Existing Neoliberalism.'" In *Spaces of Neoliberalism: Urban Restructuring in North America and Western Europe*, 2–32. Oxford: Blackwell, 2012.

Chambers, Samuel. There's No Such Thing as "The Economy": Essays on Capitalist Value. Goleta, CA: Punctum, 2018.

Close-Up Film Centre. "Utopia." Film programmes, 18 November 2017. https://www.closeupfilmcentre.com/film_programmes/2017/sohrab-shahid-saless/utopia/.

Cobley, Paul. "Narrative." In *Oxford Bibliographies in Communication*, edited by P. Moy. Oxford Bibliographies Online. Oxford: Oxford University Press, 2016. doi: 10.1093/obo/9780199756841-0088. Expanded version available at Middlesex University Research Repository. https://eprints.mdx.ac.uk/20006/1/Pre-print%20Narrative%20Oxford%20Bibliographies.pdf.

The Cow (Gaav). "1979: Revolution of the Images." Iranian Film Festival, 2019. https://www.1979ir.de/en/filme/the-cow-gaav/.

Dabashi, Hamid. "How Did Iranian Cinema Go Global?" Al Jazeera, March 21, 2018. https://www.aljazeera.com/indepth/opinion/iranian-cinema-global-180321085138324.html.

Dardenne, Luc, and Jean-Pierre Dardenne, dirs. *La Promesse*. New York: Criterion Collection, 1996. DVD. 94 min.

———. *Rosetta*. New York: Criterion Collection, 1999. DVD. 93 min.

Debord, Guy. *The Society of the Spectacle*. Translated by D. Nicholson-Smith. New York: Zone Books, 1995.

Demetrius, Michael, dir. *Cloud*. Athens: Michael Demetrius, 2019. Film. 20 min. https://vimeo.com/339640786 [trailer].

Fisher, Mark. Capitalist Realism: Is There No Alternative? Ropley, UK: Zer0 Books, 2008.

———. "Good for Nothing." *The Occupied Times*, March 19, 2014. https://theoccupiedtimes.org/?p=12841.

———. "What Is Hauntology?" *Film Quarterly* 66, no. 1 (2012): 16–24.

Fiske, John. *Television Culture*. London: Methuen, 1987.

———. Understanding Popular Culture. London: Routledge, 2011.

Fiske, John, and John Hartley. *Reading Television*. London: Routledge, 2004.

Foucault, Michel. "Of Other Spaces: Utopias and Heterotopias," *Architecture/mouvement/continuité* 5 (1984): 46–49. Translated by J. Miskowiec, October 1984. https://web.mit.edu/allanmc/www/foucault1.pdf.

———. "What Is an Author?" In *Language, Counter-memory, Practice: Selected Essays and Interviews by Michel Foucault,* 113–38. Edited by D. F. Bouchard. Ithaca, NY: Cornell University Press, 1980.

French, Philip. "*Dogtooth*" [review]. *The Guardian*, April 25, 2010. https://www.theguardian.com/film/2010/apr/25/dogtooth-film-review.

Fulton, Helen, Rosemary Huisman, Julian Murphet and Anne Dunn, eds. *Narrative and Media*. Cambridge: Cambridge University Press, 2005. doi: https://doi.org/10.1017/CBO9780511811760.

Gabri, Richard. "Recognizing the Unrecognizable in Dariush Mehrjui's 'Gav.'" *Cinema Journal* 54, no. 2 (Winter 2015): 49–71.

Georgakas, Dan. "Greek Cinema for Beginners: A Thumbnail History." *Film Criticism* 27, no. 2 (2002–03): 2–8.

Ghorbankarimi, Maryam. "Redefining the Filmic Genres of Iranian Cinema: The Generic Qualities of New Iranian Cinema." Association for Iranian Studies. Accessed 14 May 2019. https://associationforiranianstudies.org/node/124.

Gordon, Avery F. "Some Thoughts on Haunting and Futurity." *Borderlands* 10, no. 2 (2011): 1–21.

"Haft Tappeh Workers Urge International Labor Organization to Investigate Suppression of Labor Protests." Human Rights in Iran, June 7, 2019. https://iranhumanrights.org/2019/06/haft-tappeh-workers-urge-international-labor-organization-to-investigate-suppression-of-labor-protests/.

Hay, James, and Nick Couldry. "Rethinking Convergence/Culture: An Introduction." *Cultural Studies* 25, no. 4/5 (2011): 473–86.

Hayek, Friedrich A. *The Road to Serfdom: Text and Documents; The Definitive Edition*. Edited by Bruce Caldwell. Chicago: University of Chicago Press, 2007.

Healy, Alice. "Altering Horizons: An Aesthetic of Reception and Reproduction in *Oscar and Lucinda*." In *Australian Literary Studies in the 21st Century: Proceedings of the 2000 ASAL Conference*, edited by P. Mead, 145–50. Hobart, Australia: AASL, 2000. https://openjournals.library.sydney.edu.au/index.php/JASAL/article/view/9601.

Horton, Andrew. "Theodor Angelopoulos and the New Greek Cinema." *Film Criticism* 11, no. 1/2 (Fall/Winter 1986–87): 84–94.

Human Rights Watch. "Iran: Targeting of Dual Citizens, Foreigners, Prolonged Detention, Absence of Due Process." Press release, September 26, 2018. https://www.hrw.org/news/2018/09/26/iran-targeting-dual-citizens-foreigners.

Jauss, Hans Robert. *Toward an Aesthetic of Reception*. Translated by T. Bahti. Minneapolis: University of Minnesota Press, 1982.

Jauss, Hans Robert, and Elizabeth Benzinger. "Literary History as a Challenge to Literary Theory." *New Literary History* 2, no. 1 (1970): 7–37.

Jenkins, Henry. *Convergence Culture: Where Old and New Media Collide*. New York: New York University Press, 2006.

———. "The Cultural Logic of Media Convergence." *International Journal of Cultural Studies* 7, no. 1 (2004): 33–43.

———. "John Fiske: Now and the Future." *Confessions of an ACA-Fan* (blog), June 16, 2010. http://henryjenkins.org/blog/2010/06/john_fiske_now_and_the_future.html.

———. "Rethinking 'Rethinking Convergence/Culture.'" *Cultural Studies* 28, no. 2 (2014): 267–97.

Jenkins, Henry, and Nico Carpentier. "Theorizing Participatory Intensities: A Conversation about Participation and Politics." *Convergence* 19, no. 3 (2013): 265–86.

Jenkins, Henry, and David Thorburn, eds. *Democracy and New Media: Media in Transition*. Cambridge, MA: MIT Press, 2003.

Karalis, Vrasidas. *A History of Greek Cinema*. London: Bloomsbury, 2012.

Karimi, Keywan, dir. *Writing on the City.* Iran, 2015. Film. 60 min. https://www.youtube.com/watch?v=3laaKrp5ebE [trailer].

Kermode, Mark. "*The Killing of a Sacred Deer* Review: Uneasy about a Boy." *The Guardian*, November 5, 2017. https://www.theguardian.com/film/2017/nov/05/killing-of-sacred-deer-review-yorgos-lanthimos-colin-farrell-nicole-kidman.

Kosmidou, Eleftheria Rania. "Theo Angelopoulos's *O Thiasos/The Travelling Players* (1975) and *Oi Kynigoi/The Hunters* (1977) and How They Affect the Brechtian Project." *Journal of Modern Greek Studies* 35, no. 2 (October 2017): 513–38.

Kotsko, Adam. Neoliberalism's Demons: On the Political Theology of Late Capital. Redwood City, CA: Stanford University Press, 2018.

Koutsourakis, Angelos, and Mark Steven, eds. *The Cinema of Theo Angelopoulos.* Edinburgh: Edinburgh University Press, 2015.

Lanthimos, Yorgos, dir. *Alps.* New York: Kino Video, December 2012. DVD. 123 min.

———. *Dogtooth*. New York: Kino Entertainment, May 2009. DVD. 97 min.

———. *The Killing of a Sacred Deer*. Toronto: Elevation Pictures, 2017. DVD. 121 min.

Larner, Wendy, and Maria Butler, "The Places, People, and Politics of Partnership: After Neoliberalism in Aotearoa, New Zealand." In Leitner et al., *Contesting Neoliberalism*, 71–89.

Leathem, Hilary M. V. "Ghostly Excesses: Ethnography and Experimental Cinema." Society for Cultural Anthropology, December 30, 2019. https://culanth.org/fieldsights/everything-is-full-of-ghosts-experimental-cinema-and-ethnography.

Leitner, Helga, Jamie Peck, and Eric S. Sheppard, eds. *Contesting Neoliberalism: Urban Frontiers*. New York: Guilford, 2007.

———. "Squaring Up to Neoliberalism." In Leitner et al., *Contesting Neoliberalism*, 311–27.

Leitner, Helga, Eric S. Sheppard, Kristin Sziarto and Anant Maringanti. "Contesting Urban Futures: Decentering Neoliberalism." In Leitner et al., *Contesting Neoliberalism*, 1–25.

Lilith. "A Response to the Meritocratic Revolution." *Queen Mob's Teahouse*, May 28, 2020. https://queenmobs.com/2020/05/a-response-to-the-meritocratic-revolution/?fbclid=IwAR0ZRC8hiAK9-JJgHb-r91arvYthV8z7ko2lOv2oj_krjn8K0KONRLXk5-g.

Lykidis, Alex. "Crisis of Sovereignty in Recent Greek Cinema." *Journal of Greek Media and Culture* 1, no. 1 (2015): 9–27. doi: 10.1386/jgmc.1.1.9_1.

Macpherson, Charles Brough. *The Political Theory of Possessive Individualism: Hobbes to Locke*. 1962. Reprint, Oxford: Oxford University Press, 2010.

MacWhirter, Ian. "How to Survive the Recession." *New Statesman*, August 21, 2008. Accessed 27 May 2018. https://www.newstatesman.com/economy/2008/08/government-credit-banks.

Mair, Kimberly. Guerrilla Aesthetics: Art, Memory, and the West German Urban Guerrilla. Montreal: McGill-Queen's University Press, 2016.

Malabou, Catherine. "Superhumanity." *Repetition, Revenge, Plasticity*. e-flux Architecture, February 21, 2018. https://www.e-flux.com/architecture/superhumanity/179166/repetition-revenge-plasticity/.

Manent, Pierre. "Between Athens and Jerusalem." *First Things*, February 2012. https://www.firstthings.com/article/2012/02/between-athens-and-jerusalem.

Mayer, Margit. "Contesting the Neoliberalization of Urban Governance." In Leitner et al., *Contesting Neoliberalism*, 90–115.

Mbembe, Achille. "Necropolitics." Translated by L. Meintjes. *Public Culture* 15, no. 1 (Winter 2003): 11–40.

Mehrjui, Dariush, dir. *The Cow (Gaav)*. 1969. Toronto: Knightscove-Ellis International, 2004. DVD. 105 min.

———. *The Cycle*, London: IMVBox, 1975. Film. 101 min. https://www.imvbox.com/watch-persian-movie-iranian-movies/the-cycle-dayereh-mina.

Miaojin, Qiu. *Notes of a Crocodile*. Translated by B. Huie. New York: New York Review Books, 2017.

Mikos, Lothar. "Analysis of Film." In *The SAGE Handbook of Qualitative Data Analysis*, edited by Uwe Flick, 409–23. Thousand Oaks, CA: SAGE, 2014. doi: http://dx.doi.org/10.4135/9781446282243.n28 .

Mirowski, Philip. Interview by Bruce Livesey. In "Is Neoliberalism Destroying the World?" *Ideas*. CBC Radio, August 29, 2019. https://www.cbc.ca/radio/ideas/is-neoliberalism-destroying-the-world-1.4839399.

Mirowski, Philip, and Dieter Plehwe, eds. *The Road from Mont Pèlerin: The Making of the Neoliberal Thought Collective.* Cambridge, MA: Harvard University Press, 2015.

Moores, Shaun. "Texts, Readers and Contexts of Reading: Developments in the Study of Media Audiences." *Media, Culture and Society* 12, no. 1 (1990): 9–29.

Naderi, Amir, dir. *Tangsir*. Iran, 1973. Film. 118 min. https://www.youtube.com/watch?v=RwxICKH07wA.

Naficy, Hamid. *An Accented Cinema: Exilic and Diasporic Filmmaking*. Princeton, NJ: Princeton University Press, 2001.

———. "Making Films with an Accent: Iranian Émigré Cinema." *Framework* 43, no. 2 (Fall 2002): 15–41.

———. A Social History of Iranian Cinema. Vol. 1, The Artisanal Era, 1897–1941. Durham, NC: Duke University Press, 2011.

Nategh, Homa. "Women: The Damned of the Iranian Revolution." In *Caught Up in Conflict*, edited by Rosemary Ridd and Helen Callaway, 45–60. London: Macmillan, 1986.

Noys, Benjamin. "Gestural Cinema? On Two Texts by Giorgio Agamben, 'Notes on Gesture' (1992) and 'Difference and Repetition: On Guy Debord's Films' (1995)." *Film-Philosophy* 8, no. 2 (2004). https://www.euppublishing.com/doi/full/10.3366/film.2004.0012.

Oud, G. J., A. Weijers and F. Wester. *Narrative and Culture; The WOW Method: An Approach to Textual Analysis of Television Drama*. Nijmegen: Instituut voor Masscommunicatie, Katholieke Universiteit Nijmegen (1997), 1–19. https://www.academia.edu/3248939/Narrative_and_culture_the_WOW_method_an_approach_to_texual_analysis_of_television_drama.

Page, Janis Teruggi. "Towards a Theory of Visual Narrative Analysis: What We See on HGTV." PhD diss., University of Missouri–Columbia, 2005. https://www.proquest.com/openview/1dfd8ed52ac871f8cd5e0210a579a9d2/1?pq-origsite=gscholar&cbl=18750&diss=y.

Papadimitriou, Lydia. "Greek Film Studies Today: In Search of Identity," *Kambos Cambridge Papers in Modern Greek* 17 (2009): 49–78. https://www.academia.edu/1272469/Greek_Film_Studies_Today_In_Search_of_Identity.

Papadimitriou, Lydia, and Y. Tzioumakis, eds. *Greek Cinema: Texts, Histories, Identities.* Bristol: Intellect, 2012.

Pavsek, Christopher, dir. *To Those Born After.* Vancouver, BC: Christopher Pavsek, 2005. Film. 28 min. http://www.sfu.ca/~cpavsek/.

Peck, Jamie, and Adam Tickell. "Conceptualizing Neoliberalism, Thinking Thatcherism." In Leitner et al., *Contesting Neoliberalism*, 26–50.

———. "Neoliberalizing Space." In Spaces of Neoliberalism: Urban Restructuring in North America and Western Europe, 33–57. Oxford: Blackwell, 2012.

Persson Sarvestani, Nahid, dir. *Four Wives – One Man.* New York: Women Make Movies, 2007. DVD. 76 min. https://www.wmm.com/catalog/film/four-wives-one-man/.

Phillis, Philip. E. *Greek Cinema and Migration, 1991–2016.* Edinburgh: Edinburgh University Press, 2020.

Polanyi, Karl. *The Great Transformation: The Political and Economic Origins of Our Time.* Boston: Beacon, 2001.

Poster, Mark. *The Mode of Information: Poststructuralism and Social Context.* Chicago: University of Chicago Press, 1990.

Prince, Stephen. "The Discourse of Pictures: Iconicity and Film Studies." *Film Quarterly* 47, no. 1 (1993): 16–28.

Psaras, Marios. "Weirdly/Queerly Ethical: Contemporary Greek Cinema and the Crisis of Meaning." *E-International Relations*, February 14, 2018. https://www.e-ir.info/pdf/72752.

Ramp, William. "Heads and Tales: Story in an Age of (Dis)information." *Weekly Hubris*, February 3, 2017. https://weeklyhubris.com/heads-tales-story-in-an-age-of-disinformation/.

———. "Heroes, Archetypes and Politics." *Weekly Hubris*, March 1, 2017. https://weeklyhubris.com/heroes-archetypes-politics/.

Rose, Steve. "*Attenberg, Dogtooth* and the Weird Wave of Greek Cinema." *The Guardian*, August 27, 2011. https://www.theguardian.com/film/2011/aug/27/attenberg-dogtooth-greece-cinema.

Rosenbaum, Jonathan. "The World Is Watching." Chicago Reader, March 8, 2001. https://chicagoreader.com/film/the-world-is-watching/.

Russell, Andrew. "Slow Cinema: What It Is and Why It's on a Fast Track to the Mainstream in a Frenetic World." The Conversation, April 29, 2019. https://theconversation.com/slow-cinema-what-it-is-and-why-its-on-a-fast-track-to-the-mainstream-in-a-frenetic-world-114769.

Saljoughi, Sara. "The Boundaries of Community: Sara Saljoughi on Dariush Mehrjui's *The Cow*." *Crosscuts.* Walker Art Gallery, July 19, 2017. https://walkerart.org/magazine/sara-saljoughi-dariush-mehrjui-the-cow.

Sandburg, Carl. "Chicago." *Poetry* 3, no. 6 (March 1914): 191–92.

Sayer, Derek. Capitalism and Modernity: An Excursus on Marx and Weber. London: Routledge, 1991.

Schmitt, Carl. *Political Theology: Four Chapters on the Concept of Sovereignty.* 1922. Translated by G. Schwab. Chicago: University of Chicago Press, 2005.

Shahid Saless, Sohrab, dir. *Utopia.* Hamburg: Multimedia Gesellschaft für audiovisuelle Information, May 1983. Film. 198 min. https://www.filmportal.de/video/utopia-1983 [trailer].

Shakhsari, Sima. *Politics of Rightful Killing: Civil Society, Gender, and Sexuality in Weblogistan.* Durham, NC: Duke University Press, 2020.

Sites, William. "Contesting the Neoliberal City? Theories of Neoliberalism and Urban Strategies of Contention." In Leitner et al., *Contesting Neoliberalism*, 116–38.

Steiner, Philippe. *Durkheim and the Birth of Economic Sociology.* Translated by K. Tribe. Princeton, NJ: Princeton University Press, 2011.

Tkalec, Gordana, Iva Rosanda Žigo and Žarka Dolinara. "Film Reception by Means of New Media, or How the Film Escaped from the Cinema." *European Journal of Interdisciplinary Studies* 3, no. 2 (2017): 105–11.

Tsangari, Athina Rachel, dir. *Attenberg.* London: Curzon Artificial Eye, 2010. DVD. 97 min. https://www.curzonartificialeye.com/attenberg/.

Uhler, Rodney. "'The Lobster,' 'Chevalier,' and the Importance of New Greek Cinema." IndieWire, October 19, 2015. https://www.indiewire.com/2015/10/the-lobster-chevalier-and-the-importance-of-new-greek-cinema-129248/.

Vaneigem, Raoul. "The Wall Is a Mirror." Punto de Vista, December 2, 2015. http://www.puntodevistafestival.com/en/noticias.asp?IdNoticia=399.

Varoufakis, Yanis. *And the Weak Suffer What They Must: Europe's Crisis and America's Economic Future.* New York: Nation, 2016.

———. "Bankruptocracy: How Bankrupt Banks Rule the Economy Today; Explained by Yanis Varoufakis." acTVism Munich, n.d. YouTube video. 0:3:42. https://www.youtube.com/watch?v=jlW9DCRQeiE.

———. "The Deep State Part 5: From Goebbels to Donald Trump's Campaign Against the Deep State." Soundcloud. 2019. https://soundcloud.com/yanisv/the-deep-state-part-5-from-goebbels-to-donald-trumps-campaign-against-the-deep-state.

———. Interview by Brian Livesey. In "Is Neoliberalism Destroying the World?" *Ideas.* CBC Radio, August 29, 2019. https://www.cbc.ca/radio/ideas/is-neoliberalism-destroying-the-world-1.4839399.

———. *Talking to My Daughter about the Economy: A Brief History of Capitalism.* London: Bodley Head, 2018.

———. "2008 and the International New Deal We Need for the Post-2018 World World: OECD Keynote, 14 Sep 2018." Yanis Varoufakis (website), September 18, 2018. https://www.yanisvaroufakis.eu/2018/09/18/2008-and-the-international-new-deal-we-need-for-the-post-2018-world-oecd-keynote-14-sep-2018/?fbclid=IwAR0gOBYjLSrft6jZvoBfnFE2-I9yNqZnlYpFA7Aou4fVafAonminJ8rSBqo.

Voulgaris, Pantelis, dir. *Little England.* Riegelsville, PA: Corinth Films, 2013. DVD. 132 min. http://corinthfilms.com/films/little-england/.

Wildfeuer, Janina. *Film Discourse Interpretation: Towards a New Paradigm for Multimodal Film Analysis.* London: Routledge, 2014.

Williams, Raymond. *Modern Tragedy.* Edited by P. McCallum. Peterborough, ON: Broadview, 2006.

Zeydabadi-Nejad, Saeed. *The Politics of Iranian Cinema: Film and Society in the Islamic Republic.* London: Routledge, 2010.

Chapter 5

Decolonizing the Boundaries of Belonging and Citizenship: Turning to Ancient Hellenic and Indigenous Cosmopolitanisms during the Climate Crisis

Cynthia J. Alexander

Acadia University, Canada

Abstract

Decolonizing ourselves necessitates fundamental shifts in ideas about belonging and about the civic responsibilities we owe each other as humans ... and vis-à-vis Nature. In this chapter I explore the idea of cosmopolitanism with a focus on two cultures that at first glance seem to be worlds apart. That is, I provide a brief examination of Hellenic cosmopolitanism to set the foundation for an exploration of the values, principles and ways of being that underpin Indigenous cosmopolitanism. The chapter is informed by the invaluable opportunities I have had to listen to and learn from First Nations peoples and from Inuit of Nunavut in the eastern Arctic in Canada. As a settler scholar, living on unceded land on the East Coast of Canada, I focus on the need for epistemological and ontological pluralism rather than for the persistence of Eurocentric worldviews. In this chapter I share the connections I have been making between my study of Greek philosophy and what I have been working to learn from Indigenous peoples across Canada. *Inuit Qaujimajatuqangit* (*IQ*) is a term for Inuit traditional knowledge (TK) and ways of being, and cultural values that continue to be shared from generation to generation, despite colonial policy actions to assimilate Inuit. Inuit principles and practices of interdependence, interconnectedness among humans and more-than-humans, and respect for intergenerational relationships, reveal a simple thesis: nationalistic and other exclusionary ideas about citizenship that propagate an 'Us versus Other' mentality is antithetical to the kind and quality of civic engagement and policy action required to address the planetary climate emergency. I share a case study of the humanitarian crisis that persists in the Mediterranean—the world's deadliest migration route by sea—to illustrate how addressing the climate crisis merits consideration of the urgency to recentre ancient ever-evolving Indigenous knowledges which honour all life forms. I conclude by illustrating how Inuit have created interactive digital designs that provide global citizens with immersive learning experiences that can expand and deepen our civic awareness, and our ability to become contemporary cosmopolitans, in ways that support decolonizing journeys vis-à-vis Nature, and with each other as humans.

Keywords: cosmopolitanism, Hellenic cosmopolitanism, Indigenous cosmopolitanisms, Indigeneity, Indigenous knowledges, Nunavut, Arctic, Circumpolar, Inuit, Inuit values, interconnectedness, refugees, climate migration, climate refugees, climate crisis, eco-justice, sharing economy, Mediterranean region, humanitarian crisis, public policy, policy inaction, austerity, systemic racism, Islamophobia, authoritarianism, United Nations, organizational sclerosis, human rights violations, state-based violence, proxy wars, North Africa, Libya, citizenship, ethics, virtuous action, moral compass, active hope, citizen engagement, civic obligations, civic duty.

***

Introduction

If ever there were a time to be "living in accordance with nature and rejecting what is conventional,"[1] as Diogenes and the Cynics asserted in Greece during the fourth century BCE, it is during the climate crisis in the early 21st century. The climate crisis underpins the animating question addressed in this chapter: how do the legacies of ancient peoples provide insights to inform a tidal change of moral and ethical engagement vis-à-vis Nature and among humans? In this chapter, inspired by Hellenic cosmopolitanism, I explore the value of seeking an understanding of Indigenous cosmopolitanism during the climate crisis. Hellenic and Indigenous cosmopolitanisms offer timely and urgent insights from the legacies of peoples who live worlds apart, temporally, spatially and culturally.

On June 21, 2021, Mary Simon became the first Indigenous Governor General in Canadian history. She had previously served as the national Inuit leader in Canada. During the installation ceremony, the newly appointed Governor General stated:

> The twin global crises of nature destruction and climate change are undoubtedly the challenge of our time. For evidence, we need only look at the Arctic, and what has happened this past month across the country: the devastating impacts of forest fires, prolonged droughts, record heat waves. ... [I]n order to have a healthy future, we must reset our thinking to understand that nature contains and

---

1. Pauline Kleingeld and Eric Brown, "Cosmopolitanism," *Stanford Encyclopedia of Philosophy*, rev. October 17, 2019, https://plato.stanford.edu/entries/cosmopolitanism/.

creates our climate. Our climate allows society to be possible, and within our society is our economy.[2]

Ongoing efforts by Indigenous peoples and their allies to introduce a seismic cultural shift away from dominant European metanarratives are challenged by the persistence of neo-colonialism, which continues to harm Indigenous peoples around the world. To provide some insight into the urgency of changing the dominant mindset, which continues to move us rapidly along the path of least resistance towards an unlivable planet, I begin with a brief overview of the impacts of the climate emergency on human health and well-being. I offer a case study of a policy issue that tends to be ignored by policymakers and the public alike in Europe, North America and elsewhere: the persistent dehumanization of climate refugees in the Mediterranean. The United Nations has urged governments around the world to learn from Indigenous peoples in the face of the accelerating planetary crisis. The following fact is recognized by too few policymakers, scholars and citizens alike:

> Indigenous peoples account for most of the world's cultural diversity. Throughout the world, there are approximately 370 million indigenous peoples occupying 20 per cent of the earth's territory. It is also estimated that they represent as many as 5,000 different indigenous cultures. The indigenous peoples of the world therefore account for most of the world's cultural diversity, even though they constitute a numerical minority.[3]

Given the existential threat posed by the climate crisis, I argue that there is a pressing need for non-Indigenous policy officials, academics and citizens alike to listen to and learn from Indigenous peoples with the kind and quality of interest, respect and even reverence with which we learn from ancient Greeks. The chapter concludes by providing an example of the invaluable insights that we can learn from Inuit about how to reconcile with Nature and with each other, based on the principles of *Inuit Qaujimajatuqangit* (IQ). I share an example of how Inuit are creating immersive digital content that shares the legacies of their ancestors with world citizens in ways that can support our individual and collective decolonizing journeys away from persistent neo-colonialism. Shelby Ward cautions that "the Anthropocene already operates within a cosmopolitan geospatial imaginary, which not only collapses blame and responsibility in the face of global environmental crises but also silences and erases the historical contexts of exploitation

---

2. The Energy Mix, "'Climate Allows Society', Governor General Mary Simon Tells Official Ceremony," July 29, 2021, https://www.theenergymix.com/2021/07/29/climate-allows-society-governor-general-mary-simon-tells-official-ceremony/.

3. United Nations Department of Economic and Social Affairs, "Indigenous Peoples," n.d., https://www.un.org/development/desa/indigenouspeoples/mandated-areas1/environment.html.

and extraction that follow within north-south lines of coloniality."[4] Willful blindness to Indigenous peoples' ancient knowledge forms as original eco-stewards and violent reactions to their actions as land guardians and water protectors reflect the persistence of climate denialism and the defensiveness of global systems of resource extractivism in the face of scientific expertise that the planet is in a "code red" state; such responses are among the key manifestations of persistent neo-colonialism that created, and perpetuate, the climate crisis.

The epistemological and ontological frameworks that underpin Eurocentric metanarratives and sustain neo-colonial governance systems in the West continue to marginalize Indigenous ways of knowing and ways of being. The United Nations University has reiterated that Indigenous peoples must play a crucial role in addressing the climate crisis: "With collective knowledge of the land, sky and sea, these peoples are excellent observers and interpreters of change in the environment. The ensuing community-based and collectively-held knowledge offers valuable insights."[5] Inspired by the ancient Greek philosopher Diogenes, who created the concept of cosmopolitanism, I provide an illustration in this chapter of how Indigenous traditional knowledge informs cosmopolitanism during a time of climate crisis.

Pale Blue Dot: κλιματική κρίση![6]

The global climate emergency presents an ultimatum to humanity, a challenge that was thoughtfully articulated by the former president of Colombia, Juan Manuel Santos:

> The day I became president of Colombia in 2010, our "older brothers"—the indigenous peoples that inhabit the mountains of the Sierra Nevada de Santa Marta—gave me some important advice: "Seek peace and reconciliation among Colombians but also with Mother Nature because she is mad, and she is mad because she has been severely mistreated." Today, that advice is an urgent warning, one that every person and government on Earth must heed. ... These global threats can be addressed only through global action. Yet most nations still

---

4. Shelby E. Ward, "Decolonizing the Cosmopolitan Geospatial Imaginary of the Anthropocene: Beyond Collapsed and Exclusionary Politics of Climate Change," *Pivot* 7, no. 1 (2019): 139.

5. Gleb Raygorodetsky, "Why Traditional Knowledge Holds the Key to Climate Change," United Nations University, December 13, 2011, https://unu.edu/publications/articles/why-traditional-knowledge-holds-the-key-to-climate-change.html.

6. "Climate crisis!" *Pale Blue Dot* is a photograph of Earth taken on February 14, 1990, by the *Voyager 1* space probe, from a record distance of about 6 billion kilometers.

cling to the illusion that they can survive in isolation, that their borders can somehow magically protect them while the rest of the planet burns.[7]

The term "crisis" comes from the Greek word *krino*, which means "to choose." The climate crisis definitively reflects the globally collective urgent need to change course, starting with a new mindset that recognizes and honors the interdependence between humanity and Nature. As Washington and Ehrlich state, "Humanity is dependent on Nature to survive, yet our society largely acts as if this is not the case."[8] Around the world, a growing number of people are suffering from eco-anxiety, climate grief or eco-paralysis (among other terms that are considered to be "psychoterratic syndromes"):

> The term "psychoterratic," coined by the philosopher Glenn Albrecht, refers to mental conditions arising from our relationship with the natural world. One so-called psychoterratic syndrome is "solastalgia," another term coined by Albrecht. The word "solastalgia" joins the Latin word for comfort with the Greek word meaning pain. It refers to the distress one experiences when a well-known environment has changed and no longer offers the same solace. It is a kind of nostalgia one can feel while still at home, an experience of loss that can be very difficult to put into words.[9]

Solastalgia is warranted, as evidenced by the Climate Clock website launched in 2015, which records how quickly the time to choose to respond to the climate crisis is passing.[10] The Climate Clock visually represents how rapidly the planet is warming; specifically, it reveals how quickly, with current emissions trends, we are approaching 1.5°C of global warming. The clock's co-creator, David Usher, explains: "If emissions keep rising, the date we reach 1.5°C will move closer. If emissions start to decrease, the date for 1.5°C will move further away."[11] Usher is collaborating with Damon Mathews, who holds the Concordia University Research Chair in Climate Science and Sustainability, to create an interactive website for the Countdown 2°C Clock to help the public understand whether

---

7. Juan Manuel Santos, "Colombia's Former President Says COVID-19 Shows the Importance of Listening to Indigenous Peoples on How We Treat the Planet," World Economic Forum, May 7, 2020, https://www.weforum.org/agenda/2020/05/juan-manuel-santos-colombia-indigenous-peoples-coronavirus-pandemic-climate-change-environment-nature/.

8. Hayden Washington and P. R. Ehrlich, "Human Dependence on Nature: How to Help Solve the Environmental Crisis," May 2013, doi: 10.4324/9780203095560; https://www.researchgate.net/publication/287322965_Human_Dependence_on_Nature_How_to_Help_Solve_the_Environmental_Crisis.

9. Janet Lewis, "In the Room with Climate Anxiety," *Psychiatric Times* 35, no. 11 (November 28, 2018), https://www.psychiatrictimes.com/view/room-climate-anxiety.

10. Climate Clock, https://climateclock.net.

11. H. Damon Matthews et al., "The Climate Clock: Counting Down to 1.5°C," The Conversation, December 5, 2018, https://theconversation.com/the-climate-clock-counting-down-to-1-5-107498.

we have gained or lost time in our collective efforts to address the climate crisis before we cross the 2°C threshold—a target that can seem too abstract to many people. The Countdown 2°C Clock is designed to serve as a measuring stick to evaluate whether humanity, working collectively, adds time to the clock to avoid crossing the 2°C threshold.

One of the 11,258 scientists who signed the Climate Emergency Declaration, Australian epidemiologist Fiona Stanley, states that she is already measuring the health impacts of global warming: "We are doing too little, too late. As a society, we need to step up."[12] There is precious little time to choose to act in concert together to mitigate the catastrophic implications of inaction and/or half-hearted policy actions for our species, and for the planet. Christos Zerefos, a professor of atmospheric physics, states: "Our models show annual mean temperatures across the Mediterranean increasing by up to 2°C over the next 30 years. ... In the summer, the air temperature will rise by more than 3°C. Ecosystems will suffer."[13] The need to choose to address the climate emergency with immediate action is evident in Greece and around the world.

The term "environmental refugee" was coined in the late 1980s by the United Nations Environment Programme. A United Nations body called the Intergovernmental Panel on Climate Change (IPCC) was established in 1988. In 1990 the IPCC reported that the greatest single impact of climate change would be the millions of humans who would be displaced. On April 22, 2021, the United Nations High Commissioner for Refugees (UNHCR) reported that "roughly 90 per cent of refugees come from countries that are the most vulnerable and least ready to adapt to the impacts of climate change."[14] The hundreds of millions of people around the world who are most vulnerable to the climate crisis live outside the so-called developed world, which is overwhelmingly to blame for the catastrophic conditions leading to the vulnerable people's need to flee and seek refuge.

The legacy of colonialism persists around the world, from Brazil to Canada to North Africa to Australia. Indigenous peoples are particularly vulnerable to the climate crisis, as described in the following excerpt from a United Nations document:

> Climate change threatens the very existence of indigenous peoples. For many indigenous peoples, climate change is already a reality, and they are increasingly realizing that climate change is clearly not just an environmental issue, but one

---

12. David Spratt, "Climate Emergency Public Statement Key Messages," Climate Emergency Declaration, June 20, 2016, https://climateemergencydeclaration.org/media/#keymessages.

13. Helena Smith, "The Next Decade Will Be All About Heat: Can Athens Head Off the Climate Crisis?" *The Guardian*, May 10, 2021, https://www.theguardian.com/world/2021/may/10/heat-athens-climate-crisis-mayor.

14. United Nations International Day of the World's Indigenous Peoples, August 9, 2021, https:// www.un.org/en/observances/indigenous-day.

with severe socioeconomic implications. The World Bank also sees climate change as having the potential to hamper achievement of the Millennium Development Goals, including those on poverty eradication, child mortality, combating malaria and other diseases, as well as environmental sustainability. For many indigenous peoples, climate change is a potential threat to their very existence and a major issue of human rights and equity.[15]

The knowledge forms, values and ways of being, policy needs and interests of Indigenous peoples in northern Canada tend to remain ignored by southern-based public officials, academics and citizens alike in ways that are complicit in perpetuating neo-colonialism. The time is long overdue to make space to listen to and learn from Inuit, given that the Arctic is melting at *three times* the global rate.

Climate change is rapidly impacting Inuit, who have served as eco-stewards for millennia across their circumpolar homelands. Nunavummuit (those people who call Nunavut, in the eastern Arctic in Canada, home) are intimately familiar with the finding of the "first-ever national survey examining the human impact of the climate emergency" that "[t]emperature change is magnified in circumpolar regions. There is no question Arctic people are now showing symptoms of anxiety, 'ecological grief' and even post-traumatic stress related to the effects of climate change."[16] The "declaration of a climate emergency," which 11,258 scientists around the world endorsed in the fall of 2019, speaks to the fact that the climate crisis represents an existential threat.

John Borrows, a renowned Anishinaabe scholar and an expert in Indigenous law, sheds some light on the Indigenous epistemological and ontological frameworks that have been silenced by ongoing colonialism:

> If we, as human beings, reconcile ourselves with the earth, it will be much easier for Indigenous and non-Indigenous people to identify the earth as the source to help correlate how we relate together. ... You can think of yourself as an ally with the fish and the birds and the trees. We are citizens together because we are part of a community that is mutually participatory with the impulse to ensure that it isn't being hierarchal and neglecting voices.[17]

---

15. UN Department of Economic and Social Affairs, "Indigenous Peoples."

16. Dan McDougall, "'Ecological Grief': Greenland Residents Traumatised by Climate Emergency," *The Guardian*, August 12, 2019, https://www.theguardian.com/world/2019/aug/12/greenland-residents-traumatised-by-climate-emergency.

17. University of Calgary, "Reconcile Yourself with the Earth," UCalgary News, November 17, 2021, https://ucalgary.ca/news/reconcile-earth.

Indigenous cosmopolitanism recognizes that the circle of belonging and citizenship includes reconciling our relationships with the full diversity of "more-than-humans" in Nature, as Borrows eloquently explains above. The journey that redirects our focus from Hellenic cosmopolitanism to explore Indigenous values, innovations and interactions represents a path to decolonize ourselves in our relationships both with each other as human beings and vis-à-vis Nature. There is a common thread that travels around the world, shaped by a "diverse legacy of epistemologies, ontologies, methodologies, and imaginaries other than those developed in the Western academy."[18] While this fact was not highlighted in the readings I was required to study as an undergraduate student 40 years ago, it is increasingly recognized in the literature that cosmopolitan thought can be found within the diverse ancient works of numerous Egyptians, Hebrews, Chinese, Ethiopians, Assyrians and Persians. Here is one example:

> Historically, another cry for human connectedness was formulated alongside that of Diogenes and comes from Buddhism. As Dharwadker (2001: 7) states, the cosmopolitan argument of an inclusive idea of humanity and our interconnectedness put forward by the Buddha foreshadows the Greek formulation of cosmopolitanism in interesting ways.[19]

Epistemological and ontological pluralism is central to decolonizing our relationships with each other and with Nature. Ward suggests:

> Perhaps considering the relationship more rhizomatically would help as well. We have never been individuals, but always sympoiesis, or "making-with" one element or another (Haraway, Trouble 67; 58). "Sympoiesis" is also meant to convey "complex, dynamic, responsive, situated, historical systems. It is a word for wording-with, in company" (Haraway, Trouble 58). The human body is always renegotiated and remembered in these instances. Work is done to carve it back out of its rhizomatic and performative existences. And perhaps, then, reconceptualizing the Anthropocene is really a decolonization of the self in space.[20]

The theme of the 2021 United Nations International Day of the World's Indigenous Peoples is "[l]eaving no one behind: Indigenous peoples and the call for a new social contract. But what does this mean? ... the building and redesigning of a new social contract as an expression of cooperation for social interest and common good for humanity and nature, is needed."[21] We can learn from Diogenes how cosmopolitanism

---

18. Michael Murphy, "Cosmopolitanism," Global Social Theory, 2014, https://globalsocialtheory.org/concepts/cosmopolitanism/.
19. Murphy.
20. Ward, 163.
21. UN International Day of the World's Indigenous Peoples.

provides fertile ground to reject the neo-colonialism that has paved the way, literally and figuratively, to the climate crisis.

In the tradition of Western political thought, the word "cosmopolitanism" is rooted in two ancient Greek words: *cosmos* (world) and *polites* (citizen). Diogenes (c. 412–323 BCE), one of the founders of the Cynic school of philosophy, offered a radical alternative to the dominant narratives and realities of his time, including social norms. He was deviant in his behavior and in his ideas. Compared to the traditional Greek man, who defined himself by his relationship to the state, to his family and to his local origins, Diogenes would assert that he was a "citizen of the world": *kosmopolitês* in Greek. He rejected the conventions that separated people. Instead, Diogenes asserted that humans everywhere were not so different from one another. He held that "our first and foremost form of affiliation should be to our common humanity, not our uncontrollable secondary characteristics of race, gender or class."[22]

Paul Meany recounts a story of Alexander the Great meeting Diogenes: "Alexander approaches Diogenes who is attentively scanning through an immense pile of human bones. When Alexander asks him what he is doing, Diogenes replies, 'I am searching for the bones of your father but cannot distinguish them from those of a slave.'"[23] Meany notes that "Alexander the Great was accustomed to the practice of respecting philosophers, having been tutored by Aristotle. Surprisingly, the young king had a deep admiration for Diogenes. Once he even stated that if he had not been born as Alexander he would like to have been born as Diogenes."[24] Diogenes influenced the Stoics through Chrysippus, a student of the Stoic school of philosophy's founder, Zeno of Citium. Significantly, "Chrysippus ambitiously explained that since all people possess reason to understand how law ought to be, they must be part of a larger city composed of all rational beings. The unity of human rationality is a key aspect of Stoic thought."[25]

It is beyond the scope of this chapter to explore Western cosmopolitanism further before leaping forward to the ancient teachings that underpin Indigenous cosmopolitanism. Suffice it to note that a cosmopolitan is a citizen of the world who brings a normative perspective, looking beyond how the world is to a focus on how the world ought to be. The idea of taking equal account of all human beings provides an ethical compass for cosmopolitanism. The focus on the responsibility of the individual lies beyond the border walls of the *polis* (city-state in ancient Greece); that is, the concept comes infused with a gaze that focuses

---

22. Paul Meany, "The Stoic Origins of Cosmopolitanism: An Idea More Important Now Than Ever Before," Medium, accessed September 18, 2018, https://medium.com/@meanyp/the-stoic-origins-of-cosmopolitanism-25662d179311.
23. Meany.
24. Meany.
25. Meany.

on the international horizon, envisioning a "cosmopolis." The common thread among the diverse modern theorists of cosmopolitanism lies in an ethic that transcends parochial worldviews, relationships and social organization by engaging with alterity—the state of being other, or Otherness—often, however, within narrowly defined universalizing parameters.

Given the focus in this chapter on Indigenous cosmopolitanism, it is crucial to offer the cautionary note that Maximilian C. Forte articulates: "Tributes to Kantian cosmopolitanism often leave out Kant's unvarnished racism, his classification of peoples according to their skin colour, moral character, and presumed industriousness (or lack thereof), usually reserving the best attributes for Europeans, the worst for Amerindians and Africans."[26] Among the critiques of cosmopolitanism is first, that "it is closely associated with privileged forms of mobility tied to circuits of transnational capital … even as large swaths of humanity are precluded from such mobility by the economic and juridical structures of contemporary neoliberalism," and second, that "cosmopolitanisms are historically deeply grounded in the formation of the European nation as a unit of difference fragmenting the planetary space of humanity."[27] Eurocentrism—which often serves as shorthand for Western-centrism—prevails in the contemporary "global village" despite centuries of resistance that persist, including social movements from #BlackLivesMatter to #IdleNoMore that resonate globally in an era of digital solidarity.

In the spirit of Diogenes, the ancient Greek gadfly who advanced the idea of cosmopolitanism, there are growing counternarratives to the Western values of individualism, the "traditional" nuclear family structure, a belief in control over nature, dualistic thinking, competitiveness, private property, patriarchy. The growing chorus of diverse voices is represented by the meme in Figure 5.1. The meme went viral on social media in 2013 because it demonstrated in a visual way that most of the world's population lives within a circle in the southeast corner of Asia. As exemplified by the points in the quotation below, the human and ecological diversity represented within the circle is staggeringly dense, rich in cultures, and burdened by enormous policy challenges such as poverty, inadequate housing and food insecurity that are exacerbated by the climate crisis.

---

26. Maximilian Forte, "Introduction: Indigeneities and Cosmopolitanisms," in *Indigenous Cosmopolitans: Transnational and Transcultural Indigeneity in the Twenty-First Century*, ed. Maximilian C. Forte (New York: Peter Lang, 2010), 4–5.

27. Neel Ahuja, "Species in a Planetary Frame: Eco-cosmopolitanism, Nationalism and *The Cove*," *Tamkang Review* 42, no. 2 (June 2012): 25–26.

Decolonizing the Boundaries of Belonging and Citizenship   147

Figure 5.1. The Majority of the World's Population Lives in this Circle.

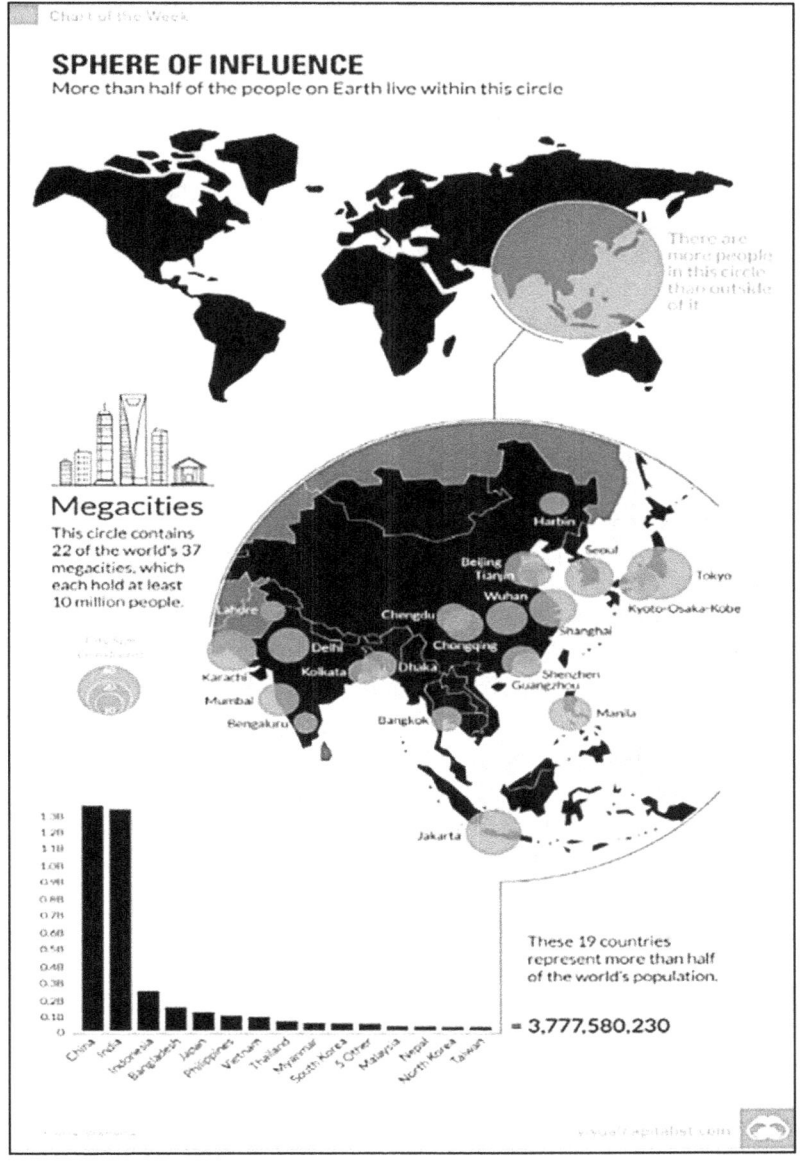

The circle contains a lot of people, but it also has

- The highest mountain (Everest)
- The deepest ocean trench (Mariana)
- More Muslims than outside of it.

- More Hindus than outside of it.
- More Buddhists than outside of it.
- More communists than outside of it.
- The most sparsely populated country on earth (Mongolia).[28]

Furthermore, the circle holds 22 of the world's 37 megacities, including the five most populous municipalities on Earth. In 2019 the Indonesian government announced that the country's capital will move from Jakarta to a new city that will be built, given that Jakarta is the fastest-sinking city on the planet because of rising sea levels. Heri Andreas, an expert in Jakarta's land subsidence at the Bandung Institute of Technology, explains: "If we look at our models, by 2050 about 95% of North Jakarta will be submerged."[29] The circle in Figure 5.1 represents a region containing more than 640 million people. As illustrated by Jakarta, heavily populated cities in low-lying areas in a region characterized by long coastlines make Southeast Asians among the world's most vulnerable to weather extremes and rising sea levels associated with global warming.

The challenge is that compassion fatigue is compounded when we know little—and perhaps care to know little—about Otherized peoples in our own backyards and around the world; however, there have been some efforts to address the gaps in awareness, interest and understanding. Beginning in the early 1990s, for example, universities in Canada and abroad began working to "internationalize the curriculum" with the objective that the campus community would gain global and intercultural competencies, moving closer to the goal of graduating students who were prepared to be global citizens. Significantly, perhaps, one comparative assessment of Canadian universities reported the following finding:

> Students overall appreciate faculty members who take advantage of the presence of international students and other students with international experience in the classroom to broaden understanding of their discipline. More importantly, students' sense of justice and social responsibility drives the need for internationalization. Yet one recent study suggests that students enter university with a more internationalized view of the world than when they graduate.[30]

---

28. Jeff Desjardins, "The Majority of the World's Population Lives in This Circle," *Visual Capitalist*, September 9, 2016, https://www.visualcapitalist.com/majority-worlds-population-lives-circle/.

29. Merrit Kennedy, "Indonesia Plans to Move Its Capital Out of Jakarta, a City That's Sinking," NPR, April 29, 2019, https://www.npr.org/2019/04/29/718234878/indonesia-plans-to-move-its-capital-out-of-jakarta-a-city-thats-sinking.

30. Association of University and Colleges in Canada (AUCC), *Internationalization of the Curriculum: A Practical Guide to Support Canadian Universities' Efforts* (n.p., March 2009), 6, https://www.massey.ac.nz/massey/fms/NCTL/VC%20symposium/curriculum-primer_e.pdf.

Similarly, universities across Canada have been working to "Indigenize" their curricula, in line with the Calls to Action in the 2015 report of the National Truth and Reconciliation Commission (TRC), which found that education institutions have been part of the problem in perpetuating neo-colonialism. The former chair of the TRC, the Honorable Murray Sinclair, has stated, "Education has been used to harm everybody." Sinclair reports "that in school textbooks, Indigenous people are not seen as evolved or evolving, they are parked out of the way, out of sight. Their full history is not told. People were educated to believe Indigenous people were less than other Canadians."[31] At the 2018 Belong Forum held at Dalhousie University, Sinclair was asked to address the question "What would it take to create a world where we all feel we truly belong?" He replied that "true belonging means there are people around you who will help you when you need it—and you, in turn, will help them" and emphasized that "[f]or a long time now, Indigenous people have not felt like they belong in the same circles as the rest of Canada because the history of our relationship has been about rejection."[32]

> Sinclair discussed a fascinating paradox: that the greatest hope for change is education, but at the same time, "Education has been a primary tool of assimilation, and ... continues to be." This is because children are still taught from the misguided and inaccurate perspective that a superior race of people settled and civilized this nation. And so, he said, "We need to change the way we think, talk and act." Schools need to help students address four fundamental questions: Where do I come from? Where am I going? Who am I? And why am I here? If we don't address the fundamental assumption of racial and cultural superiority, along with all the negative stereotypes about Indigenous people that our children are exposed to in media and conversation, Sinclair says, we'll be having the same conversations for many more years. And that will mean Indigenous people will continue to feel they don't belong, will continue to be angry, and their communities will continue to suffer the same problems.[33]

It is in this context that exploring Indigenous cosmopolitanism is an urgent endeavor, given the global climate emergency.

---

31. "Education, Respect for Each Other, Keys to Reconciliation, Senator Murray Sinclair Says in Powerful Keynote at StFX," St. Francis Xavier University, November 8, 2016, https://www.stfx.ca/about/news/senator-murray-sinclair-delivers-powerful-message.

32. Chris Benjamin, "Belong Forum: Senator Murray Sinclair Urges Canada to Think, Talk, Act Differently," Dalhousie University, September 6, 2018, https://www.dal.ca/news/2018/09/06/belong-forum--senator-murray-sinclair-urges-canada-to-think--tal.html.

33. Benjamin.

Terra Nova: the human dimensions of the climate crisis

Greece is experiencing deadly floods and forest fires. In addition, thousands of exposed ancient Greek archeological sites are eroding because of sudden swings from periods of flooding to drought. By 2050 Greece could be 2°C warmer, with 18% less rainfall. Indeed, Greece is "ranked 26th for water stress in the world and its climate change predictions are bleak: around 30 percent of Greece could become desert over the next few decades."[34] In 2016, the first major global assessment of soil health found that 33% of the land was "moderately or highly degraded," which impacts food security, biodiversity and, of course, the ability to reduce carbon emissions.[35] Among the critical issues that John Podesta identifies is the already evident fact that "[i]ntensifying intra- and inter-state competition for food, water, and other resources, particularly in the Middle East and North Africa," will "test the limits and scale of national and global governance as well as international cooperation."[36]

In recent years the Earth's oceans have kept hitting their warmest levels, accelerating each year since 2015. The scientific director of the French-based Mediterranean Institute for Biodiversity and Ecology, Wolfgang Cramer, led a team of more than 80 scientists whose comprehensive research study informed a ground-breaking report on the impact of climate and environmental change in the Mediterranean region. Cramer states that the "Mediterranean basin is one of the hot spots of this global crisis," and further, that in some ways "it is being hit harder than other parts of the world."[37] Among all the climate change effects identified in his team's study, Cramer is particularly concerned about rising sea levels: "By 2100 the waters of the Mediterranean will swell over a meter ... This will affect a third of the population living on the Mediterranean coast: in North Africa alone, the livelihood of at least 37 million people is at risk."[38]

The United Nations Human Rights Committee anticipates the possibility by 2050 of a billion environmental refugees. The U.N. cautions that this catastrophic flow of desperate people may soon result in governments' being prohibited from sending people back to their home countries when there are immediate threats to life due to climate change. Furthermore, the U.N. committee suggests that potential human rights violations caused

---

34. Jon Heggie, "Preventing a Water Crisis in Greece," *National Geographic*, May 27, 2020, https://www.nationalgeographic.com/science/2020/05/partner-content-where-our-water-goes-greece/.

35. Adam Wentworth, "Climate and Hunger Solutions Are on Terra Firma, Says UN," ClimateAction, August 15, 2018, http://www.climateaction.org/news/climate-and-hunger-solutions-are-on-terra-firma-says-un.

36. John Podesta, "The Climate Crisis, Migration, and Refugees," Brookings Institute, July 25, 2019, https://www.brookings.edu/research/the-climate-crisis-migration-and-refugees/.

37. Manuel Planelles, "Mediterranean Is Warming Up Faster Than the Rest of the Planet, Report Warns," *El País*, October 10, 2019, https://english.elpais.com/elpais/2019/10/10/inenglish/1570692096_073306.html.

38. Planelles.

by climate change should be taken into consideration by states that intend to deport asylum seekers. For example, a paper included in the 2016 Proceedings of the National Academy of Sciences offers insight into how a prolonged drought linked to climate change devastated rural areas in war-torn Syria. In countries like Syria and Libya (which has the world's longest Mediterranean coastline), devastated by brutal, drawn-out proxy wars between regional and world powers, climate change may be

> a malign background presence, nudging things in the wrong direction and weighting the dice in favour of disruptive, unpredictable chains of events. For this reason, the security community has labelled climate change a "threat multiplier." As such, climate change's influence on displacement will be difficult to disentangle from the web of other social, economic and environmental factors that shape migration patterns.[39]

Writing for the Brookings Institute, Podesta confirms that "[a]lthough there are few instances of climate change as the sole factor in migration, climate change is widely recognized as a contributing and exacerbating factor in migration and conflict."[40] While it is beyond the scope of this chapter to dig deeper into the issue, in a chapter focused on cosmopolitanism in a time of climate crisis it is imperative to recognize that a rapidly growing number of people are seeking refuge on Greek shores and elsewhere around the world. It is important to note that at the same time as vulnerable people are fleeing, there are those who are immobile, despite the dangers introduced by the climate crisis, including "poverty, food insecurity, and water shortages."[41]

In October 2020, a Greek court ruled that a neo-Nazi political party called Golden Dawn was a criminal organization, and sentenced its leaders for crimes ranging from murders to attacks on migrants. In Greece, as elsewhere in Europe and in North America, some public officials assert "that the refugees will infect and rot the population, and they cannot adapt to the western way of life," to which Petros Constantinou counters:

> We're going to be campaigning for the refugee children to get into the schools, and for everyone to be able to access hospitals. We're going to build a movement to bring the refugees inside of the cities into public housing, to close the camps and the ghettos. ... So I'm very proud that we started all this tradition of international mobilisation because the fight against Fortress Europe and the fight

---

39. Rob Bailey and Emma Green, "Should Europe Be Concerned about Climate Refugees?" Chatham House, May 23, 2016, https://www.chathamhouse.org/expert/comment/should-europe-be-concerned-about-climate-refugees#.

40. Podesta.

41. Kira Walker, "Immobility: The Neglected Flipside of the Climate Displacement Crisis," The New Humanitarian, April 26, 2021, https://www.thenewhumanitarian.org/analysis/2021/4/26/the-climate-displacement-crisis-has-a-neglected-flipside.

in 2015 was based on that movement and we managed to open the borders for some moments in Greece because of the solidarity movement for refugees. The anti-fascist movement opened the way for that.[42]

Human Rights Watch issued a report that Greece continues to "host large numbers of asylum seekers while failing to protect their rights,"[43] while Amnesty International reports that Greece has "responded with a package of inhumane measures that violate EU and international law."[44] Angelo Tramountanis, a researcher at the National Centre for Social Research in Athens, observes that "a crucial protection gap exists for the refugee population in Greece. ... This situation is likely to deteriorate further, since significant budget cuts are expected in the assistance provided by the EU in the coming years."[45]

Award-winning novelist Leïla Slimani looks at Greece from the vantage point of a different Mediterranean coast, reminding us of the view of Greece from North Africa. Slimani poignantly shares her insights about the daily horrors that occur at sea, to which most world citizens are willfully blind:

> I am from the Maghreb; I am from the Mediterranean. My attachment to Europe was built across that sea. For me, *mare nostrum* was not a border and not yet a cemetery; it was the outline of a community. In Homer, the Mediterranean is *hygra keleutha*, the liquid road, a space of transition and sharing. It is our common heritage. Odysseus made stopovers on the coast of Africa just as he did in the Greek islands. When I first visited Spain, Portugal and Italy, I was struck by this feeling of familiarity. So how can we explain Europe's current inability to face that sea? How can we understand the way it has deliberately turned its back on the Mediterranean, when this southward tropism is one of the most fortunate aspects of our continent? We have lost the sea and betrayed that essential part of our identity. How devastating to see the youth of the Maghreb and Africa turning away from the continent that has rejected them and let them down.[46]

---

42. Marc Goudcamp, "Ten Years of Fighting Racism and Fascism in Greece," Solidarity, October 31, 2019, https://www.solidarity.net.au/racism/ten-years-of-fighting-racism-and-fascism-in-greece/.

43. Human Rights Watch, "Greece: Events of 2020," World Report 2021, https://www.hrw.org/world-report/2021/country-chapters/greece.

44. Amnesty International, "Explained: The Situation at Greece's Borders," March 5, 2020, https://www.amnesty.org/en/latest/news/2020/03/greece-turkey-refugees-explainer/.

45. Angelo Tramountanis, "Addressing the Protection Gap in Greece," ODI [Overseas Development Institute], July 21, 2021, https://odi.org/en/insights/addressing-the-protection-gap-in-greece/.

46. Leïla Slimani, "Europe Has Turned Its Back on the Mediterranean—But There Is Still Hope," *The Guardian*, March 2, 2020, https://www.theguardian.com/books/2020/mar/02/leila-slimani-divided-territory-mediterranean.

As I took an evening ferry from Mykonos to Paros in June 2019, to join my fellow participants at the Symposium on the Greeks, the kinds of questions and concerns expressed by Slimani weighed heavily on me. It seemed unimaginable that out there on the same expanse of dark waters were overcrowded, leaky vessels full of strong, resilient and actively hopeful but inconceivably vulnerable humans of all ages, including desperate parents, traumatized children and others seeking refuge, all of whom are dehumanized collectively with words such as "swarms" and even "migrants" as they seek a shoreline of humanity. The seas and landscapes that inspired me over the past 40 years of studying and living in Greece were replaced with a deep concern and shame, thoughtfully articulated by Zoe Todd, a professor in the School of Indigenous and Canadian Studies at Carleton University in Ottawa, Canada:

> There are forms of time that shape the world and refuse its current accretions of hate, violence, violation. Christina Sharpe (2016) contemplates the enslaved people who were deliberately drowned in the Middle Passage, who died in that violent rending of worlds: "The amount of time it takes for a substance to enter the ocean and then leave the ocean is called residence time. Human blood is salty, and sodium, Gardulski tells me, has a residence time of 260 million years. And what happens to the energy that is produced in the waters? It continues cycling like atoms in residence time. We, Black people, exist in the residence time of the wake, a time in which 'everything is now. It is all now.'"[47]

The apt description in the quotation above—"exist in the residence time of the wake"— merits repeating in the context of the profound loss of life in the Mediterranean. Given that the global climate crisis exacerbates challenges ranging from food security and/or limited access to clean drinking water to agricultural degradation to violent conflict, there is clearly an intersection between climate change and migration. Podesta observes:

> As severe climate change displaces more people, the international community may be forced to either redefine "refugees" to include climate migrants or create a new legal category and accompanying institutional framework to protect climate migrants. However, opening that debate in the current political context would be fraught with difficulty. Currently, the nationalist, anti-immigrant, and xenophobic atmosphere in Europe and the U.S. would most likely lead to limiting refugee protections rather than expanding them.[48]

How are individual and collective efforts resisting such waves of human rights abuses? Euromed Rights (formerly the Euro-Mediterranean Human Rights Network) is a network representing 80 non-governmental human rights organizations in over 30 countries, with

---

47. Zoe Todd, "On Time," *Speculative Fish-ctions* (blog), November 7, 2018, https://zoestodd.com/2018/11/07/on-time/.

48. Podesta.

a permanent working group on migration and asylum. In the wake of the Arab Spring uprisings that began in 2011, the European Union (E.U.) announced a new approach to a "new neighbourhood," resulting in a "shrinking space for civil society, militarisation of borders ... and mass displacement from Syria or Libya," all of which have "pushed the question of universal rights back to the bottom of the political agenda, especially for foreign nationals."[49] According to the U.N.'s International Organization for Migration (IOM), at least 57 people drowned in July 2021 after a boat capsized off the Libyan coast. Europe has ceded responsibility to the Libyan coastguard, and survivors are returned to Libyan detention centers—in a country that has been suffering from proxy wars and instability since the civil uprising in 2011 that successfully toppled the country's dictator, Muammar Gaddafi. The regular, and at times weekly, recovery of bodies along the Tunisian and Libyan coastlines reflects the ongoing inhumane and, some experts say, illegal E.U. policy. E.U. policies continue to focus on protecting borders rather than protecting the refugees' human rights, going to the extreme of condemning rescue boats for assisting drowning refugees in the Mediterranean. A U.N. report in May 2021 identified the E.U. and member states as partly responsible for migrant deaths, given their policy responses, which include the obstruction of humanitarian rescue efforts.[50]

There are acts of individual resistance to the dehumanization refugees increasingly face that might exemplify contemporary cosmopolitanism. For example, Carola Rackete, a German, served as captain of the migrant rescue ship *Sea-Watch 3*. She defied Italian law and was arrested for violating a naval blockade that tried to stop her from taking 42 migrants, whom she had rescued from an inflatable raft drifting off the coast of Libya, to Lampedusa, a port in Italy. Rackete explains: "For two weeks, we had been informing the authorities that the situation of the people onboard was becoming more and more critical and that the medical conditions of migrants were getting worse, day after day. ... But it was like talking to a brick wall."[51] Italy's then interior minister Matteo Salvini declared the incident to be an "act of war" by an outlaw and a pirate. Demonstrations in Germany called for her release, while her online supporters used the hashtag #FreeCarola and crowds cheered her outside a courthouse in the Sicilian city of Agrigento. The Italian court found her not guilty of endangering lives when Rackete's ship hit an Italian patrol boat. In a statement she released prior to the verdict, Rackete stated: "It is a disgrace to

---

49. EuroMed Rights, "Migration and Asylum," 2020, https://euromedrights.org/theme/migration-refugees-and-asylum-seekers/.

50. Emma Farge, "MSF Denounces Seizure of Migrant Rescue Vessel in Italy," Reuters, July 5, 2021, https://www.reuters.com/world/europe/msf-denounces-seizure-migrant-rescue-vessel-italy-2021-07-05/.

51. Lorenzo Tondo, "Captain Who Rescued 42 Migrants: I'd Do It Again Despite Jail Threat," *The Guardian*, July 5, 2019, https://www.theguardian.com/world/2019/jul/05/captain-who-rescued-42-migrants-id-do-it-again-despite-jail-threat.

Decolonizing the Boundaries of Belonging and Citizenship 155

both words, European and union ... not a single European institution was willing to assume responsibility, until I was forced to do so myself."[52]

Notably, in September 2021 Salvini, the chairman of Italy's right-wing Northern League Party, was to stand trial in Sicily on migrant-kidnapping charges, given his decision as interior minister to prevent more than 100 refugees from landing in Italy, leaving them stranded at sea until prosecutors ordered seizure of the ship and evacuated the refugees—a decision he took multiple times during his tenure. In response to the charge against Salvini, Oscar Camps, the founder of Proactiva Open Arms, a Spanish non-governmental organization that operates rescue ships in the Mediterranean, states that the trial will be "an opportunity to judge a period of European history."[53]

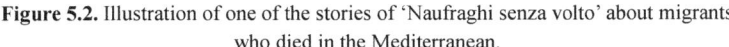

Figure 5.2. Illustration of one of the stories of 'Naufraghi senza volto' about migrants who died in the Mediterranean.

ANSA 2019, https://www.infomigrants.net/en/post/14626/deceased-migrants-found-carrying-report-cards-soil-from-home.

Individuals have also developed initiatives to humanize the migrants in ways that might inspire more citizens to become cosmopolitan in the face of policies that seek to impede cosmopolitan intent. The daily humanitarian toll in the Mediterranean is increasingly met with compassion fatigue, if it makes the news at all. This horrific reality is illustrated

---

52. "Italy Migrant Rescue Boat: Captain Carola Rackete Freed," BBC News, July 2, 2019, https://www.bbc.com/news/world-europe-48838438#:~:text=The%20German%20boat%20captain%20who,patrol%20boat%20at%20a%20quayside.

53. Wladimiro Pantaleone and Gavin Jones, "Italy's Salvini Sent to Trial on Migrant Kidnapping Charge," Reuters, April 17, 2021, https://www.reuters.com/world/europe/italys-salvini-sent-trial-migrant-kidnapping-charge-2021-04-17/.

powerfully by an Italian cartoonist, Mattox, for the paper *Il Foglio* (see fig. 5.2). Mattox portrays a child who has pinned his report card inside his jacket, hoping perhaps that it will assist his entry into Europe when he crosses the Mediterranean, only to find himself coming back to life at the bottom of the sea; sea creatures are examining his school report, the shark saying, "Wow, all tens," and the octopus observing, "A rare pearl." The cartoon may represent a child described in a book about migrants who died trying to reach Europe via the Mediterranean, called *Naufraghi senza volto* (Faceless castaways), written by an Italian coroner, Christina Cattaneo. Mati, from Mali, had his school report card, called "bulletin scolaire," with him when he, at 14 years old, died in a boat in the Mediterranean on April 18, 2015. In her book, Cattaneo also shares stories of finding the "body of an Eritrean boy who had been carrying a sack of earth from his native land and another one of a boy from Ghana who had taken a library card with him."[54] Vast human tragedies are re-counted as persistent, growing data inform the ongoing U.N. chorus of "victims swallowed up by the waves" and insistent warnings that the "upcoming season could be deadlier," year by year. Western ideals of human rights appear to have sunk to new depths, along with the lives of children like Mati from Mali.

Yet cosmopolitans persist. For example, Migrants of the Mediterranean (MotM), founded by Pamela Kerpius in February 2017, is an initiative that draws on humanitarian storytelling to recognize, record, honor and share individual migrants' journeys with all "the emotion of what it means to move across borders and through the central Mediterranean as one of the world's most vulnerable. And when we are connected to that journey and the individual who lived it, we are enabled to see ourselves on parallel human terms."[55] Kerpius's MotM initiative reflects the heart of cosmopolitanism:

> Migrants of the Mediterranean believes in mobility and free movement for all. We believe that by illustrating through Humanitarian Storytelling the difficult and dehumanizing passages people must make—from Africa, the Middle East, and beyond—we can develop empathy for our fellow human beings, thus inspiring urgency to create alternative, safe migration routes, and affect social policy that speaks to the realities of how we live together now.[56]

Importantly, MotM illustrates how one cosmopolitan-minded citizen can identify and choose a course of action in response to state inaction (or to state actions such as caging

---

54. ANSA, "Deceased Migrants Found Carrying Report Cards, Soil from Home," January 21, 2019, https://www.infomigrants.net/en/post/14626/deceased-migrants-found-carrying-report-cards-soil-from-home.

55. [Pamela Kerpius], "About Migrants of the Mediterranean," Migrants of the Mediterranean, 2020, http://www.migrantsofthemed.com/about.

56. Kerpius.

migrants in the United States): "Only by combining our efforts will we find solutions to the challenges of the future, and the best example of this is obviously the planet's ecological ultimatum."[57]

It is with respect to civic responsibility extended to fellow humans everywhere, as well as to the "more-than-humans" that constitute Nature, that Indigenous cosmopolitanism, based on ancient and ever-evolving teachings, can extend our understanding of belonging. For example, from Canada to Aotearoa (New Zealand), Indigenous peoples around the world are successfully working to have the legal "personhood" rights of rivers, lakes and mountains recognized, as Kesler-D'Amours writes:

> Jean-Charles Pietacho says the belief that nature is a living thing that must be respected, has been at the heart of the Innu people's way of life for generations. But now, that idea has been applied in a new way as the Innu Council of Ekuanitshit in February recognised the Magpie River, a 300km (186 miles) waterway in the Côte Nord region of the Canadian province of Quebec, as a "legal person."[58]

The landscape is shifting as we decolonize ourselves by listening to and learning from Indigenous peoples in ways that may slow the Countdown 2°C Clock.

Terra Nullius? Indigenous resurgence in the face of neo-colonialism

Despite the persistence of neo-colonialism globally, from Canada to Brazil to Australia to Tunisia and Libya, Indigenous legacies—from knowledge forms to governance and legal systems to languages and cultures and ways of being—are experiencing a resurgence, even in the face of ongoing state-sponsored violence and systemic racism. In 2015, then Supreme Court Chief Justice Beverley McLachlin stated that Canada had attempted to commit "cultural genocide" against Indigenous peoples, calling it "the worst stain on Canada's human-rights record."[59] Intergenerational trauma takes a toll on the survivors (and their descendants) of residential schools, where Indigenous children and youth kidnapped from their families and communities experienced horrific treatment at the hands of religious administrators who ran the state-based "schools." In 2013, United Nations Special Rapporteur Dr. James Anaya investigated the human rights situation of Indigenous peoples in Canada, concluding that

---

57. Slimani.
58. Jillian Kesler-D'Amours, "This River in Canada Is Now a 'Legal Person,'" Al Jazeera, April 3, 2021, https://www.aljazeera.com/news/2021/4/3/this-river-in-canada-now-legal-person.
59. Sean Fine, "Chief Justice says Canada Attempted 'Cultural Genocide' on Aboriginals," *Globe and Mail*, May 28, 2015, https://www.theglobeandmail.com/news/national/chief-justice-says-canada-attempted-cultural-genocide-on-aboriginals/article24688854/.

Canada faces a continuing crisis when it comes to the situation of indigenous peoples of the country. The well-being gap between aboriginal and non-aboriginal people in Canada has not narrowed over the last several years, treaty and aboriginals' claims remain persistently unresolved, indigenous women and girls remain vulnerable to abuse, and overall there appear to be high levels of distrust among indigenous peoples toward government at both the federal and provincial levels.[60]

The crisis continues in Canada. For example, while former federal Crown–Indigenous Relations Minister Carolyn Bennett affirmed the national government's commitment to upholding and advancing the "calls for justice" stemming from the recommendations of the national Missing and Murdered Indigenous Women and Girls Inquiry, a plan of action has yet to be announced by the Government of Canada. Similarly, in 1996 the Report of the Royal Commission on Aboriginal Peoples (RCAP) included a 20-year agenda for implementing its recommendations to improve the lives of Indigenous peoples across Canada. In 2016, Paul Chartrand, one of the original commissioners of the RCAP, stated: "There is a very powerful lesson there, which is that today still, I don't think it's changed much."[61] The Truth and Reconciliation Commission of Canada listened to the testimony of residential school survivors across Canada and recommended 94 Calls to Action. To those Canadians who call on Indigenous peoples to "get over it," Murray Sinclair responds:

And until people show that they have learned from this, we will never forget, and we should never forget, even once they have learned from it, because this is part of who we are. It's not just a part of who we are as survivors and children of survivors and relatives of survivors, it's part of who we are as a nation. And this nation must never forget what it once did to its most vulnerable people.[62]

While Indigenous peoples remain vulnerable in neo-colonial countries globally, it may surprise people to hear that systemic discrimination runs across Canada throughout diverse institutions, from the justice system to health and education, with the social determinants of health and well-being for Indigenous peoples characterized by underfunding and policy inaction. With reference to the "residence times" briefly

---

60. James Anaya, *Report of the Special Rapporteur on the Rights of Indigenous Peoples, James Anaya*, United Nations Human Rights Council (Geneva: United Nations General Assembly, 2014), 23, https://www.ohchr.org/Documents/Issues/IPeoples/SR/A.HRC.27.52.Add.2-MissionCanada_AUV.pdf.

61. Martha Troian, "20 Years Since Royal Commission on Aboriginal Peoples, Still Waiting for Change," CBC News, March 3, 2016, https://www.cbc.ca/news/indigenous/20-year-anniversary-of-rcap-report-1.3469759.

62. Emma Prestwich, "Murray Sinclair Responds to People Who Want Indigenous People to Get Over It," Huffington Post, March 30, 2017, https://www.huffingtonpost.ca/2017/03/30/murray-sinclair-residential-schools_n_15708156.html.

examined above, Zoe Todd extends her analysis of the depths of inhumanity in the twenty-first century beyond the Mediterranean:

> These are residence times that Indigenous women like me must heed. Residence times of what Sharpe calls "the wake" of the Middle Passage (in its plural registers), which my ancestors did not survive or endure. But these are residence times I must honour, and I must take care to listen to those whose ancestors are intimately bound to the residence time of those atoms and energy, in those columns of water that bore and bear witness to the worst violations and impulses of the white supremacist/capitalist/colonial craton congealing thought and power in the world today.[63]

There are seismic shifts that appear to be re-forming cosmopolitanism into a moral and ethical mode for world citizens to engage with each other. Such shifts are illustrated by the #IdleNoMore and #BlackLivesMatter movements, which went global, and importantly with respect to more-than-humans, by the #FridaysforFuture youth climate action movement.

Terra Firma: Indigenous cosmopolitanism

In the fall of 2019, the Lheidli T'enneh First Nation held a potlatch—a spiritual and cultural ceremony integral to governance, sharing wealth and strengthening clans—for the first time in 73 years. In Canada, the potlatch had been banned for over half a century; indeed, gathering for a potlatch feast had been a criminal offence. Reclaiming such traditions is key to healing from the trauma that has persisted for centuries, since the first settlers arrived. Elder Monica Paul hopes the traditions will bring youth off the streets: "We need to bring them home ... we need to teach them our ceremonies to bring them back. ... They need to learn what they missed and start working with them to remember."[64]

A growing number of Indigenous youth are learning from the legacies of their ancestors. For example, Autumn Peltier is a teen from Wikwemikong First Nation (Manitoulin Island) of Ojibway/Odawa heritage. She lives on one of the largest freshwater lakes on the planet, Lake Huron, in Ontario, Canada. As a young warrior who speaks for the water, she has been an actively engaged citizen her entire life and has been nominated for the Children's International Peace Prize. At the age of 13, she spoke before the United Nations General Assembly on World Water Day, March 22, 2018, during which she explained a cornerstone of Indigenous cosmopolitanism: "Many people don't

---

63. Todd.
64. Betsy Trumpener, "Lheidli T'enneh First Nation to Hold First Potlatch in 73 Years," CBC News, November 2, 2019, https://www.cbc.ca/news/canada/british-columbia/once-banned-potlatch-now-makes-comeback-in-prince-george-1.5342833.

think water is alive or has a spirit. My people believe this to be true. Our water deserves to be treated as human with human rights. We need to acknowledge our waters with personhood so we can protect our waters."[65] Autumn asked the U.N. delegates: "With what Mother Earth is going through right now, imagine that in 10 years."[66] She pointed out that several Indigenous communities in Canada near her own community do not have potable water, as is the case from coast to coast to coast for many Indigenous communities across Canada. As one elder explains, "They didn't put in roads, housing or infrastructure because they thought we were going to die out … they never thought we would still be here. The fact that we are is a testimony to our resilience and our strength as a people."[67]

Indigenous peoples around the globe have knowledge forms and ways of being that have been silenced by the epistemological and ontological hegemony that underpins Euro-cosmopolitanism, and also the hate that is obscured by dominant Eurocentric narratives about the worldly citizen, the cosmopolitan. Quoting Sylvia Wynter, Métis scholar Zoe Todd describes the impact of the colonial gaze for humans and more-than-humans:

> [I]t was to be the peoples of Black African descent who would be constructed as the ultimate referent of the "racially inferior" Human Other, with the range of other colonized dark-skinned peoples, all classified as "natives," now being assimilated to its category—all of these as the ostensible embodiment of the non-evolved backward Others—if to varying degrees and, as such, the negation of the generic "normal humanness," ostensibly expressed by and embodied in the peoples of the West.

Todd goes on to say:

> Through the reformation of the earth as a "vile and base matter," as Wynter (2003: 267) points out, white supremacy and imperialism and colonialism and capital try to imbue all of Life and NonLife (Povinelli 2016) [6] with these flimsy euro-western notions of hierarchy and extraction. White supremacy, capitalism, colonialism all work to render the rocks, cliffs, trenches, continents, tectonic plates as things that can be acted upon, claimed, owned, extruded, mined, fracked, and burnt—rather than as beings that act mutually upon us and

---

65. Melissa Kent, "Canadian Teen Tells UN 'Warrior Up' to Protect Water," CBC News, March 22, 2018, https://www.cbc.ca/news/canada/autumn-peltier-un-water-activist-united-nations-1.4584871.
66. Kent.
67. Jane Gerster and Krista Hessey, "Why Some First Nations Still Don't Have Clean Drinking Water—Despite Trudeau's Promise," Global News, September 28, 2019, https://globalnews.ca/news/5887716/first-nations-boil-water-advisories/.

everything around us, reciprocally stretching through folds of space and time to carve out the very realities that manifest this existence (or existences).[68]

The challenge is to learn from but not to appropriate the insights, values and ways of being of Indigenous peoples who have long been labeled "pre-civilized."

Indigenous political processes, legal systems and cultural legacies are increasingly influential, resituating relationality and connectedness among humans and more-than-humans and emphasizing our responsibilities to each other as humans and to the more-than-humans. For example, there is a growing literature on "Earth jurisprudence" that "places the ecological integrity of Earth at its heart," and on "wild law," which promotes "an emotional and empathic relationship with the rest of the natural world and a perception of interdependence."[69] The legal significance of Indigenous peoples' persistence is epitomized by the Maoris' more than 140 years of resistance and resurgence in Aotearoa (New Zealand) and their fight to have the rights of the third largest river in their homeland recognized as those of an ancestor. Gerrard Albert, the lead negotiator for the Whanganui *iwi* ("people"), states:

> We have fought to find an approximation in law so that all others can understand that from our perspective treating the river as a living entity is the correct way to approach it, as in indivisible whole, instead of the traditional model for the last 100 years of treating it from a perspective of ownership and management.[70]

The river, Te Awa Tupua, has its own legal identity, with all the corresponding rights, duties and liabilities of a legal person, and with two guardians appointed to act on behalf of the river. The idea of belonging is expanded to include more-than-humans. For example, "Albert said all Māori tribes regarded themselves as part of the universe, at one with and equal to the mountains, the rivers and the seas. ... 'that is not an anti-development, or anti-economic use of the river but to begin with the view that it is a living being, and then consider its future from that central belief.'"[71]

The shift toward Indigenous cosmopolitanism is challenging the status quo. In Brazil, for example, "deforestation in indigenous reserves demarcated in the Amazon increased 32 percent from August 2016 to July 2017, compared to the previous period, while

---

68. Todd.

69. Helena R. Howe, "Making Wild Law Work: The Role of 'Connection with Nature' and Education in Developing an Ecocentric Property Law," *Journal of Environmental Law* 29, no. 1 (March 2017): 19, https://academic.oup.com/jel/article/29/1/19/2585049.

70. Eleanor Ainge Roy, "New Zealand River Granted Same Legal Rights as Human Beings," *The Guardian*, March 16, 2017, https://www.theguardian.com/world/2017/mar/16/new-zealand-river-granted-same-legal-rights-as-human-being.

71. Roy.

throughout the Amazon region, made up of nine states, there was a 16 percent reduction,"[72] and the battle has been intensifying under President Bolsonaro. In August 2019 the National Space Research Institute in Brazil "estimated that 3,553 fires were burning on 148 Indigenous territories,"[73] with over 97% of their territories situated in the Amazon rainforest, the lungs of the world. As the original eco-stewards of their homelands over millennia, Indigenous peoples worldwide continue to face violent responses as they fulfill their civic responsibilities with more-than-humans. Land defenders face strong state-based resistance across Canada—from Elsipogtog First Nation in New Brunswick, who were confronted by heavily armed police when they peacefully protested fracking by a Texas-based corporation in 2013, to the arrests of members of the Unist'ot'en camp, who have long been protesting fossil-fuel pipeline construction through the Wet'suwet'en First Nation's unceded territory in northern British Columbia, leading to a national solidarity movement that went global in early 2020. On February 10, 2020, it was reported that a helicopter delivered RCMP officers and snowmobiles behind the Unist'ot'en gate. They watched from a hill overlooking the camp as more officers approached from the road. Surrounded on all sides, Dr. Karla Tait, who works in the healing center, her mother, her aunt and four supporters stood near the barrier, praying and drumming. Tait was the third to be arrested. "Two officers came around me and held my arms to try to prevent me from drumming," she said. They continued to sing even as they were being loaded into the police van.

> "The violence of Canada and the emptiness of its commitments to us as Indigenous people were laid bare in their actions, and their forcible removal of us in the midst of ceremony," Tait said. "The events we experienced leading up to February 10 are another culmination of the efforts of Canada to discredit and criminalize us for simply existing on our land as we always have."[74]

Given the growing conflicts between Indigenous land protectors and water warriors and state police and military forces worldwide, from Hawaii to Peru to the Congo, the recommendations of a United Nations panel of climate-change science experts are timely, and their voices need to be amplified.

---

72. Mario Osava, "Indigenous People, Guardians of Threatened Forests in Brazil," Inter Press Service, December 4, 2017, http://www.ipsnews.net/2017/12/indigenous-people-guardians-threatened-forests-brazil/.

73. Leo Correa, Mario Lobao and Anna Jean Kaiser, "Brazilian Indigenous People Speak Out as Amazon Fires Rage," PBS News Hour, August 29, 2019, https://www.pbs.org/newshour/world/brazilian-indigenous-people-speak-out-as-amazon-fires-rage.

74. Alleen Brown and Amber Bracken, "No Surrender: After Police Defend a Gas Pipeline over Indigenous Rights, Protesters Shut Down Railways across Canada," The Intercept, February 23, 2020, https://theintercept.com/2020/02/23/wetsuweten-protest-coastal-gaslink-pipeline/.

On August 8, 2019, the Intergovernmental Panel on Climate Change (IPCC) issued a "Special Report on Climate Change and Land," which cited, for the first time, strong land rights for Indigenous peoples and local communities as a solution to the climate crisis. Indigenous leaders and communities from 42 countries issued a response to the IPCC report, stating:

> Finally, the world's top scientists recognize what we have always known. We—Indigenous Peoples and local communities—play a critical role in stewarding and safeguarding the world's lands and forests. For the first time, the Intergovernmental Panel on Climate Change (IPCC) report released today recognizes that strengthening our rights is a critical solution to the climate crisis.[75]

Levi Sucre Romero is a leader of the Bribri, one of Costa Rica's largest Indigenous groups. He coordinates the Executive Commission of the Mesoamerican Alliance of Peoples and Forests (AMPB), one of the most important land-rights platforms for Indigenous communities in Central America and Mexico, representing more than 50,000 people who live in densely forested lands. Romero states that Indigenous peoples offer a different vision: "We put at the disposal of humanity our traditional knowledge and experience of how to coexist with nature—to meet the needs of both people and planet."[76] In the modern era, Indigenous peoples have been speaking up for the environment, with deep concern, for generations: "For years, Romero and other indigenous leaders have been urging the rest of the world to adopt a more indigenous-inspired way of coexisting with nature, including leaving habitats intact, harvesting plants and animals at sustainable levels and acknowledging and respecting the connection between human and planetary health."[77]

Erin Mordecai, a biologist at Stanford University, identifies the crucial role that Indigenous peoples play as ecological stewards: "By protecting indigenous landscapes, you're protecting not only those people and their way of life, but also preventing really rapid transformation of landscapes," notably adding that such "rapid transformation has huge-scale cultural and environmental consequences, but also disease-transmission

---

75. Rights and Resources Initiative, "UN IPCC Report Recognizes Indigenous and Community Land Rights as Vital to Slowing Climate Crisis," YubaNet, August 8, 2019, https://yubanet.com/world/un-ipcc-report-recognizes-indigenous-and-community-land-rights-as-vital-to-slowing-climate-crisis/.

76. Rights and Resources Initiative.

77. Rachel Nuwer, "The Indigenous Communities That Predicted Covid-19," BBC, May 4, 2020, http://www.bbc.com/travel/story/20200503-the-indigenous-communities-that-predicted-covid-19.

consequences."[78] Mary Menton, a research fellow in environmental justice at the University of Sussex, astutely links the ecological threat with racism, arguing that

> indigenous people face additional threats because of racism and "perceptions that they're second-class citizens." Often, this is a problem promoted from the top down. For instance, Brazil's president, Jair Bolsonaro, recently said, for example, that "Indians are evolving" to become "increasingly human, like us." Indigenous people, in other words, are "facing threats both in terms of actual physical conflicts over land, but also cultural threats and attacks over their right to exist."[79]

Romero "hopes that people will be more receptive to the knowledge that he and other indigenous leaders have to offer, and that humanity will begin to re-evaluate its relationship with nature."[80]

In this context of overlapping international crises—a global climate crisis, a spike in human rights deficits illustrated by the human rights violations of refugees, and the global COVID-19 pandemic—cosmopolitanism may gain further traction. Offering her observations on "Cosmopolitanism, Nationalism, and Closed Borders in the Covid-19 Era", Gillian Brock advises that

> what the cosmopolitans get right is that on so many issues, we are interdependent, our fates intertwined, and that sustained, cooperative action is necessary to address our shared problems effectively. We need the institutional structures that can help us address our common problems, coordinate efforts and share associated responsibilities in ways that are sensitive to many different features, such as our varying capacities to assist. And to help in making all of this happen we need to nurture not just an awareness that we sink or swim together, but a sense of compassion and empathy for our fellow human beings who may be suffering in near and faraway places.[81]

Yenny Vega Cardenas, president of the International Observatory on the Rights of Nature, cautions: "We've become aware of the weaknesses of our system. ... And if we don't change now, when? We cannot wait any longer."[82] More specifically, in what ways does *Indigenous* cosmopolitanism provide insight and direction that deepens our humanity, extends our temporal and spatial zone of "response-ability" and resets our eco-justice compass to include more-than-humans?

---

78. Nuwer.
79. Nuwer.
80. Nuwer.
81. Gillian Brock, "Cosmopolitanism, Nationalism and Closed Borders in the Covid-19 Era," *fifteeneightyfour* (blog), Cambridge University Press, June 1, 2020, http://www.cambridgeblog.org/2020/06/cosmopolitanism-nationalism-and-closed-borders-in-the-covid-19-era/.
82. Kestler-D'Amours.

Terabyte: the North Star as a compass point during the climate crisis

Fabián Flores Silva asks a timely and inspiring question: "Therefore, by paraphrasing Latour, is it possible to find cosmopolitan theories whose politics recognise at least more than one entity as a part of its cosmos, and whose cosmos recognises that politics as not being exclusively human?"[83] Marina Tyquiengco presents the Alaskan Native Heritage Center as a site of cosmopolitanism, based on "its stated purpose and authorship," and as a site of "cosmopolitan curiosity":

> Many sources point to the seeming dichotomy between indigeneity as highly localized and spatially bounded, and cosmopolitanism, at its roots meaning citizen of the cosmos who is somehow simultaneously above the cosmos. Scholar Elizabeth Povinelli, who has written extensively on Indigenous issues, asks succinctly, "Are indigeneity and cosmopolitanism two different ways of being a citizen of the earth?"[84]

Internationally renowned Anishinaabe scholar John Borrows is a member of the Chippewa of the Nawash First Nation in Ontario. He holds a Canada Research Chair in Indigenous Law and teaches at the University of Victoria in British Columbia, a campus that offers the world's first Indigenous law degree. Borrows explains that "Indigenous law is the way that people organize their relationships in patterns," and "those patterns flow from views of the Earth, from stories and songs—and are applied to dispute resolution and regulation."[85] He says that "Indigenous peoples' relationships with lands and resources stems [sic] from their legal traditions."[86] In a more recent work, *Canada's Indigenous Constitution*, Borrows clarifies how

> Indigenous peoples find and develop law from observations of the physical world around them, making analogies drawn from the behaviours of watersheds, rivers, mountains, valleys, meadows or shorelines to guide legal actions. As such, these laws may be regarded as literally being written on the Earth. ... For many

---

83. Fabián Flores Silva, "Cosmopolitanism, Cosmopolitics and Indigenous Peoples: Elements for a Possible Alliance" (blog), *Alternautas*, 2017, http://www.alternautas.net/blog/2017/2/6/cosmopolitanism-cosmopolitics-and-indigenous-peoples-elements-for-a-possible-alliance.

84. Marina Tyquiengco, "Indigenous Cosmopolitanism: The Alaska Native Heritage Center," *Lateral* 7, no. 2 (Fall 2018), https://csalateral.org/issue/7-2/indigenous-cosmopolitanism-alaska-native-heritage-center-tyquiengco/.

85. David P. Ball, "University of Victoria to Offer World's First Indigenous Law Degree," *Toronto Star*, September 25, 2018, https://www.thestar.com/vancouver/2018/09/25/university-of-victoria-to-offer-worlds-first-indigenous-law-degree.html.

86. John Borrows, "Indigenous Legal Traditions in Canada," *Washington Journal of Law and Policy* 19 (January 2005); 206, https://openscholarship.wustl.edu/cgi/viewcontent.cgi?article=1380&context=law_journal_law_policy.

Indigenous people, the casebook for learning natural law requires an intimate knowledge of how to read the world.[87]

The challenge lies in restoring equilibrium among humans and more-than-humans, which depends on an epistemological and ontological seismic shift. The epistemic silencing of Indigenous peoples has impacted us all as humans and has harmed Nature profoundly and, perhaps, irreversibly. U.N. General Assembly president María Fernanda Espinosa Garcés of Ecuador has warned: "We are the last generation that can prevent irreparable damage to our planet."[88] The field of postcolonial studies has been

> calling for a critical cosmopolitanism that unveils the reliance of liberal-managerial forms of cosmopolitanism on a history of coloniality (Mignolo 723), [and] such moves invert the presumed civilizational debt the colonized owe to European "modernity" and situate decolonial praxis as a site of worldmaking ... any vision of a multispecies planetary ethic would have to navigate the post-Enlightenment division of "species" and "nation" such that solidarity and belonging constitute an ethical orientation across *both* national borders and the taxonomic lines that separate humanity from multispecies lifeworlds.[89]

Inuit have long navigated distinctive temporal and spatial realities on Earth, and their knowledge systems are helping them broach new realities with a spirit of innovation, recognition of the interconnectedness of all life, and an appreciation for interdependence that underpins the ongoing legacy of Arctic peoples, who have been circumpolar eco-stewards since time immemorial. What can we learn from Inuit to inform and inspire "cosmopolitanism" in ways that deepen and extend belonging and citizenship among humans, and in regard to more-than-humans?

The homelands of Inuit in Canada's eastern Arctic are changing rapidly, given the climate crisis, with evident changes ranging from wildly fluctuating weather patterns to rising sea levels, thinning sea ice and unprecedented coastal erosion due to storm surges. Inuit confront food insecurity alongside ongoing housing and health crises and other policy challenges that the federal government, based in southern Canada, continues to ignore. Inuit are innovative and resilient, drawing upon *Inuit qauijimajatuqangit* (pronounced *khao-yee-muh-yah-tut-khang-geet*), or IQ, which represents an ever-evolving knowledge system, principles and ways of being that Inuit have developed over millennia.

The Government of Nunavut (GN) was created on April 1, 1999, following the Nunavut Land Claims Agreement signed in 1993, the largest such agreement in Canadian

---

87. John Borrows, *Canada's Indigenous Constitution* (Toronto: University of Toronto Press, 2011), 28–29.

88. United Nations, "Only 11 Years Left to Prevent Irreversible Damage from Climate Change, Speakers Warn During General Assembly High-Level Meeting," March 28, 2019, https://www.un.org/press/en/2019/ga12131.doc.htm.

89. Ahuja, 15.

history. From the outset, the GN has placed IQ as a pillar of government and governance, with the goal of creating a "made in Nunavut" public sector with IQ infused throughout policy systems and processes. Nunavut's Department of Environment created the Nunavut Climate Change Center (NC3) to "share and distribute climate change knowledge" and to offer information and insight into the relationship between IQ and climate change, illustrated in the following quotation from the NC3 website:

> Inuit Qaujimajatuqangit, the system of Inuit traditional knowledge and social values, is based on a long and close relationship with the land and environment. It gives us rich and detailed insight into climate change and adaptation, as well as context to help understand how climate change will impact Inuit culture, communities, and individuals.[90]

Figure 5.3. The IQ Adventure!

Alexander, The *Nanisiniq Inuit Qaujimajatuqangit* (The IQ Adventure!)

"Traditional knowledge" (TK), including "traditional ecological knowledge" (TEK), is too often misrepresented by non-Indigenous academics and policymakers alike as static, frozen in time; rather, TK/TEK is ever evolving. A useful definition is that "tradition is the dynamic enactment of values and forms (what folklorists refer to as expressive culture) by all human beings."[91] At a roundtable of Inuit elders, public officials and

---

90. Nunavut Climate Change Secretariat, "Climate Change IQ," Nunavut Climate Change Centre, n.d., https://www.climatechangenunavut.ca/en/knowledge/voices-land.

91. Tyquiengco.

community members came from across Nunavut to Acadia University in 2005 to reflect on the first five years of the Government of Nunavut and to share their research priorities. In the face of diverse urgent policy issues that merited attention, Inuit at the Nunavut@5 Policy Symposium agreed that the top priority was to connect Inuit youth with the legacy of their ancestors.

In partnership with the Government of Nunavut, and under the leadership of Inuk elder and former commissioner of Nunavut Dr. Piita (Peter) Irniq, along with a team of Inuit and non-Indigenous artists, filmmakers and other talented people, including university students, I co-developed an online resource called the Nanisiniq Inuit Qaujimajatuqangit or IQ Adventure website (fig. 5.3).[92] Among the diverse resources offered on the website is an interactive film that takes the user on a virtual voyage by ship that departs from Iqaluit, the capital of Nunavut, after exploring the Nunavut legislature.

The GN is an important starting place in trying to understand how Inuit are working to infuse Indigenous cosmopolitanism into policy processes. As a tour through the photographs on the Nanisiniq Inuit Qaujimajatuqangit website illustrates, the beautifully designed legislature positions the representatives from across the territory—elected without political parties—in a circle, reflecting the emphasis in IQ on consensus-based decision-making rather than adversarial politics. In the legislature, there are seats designated for Inuit elders, just as there are Inuit IQ coordinators within each of the government departments from whom public policy officials seek insight and counsel. As stated on the GN's website,

> From its start in 1999, our government has been guided by Inuit societal values. We continue to be guided by these principles as we address our challenges and step forward together towards a brighter future:
> - Inuuqatigiitsiarniq: Respecting others, relationships and caring for people.
> - Tunnganarniq: Fostering good spirits by being open, welcoming and inclusive.
> - Pijitsirniq: Serving and providing for family and/or community.
> - Aajiiqatigiinniq: Decision-making through discussion and consensus.
> - Pilimmaksarniq/Pijariuqsarniq: Development of skills through observation, mentoring, practice, and effort.
> - Piliriqatigiinniq/Ikajuqtigiinniq: Working together for a common cause.
> - Qanuqtuurniq: Being innovative and resourceful.[93]

How, if at all, might these values inform and reflect Indigenous cosmopolitanism? During an announcement of federal funding support for the creation of a National Inuit Climate Change Strategy on June 7, 2019, the national Inuit leader in Canada, Natan Obed, stated:

---

92. Nanisiniq Inuit Qaujimajatuqangit (website), www.inuitq.ca.
93. Nunavut, "Inuit Societal Values," https://www.gov.nu.ca/information/inuit-societal-values.

Inuit have a relationship with the environment that is steeped in meaning. It shapes our identity, values and world view. Our environment is a fundamental source of learning, memories, knowledge and wisdom. The National Inuit Climate Change Strategy is a response to an unprecedented global climate crisis. It is a hopeful, forward-looking plan in the face of potentially catastrophic change that welcomes unique partnerships that are respectful of Inuit rights and knowledge.[94]

Inuit were early adopters of new media technologies, connecting with the world and, importantly, using social media and other digital resources to amplify their voices. Throughout the virtual voyage on the Nanisiniq Inuit Qaujimajatuqangit website (see Figure 5.3), the user can draw upon the insights and wisdom of Inuk elder Piita (Peter) Irniq. He acts as a personal guide throughout the journey, guiding users to listen to and learn from Inuit about environmental stewardship, restorative justice, sustainable communities and more. Importantly, as users learn about IQ from Inuit in Inuktitut and/or in English, opportunities arise throughout the virtual voyage for them to demonstrate how to apply ancient IQ knowledge forms, values and approaches to contemporary policy issues, including environmental stewardship. Inuit elders and wisdom keepers such as Piita Irniq have been sharing their wisdom with the world about how their epistemological and ontological frameworks have helped Inuit live harmoniously with each other and with the land, in the harshest conditions on the planet. Inuk leader and climate activist Sheila Watt-Cloutier, a 2007 Nobel Peace Prize nominee and author of the acclaimed 2018 book *The Right to be Cold*, states:

Inuit and Indigenous peoples provided life-saving guidance to early European visitors unfamiliar with the severe conditions of this land, which they ignored at their peril. The whole planet benefits from a frozen Arctic and Inuit still have much to teach the world about the vital importance of Arctic ice, not only to our culture, but to the health of the rest of the planet.[95]

Siri Veland elaborates on the kind of transformation that is needed in environmental policy, asserting that we must "consider our relations with each other and with Earth systems under rapid change":[96]

---

94. Canada, Department of Environment and Climate Change, "Government of Canada Supports Inuit-Led Climate Change Strategy," news release, June 7, 2019, https://www.canada.ca/en/environment-climate-change/news/2019/06/government-of-canada-supports-inuit-led-climate-change-strategy.html.

95. Sheila Watt-Cloutier, "It's Time to Listen to Inuit on Climate Change," *Canadian Geographic*, November 15, 2018, https://www.canadiangeographic.ca/article/its-time-listen-inuit-climate-change.

96. Siri Veland, "Transcending Ontological Schisms in Relationship with Earth, Water, Air, and Ice," *Weather, Climate, and Society* 9, no. 3 (2017): 607.

Drawing on "concepts of emergence, connectivity and space-time relationality," this "situated, non-relativist response to people–landscape connections" (Wilcock et al. 2013, p. 573) considers interactions with dynamic earth processes as moments of possible convergence across knowledge systems. In risk research, it has long been recognized that "environmental" problems are really social problems that concern the distribution of goods between social groups (Hewitt 2014, 1995). Similar recognition in environmental policy says we are not really managing Earth systems, but rather human relationships. ... Veland and Lynch (2017) agree, "we cannot renew our relationship with nature without renewing our relationship with each other ... the 'natural' world is created by, through and with the same human concepts, ideas and emotions that create the 'social.'"[97]

Nunavummuit have worked to infuse Inuit Qaujimajatuqangit into the government and governance processes, including in the field of environmental policymaking. Within the territorial government and at the local community level, "mobilizing IQ in management decision making requires that Inuit be empowered at the local level to make decisions that reflect their experiential knowledge of the resource."[98] Frank Tester and Peter Irniq clarify what is on the line:

> The promotion of IQ and a cosmology that melds the distinction between human and other living forms and that requires special (i.e. non-Western) consideration of other living and non-living forms in the course of human activity constitutes a social cost for those interested in conventional resource development. Treating other living forms in this way is an impediment to development within the logic of Western capitalist economies. Operating with a seamless definition of IQ clearly involves struggle and resistance.[99]

From an international perspective, Nunavut remains a site of policy innovation and the incorporation of IQ into decision-making processes in ways that reflect Indigenous cosmopolitanism, given the recognition that "[o]ntological separations made between earth, water, air, and ice can surreptitiously produce high-risk outcomes in environmental policy processes."[100]

---

97. Veland, 616.

98. Erin Keenan, Lucia M. Fanning and Chris Miley, "Mobilizing Inuit Qaujimajatuqangit in Narwhal Management Through Community Empowerment: A Case Study in Naujaat, Nunavut," Free Library, March 1, 2018, https://www.thefreelibrary.com/Mobilizing+Inuit+Qaujimajatuqangit+in+Narwhal+Management+through....-a0535418557.

99. Frank Tester and Peter Irniq, "Inuit Qaujimajatuqangit: Social History, Politics and the Practice of Resistance," *Arctic* 61 (2009): 57, http://caid.ca/Arctic612008.pdf.

100. Veland, 607.

Conclusion: decolonizing ourselves

Over several centuries, the ancient Greeks developed an elaborate cosmology. Concepts such as Hellenic cosmopolitanism continue to inspire undergraduate students in liberal arts universities and inform political and policy dialogues. Over millennia, Inuit have been developing their own elaborate cosmology, as Indigenous peoples around the world have been doing in their homelands. As in the United States and Australia, education systems at all levels in Canada have sought to assimilate Indigenous peoples, uprooted them from their homelands, appropriated or marginalized their knowledge forms, and sought to silence their languages, cultures and ways of being. In Canada, efforts are underway to respond to the national TRC's Calls to Action, which include working to decolonize education systems, including post-secondary education. Call to Action 62 emphasizes the imperative to "educate teachers on how to integrate Indigenous knowledge and teaching methods into the classroom."[101] Academic professional associations, such as the Canadian Political Science Association (CPSA), have asserted that "[u]npacking assumptions that ignored, stereotyped and demonized Indigenous peoples in the development of the Canadian state and its policies will allow scholars to consider critical materials challenging the canon, and materials that envision new political possibilities through engagement with Indigenous scholarship, perspectives and content resources."[102]

The focus in Canada in 2021 is on the need for settler Canadians to recognize the ugly truths about Canada's persistent colonialism—before reconciliation can begin vis-à-vis Indigenous peoples. The movement out of the default mode of colonialism is happening slowly among non-Indigenous Canadians. For example, despite the national TRC inquiry, which issued its final report in 2015 based on testimonies of residential "school" survivors and their families, a step toward recognition by settler Canadians of the horrors of Canada's residential "schools" occurred only in the spring of 2021, after the discovery of mass graves on the sites of former "schools" in British Columbia and elsewhere across North America.

The climate crisis provides a timely incentive to learn from Indigenous peoples, as James T. Gathii concludes:

> It is time we put an end to the epistemic silences in predominant climate change discourses, which erase and ignore the agency, knowledge, and experiences of

---

101. Truth and Reconciliation Commission of Canada, *Truth and Reconciliation Commission of Canada: Calls to Action* (Winnipeg: TRC, 2015), 7, https://ehprnh2mwo3.exactdn.com/wp-content/uploads/2021/01/Calls_to_Action_English2.pdf.

102. Canadian Political Science Association Reconciliation Committee, *Indigenous Content Syllabus Materials: A Resource for Political Science Instructors in Canada* (Ottawa: CPSA, 2018), 4, https://cpsa-acsp.ca/wp-content/uploads/2020/02/Indigenous-Content-Syllabus-Materials-November-27-2019.pdf.

non-Western, non-White peoples, and Indigenous communities. Effectively responding to the immense challenges posed by climate change requires a climate justice approach that centers the voices and experience of those most vulnerable.[103]

Indigenous cosmopolitanism provides an invaluable framework to begin to examine how to change our mindsets to advance human and ecological rights in the face of the climate crisis. In April 2021, the International Circumpolar Council (ICC) became the first Indigenous peoples' organization to hold observer status with the IPCC. ICC Canada vice-president (international) Lisa Koperqualuk states:

> Given the diverse impacts of climate change upon us and our region of the world, this is one example of how we have been bringing the Inuit voice to contribute to the findings of hundreds of scientists working in collaboration on the special reports of the IPCC. ... Observer Status will strengthen the Inuit voice in this climate forum and support greater access for Inuit input into the work of the IPCC. ICC has been working with the IPCC to ensure that proper consideration is given to Indigenous Knowledge in future assessments. ... We anticipate that having Observer Status will help us to build an understanding among climate scientists of the importance of the co-production of knowledge.[104]

Around the world, citizens of all ages from diverse walks of life are mobilizing together, based on their discontent with piecemeal public policy responses and corporate inaction to address the climate crisis and a range of sociocultural, political, economic and eco-justice issues. Persistent resistance to climate action is illustrated in the following quotation, revealing the ongoing intense lobbying faced by the Biden administration in the United States:

> a recent investigative report into ExxonMobil revealed that the fossil fuel giant has actively lobbied against any climate action, speaking weekly to influential senators, such as Democratic senator Joe Manchin, in an effort to drastically reduce the scope of Biden's plan to benefit the corporation and their shareholders. In an interview with an undercover reporter, Exxon lobbyist Keith McCoy describes their campaigns to subvert climate change actions. "Did we join some

---

103. James Gathii, "Without Centering Race, Identity, and Indigeneity, Climate Responses Miss the Mark," Wilson Center, September 30, 2020, https://www.wilsoncenter.org/article/without-centering-race-identity-and-indigeneity-climate-responses-miss-mark.

104. Inuit Circumpolar Council, "Ahead of Earth Day 2021, ICC Obtains Observer Status within the Intergovernmental Panel on Climate Change," April 21, 2021, https://www.inuitcircumpolar.com/news/ahead-of-earth-day-2021-icc-obtains-observer-status-within-the-intergovernmental-panel-on-climate-change-ipcc/.

of these 'shadow groups' to work against some of the early efforts on climate? Yes'".[105]

The above quotation reflects the challenge of unsettling the dominant modes of being and belonging in a globalized world. Given the existential threat that the climate crisis presents to humans and ecosystems, it is timely to revisit Diogenes' teachings about cosmopolitanism, and it is long overdue for settlers like myself to learn from Indigenous peoples, starting with how ancient, ever-evolving traditional knowledge underpin Indigenous cosmopolitanism. New research reveals the following relationship between a connection with Nature and reconciliation among humans:

> Researchers have found that those who feel more connected to nature tend to feel more connected to all of humanity. They hold that framing animals as similar to humans not only increases moral concern for other animals, but increases concern for other humans. And social dominance orientation, or one's preference for hierarchy among groups, accounts for the relationship between speciesism and ethnic prejudice. ... Given our current reality—that we live within a changing and destabilizing climate—it is important to move beyond our human-centric approach to addressing social issues.[106]

To address the climate crisis, we can learn from Indigenous leaders such as Inuk elder Piita Irniq, Nobel Prize nominee Sheila Watt-Cloutier, and water warrior Autumn Peltier, who remind us that reconciliation with Nature and with each other as humans are interconnected goals. Indigenous peoples are reaching out to the world in innovative ways. As sophisticated digital content producers and filmmakers, policy innovators and eco-stewards, Inuit and Indigenous peoples around the world offer the profound insights that we need to become contemporary cosmopolitan citizens facing an existential crisis. Indigenous cosmopolitanism can inform our individual and collective decolonizing journeys in ways that might help slow down the Countdown 2°C Clock. Just as we learn from ancient Greeks about cosmopolitanism, so too must we listen to and learn from Inuit, together with other Indigenous peoples around the world, who are drawing on the legacies of their ancestors to protect planet Earth in a time of crisis.

---

105. Amali Towe and Moriah Prescia, "Who Is Accountable When Climate Change Displaces Indigenous People?" Climate Refugees, July 9, 2021, https://www.climate-refugees.org/spotlight/2021/9/7 indigenousdisplacement.

106. Aleah Fontaine and Katherine B. Starzyk, "People Who Feel More Connected to the Natural World Are More Likely to Support Reconciliation," CityNews, August 22, 2021, https://www.halifaxtoday.ca/local-news/people-who-feel-more-connected-to-the-natural-world-are-more-likely-to-support-reconciliation-4240929.

Bibliography

Ahuja, Neel. "Species in a Planetary Frame: Eco-cosmopolitanism, Nationalism and *The Cove*." *Tamkang Review* 42, no. 2 (June 2012): 13–32.

Alexander, Cynthia J. The Nanisiniq Inuit Qaujimajatuqangit/The IQ Adventure! (website). 2019. www.inuitq.ca.

Amnesty International. "Explained: The Situation at Greece's Borders." March 5, 2020. https://www.amnesty.org/en/latest/news/2020/03/greece-turkey-refugees-explainer/.

Anaya, James. *Report of the Special Rapporteur on the Rights of Indigenous Peoples, James Anaya*. United Nations Human Rights Council. Geneva: United Nations General Assembly, 2014. https://www.ohchr.org/Documents/Issues/IPeoples/SR/A.HRC.27.52. Add.2-MissionCanada_AUV.pdf.

ANSA. "Deceased Migrants Found Carrying Report Cards, Soil from Home." Infomigrants, January 21, 2019. https://www.infomigrants.net/en/post/14626/deceased-migrants-found-carrying-report-cards-soil-from-home.

Association of University and Colleges in Canada (AUCC). March 2009. *Internationalization of the Curriculum*. https://www.massey.ac.nz/massey/fms/NCTL/VC%20symposium/curriculum-primer_e.pdf.

Bailey, Rob, and Emma Green. "Should Europe be Concerned about Climate Refugees?" Chatham House, May 23, 2016. https://www.chathamhouse.org/expert/comment/should-europe-be-concerned-about-climate-refugees#.

Ball, David P. "University of Victoria to Offer World's First Indigenous Law Degree." *Toronto Star*, September 25, 2018. https://www.thestar.com/vancouver/2018/09/25/university-of-victoria-to-offer-worlds-first-indigenous-law-degree.html.

BBC News. "Italy Migrant Rescue Boat: Captain Carola Rackete Freed." July 2, 2019. https://www.bbc.com/news/world-europe-48838438#:~:text=The%20German%20boat%20captain%20who,patrol%20boat%20at%20a%20quayside.

Benjamin, Chris. "Belong Forum: Senator Murray Sinclair Urges Canada to Think, Talk, Act Differently." Dalhousie University, September 6, 2018. https://www.dal.ca/news/2018/09/06/belong-forum--senator-murray-sinclair-urges-canada-to-think--tal.html.

Borrows, John. *Canada's Indigenous Constitution*. Toronto: University of Toronto Press, 2011.

———. "Indigenous Legal Traditions in Canada." *Washington Journal of Law and Policy* 19 (January 2005): 166–223. https://openscholarship.wustl.edu/cgi/viewcontent.cgi?article=1380&context=law_journal_law_policy.

Brock, Gillian. "Cosmopolitanism, Nationalism and Closed Borders in the Covid-19 Era." *fifteeneightyfour* (blog). Cambridge University Press, June 1, 2020. http://www.cambridgeblog.org/2020/06/cosmopolitanism-nationalism-and-closed-borders-in-the-covid-19-era/.

Brown, Alleen, and Amber Bracken. "No Surrender: After Police Defend a Gas Pipeline over Indigenous Rights, Protesters Shut Down Railways across Canada." The Intercept, February 23, 2020. https://theintercept.com/2020/02/23/wetsuweten-protest-coastal-gaslink-pipeline/.

Canada, Department of Environment and Climate Change. "Government of Canada Supports Inuit-Led Climate Change Strategy." News release, June 7, 2019. https://www.canada.ca/en/environment-climate-change/news/2019/06/government-of-canada-supports-inuit-led-climate-change-strategy.html.

Canadian Political Science Association Reconciliation Committee. *Indigenous Content Syllabus Materials: A Resource for Political Science Instructors in Canada*. Ottawa: CPSA,

2018. https://www.cpsa-acsp.ca/documents/committees/Indigenous%20Content%20 Syllabus%20Materials%20Sept%2024%202018[27].pdf .

Correa, Leo, Mario Lobao and Anna Jean Kaiser. "Brazilian Indigenous People Speak Out as Amazon Fires Rage." PBS News Hour, August 29, 2019. https://www.pbs.org/newshour/world/brazilian-indigenous-people-speak-out-as-amazon-fires-rage.

Desjardins, Jeff. "The Majority of the World's Population Lives in This Circle." Visual Capitalist, September 9, 2016. https://www.visualcapitalist.com/majority-worlds-population-lives-circle/.

Energy Mix. "'Climate Allows Society', Governor General Mary Simon Tells Official Ceremony." July 29, 2021. https://www.theenergymix.com/2021/07/29/climate-allows-society-governor-general-mary-simon-tells-official-ceremony/.

Euromed Rights. "Migration and Asylum." 2020. https://euromedrights.org/theme/migration-refugees-and-asylum-seekers/.

Farge, Emma. "MSF Denounces Seizure of Migrant Rescue Vessel in Italy." Reuters, July 5, 2021. https://www.reuters.com/world/europe/msf-denounces-seizure-migrant-rescue-vessel-italy-2021-07-05/.

Fine, Sean. "Chief Justice Says Canada Attempted 'Cultural Genocide' on Aboriginals." *Globe and Mail*, May 28, 2015. https://www.theglobeandmail.com/news/national/chief-justice-says-canada-attempted-cultural-genocide-on-aboriginals/article24688854/.

Fontaine, Aleah, and Katherine B. Starzyk. "People Who Feel More Connected to the Natural World Are More Likely to Support Reconciliation," City News, August 22, 2021. https://www.halifaxtoday.ca/local-news/people-who-feel-more-connected-to-the-natural-world-are-more-likely-to-support-reconciliation-4240929.

Forte, Maximilian C. "Introduction: Indigeneities and Cosmopolitanisms." In *Indigenous Cosmopolitans: Transnational and Transcultural Indigeneity in the Twenty-First Century*, edited by Maximilian C. Forte, 1–16. New York: Peter Lang, 2010.

Gathii, James. "Without Centering Race, Identity, and Indigeneity, Climate Responses Miss the Mark." Wilson Center, September 30, 2020. https://www.wilsoncenter.org/article/without-centering-race-identity-and-indigeneity-climate-responses-miss-mark.

Gerster, Jane, and Krista Hessey. "Why Some First Nations Still Don't Have Clean Drinking Water—Despite Trudeau's Promise." Global News, September 28, 2019. https://globalnews.ca/news/5887716/first-nations-boil-water-advisories/.

Goudcamp, Marc. "Ten Years of Fighting Racism and Fascism in Greece." Solidarity, October 31, 2019. https://www.solidarity.net.au/racism/ten-years-of-fighting-racism-and-fascism-in-greece/.

Heggie, Jon. "Preventing a Water Crisis in Greece." *National Geographic*, May 27, 2020. https://www.nationalgeographic.com/science/2020/05/partner-content-where-our-water-goes-greece/.

Howe, Helena R. "Making Wild Law Work: The Role of 'Connection with Nature' and Education in Developing an Ecocentric Property Law." *Journal of Environmental Law*. 29, no. 1 (March 2017): 19-45. https://academic.oup.com/jel/article/29/1/19/2585049.

Human Rights Watch. "Greece: Events of 2020." World Report 2021. https://www.hrw.org/europe/central-asia/greece.

Inuit Circumpolar Council. "Ahead of Earth Day 2021, ICC Obtains Observer Status within the Intergovernmental Panel on Climate Change." April 21, 2021. https://www.inuitcircumpolar.com/news/ahead-of-earth-day-2021-icc-obtains-observer-status-within-the-intergovernmental-panel-on-climate-change-ipcc/.

Keenan, Erin, Lucia M. Fanning and Chris Miley. "Mobilizing Inuit Qaujimajatuqangit in Narwhal Management Through Community Empowerment: A Case Study in Naujaat, Nunavut." Free Library, March 1, 2018. https://www.thefreelibrary.com/Mobilizing+Inuit+ Qaujimajatuqangit+in+Narwhal+Management+through...-a0535418557.

Kennedy, Merrit. "Indonesia Plans to Move Its Capital Out of Jakarta, a City That's Sinking." NPR, April 29, 2019. https://www.npr.org/2019/04/29/718234878/indonesia -plans-to-move-its-capital-out-of-jakarta-a-city-thats-sinking.

Kent, Melissaa. "Canadian Teen Tells UN 'Warrior Up' to Protect Water." CBC News, March 22, 2018. https://www.cbc.ca/news/canada/autumn-peltier-un-water-activist-united-nations -1.4584871.

Kerpius, Pamela. Migrants of the Mediterranean (website). 2020. http://www.migrantsoft hemed.com/.

Kesler-D'Amours, Jillian. "This River in Canada Is Now a 'Legal Person.'" Al Jazeera, April 3, 2021.https://www.aljazeera.com/news/2021/4/3/this-river-in-canada-now-legal-person.

Kleingeld, Pauline, and Eric Brown. "Cosmopolitanism." *Stanford Encyclopedia of Philosophy.* 2019. https://plato.stanford.edu/entries/cosmopolitanism/.

Lewis, Janet. "In the Room with Climate Anxiety." *Psychiatric Times* 35, no. 11 (November 2018). https://www.psychiatrictimes.com/view/room-climate-anxiety.

Matthews, H. Damon, Glen Peters, Myles Allen and Piers Forster. "The Climate Clock: Counting Down to 1.5°C." The Conversation, December 5, 2018. https://theconversation. com/the-climate-clock-counting-down-to-1-5-107498.

McDougall, Dan. "'Ecological Grief': Greenland Residents Traumatised by Climate Emergency." *The Guardian*, August 12, 2019. https://www.theguardian.com/world/2019/ aug/12/greenland-residents-traumatised-by-climate-emergency.

Meany, Paul. "The Stoic Origins of Cosmopolitanism: An Idea More Important Now Than Ever Before." Medium. Accessed September 18, 2018. https://medium.com/@meanyp/the-stoic-origins-of-cosmopolitanism-25662d179311.

Murphy, Michael. "Cosmopolitanism." Global Social Theory, 2014. https://globalsocial theory.org/concepts/cosmopolitanism/.

Nanisiniq Inuit Qaujimajatuqangit (website). www.inuitq.ca.

Nunavut. "Inuit Societal Values." https://www.gov.nu.ca/information/inuit-societal-values.

Nunavut Climate Change Secretariat. "Climate Change IQ." Nunavut Climate Change Centre. https://www.climatechangenunavut.ca/en/knowledge/voices-land.

Nuwer, Rachel. "The Indigenous Communities that Predicted Covid-19." BBC, May 4, 2020. http://www.bbc.com/travel/story/20200503-the-indigenous-communities-that-predicted-covid-19.

Osava, Mario. "Indigenous People, Guardians of Threatened Forests in Brazil." Inter Press Service, December 4, 2017. http://www.ipsnews.net/2017/12/indigenous-people-guardians-threatened-forests-brazil/.

Pantaleone, Wladimiro, and Gavin Jones. "Italy's Salvini Sent to Trial on Migrant Kidnapping Charge." Reuters, April 17, 2021. https://www.reuters.com/world/europe/ italys-salvini-sent-trial-migrant-kidnapping-charge-2021-04-17/.

Planelles, Manuel. "Mediterranean Is Warming Up Faster Than the Rest of the Planet, Report Warns." *El País*, October 11, 2019. https://english.elpais.com/elpais/2019/10/ 10/inenglish/1570692096_073306.html.

Podesta, John. "The Climate Crisis, Migration, and Refugees." Brookings Institute, July 25, 2019. https://www.brookings.edu/research/the-climate-crisis-migration-and-refugees/.

Prestwich, Emma. "Murray Sinclair Responds to People Who Want Indigenous People to Get Over It." Huffington Post, March 30, 2017. https://www.huffingtonpost.ca/2017/03/30/murray-sinclair-residential-schools_n_15708156.html.

Raygorodetsky, Gleb. "Why Traditional Knowledge Holds the Key to Climate Change." United Nations University, December 13, 2011. https://unu.edu/publications/articles/why-traditional-knowledge-holds-the-key-to-climate-change.html.

Rights and Resources Initiative. "UN IPCC Report Recognizes Indigenous and Community Land Rights as Vital to Slowing Climate Crisis." Yubanet, August 8, 2019. https://yubanet.com/world/un-ipcc-report-recognizes-indigenous-and-community-land-rights-as-vital-to-slowing-climate-crisis/.

Roy, Eleanor Ainge. "New Zealand River Granted Same Legal Rights as Human Beings." *The Guardian*, March 16, 2017. https://www.theguardian.com/world/2017/mar/16/new-zealand-river-granted-same-legal-rights-as-human-being.

Santos, Juan Manuel. "Colombia's Former President Says COVID-19 Shows the Importance of Listening to Indigenous Peoples on How We Treat the Planet." World Economic Forum, May 7, 2020. https://www.weforum.org/agenda/2020/05/juan-manuel-santos-colombia-indigenous-peoples-coronavirus-pandemic-climate-change-environment-nature/.

Silva, Fabián Flores. "Cosmopolitanism, Cosmopolitics and Indigenous Peoples: Elements for a Possible Alliance" (blog). *Alternautus*, 2017. http://www.alternautas.net/blog/2017/2/6/cosmopolitanism-cosmopolitics-and-indigenous-peoples-elements-for-a-possible-alliance.

Slimani, Leïla. "Europe Has Turned Its Back on the Mediterranean—But There Is Still Hope." *The Guardian*, March 2, 2020. https://www.bing.com/profile/history?form=edgehs.

Smith, Helena. "The Next Decade Will Be All about Heat: Can Athens Head Off the Climate Crisis?" *The Guardian*, May 10, 2021. https://www.theguardian.com/world/2021/may/10/heat-athens-climate-crisis-mayor.

Spratt, David. "Climate Emergency Public Statement Key Messages." Climate Emergency Declaration, June 20, 2016. https://climateemergencydeclaration.org/media/#keymessages.

St. Francis Xavier University. "Education, Respect for Each Other, Keys to Reconciliation, Senator Murray Sinclair Says in Powerful Keynote at StFX." November 8, 2016. https://www.stfx.ca/about/news/senator-murray-sinclair-delivers-powerful-message.

Tester, Frank, and Peter Irniq. "Inuit Qaujimajatuqangit: Social History, Politics and the Practice of Resistance." *Arctic* 61 (2009): 48–61. http://caid.ca/Arctic612008.pdf.

Todd, Zoe. "On Time." *Speculative Fish-ctions* (blog), November 7, 2018. https://zoestodd.com/2018/11/07/on-time/.

Tondo, Lorenzo. "Captain Who Rescued 42 Migrants: I'd Do It Again Despite Jail Threat." *The Guardian*, July 5, 2019. https://www.theguardian.com/world/2019/jul/05/captain-who-rescued-42-migrants-id-do-it-again-despite-jail-threat.

Towe, Amali, and Moriah Prescia. "Who Is Accountable When Climate Change Displaces Indigenous People?" Climate Refugees, July 9, 2021. https://www.climate-refugees.org/spotlight/2021/9/7indigenousdisplacement.

Tramountanis, Angelo. "Addressing the Protection Gap in Greece." ODI [Overseas Development Institute], July 21, 2021. https://odi.org/en/insights/addressing-the-protection-gap-in-greece/.

Troian, Martha. "20 Years Since Royal Commission on Aboriginal Peoples, Still Waiting for Change." CBC News, March 3, 2016. https://www.cbc.ca/news/indigenous/20-year-anniversary-of-rcap-report-1.3469759.

Trumpener, Betsy. "Lheidli T'enneh First Nation to Hold First Potlatch in 73 Years." CBC News, November 2, 2019. https://www.cbc.ca/news/canada/british-columbia/once-banned-potlatch-now-makes-comeback-in-prince-george-1.5342833.

Truth and Reconciliation Commission of Canada. *Truth and Reconciliation Commission of Canada: Calls to Action*. Winnipeg: TRC, 2015. https://ehprnh2mwo3.exactdn.com/wp-content/uploads/2021/01/Calls_to_Action_English2.pdf.

Tyquiengco, Marina. "Indigenous Cosmopolitanism: The Native Alaskan Heritage Center." *Lateral* 7, no. 2 (Fall 2018). https://csalateral.org/issue/7-2/indigenous-cosmopolitanism-alaska-native-heritage-center-tyquiengco/.

United Nations. "Only 11 Years Left to Prevent Irreversible Damage from Climate Change, Speakers Warn During General Assembly High-Level Meeting." March 28, 2019. https://www.un.org/press/en/2019/ga12131.doc.htm.

United Nations, Department of Economic and Social Affairs. "Indigenous Peoples." n.d. https://www.un.org/development/desa/indigenouspeoples/mandated-areas1/environment.html.

United Nations International Day of the World's Indigenous Peoples (website). August 9, 2021. https://www.un.org/en/observances/indigenous-day.

University of Calgary. "Reconcile Yourself with the Earth." UCalgary News, November 17, 2021. https://ucalgary.ca/news/reconcile-earth.

Veland, Siri. "Transcending Ontological Schisms in Relationship with Earth, Water, Air, and Ice." *Weather, Climate, and Society* 9, no. 3 (2017): 607–19.

Walker, Kira. "Immobility: The Neglected Flipside of the Climate Displacement Crisis." The New Humanitarian, April 26, 2021. https://www.thenewhumanitarian.org/analysis/2021/4/26/the-climate-displacement-crisis-has-a-neglected-flipside.

Ward, Shelby E. "Decolonizing the Cosmopolitan Geospatial Imaginary of the Anthropocene: Beyond Collapsed and Exclusionary Politics of Climate Change." *Pivot* 7, no. 1 (2019): 139–68.

Washington, Hayden, and P. R. Ehrlich. "Human Dependence on Nature: How to Help Solve the Environmental Crisis." May 2013. doi: 10.4324/9780203095560; https://www.researchgate.net/publication/287322965_Human_Dependence_on_Nature_How_to_Help_Solve_the_Environmental_Crisis.

Watt-Cloutier, Sheila. "It's Time to Listen to Inuit on Climate Change." *Canadian Geographic*, November 15, 2018. https://www.canadiangeographic.ca/article/its-time-listen-inuit-climate-change.

Wentworth, Adam. "Climate and Hunger Solutions Are on Terra Firma, Says UN." ClimateAction, August 15, 2018. http://www.climateaction.org/news/climate-and-hunger-solutions-are-on-terra-firma-says-un.

Chapter 6

Common Divine Healing Themes in Ancient Greek and Traditional Zulu Culture

Stephen Edwards

University of Zululand, South Africa

Abstract

This chapter is based on a meeting of an Australian shaman and Zulu divine healer as organized by the author. The approach may be termed memorial and reflective. The chapter explores some common themes in divine healing in traditional Zulu and classical Greek culture. Themes include indigenous knowledge, ancestral and divine consciousness, truth, harmony, ecology, transformation of the psyche and energy healing. The chapter calls for further study into divine healing, as well as the transformational effects of the legacies of Ancient Greece on the consciousness of researchers, teachers and students.

Keywords: Indigenous Knowledge, South Africa, Divine Healing, Shaman, Spirituality, Ancestral Consciousness, Ancient Greek, Culture, truth, harmony, ecology, transformation of the psyche, energy healing.

***

Introduction: common themes in divine healing

Accompanied by an Australian shaman and a local clinical psychologist, I once visited a traditional Zulu divine healer (*isangoma*) whom I had known for some 20 years. At the University of Zululand, colleagues and I had been discussing African, Asian and Australian forms of Indigenous and shamanic energy healing, with special reference to *umbilini*, when we were invited by the healer, Mr. M., to continue our discussions at his home (*umuzi*) near the small Zululand village of Mthunzini. The atmosphere in the hut brought back many memories of the *isangoma* who had trained Mr. M., with whom I had shared many experiences.

Mrs. M., who had passed on 10 years previously, was a typical example of an *isangoma,* or Zulu diviner. She had undergone a spiritual, cultural and religious conversion experience after receiving an ancestral call to become a divine healer, undergoing a creative illness (*ukuthwasa*), and receiving intensive instruction and supervision from a qualified diviner. Practicing in the community, she had earned widespread respect and recognition as a medium with the ancestral shades (*amadlozi*) and the original being (*uMvelingqangi*). On many occasions, Mrs. M. had also been a caring host to overseas visitors to the university, who invariably wish to encounter a traditional Zulu healer. Those visits turn out to be deeply meaningful and mutually beneficial intercultural learning experiences.

During one such encounter with a group of overseas visitors, we were discussing the *ukuthwasa* process in terms of the calling to become a healer, which invariably involves dreams and/or lived experiences of ancestors, snakes and water. A student (*ithwasa*), Mrs. G., who was undergoing supervision at Mrs. M.'s *umuzi*, began the sharing of meaning of her *ukuthwasa* experience in a most dramatic way—by unrolling an African python skin, some four meters long, across the floor of the diviner's hut. The *ithwasa* related how she had met the python on a rocky outcrop and how it was made powerless by the ancestors in order to be killed by Mrs. G., thereby proving itself to be an ancestral assistant to her and to the community in divine healing.

Such experiences provide infinite interpretive possibilities: phenomenological, evolutionary, ecological, mythological, psychodynamic, existential, feministic, ethnographical, medical and theological. However exceptional the *ithwasa* encounter may seem, the catching of a snake in order to create a snake-vertebra necklace is in fact the rule.[1] Reflection reveals that this is simply a radically concrete instance of a universal process of being called to become a healer, and that the serpent is a time-honored and universal symbol of creative healing and medicine. It was at Delphi that Apollo slew Python and took possession of the oracle from which the priestess Pythia thenceforth interpreted divine messages.

"Divine healing" fundamentally refers to holistic healing inspired by some form of divinity such as ancestors, gods or an original being. It essentially consists of two processes: the diviner being healed and the diviner as healer. The aim of this chapter is to explore some universal themes in divine healing as revealed in both traditional Zulu and ancient Greek culture. Although the focus is on traditional Zulu culture, very similar patterns are found among other South African cultural groups.

Characteristics of healing include healing dialogue, spirituality, power, exchange, community, shared worldview, emotional arousal, new information, learning, approach, methods and holism. Divine healing is a holistic form of healing that includes all these and more. The following themes are chosen for their instructional value.

---

1. Axel-Ivar Berglund, *Zulu Thought Patterns and Symbolism* (Cape Town: David Philip, 1976), 156.

Indigenous knowledge systems

Indigenous knowledge systems are the time-honored traditional cultural ways of local people employing local knowledge to survive. Though local in their manifestation, Indigenous knowledge systems may or may not be derived from evidence-based, consensually validated scientific methods. They are of global interest for their heuristic, creative practicality and contextualization. Whether the systems are traditional, conservative, dynamic and/or activist in intent and effect, in the absence of writing their products inevitably originate in oral communities. Breath-based speech, song, meditative, contemplative and/or intercessory traditions form an essential historical context for all forms of knowledge and culture.[2]

Recognition and appreciation of those oral traditions that informed and shaped literature are critical in any hermeneutic endeavor. It is particularly crucial to understand the evolving role of breath, speech and writing in the human psyche and consciousness. For example, compare Homer's understanding of "psyche"—as the breathing life force without which one is dead—with the objective abstract consciousness involved in understanding the written word *psyche*. Indigenous knowledge systems play an integral role in the experiential, behavioral, cultural and social life of communities, as attested by the unprecedented rise of the African Indigenous church movement, which readily incorporates and integrates traditional ancestral and Christian-oriented consciousness, beliefs and practices.

Divine ancestral consciousness

The many deities of ancient times are still revered at virtually every hill and spring in Greece today, although the Greek Orthodox Church houses the official state religion. Delphi, the temple of Apollo on Mount Parnassus—traditionally believed to be the center of the world—still attracts and realigns the inner nature of pilgrims from all over the world. Besides reverence for the old gods such as Zeus, Poseidon, Hera and Athena, animal sacrifice is still practiced in Greece as it is in Kwa-Dlangezwa.

Alan Johnston classifies Greek religious practices into three broad categories. First, city (*polis*) cults involved the Olympian deities as overseers and protectors, such as Apollo at Delphi and Athena at Athens. Second, more local, personalized practices were mostly concerned with the fertility of crops and animals and centered on demigods or nymphs residing in caves or springs, for example, Demeter at Eleusis. Third were ancestor-reverence, hero and founder cults such as those of Agamemnon at Sparta and Odysseus on Ithaca.[3]

---

2. Stephen Edwards, "A Psychology of Indigenous Healing in Southern Africa," *Journal of Psychology in Africa* 21, no. 3 (2011): 335–47.
3. Alan Johnston, *The Emergence of Greece* (Oxford: Elsevier-Phaidon, 1976), 137.

Apparently, Delphi (meaning "wombs") was a sacred site even in the Bronze Age, well before Apollo took over the oracle from Ge, the earth, when he slew Python. In the archaic period, the sanctuary really flourished, with many foreign states and individuals consulting the oracle before embarking on major undertakings. On such occasions, the priestess would go through an elaborate ritual, drinking from the spring of Cassotis, chewing bay leaves, sitting on a holy tripod and going into an inspired trance. Her utterances would be interpreted by attending priests to those who had paid the appropriate fee and made the correct sacrifices in order to consult the oracle.

Traditional Zulu ancestral reverence and communal spirituality have already been discussed in other, related work.[4] It is interesting here merely to draw parallels between Zeus and Athena on the one hand and uNkhulunkulu and Nomkhubulwana on the other hand. In the Greek conception, Zeus was the supreme deity who ruled the other gods from Mount Olympus. Athena, the virgin princess, goddess of wisdom and civilization, art, literature, philosophy, poetry and music, was believed to have sprung fully grown from the brow of Zeus. During the governance of Pericles (461–43 BCE), a 38-foot-high statue of Athena graced the Parthenon Temple on the Acropolis.[5]

In traditional Zulu cosmology there is a remarkable similarity in the interpretation of the same phenomena. uNkhulunkulu is described as God, Lord or father of the sky, responsible for thunder and lightning. His daughter, Nomkhubulwana, is the virgin princess responsible for the soft, misty spring rain and fertilization of crops. There are many rituals surrounding this deity, such as young girls dressing up in their boyfriend's clothing and stealing out of the homestead to meet and sacrifice to Nomkhubulwana. More recently, Nomkhubulwana ceremonies have been reintroduced as a means of emphasizing purity, sexual abstinence, safe sex practices (*ukusoma*) and prevention of contracting HIV/AIDS.

Truth: divination of the truth in cause, diagnoses and treatment

"'Beauty is truth, truth beauty,'—that is all / Ye know on earth, and all ye need to know." These lines from Keats's "Ode to a Grecian Urn" portray the Greek aesthetic conception of truth as it unfolds in many forms, including art, sculpture, the ordering principle of the universe (*nous*), logic and the law of nature (*logos*). The Zulu conception of truth (*iqiniso*) generally implies similar concepts, as well as a more human-designed, consensually validated version of reality as truth. For example, in the *vumisa* technique of the *isangoma*, the truth as to cause, diagnosis and treatment is agreed upon through successive enthusiastic agreements by the client and his/her family in response to the divination.

---

4. See, for example, Edwards.
5. Alexander Eliot, *Greece: A History* (New York: Time-Life International, 1964), 40.

In the case of both the Delphian oracle and *isangoma* such as *sabalozi*, supernatural/divine messages can be directly received and directly accepted by clients; no negotiation as to truth is expected, asked or given, and from there, clients leave strengthened (*uqinisiwe*). In this regard, unlike glass-mirror diviners (*isangoma sesibuko*), Mrs. M. is more psychological, asking her clients to use an imaginary mirror in her divination.

The great recognition given to authentic diviners has unfortunately found its way into commercialization. In eShowe, a market town in Zululand, I once found a commercial divining kit that sold for three rands. The kit included bones representing positive and negative forces, men, women and children; small model huts to represent his and her ancestors; and crocodile bones to represent the unconscious. Maps and instructions were provided for the interpretation of romance, health and prosperity scenarios. Without skillful interpretation by an authentic *isangoma* such as Mrs. M., one can only hope that such commercialized kits will be insightfully and responsibly used.

Harmony

As harmony is achieved through melody, rhythm and many other facets in music, so health is believed to consist of harmonious order and balance among all the elements of the universe, the original being, ancestors, persons in community, plants, animals and all creatures in cosmic time and space and the here-and-now earth, air, fire and water. Harmony is implied in various Zulu terms such as *ukuthula* (peace), *ukulungisa* (balance) and *uhlelo* (order). While not an exact equivalence, the Greek term *arete* implies a striving for perfection through harmonious development of body, mind and spirit, leading to glorious excellence, which is probably more exactly translated by the Zulu word *hlambuluka*—to become free of imperfections, as in recovery after illness or as in full confession.

The Greeks believed that the true poles of wisdom were found at Delphi in the inscriptions "Know thyself" and "Nothing in excess." If harmony became too disturbed by *hubris* (excess, pride, corruption), illness would certainly follow. The concept is expressed as *ukudlula* in Zulu. Becoming out of synchrony with one's world implies vulnerability to fate, the gods, pollution (*umnyama*), ancestral displeasure (*abaphansi basifulathele*), witchcraft and sorcery (*ubuthakathi*), and ecological health hazards (*umkhondo omubi*).

The dynamic nature of harmony is clear in both the Zulu and Greek cosmologies. Individuals, communities, the ancestors and gods are continually disrupting and creating new forms of balance in the ongoing creative/destructive struggle for melody, rhythm, existence, becoming and greater being (*uBukhona*). This has been the shared experience of many visitors to Mrs. M.'s divining hut and cluster of dwelling places, which are set against a small hill like a miniature replica of the design of the temple at Delphi.

Figure 6.1. The Delphi oracle.

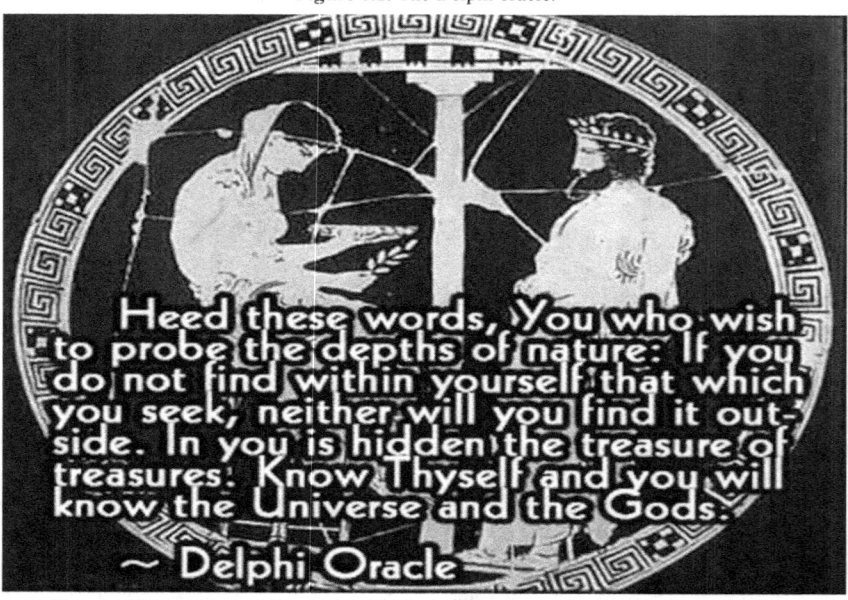

Source: Pinterest (public domain), https://za.pinterest.com/pin/545709679847700209/.

Ecology

Greece has been described as a land of clear air (*aera*) where colors are pure and the forms of things fine. The people have traditionally been closely attuned to nature, as evidenced in their shrines and temples in the hills and streams. As Alexander Eliot puts it,

> Science tends to treat nature as fairly neutral material. Human instinct, however, feels that living, though invisible, presences must inhabit the air, streams and mountains. This instance has always been especially strong in Greece. Here nature still comes close to man. Here men find it difficult not to believe that glances dart upon the air like transparent fish with good and evil intent, that Nymphs are dancing and splashing in the waterfalls, that some islands are holy and that whole mountains can feel motherly sympathy for men.[6]

This close harmony with nature also led to the early Greek philosophers' search in the life of matter for prime substances such as air (Thales), fire (Heraclitus) and atoms (Democritus).

Traditional Zulu worldviews are of a similar undivided cosmos where plants, animals, humans, ancestors, earth, air, sky, stars, plants and sun all form a harmonious universe.

---

6. Eliot, 131.

Moving, breathing creatures are especially believed to leave winds or tracks (*imimoya, imikhondo*) as signs of their passing that can influence others in the sense of healthy or unhealthy germs. For example, the illness *umeqo* is believed to result from stepping over a harmful track or a sorcerer's medicines (*muthi*); it typically presents in the form of hemiparesis, edema, pain in the lower leg and the associated psychosocial sequelae of conversion disorder. While some illnesses may present with a relatively large psychosocial/cultural/spiritual/ecological component, others (such as malaria) are clearly more natural and somatic in their etiology, diagnosis and treatment. Traditional healers emphasize healthy diet, exercise and hygienic environments for the latter type of illness.

Experience in such a harmonious ecology enables us to deconstruct artificial academic distinctions and arbitrary categories such as "nature," "human nature" and "the supernatural." Let us consider some examples:

- *The relationship between animals and people*. Before Shakespeare described man as "the paragon of animals," through the works of Sophocles a winged lion with a human female head—the sphinx—posed a riddle to Oedipus concerning a child, an adult and an old person. Before that, the Minotaur of Knossos was regularly portrayed as a bull-headed man.
- *The relationship between natural and supernatural*. In 2022 CE scientists might travel to other planets and predict tsunami waves and continental rainfall patterns, yet still be struck by the supernatural awesomeness of an electrical storm when alone in the wilderness with lightning, which has onomatopoeic sounds like the word *Zeus*. Axel-Ivar Berglund describes the elaborate ritual of the Zulu lightning doctor (*izinyanga zezulu*) or heaven herd (*adelusi bezulu*). Some points of interest include:
- a herdsman's stick (*eyokwelusa*)—a branch of an *umunga* tree (*Maerua angolensis*)—to drive away the anger of the sky;
- a flute made of reeds (*umtshingo*) to blow while driving away storms; and
- training in medicine for driving away storms.

Berglund describes 10 different medicines to be used in compound form, the most essential of which is the fat of the lightning bird *inyoni yezulu* (or *impundulu*). If the latter is not available, the fat of a bateleur eagle, which makes a sound that resembles thunder when it flies, can be used. All of the above makes sound psychological sense in terms of the possibility of being struck by lightning in the form of a bird!

Transformation of the psyche

The Greek term *psyche* literally refers to breath, soul or spirit. It is a metaphor for human existence or the universal being that appears in particular individuals, couples, families, communities and nations. The equivalent Zulu terms are *umphefumulo* (breath/soul), *umoya* (spirit) and *uBukhona* (presence/being). Divine healing is concerned with healing as transformation at various levels of the psyche:

- *Holistic healing of an essentially spiritual and communal nature.* The divine healer is sanctioned by her community as an accepted medium with the spiritual world and ancestral shades. This also reflects culture, traditions and belief systems. The healing is both universal and local, involving, for example, belief in ancestors (*amadlozi*) and a god (Zeus, *uNkhulunkulu*). Divination and healing take place in a family or community context, at either the diviner's home (or shrine, as at Delphi) or the home of the person seeking divination and help. This does not exclude bodily, material, earthly or other aspects of the psyche that also become transformed. I visited a diviner in Uganda who cared for more than 100 clients in a traditional hospital, all of whom were brought in and cared for by a relative during their stay. Over time, different rooms had been built for the hospital: for divination, demon exorcizing and physical treatments such as bathing and purification. All clients were treated free of charge but would pay the healer in some form according to their conscience, and only after successful treatment. The healer himself had no professional qualifications besides his spiritual calling, community recognition and obvious effectiveness.

- *Interpersonal change in the psyche through the ongoing healing event.* Research has indicated increased levels of empathy, warmth and genuineness in divine healing interviews. These three variables have been shown in various studies to be universally essential ingredients of beneficial interpersonal effectiveness. Aristotle described friendship as a single soul (*psyche*) dwelling in two bodies, before empathy became empirically validated. In the *vumissa* technique, consensual validation is arrived at by both *isangoma* and client with regard to cause, diagnosis and management of illness. This is a universal example of effective interpersonal transformation and the essence of effectively helping human relationships and healing.

- *Individual change in the healer and the community.* The diviner may be changed by the calling to become a divine healer, and other individuals, couples, families, groups and communities also become changed through the diviner's healing. Despite the creative illness, the call bestows great spiritual empowerment. In fact, power is an important factor in divine healing—power as a medium with ancestors/gods; power as specialist in social and community relations; therapeutic power to transform others; power as an ecologist; and the power of knowledge and experience in those boundary situations that involve life and death.

- *Change over time in healing methods.* Processes of healing change with new divination and healing approaches and improve techniques, skills and tools.

Modern medicine is based upon traditional medicine derived from plants and herbs. Although divine healers do not necessarily specialize in medicines, most have a thorough working knowledge of medicinal plants. The processes of healing rituals also have a marked transformational effect on the psyche. The essence of Greek religious practice was the sacrifice of animals, usually burned on an altar dedicated to the deity. Harriet Ngubane lists various Zulu sacrificial rituals, such as *ukubuyisa* (to bring home the spirit of a person who died away from home, in order to be integrated with the body of ancestral spirits), *ukushweleza* (to appease ancestors) and *ukubonga* (thanksgiving).[7] In both Greek and Zulu customs, the special transformational power of ritual sacrifice, cleansing purification and healing was experienced at community gatherings to mark major life occasions such as birth, adolescence, adulthood, marriage, death, first fruits, harvest, going to war, the Olympic games and so forth. Divine healers are called on at all such occasions.

- *Communal, social and cosmic transformation*. The community gatherings described above were filled with music, dance and drama in a cycle that involved growth and health on all levels—physical, psychological, social, spiritual—for the individual, the group, the surrounding environment and the cosmos. Divine healing is an integrating and enhancing force, far more fundamental than a simple cure or the application of medicine. For example, Greek homes had shrines to Hestia, the goddess of home life, and Zeus, who protected the building. Zulu homesteads (*imizi*) have sacred ancestral places (*umsamo*). Divine healers are called in to sprinkle medicines around the homes in order to cleanse, strengthen, protect and purify.[8]

Energy healing

The World Health Organization has defined health as not merely the absence of disease but a state of complete physical, mental and social wellbeing. As implied in this definition, *health* has a positive, energized meaning and vitality, as conveyed in the Nguni/Zulu/Xhosa term *impilo*. Graham notes that the term "energy healing" is derived from the Greek *energeia,* German *heilin* (whole) or *helig* (holy), and the related Old English words *hael* (whole), *haelen* (heal) and *halig* (holy).[9] Etymologically speaking, therefore, to heal is to make whole or holy. The term holistically embraces both physical and spiritual aspects of humanity, as instructively portrayed in the related Nguni/Xhosa/Zulu terms *ukuphilisa* or *elapha* (heal) and *philile* (whole).

---

7. Harriet Ngubane, *Body and Mind in Zulu Medicine* (London: Academy Press, 1977), 167.
8. Ngubane, 167.
9. Helen Graham, *Time, Energy and the Psychology of Healing* (London: Jessica Kingsley, 1990), 183.

However it is conceptualized, *energy* refers to the experience of a vital and variable phenomenon necessary for all forms of life. The terms *energy* and *healing* are used in this chapter in an essentially experiential, phenomenological and psychological sense. Healing typically involves some transformation from illness to health. Such transformation is graphically and energetically portrayed in the San notion of *twe*, a term that explicitly captures the tensile, organismic healing experience of "pulling out" an illness.

According to Graham, traditional forms of energy healing have their origins in observations of the perennial rhythms, balances, harmony, blockages and flow of forces that occur in nature. These forces include the polarity of earth and sky, day and night, man and woman and the regularity of the seasons of spring, summer, autumn and winter, as well as the eternal creative and destructive cycles in the relationships between the elements such as air, earth, water and fire, which includes the resilience of the earth to flooding rivers, ravaging tidal waves and volcanoes and the power of wind to spread fire and of water to put out fire and generate life. Throughout the ages, energy healers have observed and experienced such forces in the human microcosm as in masculine and feminine dimensions, the fiery emotions of the psyche, rivers of blood in the body and seasons of life from birth to death. They have traditionally viewed their role as attendants, helping nature to heal itself through facilitating the energy balance and flow disturbed by disease, but not interfering with the disease itself. Their traditional role was thus literally that of attendants (from the Greek *therapeia*, "attendance") in the healing process.[10]

Contemporary Indigenous Zulu healing is based on the spiritual energy of the ancestors. This energy takes different forms as reflected in *ukububula/nokubhonga kwedlozi*, the religious spirit power and supernatural force of the ancestors breathing through the *isangoma*. The energy is strengthened by healing and good deeds and is weakened by evil spirits and abuse. During a typical divinatory session, or *vumisa*, after contacting the spirit of the ancestors, the *isangoma* may breathe this spirit into the divinatory bones before throwing them. Likewise, clients may be required to inhale this ancestral spiritual breath energy from the bones and use it in various healing rituals. Depending on the depth of the past evolutionary ancestral call, diviners may breathe like roaring lions (*ukubhodla kwengonyama*) or even pythons in their silent communication (*inhlwathi igingile*). Typically, however, the *isangoma* is breathed by recently departed ancestors who have previously appeared to her in dreams, called her to become a diviner and accompanied her through a creative illness in the form of a religious conversion experience, until she completed her apprenticeship under a qualified diviner in a spiritual rebirth macro process called *ukuthwasa*. This is a perennial form of a society caring for and being cared by persons who are first spiritually afflicted and then purified.

The micro process of being breathed by the ancestors during divination occurs in response to a request by clients, who consult the diviner for various reasons such as

---

10. Graham, *Time, Energy*, 185.

illness prevention, health promotion, prosperity or romance. While diviners differ in divinatory methods, the essence of the process consists of the diviner invoking her ancestors and acting as a medium for their messages concerning the client. In an ongoing emotionally charged dialogue, clients' verbal and nonverbal responses become progressively more enthusiastic, with the divination being experienced as becoming more true and real, in a form of consensual validation of the assessment of the problem and solutions offered. The end result is typically agreement as to some form of culturally accepted ritual ceremony for the ancestors, for example, involving protection, appeasement and/or thanksgiving.

Figure 6.2. Zulu divination.

Source: University of Zululand Media Centre, KwaDlangezwa, South Africa, 3886.

In everyday life, the exclamation "*Makhosi*" (ancestors) is made after a sneeze, in recognition of ancestral spirits working their way through the descendant. Ancestors are experienced as living dead, continuing to care for descendants in an extended link with the Source. Such consciousness may ultimately bring awareness of all humanity, the world and the inhabitants of planet Earth, being breathed by the Cosmic Breath. The spiritual calling by recently departed ancestors and/or God often occurs in dreams. The call is followed by a spiritual rebirth experience until the completion of an apprenticeship under a qualified diviner. Thereafter the divine healer experiences being breathed by the ancestors and/or God during the divine healing process.

With their time-honored spiritual healing traditions as evident in such isiZulu terms as *umphefumulo* (breath/soul) and *umoya* (spirit), divine healers essentially honor the subtle energetic functions of the breath as consciousness, psyche, soul and spirit, in both immanent and transcendent form. For example, Credo Mutwa graphically describes his maternal grandfather's teaching during his initial *isangoma* apprenticeship:

He taught me the art of breathing properly. He taught me the secret art of joining my mind to that of the great gods in the unseen world. He taught me how to sit still—very, very still—and eliminate all the thought from my mind and call upon the hidden powers of my soul. In short, my grandfather taught me the Zulu version of what is called in English, "meditation." How to breathe softly and gently like a whisper until you feel something like a hot coiled snake ascending up your spine and bursting through the top of your head—a fearsome thing that is known as umbilini. This umbilini, my grandfather told me, is the source of the sangoma's powers. A sangoma must be able to summon this umbilini at will through the beating of the drum and through meditation, very, very deep meditation.[11]

Umbilini, also known as *kundalini* in Asian yogic traditions, can be traced back to ancient Egyptian views on energy healing, which were based on the vision of a harmoniously interrelated universe suffused with the energies of heaven and earth. The sun god Ra radiated cosmic forces of light onto microcosmic humanity, whose ultimate purpose in life was to become enlightened, through opening to the light and channeling, distributing and merging that light with earth energy, which was symbolized in the form of a rearing serpent. Successful energy channeling was depicted in Egyptian paintings and sculpture as a snake rising from the forehead of enlightened healers such as Mr. M. and Mrs. M. The vital energies of heaven and earth were believed to merge in a vital human energy body called *ka*. The aim of the Egyptian mystery system some 5,000 years ago was to educate and to enlighten humanity with regard to such energy beliefs and practices. Energy healers recognized cycles of the sun, seasons—especially those related to the flooding of the Nile—and other rhythms of life, music and movement.

Divine healing is a fertile field for future research. There is a need for further in-depth qualitative and quantitative, conceptual and empirical research into various themes and issues, such as perennial healing components that include empathy, transpersonal spirituality and especially ancestral consciousness and intuition. In this regard, psychokinetic research using sophisticated experimental methodology and randomized controlled trials with indigenous Zulu healers has provided evidence that healers who beam spiritual healing energy into a computerized random events generator are able to effect significant differences in random number distributions. This finding also provides evidence that traditional Zulu healing incorporates some level of psi functioning. Healers themselves believe that the healing power works through both internal and external ancestral forces. Healers' perceptions are supported by empirical research conducted at the HeartMath Institute in the United States, which has provided significant electrophysiological evidence of intuition as a system-wide energetic process, involving

---

11. Credo Vusa'mazulu Mutwa, *Zulu Shaman Dreams: Prophecies and Mysteries* (Rochester, VT: Destiny Books, 2003), 13.

a non-local realm outside the space-time world that is initially mediated by the heart and then the brain.12

Conclusion

This chapter has been concerned with an exploration of some common themes in divine healing, with special reference to ancient Greek and traditional Zulu culture in particular. Although these contexts are distinct in many ways (such as time, place, history, geography and culture), there are marked similarities with regard to universal themes in the perennial process of divine healing.

Years after the incident of the unrolled python skin, I met Mrs. M.'s former *ithwasa* student Mrs. G., who reported a successful community practice near her home, where she had caught the python. On subsequent visits to Mrs. M., she reported her student's continued success. They met on a fairly regular basis with other divine healers for refresher and re-education courses. Apollo commemorated his killing of Python by founding the Delphic oracle and Pythian games. The cycle continued; many memories flooded back as I observing the python skin hanging in the divination hut of Mr. M., who carries on the tradition and is now recognized as the leader of the local *izangoma*, just as his mentor/trainer, Mrs. M., had been.

The main focus of this book is on legacies of ancient Greece in contemporary perspectives. The historical extent to which ancient Greek divine healing legacies might have infiltrated traditional Zulu culture—for example, via trade routes and oral transmission—is unknown. Certainly, the reverse may have occurred through the African diaspora. Such speculation is beyond the scope of the present chapter, which materialized through the reflections and interpretations of the author. However, the chapter does call for further study into divine healing.

At a meta-reflective level, the legacies of ancient Greece continue to transform the consciousness of researchers, teachers and students. A heuristic phenomenological study by the various authors of this book into the influence of ancient Greek culture on their academic and personal lives would constitute a valuable sequel to this book.

Acknowledgment

An earlier version of this chapter appeared in *Indilinga: African Journal of Indigenous Knowledge Systems* 12, no. 2 (2013), 263–76, under the title "Reflections on Divine Healing with Special Reference to Zulu and Greek Culture."

---

12. Rollin McCraty, Mike Atkinson, Dana Tomasono and Raymond Bradley, *The Coherent Heart* (Boulder Creek, CA: Institute of HeartMath, 2006), 22.

Bibliography

Berglund, Axel-Ivar. *Zulu Thought Patterns and Symbolism.* Cape Town: David Philip, 1976.

Edwards, Stephen. "A Psychology of Indigenous Healing in Southern Africa." *Journal of Psychology in Africa* 21, no. 3 (2011): 335–47.

Eliot, Alexander. *Greece: A History.* New York: Time-Life International, 1964.

Graham, Helen. *Time, Energy and the Psychology of Healing.* London: Jessica Kingsley, 1990.

Johnston, Alan. *The Emergence of Greece.* Oxford: Elsevier-Phaidon, 1976.

McCraty, Rollin, Mike Atkinson, Dana Tomasono and Raymond Bradley. *The Coherent Heart.* Boulder Creek, CA: Institute of HeartMath, 2006.

Mutwa, Vusa'mazulu Credo. *Zulu Shaman: Dreams, Prophecies and Mysteries.* Rochester, VT: Destiny Books, 2003.

Ngubane, Harriet. *Body and Mind in Zulu Medicine.* London: Academy Press, 1977.

Chapter 7

Athens is Burning:
A Tragedy in Three Acts

Gabrielle Moyer
Stanford University, U.S.A.

Abstract

Neoliberalism, a post-World War II philosophy that has come to dominate global economics, has gained critical attention since the 2008 financial crisis. Framed alternately as a threat to American hegemony (Duménil and Lévy) or as a threat to the other 99% (what Giroux describes as the politics of disposability), projected solutions have turned to economic restructuring (Krugman, Henwood) and a revaluation of values (Reich). I turn instead to the language and rhetorical logic of neoliberalism, at its inception in 1940s Austria (Hayek, von Mises, Haberler) and in the development of austerity measures, recently levied by the Eurogroup on Greece (IMF, Lamy). I attend, specifically, to the rhetoric of tragedy, as it proliferates around these and similar sites of loss and as it comes to refer exclusively to the loss of euros not Europeans. While Aristotle's theories of tragedy and virtue ethics challenge neoliberalism's indifference to individual suffering, Hellenist ethics, like neoliberalism, remains blindered by its own structural hierarchies. I look, then, to Euripides, to his radical poetics bearing witness to those who are least pitied and suggest that his theater plays out the tragedy of neoliberalism even as it presents its obverse or a refutation of it.

Keywords: aesthetics, Aristotle, austerity, contagion, ethics, Euripides, Greece. neoliberalism, tragedy.

***

This is a tragedy and a poem of redemption.[1] It is set in Greece but has been set elsewhere.[2] Its players are neoliberal economics and Hellenist ethics, and the language of both as they gesture to the tragic but cannot see it—cannot because because of the way that we cannot see people even as they stand before us. And how poetry may not be able to avert this tragedy but may help us to see its tragedy.

Act I: Fratricide

This morning we discovered the frozen bodies of three of our men in the ravine. Their feet were sticking out of the snow, and that's how we found them. A rebel's body lay beside the soldiers, frozen too; he was wearing summer khaki, no sweater, and his feet were bare. He had been wounded in the legs and had dragged himself over to the soldiers; the four of them were huddled together, their arms around each other to keep warm.[3]

Christos Ikonomou's *Good Will Come from the Sea* tells four stories, each set in the present on an island in the Cyclades. Their silent backdrop: years of economic austerity measures that have brought the country to its knees. If this would seem a conflict waged across national boundaries, between European commissions and Greek citizens, Ikonomou shows how international conflict condenses into civil conflict, with Greeks set against Greeks in a new economy of scarcity. When Athenian Greeks come to the islands seeking work and a new life, local mafia "rats" rape, taunt and torture the "foreigners" at will, despising them with a sadism no curses can match.[4]

As the Athenians in these stories undergo psychic, spatial and physical violence, the narrative develops in a way that is at once graphic and philosophical, particular and metonymic. The first story, told as a confession, admits to incidents around the torture and death of a fellow migrant. The narrator attempts to forget but remembers how they told their friend Tasos to put his head down and comply with the mafia, Tasos who

---

1. The city of Athens looks accustomed to graffiti, but the past decade has led to a canvassing of its walls. At shoulder height, the lower levels of buildings especially speak to life and death under austerity. At the corner of Aristonikou and Charvouri Streets, not far from the Acropolis, a middle-class apartment building reads "ATHENS IS BURNING."
2. Countries across Latin America and Eastern and Western Europe have agreed to and have continued to agree to austerity measures in response to pressure by the International Monetary Fund (IMF). The unlivable conditions they effect have ignited violent mass protest, most recently in Argentina, Chile and Ecuador (May 2019 and October 2019, respectively).
3. Nikos Kazantzakis, *The Fratricides* (London: Faber and Faber, 1967), 96.
4. Christos Ikonomou, *Good Will Come from the Sea,* trans. Karen Emmerich (Brooklyn, NY: Archipelago Books, 2014), 12, 81.

refused to be a "boot licker, a yes man."[5] Adhering instead to an eschatology of solidarity, he counters: "Say each of us has come into the world to look after ourselves and only ourselves—I don't believe it, I'll never believe it, but let's just say that's how it is for the sake of argument. Why shouldn't we change that, to whatever extant we can?"[6] After the mafia puts him in the hospital for a week, "broken teeth, his body flayed by the brushes and chemicals,"[7] Tasos's wife leaves with their children to return to Athens. Finally, at a drunken late-night Easter celebration, Tasos has a chance to shoot one of the locals but does not, lowering his gun. The other man slaps him and insults him as the Athenian community watches. That night Tasos kills himself.

In another story, a father remembers his son, Petros Petrakis, whose name he cries, prays and mouths to himself as he wanders, searching the islands for him. Months earlier, driven by the promise of "buckets of money," Lazaros urges his son to take a job driving the yacht of a local "who owns the whole island," though Petros pleads with his father not to make him go. Petros is not heard from again, though in his searching Lazaros hears stories of his son being tied up, humiliated, thrown overboard.

The last story follows a young couple who come to the island with the dream of building a kind of taverna/café, home and garden on the waterfront. In an exchange between them, they negotiate their new identities as though in another country:

> "Don't expect favors from anyone [says Artemis]. ... Whatever we do we'll do it ourselves. ... That's how things work. Got it? ... We're foreigners here."
>
> "What do you mean foreigners? [replies Stavros]. Fuck that shit. Foreigners? Where do you think we are? Canada? Australia? Is it still fucking Greece here or is it not?"
>
> "What matters isn't where you are but how you are," Artemis replied. "If you're in need, if you're on the outside, you're a foreigner everywhere."
>
> Stavros stubbed out his cigarette and put on his coat.
>
> "Where are you going?"
>
> "I can't stand to listen to you talk like [your uncle]. I'm going to get some air. It stinks of Germans in here."[8]

After borrowing and investing "bit by bit, week by week," they create their dream by the sea, from plumbing to refrigeration. Inside, small lamps are hung, along with a life preserver with a message welcoming mermaids. The night it is finished, a local man, who wanted the property for himself, has it burned to the ground.

---

5. Ikonomou, 14.
6. Ikonomou, 15.
7. Ikonomou, 11.
8. Ikonomou, 204.

If these stories' violence is relentless, it is also simple, compared to the characters' responses to it as they reconfigure their relationship to life and death. In the second story, a paraplegic convinces himself to set out, knife in teeth, to stop the rape of a young girl each night, a payoff of her mother's debt. Her rape, a fact everyone knows but no one stops. While the story ends with his decision, it is the ontological quandary that absorbs Ikonomou's attention: given what we know, what do we do? As in the first story, we find our way into a suicide that may be the only chance left to escape a worse death of public shame. The narrator captures this predicament, and perhaps the tenor of *Good Will Come from the Sea*, when he thinks of Tasos's suicide. Alone in a dark cave between life and death, "he was struggling to stay human, to keep on being a person."[9] At the limits of warfare, Ikonomou suggests, something profound may come to life in our dying.

This thread of resistance, shaped in choices for human integrity or moral care, runs as much through narrative action as through narrative discourse in the interior monologues that characters tilt into, invoking Sophocles, Aeschylus, Shakespeare, ethics, poetry, songs, memories. As if through ancient shapes and forms of thought, they might seek and find their human selves again.

> After all, as John Donne would say, no man is an island—and if the sea washes away even a clod of soil here, Europe is that much smaller. ... Everyone knows everything, but no one does anything. Say that again. [...] Say it again, say it a thousand times like a riddle, an incantation, a song. [...] Everyone, everything, nothing. [...] So choose: either you're like them or you're not. [...] Are you really who you are, or perhaps you just think you're who you are, whereas you're actually someone else, someone like them? Watch what you say. Watch what you don't say too. Because unspoken words aren't words, and unperformed actions aren't actions.[10]

What sense are we to make of Ikonomou's stories? How is another person mistaken for the kind of thing that not only might but must be destroyed, and what can aesthetics offer at all in response? This chapter attempts to respond by pursuing three questions. *Good Will Come from the Sea* seems predicated on the idea that savage economic measures lead to savage neighbors, that this is only the end point of a system that began much earlier, in international referendums and negotiations where the rights of capital took precedence over the rights of communities.[11] The questions I would pose in response are:

---

9. Ikonomou, 79.
10. Ikonomou, 103.
11. Kazantzakis's *Fratricides*, published in 1963, sets the stage for Ikonomou's book. Chronicling the Greek Civil War from the vantage point of a small town caught between communist and royalist forces, it describes Greeks killing Greeks with ruthless persistence. The tragedy of *Fratricides*, though, exceeds

(1) What is this system? (2) How does an economic system become a way of life? And (3) What power can words, spoken and performed, have within this system?

To explore the first idea, let us go back 10 years. It makes sense to let Yanis Varoufakis, the former Greek finance minister and charismatic face of Greek resistance to austerity, set the stage for the country's fall into bankruptcy. In an even-handed way, he offers:

> For years, the [Greek] state had borrowed recklessly from reckless banks in Greece, Germany, and France. [In the fall of 2009] Papandreou's government announced that the previous administration had published a wildly inaccurate estimate of that year's likely deficit. Instead of six to eight per cent of [GDP], an alarming enough figure, the deficit would be 12.5 per cent. Greece was already known to have severe, long-standing economic weaknesses: tax evasion, corruption, oligarchic habits, a failure to make products that other countries desired. The country's credit rating plummeted, along with its reputation for statistical candor.[12]

By spring 2010, Greece was veering toward bankruptcy. To avert the calamity of another European financial crisis (following the 2008 U.S. financial crisis), the so-called troika—the International Monetary Fund, the European Central Bank and the European Commission—issued the first of three international bailouts for Greece that would eventually total €289 billion. But the bailouts came with conditions. Lenders, led by Germany, agreed to the loans on the condition of austerity measures. Greece, in other words, would have to "tighten its belt" in the form of deep budget cuts and steep tax increases. This would ultimately be to Greece's benefit, though. As the *New York Times* reasonably put it, the troika would help, but Greece would have to "overhaul its economy by streamlining the government, ending tax evasion and making Greece an easier place

---

brother killing brother or child killing parents. It is the uselessness of their deaths, the abiding fear and doubt that neither side is in the right, that keep their deaths from achieving meaning: "'Dying doesn't really bother me, Lenny, I swear it doesn't. As long as I know why I'm dying and for whom I'm dying. But I really don't know. Do you?' What could I answer him ... how would I know? That's the great tragedy of it all" (100). That the Greek Civil War was a proxy war between neighboring communist countries and Britain/the United States, and thus the first stage of the Cold War, further marks the interplay between Kazantzakis's novel and Ikonomou's stories; in both the deaths occur in Greece but the power play occurs elsewhere. See, for example, Niki Kitsantonis, "Greece Adopts New Austerity Measures to Placate Creditors," *New York Times*, January 15, 2018, https://www.nytimes.com/2018/01/15/world/europe/greece-austerity-bailout.html.

12. Ian Parker, "The Greek Warrior: How a Radical Finance Minister Took on Europe—and Failed," *New Yorker*, August 3, 2015, https://www.newyorker.com/magazine/2015/08/03/the-greek-warrior.

to do business."[13] And so, with each loan (May 2010, February 2012, August 2015) came more and harsher austerity measures.

To ensure that Greece's spending was always less than its income—except when paying off the debt—the troika continued to demand further cuts. The government was initially required to cut spending by €28 billion in 2010–11, then a further €13 billion (or one-third of its GDP) in 2012–14. To achieve these numbers, Greece began with €30 billion in spending cuts and tax increases; this was followed by layoffs of 25,000 public workers, along with wage cuts, tax increases and further budget cuts. These were followed by further tax reforms, cuts to public spending, the privatization of state assets and weakened labor laws, and then even deeper tax cuts and pension cuts ("reforms") along with the sale of further assets.

If these seem the strict but necessary steps to avoid another financial crisis and hold Greece accountable for its debt, other numbers, other data followed. Under austerity, the Greek economy shrank by almost a quarter between 2008 and 2012. Hundreds of thousands of jobs were lost and unemployment nearly doubled, from 12.7% in 2010 to 24.3% in 2012, peaking at 27.5% in 2013. For those under 25, unemployment rose to 58%. After two years of austerity an additional 20,000 Greeks were homeless, with one in ten Athenians visiting a soup kitchen daily. Suicide rates also increased by 40% between 2010 and 2015. In 2018 alone, suicides more than doubled for those 22 and under. Between 2013 and 2018, over 40,000 people left the country.[14] If the troika's justifying narrative was to make Greece "better for business" while making a lesson of it to the EU, to transform it from a lazy southern body to an efficient northern one, the tourniquet of austerity also had a strangling effect.

Six years into austerity, the medical journal *The Lancet* published research comparing patterns of death and disability in Greece pre-austerity (from 2000 to 2010) to post-austerity (2010 to 2016). The study concluded that cuts in health care due to austerity corresponded to increases in death and disease.[15] Perhaps most striking is the "rapid

---

13. "Explaining Greece's Debt Crisis," *New York Times*, June 17, 2016, https://www.nytimes.com/interactive/2016/business/international/greece-debt-crisis-euro.html.

14. See, for an account of austerity's impact on the right to health and the right to education, Dunja Mijatovic's "Report of the Commissioner for Human Rights Following Her Visit to Greece from 25 to 29 of June, 2018." For an assessment specific to suicide, see George Rachiotis et al., "What Has Happened to Suicides During the Greek Economic Crisis? Findings from an Ecological Study of Suicides and Their Determinants (2003–2012)," *BMJ Journals* 5, no. 3 (May 10, 2017), doi: 10.1136/bmjopen-2014-007295corr1.

15. Stefanos Tyrovolas et al., "The Burden of Disease in Greece, Health Loss, Risk Factors and Health Financing, 2000–16: An Analysis of the Global Burden of Disease Study 2016," *The Lancet* 3, no. 8 (July 25, 2018): 395–406.

increase" in death from treatable diseases and self-harm in the youngest and most vulnerable populations, the former affecting children younger than 5, the latter affecting adolescents and young adults:

> Adverse effects of medical treatment, self-harm, and several types of cancer stood out as consistently increasing in Greece across all ages. Within specific age groups, other causes are apparent, with rapid increases in deaths due to neonatal haemolytic disease and neonatal sepsis in children younger than 5 years and prominent increases in self-harm among adolescents and young adults. Greek adults aged 15–49 years had increased mortality due to HIV [needle exchange programs were closed for two years], several treatable neoplasms, all types of cirrhosis, neurological disorders (e.g., multiple sclerosis, motor neuron disease), chronic kidney disease, and most types of cardiovascular disease.[16]

In effect, when the IMF, the European Central Bank and the EC determined that austerity measures were the cost Greece had to pay for its debts and bailout, it can also be said that the country's debt was paid back not only in euros but also in bodies.

Two years after *The Lancet* published its report, and 10 years into austerity, a small article appeared in the U.S. business magazine *Forbes*. One of its writers picked up on *The Lancet*'s research and shared its numbers—numbers which were surprising to the writer and meant to be surprising to her readers. People still agree, she writes, that Greece deserves to suffer: "Some argue, and I have heard a lot of this lately … that Greeks 'deserve' poverty and deprivation. They had a massive party at other people's expense, after all. Now, it's payback time."[17] *The Lancet*'s numbers will surprise because, as she puts it, "When writing about Greece, it is all too easy to look only at the economic figures and miss the human impact."[18]

---

16. Tyrovolas et al., 399.

17. Frances Coppola, "The Terrible Human Costs of Greece's Bailout," *Forbes*, August 31, 2018, https://www.forbes.com/sites/francescoppola/2018/08/31/the-terrible-human-cost-of-greeces-bailouts/?sh=4b5261e44b31. Although Coppola expresses shock at *The Lancet*'s findings, by calling austerity measures "bailouts" she continues to position Greece (already in her headline) as an impecunious country dependent on others' massive financial assistance. In this way she misses the complex economic history that led to austerity. Finally, and perhaps not surprisingly, the *Forbes* article begins with the same premise that Pascal Lamy begins with in his NYU lecture: that all this talk about Greece is quite a puzzle—the country is insignificant economically; Pascal Lamy, "Making Trade Work for Development: Time for a Geneva Consensus," Emile Noel Lecture, New York University Law School, October 30, 2006.

18. This comes as no secret. In a report by the Hellenic League for Human Rights, the authors identify this fairly universal sense of justice at the outset: "The negative consequences of certain policies and measures taken in response to the crisis for fundamental rights and society as a whole have been underestimated or dismissed as inevitable—and therefore acceptable—collateral damage." Elena Crespi et al., *Downgrading Rights: The Cost of Austerity in Greece* (Paris: International Federation for Human

The idea that Greece was just paying back what it owed and that, whatever that looked like on the ground, we were unsure or indifferent because our eyes were fixed on numbers of euros and not numbers of people, expresses a particular notion of justice and financial logic that is not arbitrary, but rather the expression of an economic theory that gained global dominance in the 20th and 21st centuries.[19] The financial institutions that created the crisis and debt (freed by deregulation to pursue profligate lending practices that took the form of financialization or derivatives); the political and financial institutions that passed on the debt to the poorest citizens in the form of spending cuts and higher taxes; the tax loopholes that protected the affluent from sharing the burden; and the story that economists and then the public have told about this—each express this theory.

As an economic theory, neoliberalism is based on the belief that the market does not and cannot take care of itself. To safeguard capitalism at a global scale, it has sought the broad application of market solutions to social problems and the creation of a successful international network of economic and legal rules that favor global markets in lieu of national interests or workers' interests. Developed in the 1930s as a response to the end of empire—and with the end of empire, the end of Western standards and treaties that could ensure a network of global power and wealth—neoliberalism was built on the idea that the "central values of civilization" needed to be saved.[20] Admitting that there was no return to colonization, the founding international economists who first gathered in Mont Pèlerin, Switzerland, set out to recreate the world economy in the absence of empire.[21] The historical shift from empire to nation-state, though, wasn't the only crisis they sought to address. The events of the first half of the century coalesced into a shift in European and American policies away from capitalism and toward social

---

Rights/Hellenic League for Human Rights, 2014), 4, https://www.fidh.org/IMG/pdf/downgrading_ rights_the_cost_of_austerity_in_greece.pdf.

19. See, for example, some of the most prominent, if divergent, voices on neoliberalism: Gérard Duménil and Dominique Lévy, *The Crisis of Neoliberalism* (Cambridge, MA: Harvard University Press, 2011); Henry A. Giroux, *Against the Terror of Neoliberalism: Politics Beyond the Age of Greed* (Boulder, CO: Paradigm, 2008); Giroux, *Stormy Weather: Katrina and the Politics of Disposability* (Boulder, CO: Paradigm, 2006); Doug Henwood, *Wall Street: How It Works and for Whom* (London: Verso, 1997); Paul R. Krugman, *Arguing with Zombies: Economics, Politics and the Fight for a Better Future* (New York: Norton, 2020); Robert B. Reich, *The Common Good* (New York: Knopf, 2018).

20. The quotation comes from the Mont Pèlerin Society's Statement of Aims, developed from their first meeting, on April 8, 1947, in Switzerland; https://www.montpelerin.org/statement-of-aims/.

21. Brexit, for example, has been described as "empire 2.0" by government ministers in London, as reported by *The Times*: "They [Whitehall ministers] want to start talking about African free trade deals." Sam Coates and Marcus Leroux, "Ministers Aim to Build Empire 2.0 with African Commonwealth," *The Times*, March 6, 2017, https://www.thetimes.co.uk/article/ministers-aim-to-build-empire-2-0-with-african-commonwealth-after-brexit-v9bs6f6z9.

welfare and state control, evident in developments as diverse as Soviet central planning, the New Deal, the Popular Front government in France and the rise of fascism.[22] In what can be described as syllogistic logic, these movements were—and continue to be—perceived as equivalent threats to capitalism, and therefore threats to freedom. Hence their solution: "inoculate capitalism against democracy."[23] Over the next several decades, the Geneva School (as the founders of neoliberalism came to be known) developed and implemented strategies for keeping nations but disempowering them, thus depriving them of economic autonomy and, by extension, a decision-making role in the world economy.

Despite looking backward as the world was moving forward, neoliberalism's appeal is difficult to underestimate. Its effects began to be realized at both the national and international levels as early as Geneva's League of Nations. Because the League "commissioned and broadly supported emergent forms of economic research: statistics, econometrics, macro-economics, business cycle research and economic as well as scientific theory in more general terms,"[24] its decisions grew out of the work of leading economists of the time—not least those in the Geneva School of economic thought. Indeed, the central structure of the League, where countries such as Greece and China were admitted as equals but only with some sort of continued control over their finances, exemplifies a neoliberal vision where nations are allowed to retain formal political autonomy on the condition of diminished economic autonomy.[25] This model continues to describe the conditions and consequences of EU countries as they attempt to arrive at—and fall short of—economic standards as set up in the Maastricht Criteria.

It was in the 1970s, though, that neoliberal policies began to gain political popularity, under the leadership of Ronald Reagan, Margaret Thatcher and Deng Xiaoping, as each sought to revitalize their country's economy by curbing the power of labor, deregulating industry and resource extraction and liberating the powers of finance.[26] Its influence has

---

22. Ben Jackson, "At the Origins of Neoliberalism: The Free Economy and the Strong State, 1930–1947," *Historical Journal* 53, no. 1 (2010): 132.

23. Quinn Slobodian, *Globalists: The End of Empire and the Birth of Neoliberalism* (Cambridge, MA: Harvard University Press, 2018), 95.

24. Hagen Schulz-Forberg, "The Dot-Connector: How the League of Nations Incidentally Gave Birth to Neoliberalism," *The Invention of International Bureaucracy* (blog), Aarhus University, June 24, 2018, https://projects.au.dk/en/inventingbureaucracy/blog/show/artikel/the-dot-connector-how-the-league-of-nations-incidentally-gave-birth-to-neoliberalism/.

25. Slobodian, 97.

26. Milton Friedman gives some insight into this shift in economic policy. Reflecting on the reception of his book *Capitalism and Freedom*, he remarks that it went unnoticed on its first publication in 1962, but on its second publication, in 1980, it arrived in tandem with a television show (*Free to Choose*), was "reviewed by every major publication, frequently featured in a lengthy review … sold some 400,000 copies in its first year, [was] translated into twelve foreign languages,

grown consistently, particularly after the collapse of the Soviet Union (read as the death knell of socialism and the triumph of capitalism), to a degree that advocates of neoliberalism can be found across a spectrum of economic, political, media and research centers— if few claim the title. Although the mainstream press has begun to engage with it as a school of thought, political parties and institutions rarely self-identify as neoliberal. It can better be described as an assumed global net gathering nations within it, whether plutocracies or democracies.[27]

The realization of a 21st-century neoliberal order has depended on a system where the free flow of capital and goods dissolve and thus disempower planning measures "at home," thus undercutting the very "communities of interest that sustain" the flow of capital and goods.[28] One example of this is foreign extractive industries, which move wealth offshore while workers within resource-rich countries live hand to mouth.[29]

---

and was issued in early 1981 as a mass-market paperback." For Friedman, this was a shift of both economic and ethical proportions: "Those of us who were deeply concerned about the danger to freedom and prosperity from the growth of government, from the triumph of welfare-state and Keynesian ideas, were a small and beleaguered minority ... How much the intellectual climate has changed"; Milton Friedman, *Capitalism and Freedom* (Chicago: University of Chicago Press, 2002), xii.

27. Aihwa Ong, "Neoliberalism as a Mobile Technology," *Transactions of the Institute of British Royal Geographers*, n.s. 32, no. 1 (2007): 3–8. "Neoliberal rationality has floated beyond advanced liberal countries to political environments as varied as the garrison state (Roitman 2005), post-socialist oligarchy or authoritarian formation without replacing the political apparatus or ideology (Ong 2006a)." Regarding neoliberals' self-identification as neoliberals, in what was touted as a significant admission, the IMF used the term *neoliberal* to describe its policies in 2016. Given increased negative reporting on the effects of austerity, this first acknowledgement also appears to be modestly self-reflective. "In sum, the benefits of some policies that are an important part of the neoliberal agenda appear to have been somewhat overplayed"; Jonathan D. Ostry et al., "Neoliberalism: Oversold?" *Finance and Development* 53, no. 2 (June 2016): 38–41, https://www.imf.org/external/pubs/ft/fandd/2016/06/pdf/ostry.pdf.

28. Slobodian, 75. There were 39 attendees at the first Mont Pèlerin Society meeting. Half were economists; others were academics, businessmen, journalists. They included, as president, Friedrich Hayek, along with Ludwig von Mises, Fritz Machlup and Karl Popper (also Austrian); Michael Polanyi (Hungarian); Wilhelm Röpke, Alexander Rustow and Water Euche, (German ordoliberals); Lionel Robbins and John Jewkes (British); Henry Hazlitt, Frank Knight, Milton Friedman, Aaron Director and George Stigler (American); and Maurice Allais and Bertrand de Jouvenel (French).

29. Adam Hochschild, *Lessons from a Dark Time* (Oakland: University of California Press. 2018), 63–118. Hochschild calls attention, for example, to the parallels between the Congo under Dutch colonial rule and the Congo under postcolonial rule, pointing to an ongoing history of forced labor, civil war, corruption and poverty. "Multinational corporations prefer a government weak enough not to tax and regulate heavily but strong enough to guarantee order" (80–81). At the time *Lessons* was published, AngloGold Ashanti, the world's third largest gold-mining company, had finalized a series of agreements with the Congolese government where it would take an 86% share of the operation and the near-bankrupt state mining

Another example might be the 1994 North American Free Trade Agreement, which granted privileges to transnational corporations while crippling the Mexican economy; Mexico, but not the United States, was required to end agricultural subsidies for corn, rice and beans and then mandated to phase out tariffs on agricultural imports from the U.S. and Canada. The World Bank estimates that 3.5 million Mexican farmers have been driven off their land, with 20 million living in food poverty.[30] The ongoing mass migration further disempowers labor, as rights weaken if not diminish for immigrant and "illegal" migrant workers, particularly within neoliberal economies that privilege economic growth over human rights.

On the other hand, a neoliberal approach depends on loopholes for the protection of capital—evident in the emergence of offshore tax havens or safe harbors for capital (the breadth of which has been exposed by the Panama and Paradise Papers) and the expansion of investment laws designed to protect foreign investors. Similar protections have been extended to institutions in an effort to insulate market actors from democratic pressures: actors such as the IMF and the World Bank and central banks worldwide, including the European Central Bank, the EU and the World Trade Organization (WTO).

More recently, the austerity measures that the EU has framed as the "non-ideological, no alternative response" to government debt indicate the dominance of neoliberal solutions on the international stage.[31] To describe austerity as a global project to protect capital over and above national or labor interests, though, fails to capture the way financial systems were not just favored over but came at the cost of social welfare. If this seems a high claim, it marks the conclusion of the International Federation of Human Rights and the Hellenic League for Human Rights' 80-page report on Austerity Measures:

---

company would get the rest. Further, four other multinationals, "based in England, Canada, and South Africa—have concluded other closed-door agreements over mining rights ... Representatives of villages in the area, meanwhile, find it hard to get a seat at the table ... Seldom, in fact, do local communities gain much from such agreements" (81).

30. Kathryn Ferguson et al., *Crossing with the Virgin: Stories from the Migrant Trail* (Tucson: University of Arizona Press, 2010), xxii. It seems important to add that these were not unexpected consequences. Rather, the migratory pressure of displaced farmers and, by extension, the availability of cheap, "illegal" and thus disempowered labor was assumed in advance. Immigration and Naturalization Service (INS) commissioner Doris Meissner stated before Congress in 1993: "Responding to the likely short-to-medium-term impacts of NAFTA will require strengthening our enforcement efforts at the border"; Joseph Nevins, *Dying to Live: A Story of U.S. Immigration in an Age of Global Apartheid* (San Francisco: City Lights, 2008), 114. See also Laura Carlsen, "Under NAFTA, Mexico Suffered and the United States Felt Its Pain," *New York Times*, November 23, 2013, https://www.nytimes.com/roomfordebate/2013/11/24/what-weve-learned-from-nafta/under-nafta-mexico-suffered-and-the-united-states-felt-its-pain.

31. Kevin Farnesworth and Zoë Irving, "Austerity: Neoliberal Dreams Come True," *Critical Social Policy* 38, no. 3 (2018): 462.

Saving the international financial system [was] prioritized ... instead of reforming the financial sector to prevent further collapse and ensuring a minimum social protection floor to help societies cope with the crisis' devastating consequences ... human rights language has remained absent in the diagnoses and solutions put forward by governments and the international community. ... In fact curtailing rights ... appears to have been perceived as the crisis' *inevitable and therefore tolerable consequences*.[32]

When human rights language goes missing, we might fairly conclude that human rights will go missing as well.

Might we have derived the human cost of austerity at the outset, from the language of governments and the international community? To make such a claim for the premonitory power of language may seem excessive, but the inequities of austerity arguably seam its very rhetoric. In his epic history of neoliberalism, Quinn Slobodian concludes: "the main thing neoliberalism seeks to hide is asymmetries of power."[33] Labor activists, journalists, scholars and strikers have worked to expose the consequences of those asymmetries. But we might look to its very policies and proposals, lectures and tracts, to reveal the inequities subtending them, before they come to fruition.

While neoliberalism presents as a globally-minded beneficent economic theory, it is arguably built upon flawed moral theories, flawed to the degree that they are logically inconsistent. Whether or not we take it to be moral or immoral in the values it enacts, it seems critical to point out that an economic system is also an ethical system and as such proposes, indeed shapes, not only how we spend but how we live. One way to derive its ethics is to attend to neoliberal rhetorics and, in particular, to what it perceives as tragedy. In what we take to be tragic, we reveal ourselves.

Act II, scene 1: Contagion

"Our city has become a commodity."[34]

On June 29, 2012, the University of Edinburgh bestowed an honorary doctorate on Pascal Lamy, then director-general of the World Trade Organization (2005–13) and formerly trade commissioner of the European Union (1997–2005). In his speech that day he addressed the eurozone debt crisis by telling his audience a story.[35]

---

32. Crespi et al. [emphasis added].
33. Slobodian, 269.
34. Graffiti facing the Makriyiannis statue on Dionysiou Areopagitou, a heavily touristed street of souvenir shops leading up to the Acropolis entrance and the Acropolis Museum.
35. "Europe Needs a 'Legitimacy Compact' – Lamy," speech at awarding of honorary doctorate, University of Edinburgh, June 29, 2012, https://www.wto.org/english/news_e/sppl_e/sppl241_e.htm.

Lamy began with a question "puzzling" economists for some time. In the past two years, the troubles in Greece had dominated economic news around the world and captured the attention of the international community to a degree that appeared incompatible with the relative size of its economy. The Greek economy accounted for less than 2% of the EU'S GDP and had a share of 2.5 % of the euro-area economy. What could explain this global interest?

Economists had proposed an answer to their riddle, which Lamy represented to his audience in the form of a three-act play or, as he put it (playfully or ironically), "a tragedy!"

> Act One. "Investors worried that the Greek government will be unable to pay back its debt" and, ultimately, "markets begin to suspect that other European countries could find themselves in similar waters."

> Act Two. "The ... perceived risk of insolvency leads investors to demand higher interest rates on bonds of [other] highly indebted countries, such as Portugal, Spain and Italy. This, in turn, worsens public sector balance sheets and increases the risk of insolvency. Investors' fear [has the effect of a] self-fulfilling prophecy."

> Act Three. Instability spreads throughout the financial system. At this point, contagion has made its way from Greece to the EU and threatens the rest of the world.

In sum, Greece matters because it is a source of "contagion"—a suitably pestilent solution to a pestilent problem.[36] Lamy concluded that economists' theory of contagion was partly right, but only partly. "At a deeper level," he argued, "Greece is a symbol of the reversibility of the [whole] European integration process."[37] It was for this reason that it drew global attention.

Lamy's conclusion realizes the moral logic within a set of neoliberal premises: (1) A country of insignificant GDP and thus a small part of the EU economy matters little—either to economists or to the international community.[38] (2) The best explanation for

---

36. *Oxford English Dictionary* (Oxford: Oxford University Press, 2001), http://dictionary.oed.com/entrance.dtl. The first usage of *contagion* appears as a synonym for *leprosy*: "1398 J. Trevisa tr. Bartholomew de Glanville De Proprietatibus Rerum (1495) vii. lxiv. 281 Lepra also comith of fader and moder, and so this contagyon passyth in to the chylde as it were by lawe of herytage."

37. This and the preceding four quotations are from Pascal Lamy, "Making Trade Work for Development: Time for a Geneva Consensus," Emile Noel Lecture, New York University Law School, October 30, 2006.

38. It is important to identify this as a historical shift within economics. Slobodian takes pains to distinguish economists' relationship to capital in the 19th century from their relationship to capital

concern about such nations is that they matter not in and of themselves but for what they might do to "us;" in other words, Greece is the source of a plague of financial fears that affects countries with larger economies—ones that we do care about. (3) The best response to austerity's negative consequences can be found within the realm of theoretical economics, thus foreclosing attention to public health crises, unemployment, cultural and historical significance, loss of human rights or even a sense of human solidarity. (4) Finally, while there is an ostensible or explicit concern for the European Union, there is little concern for Europeans as such; Lamy makes no mention of what is happening in Greece to Greeks.[39]

To read the speech for its embedded inequities, one might begin by pointing out its asymmetrical tragedies, or tragic asymmetries. According to Lamy, economists (generally speaking) have no interest in a particular state's "troubles" unless it produces a significant GDP. Nor can economists understand why anyone else would be interested in a low-GDP nation, to the extent that a theory must be devised to explain it—namely, that wealthier nations will become interested in a low-GDP nation when it threatens their interests. Adhering to a schema where the only relevant data point is economic; the suffering of affluent nations will matter as the suffering of less affluent nations will not matter.[40]

While Lamy takes these ideas to be shared and therefore indifferent to justification, his speech helps pave the way for consensus. By reconceiving Greece from synecdoche to symbol, he shifts its indexical value from a material population of 10.77 million to an immaterial force, significant at best for its consequences elsewhere. By reconceiving Greece as a symbolic problem (as contagion or fear), Lamy clears the way for a symbolic solution, more gestural than the first; re-enchant Europeans with Europe, he says, and "Euroenthusiasm," will save the day. With this feeling of solidarity, we create a stronger multilateral solidarity and legitimacy capable of enacting stringent disciplines.

---

over the past two centuries: "In contrast to the typical policy-minded economist in the late nineteenth century, who would have been a social reformer seeking to counteract and mollify the effects of capitalism, there emerged in the interwar period a generation of economists who sought to apply their knowledge in service of capital" (48).

39. The consequences of austerity for the EU have only grown more serious since 2020, evident in the destabilization of governments and human health and welfare, increased protests and the concomitant rise of the far right (which unilaterally favors neoliberal policies—decreasing social welfare, increasing privatization and deregulation, breaking labor unions and increasing the movement of labor). "As authorities act without consultation or democratic oversight, and fail to respond to people's basic needs, their legitimacy is increasingly eroded. This has in turn pushed people to seek refuge in extremist ideologies that purport to offer alternatives to the current system. States appear to be less and less able to contain such ideologies, sometimes tolerating them as a means of channeling frustration towards traditional scapegoats, such as migrants"; Crespi et al., 5.

40. It might be argued that this is a tautology that broaches no complaint: economists care about economics. This chapter seeks to challenge the truism by pointing to the adverse political and social consequences of such an approach.

Although this solution may seem credible within a logic or diversionary strategy that equates the value of a country to its GDP, it yet remains a naive solution to the complex and volatile history of a European single currency. That said, it would be unwise to dismiss Lamy's approach. The significance and duration of his tenure alone make him a critical figure. His approach expresses the global institutions he represents.

It is important to begin with economists' metaphor of contagion, as it exposes deep divisions between nations on the basis of economic status while claiming their union is paramount. If the European Union were united, it could not be vulnerable to contagion, in the sense that one cannot be vulnerable to oneself. Contagion always begins elsewhere, outside. One of the first observations we might make, then, is that to speak of "economies of contagion" is to disaggregate the European body politic. In this sense, we might point to the belief in a European "other" that threatens contagion as an indicator that the union has already dissolved. Further, it is not until the diseased "other" threatens to affect status nations within the EU that economists sound the alarm and invoke a rhetoric of tragedy. This delay suggests the degree to which the union, as an equitable organization, has already been lost.

The Eurogroup's responses—economic quarantine and moral opprobrium—draw on traditions that conflate medical with moral sickness. A 19th-century compilation of the *Oxford English Dictionary* notes that several definitions of contagion are "figurative," including "hurtful, defiling or corrupting contact."[41] To use the language of contagion, then, is to draw on a cultural logic that perceives sickness as both a physical and moral threat. When economists describe Greece's financial crisis as contagion, Greece's responsibility and abject status in the EU are presented as not only palatable but logical. Yet Lamy's words unwittingly implicate economists in a contagion of fear, a fear of the other that will unravel the EU.

If a metaphor of viral infections depends on a hierarchy of nations where affluent nations become threatened by impoverished ones, it is simultaneously threatened, as a metaphor, by an inversion of itself. In its state of contagion, Greece exceeds the deterministic axes of economic models. Through its infectious power, the singular body exceeds its singularity, if not its meaninglessness. In this sense, contagion, by refusing to be contained, expresses a refusal to suffer what one must, alone and without consequences. Contagion may be described as at once the problem and a refutation of it.

Drawing attention to this entanglement between economics and ethics ushers us into complex zones of excess and fear. On one hand, neoliberalism involves a set of shared if implicit values, values that determine global policies that exacerbate the precarity and suffering of already vulnerable populations. On the other hand, asymmetries of power, expressed in the variable cost of human lives, allow for vulnerable populations to disappear

---

41. Martin S. Pernick, "Contagion and Culture," *American Literary History* 14, no. 4 (2002): 860, www.jstor.org/stable/3568029.

as a "cost," even as they threaten to exceed their barriers. Both are interdependent; neither can be straightforward. Like a double helix, the ladder of neoliberalism maps onto human lives, connected by a complex sequence of words, sentences and paragraphs that asks to be read. Where is the tragedy?

In 1975 George Perec published a memoir called *W, or the Memory of Childhood*. In it, two stories alternate every few pages, his memories from childhood alternating with a "fantasy adventure" he imagined as a child. The former tells of the loss of Perec's father at the French front; his separation from his mother and her death at Auschwitz; his relocation, always to another home or school or town, nobody's child. The tone of these fragments is expressed as though from a distance; they do not hurt in the way we expect them to hurt. Written in the form of psychological or photographic stills, Perec's style communicates a documentary accuracy that he also explicitly challenges, confessing that such distinct memories were maybe only imagined, probably misremembered, likely conflated.

Woven in and out of these non-factual matter-of-fact memories is the story of an imaginary place, W. Written in italics, the story is set against Perec's memories not only visually but in its attention to numbers and nomenclature, in its methodical cataloguing of the cultivation and competition of athletes in W. What begins as an aesthetics of tedious rigor describing a byzantine system of laws and hierarchies develops, however, into a story overtaken by violence—a violence as neatly systematized as the banal organization of teams, towns, games and names that begins the story. With innumerable "laws" to determine what violence will occur to whom and when and for what reason, the system enumerates its terrors reasonably. It is preordained that athletes are to be at once lionized and mocked, set upon each other to be killed and raped, feted and drawn and quartered, all as a matter of course. While W appears wholly dedicated to athletic success, one need only look to the athletes' performances to see that it is, rather, wholly dedicated to human destruction; "if you just look and see the workings of this huge machine, each cog [of] which contributes with implacable efficiency to the systematic annihilation of men, then it should come as no great surprise that the performances put up are utterly mediocre."[42] The ultimate health camp becomes a death camp.

As the stories of childhood and W flicker between one and the other, they yet remain distinct. What are we to make of these stories, bound together as they are? The autobiographical moments, grounded in the real—Avenue Junot, Montmartre, May 1945, cousin Henri—appear antithetical to W's surreal fantasy. But Perec takes pains to undeceive us, beginning with his own confession of unreliability: "My two earliest memories are not entirely implausible, even though, obviously, the many variations and

---

42. George Perec, *W, or the Memory of Childhood*, trans. David Bellos (Boston: Verba Mundi, 2017), 13.

imaginary details I have added in the telling of them—in speech or in writing—have altered them greatly, if not completely distorted them."[43]

If history cannot fully arrive as history, W's imaginary cannot, conversely, be relegated to the imaginary. Indeed, the more graphically surreal W becomes, the more the narrator insists that it is entirely real.

> How can you explain that what he is seeing is not anything horrific, not a nightmare, not something he will suddenly wake from, something he can rid his mind of? How can you explain that this is life, real life, this is what they'll be every day. … There are competitions every day, where you Win or Lose. You have to fight to live. There is no alternative. It is not possible to close your eyes to it, it is not possible to say no. There's no recourse, no mercy, no salvation to be had from anyone.[44]

This appeal situates itself within and beyond the frame of the story. Moving outside the grammar of narrative fiction, its pronouns implicate us as readers across multiple subject positions: the voice speaks to us and about us, asking us what to do even as it tells us what to do.

Finally, in the last chapter, the space between the stories collapses. W crosses over into the autobiography, shifting out of allegory and into history:

> Years and years later, in David Rousset's Univers concentrationnaire, I read the following: The structure of punishment camps is determined by two fundamental policies: no work but "sport," and derisory feeding … standing again, very fast, with both arms held out horizontally; forcing them to do press-ups fast (always fast, fast, Schnell, los Mensch), in the mud, up and down again a hundred times in a row.[45]

The contagion of W cannot be contained.

There is a way in which symbolic systems prioritizing human life cannot speak to aggregate deontological systems. Ikonomou's fiction cannot speak to the EU. The IMF cannot speak to *The Lancet*. The Italian political journalist Oriana Fallaci, reflecting on her decades of interviews, accedes to such an ontological division: "I do not understand power, the mechanism by which men or women feel themselves invested in or become invested with the right to rule over others and punish them if they do not obey … to the same degree that I do not understand power, I do understand those who oppose power, who criticize power, who contest power."[46] Few could have listened with greater critical

---

43. Perec, 13.
44. Perec, 139–40.
45. Perec, 63–64.
46. Oriana Fallaci, *Interview with History*, trans. John Shepley (Boston: Houghton Mifflin, 1976), 13.

and emotional attention to what was said by those in power, even as she could not understand what was being said.

Similarly, the Director-General of the World Trade Organization might read Euripides and appeal to the tragic without sharing at all what tragedy means in Euripides. Each exists to demolish the other. What Perec's aesthetic experiment at once proposes and enacts is the way this antagonism or separation is illusive. Even as they seem untouchable, they are interdependent:

> In this book there are two texts which simply alternate; you might almost believe they had nothing in common, but they are in fact inextricably bound up with each other, as though neither could exist on its own, as though it was only their coming together ... that could make apparent what is never quite said in one, never quite said in the other, but said only in their fragile overlapping.[47]

To imagine this is at once elusive and urgent.

When Ikonomou's characters invoke a language of human experience, drawing upon memory and philosophy, tragedy and poetry, they reject the sociopolitical as much as the rhetorical structures of austerity that would dehumanize them. And yet, as a response to austerity, their language cannot help but bear its imprint. We can read the IMF's hierarchies in Ikonomou's aesthetics as we can read the fists or cords that marked a bruised body. Conversely, neoliberalism draws from rhetorical tropes, narrative form and tragic theater to advance its global system, a system that directs our attention away from that very body. The memories of childhood ultimately collapse under W's logic as its aesthetic imaginary elides with the *Todeslager* of Bełżec, Sobibór, and Treblinka. The daring proposition of Perec's experiment, perhaps, is that these systems of thinking are at once antagonistic and enmeshed. What might such a critical methodology look like? How can we unseam these philosophies and divine the one from within the other, their denial, repression and trace?

Act II, scene 2: What Begins in One Language Ends in Another

When orthodox economists posit that firms have "neither the duty nor the right to decide what is moral behavior (Jensen 2001, Sternberg 2000), and [that their] task is to maximize profits,"[48] they might be likened to the derivatives market: untethered from the consequences of profit. Varoufakis's recent book on the European economic crisis, *And the Weak Suffer What They Must?* weighs the burden of this adage as a guide for the global economy.[49]

---

47. Perec, xiv.

48. Colin Crouch, "Sustainability, Neoliberalism, and the Moral Quality of Capitalism," *Business & Professional Ethics Journal* 31, no. 2 (2012): 364, http://www.jstor.org/stable/41705489.

49. Yanis Varoufakis, And the Weak Suffer What They Must? Europe's Crisis and America's Economic Future (London: Random House, 2016).

The title is taken from Thucydides' *The History of the Peloponnesian War*, as the Athenian generals feign negotiations with the Melians—one of the few city-states that sought to remain neutral in the war between Athens and Sparta. Even as the Melians know they will lose against the Athenians, they choose to fight and save their sovereignty rather than surrender as slaves. The Athenians duly kill all the men and enslave the women and children. The full line spoken by the Athenian general reads: "Right, as the world goes, is only in question between equals in power, while the strong do what they can and the weak suffer what they must."[50] Haunted by this idea of Thucydides, and copious in its research, Varoufakis's book ultimately argues that reaping the benefits and ignoring the consequences of asymmetrical human value does more than free economists or bankers to maximize profits; the stakes for a future democratic Europe and, conversely, the rise of supremacism could not be higher.

And yet journalists and policymakers, politicians and global leaders working within a neoliberal project deliberately assure the social good effected by its agenda (represented as free trade, globalization, laissez-faire capitalism). Such assurances would suggest that neoliberalism's moral standing in the community does matter, very much. Continuing along Lamy's career path, *The Geneva Consensus: Making Trade Work for All* finds him praising globalization as the key to global prosperity. Under benevolent chapter headings such as "Helping the poorest up the prosperity ladder," he explains: "There is a direct correlation between integration into the multilateral trading system and economic growth, and between growth and poverty reduction. We need to look no further than China, where more than 600 million people, significantly more than the population of the European Union, have been lifted out of poverty in less than thirty years."[51] To search behind these galvanizing phrases and impressive numbers, though, is to discover other stories, stories that challenge the economic achievement and hence the social good Lamy describes.

In her recent work on female sex workers in China, anthropologist Yeon Jung Yu demonstrates how market-driven reforms have led to a dramatic economic gap between rural and urban areas, resulting in large-scale migration; about 277 million internal migrant workers in China make it the largest labor flow in the world. Because these illegal migrants lack a permanent address, they have become a "floating population," excluded from local educational resources, citywide social welfare programs and many jobs. There has also been a staggering rise in sex work, with numbers now estimated at 6 to 10 million. As state welfare programs are cut and Confucian values of hierarchical gender roles persist,

---

50. Thucydides, *The War of the Peloponnesians and the Athenians*, trans. and ed. Jeremy Mynott (Cambridge: Cambridge University Press, 2013), 5.17.

51. Pascal Lamy, *The Geneva Consensus: Making Trade Work for All* (Cambridge: Cambridge University Press, 2013), 38.

the care and support of rural families has shifted onto largely unskilled, poorly educated migrant women, women whose income as a janitor or waitress cannot compare to that from illegal sex work in the cities.[52] The value of Yu's research and other research like it cannot be overestimated, because it problematizes a simple equation of economic success with human success and, further, suggests a systemic discrepancy in perspectives between economic institutions and the very communities they claim to redeem. Speaking to the effects of austerity in the Baltics, K. B. Usha writes: "their success claims arguably contradict with its [austerity's] revealing social consequences such as increased national debt, unemployment, out-migration, negative demographic changes, poverty, inequality, social exclusion, deterioration in health security and misery to the common people."[53]

In looking to explain such divergent, even antithetical, accounts of neoliberal outcomes, inattention to labor conditions would seem at fault. And yet, from the founding of neoliberalism, its adherents have been forced to contend with labor, as much in labor's demands for rights and wages as in the "stickiness" of human choice stalling the machine of perfect labor mobility.[54] With the fall of the Austro-Hungarian empire, Austria in the 1920s had become isolated politically and economically, surrounded by new sovereign nations and new trade barriers, barred from aligning with Germany, lacking the unity of the Hapsburgs, diminished geographically and militarily and unsuited industrially for a country without empire. At this turning point of empire, Ludwig von Mises, founder of the Geneva School and a political advisor postwar, argued that in order for Austria to again become competitive internationally, it would have to adjust internally. His policy proposals from the time remain a blueprint for conservative approaches to increased competition: lower wages, privatization of public enterprises, eliminating food subsidies and lifting entry and residence restrictions for foreigners (this last ushering in a population willing to accept the previous terms). That a neoliberal approach to labor took shape during this liminal moment between the fall of empire and the reconstruction of post-imperial power is not insignificant.

At the outset, Austria's strong trade unions provided a bulwark against Mises's policies, at least until the summer of 1927. Six months earlier, members of the right-wing militia had entered a Social Democratic area and, when harassed, fired into a crowd, killing a worker and a child. Their closely watched trial ended in acquittal, sparking worker

---

52. Yeon Jung Yu et al., "Flexible Labor: The Work Strategies of Female Sex Workers in Postsocialist China," *Human Organization* 77, no. 2 (2018): 146–56; and "In-Transitivity: Network Patterns of Female Sex Workers in China," *Human Organization* 75, no. 4 (2016): 358-63.

53. K. B. Usha, "Social Consequences of Neoliberal Economic Crisis and Austerity Policy in the Baltic States," *International Studies* 51, no. 1–4 (2014): 72.

54. See Friedrich A. von Hayek, *The Essence of Hayek*, eds. Chiaki Nishiyama and Kurt R. Leube (Stanford, CA: Hoover Institution Press, 1984) and Hayek, *Hayek on Hayek: An Autobiographical Dialogue*, eds. Stephen Kresge and Leif Wenar (Chicago: University of Chicago Press, 1994).

strikes. Others stormed and set fire to the Parliament. The government's response was to order police to fire on demonstrators. After three days, 89 people had been killed and over 1,000 people injured. The workers' movement was permanently weakened.[55] Mises's biographer describes him responding to events with "surprise and delight at the general failure of the strike" and a sense of triumph that the "threats" and "bully[ing]" of the Social Democratic Party had proved "less dangerous than believed."[56] This response indicates a set of values framed as economic policy: fiscal goals may require a human cost, and such a cost may be cause for celebration.

By recalling these early neoliberal perspectives on tragedy and victory, it becomes possible to generate a kind of map of relational values and forces among political policies, workers and state violence. Gottfried Haberler, a pupil of Mises and a key researcher for the Geneva School, clarified his teacher's policies and response to Vienna 1927 in his account of the trouble with and solution to disruptive labor:

> Most mettlesome of all were the obstacles that impeded the free movement of that most essential commodity: human labor. Haberler saw labor as sticky but highly versatile when forced to move. He praised workers for their ability to adapt but condemned them for wanting to stay in place. The danger lay where labor gained allies that acted as anchors. He blamed organized labor and "state intervention in labor questions in connection with unemployment insurance and unemployment relief" for decreasing labor's "mobility and adaptability." ... For free trade to work, the barriers of the trade union needed to fall.[57]

In commodifying workers, Haberler derives a system where labor's use value increases as its replaceability and powerlessness increases, and conversely, its threat increases as its power increases.

---

55. Slobodian tells a version of this story in the first chapter of *Globalists*.

56. Slobodian, 45, quoting Jörg Guido Hülsmann, *Mises: The Last Knight of Liberalism* (Auburn AL: Ludwig von Mises Institute, 2007), 580–81. The relationship between democracy and neoliberalism has been fraught since its inception, in the sense that leftist governments and labor movements are not always supportive of neoliberal policies—as Mises's policies, going back to the 1920s, show. Varoufakis's account of the Bundesbank's recent control over European countries' elections offers a simple if stark example of this tension between democracy and neoliberalism: "Chancellor Schmidt had invested enormous political capital, in collaboration with Washington, to ensure that the Left failed in its bid for power in the Iberian peninsula and of course in Italy, where a resurgent communist party under the enlightened leadership of Enrico Berlinguer was working on a 'historic compromise' with progressive elements of Italy's Christian Democrats. Monetary union and the prospect of a common currency were political gifts of great value to conservative forces"; Varoufakis, 108–09.

57. Slobodian, 53, quoting Gottfried Haberler, Alfred W. Stonier and Frederic Benham, *The Theory of International Trade, with Its Applications to Commercial Policy* (London: W. Dodge, 1936), 194.

In these accounts, the worker functions to support the uninterrupted flow of goods. Thus, the particular needs of one who labors become "mettlesome," as they disrupt the ideality of free trade, the perfect functioning of the theoretical as the actual. Mises's response to the 1927 strike and Haberler's dream of a perfect labor flow, if dehumanizing, paved the way for austerity today, to the degree that austerity derives from an economic system whose fiscal goals exceed, if not depend upon, human costs. Through a canny slip of economic magic, Haberler sees this human cost without seeing it in human terms. If we keep our eyes trained on the numbers, individuals can become a matter of irrelevance:

> "For prices to serve their function [in other words, to accurately reflect supply and demand in markets] they must not encounter resistance ... [but] real ... losses can occur in the form of strikes and unemployment." *Luckily he [Haberler] pointed out, "labor was the most mobile and diverse of all the factors of production." Even if unemployment figures remained constant, the actual mass of unemployed usually rotated in and out as people moved from position to position.* In the demand for the "faultless functioning of the price mechanism," Haberler conjured an image reminiscent of an enormous clockwork or factory apparatus, shuttling components from one location to the other. He cited earlier thinkers like Bastiat, who argued that free trade worked like an invention, constantly rearranging the landscape of production, sending workers to new places of work when one has been outmoded or squeezed out by overseas competition.[58]

From these historical events and writings, it may become easier to imagine how proponents of globalization can describe it as the "most powerful—and life-enhancing—force on earth."[59] When particular groups of people (workers, migrants, refugees, floating labor) are occluded from a theory, and when particular people as individuals are interchangeable, like so many parts in an economic machine, a system of ethics or economics arises that will likely reduce individuals to objects even as it holds up individual freedom as the highest value.

The theoretical structure of neoliberalism as a network across nations seems predicated on fiscal control, not functionaries. Reading Slobodian's *Globalists*, one expects neoliberal policymakers to avoid any mention of people, except when deferring to the broad category of labor. And yet, as an economic school of thought, its voiced allegiance is to the individual actor. From Hayek's influential 1944 text *The Road to Serfdom* (which argues that it was collectivism, not a character defect of Germans, that led to, and will

---

58. Slobodian, 50 [emphasis added]. Claude-Frédéric Bastiat (1801–50) was an anti-socialist, anti-protectionist French economist, champion of free markets and limited government. His theory of unintended consequences, in support of "economic freedom," appears in both Hayek and Friedman.

59. Lamy, "Making Trade Work."

lead again, to Nazism[60]) to Milton Friedman's 1961 *Capitalism and Freedom* (which proclaims "freedom as the ultimate goal and the individual as the ultimate entity"[61]), the protagonist for these thinkers is the individual, free of state control. The Oxford *History of Neoliberalism* takes the terms *individual* and *freedom* to be central for defining neoliberalism: "[it] proposes that human well-being can best be advanced by liberating individual entrepreneurial freedoms and skills within an institutional framework characterized by strong private property rights, free market and free trade."[62] How does the same system celebrate the individual and the death of the individual? Are some individuals devalued while others are valued? Is the individual described here simply an avatar of capital? In which case, is it not the individual per se but the potential of the individual to generate maximum profit that is the revered subject?

The methodical efficiency with which austerity dismantled systems of solidarity would seem to indicate that the answer lies somewhere between. If we take the emancipatory subject of neoliberalism to be the individual, separate from community, then the individual in solidarity with a community would lack value except as a cog. Moreover, an individual imbricated in the community stands to threaten or at least impede the individual dedicated to profit (*And the Weak Suffer What They Must?* looks to account for this structure).[63] The idea that austerity has extended the effectiveness and reach of neoliberalism more than ever before gains in credibility when we look at the speed with which it has sought to replace cultures of solidarity with cultures of individualism—all in the name of fiscal responsibility. Whether this is an economic or an ethical transition would be difficult to state.

A central component of the reforms demanded by austerity measures was that the Greek state curb public expenditure through reductions in pensions and social benefits. In her chapter analyzing the effects of reform on Greece's cultural values, Maria Mexi, an expert with the International Labour Organization (ILO) and a senior research associate at the Albert Hirschman Centre on Democracy (IHEID) in Geneva, demonstrates (as *The Lancet* does) that austerity's toll compounds for vulnerable communities. As the state shifted the cost of debt to pensioners, immigrants and working-class families, it was forced to defund and cut social welfare programs, thus shifting the responsibility of care to populations already weakened by the debt crisis. The cost of these measures on public health has come under scrutiny, but Mexi directs us additionally to the cost of austerity on Greece's cultural framework, on its deeply held system of values. She argues that, in the long term, austerity is not just about debt collection but about long-term social and

---

60. Friedrich A. von Hayek, *The Road to Serfdom: With the Intellectuals and Socialism* (London: Institute of Economic Affairs, 2005).
61. Friedman, Capitalism and Freedom, 5.
62. David Harvey, *A Brief History of Neoliberalism* (Oxford: Oxford University Press, 2007), 2.
63. Maria M. Mexi, "Greece," in *Solidarity as a Public Virtue? Law and Public Policies in the European Union*, eds. Veronica Federico and Christian Lahusen, 91–108 (Baden-Baden: Nomos, 2018).

political change. By eroding the institutional solidarity underpinning many postwar arrangements—the very solidarity that created the Greek modern social welfare state and economy—austerity seeks nothing less than a cultural exchange of values, solidarity in exchange for individualism:

> The adverse effects of this linkage have been more painful for vulnerable groups undermining a set of values such as social justice and equity and the moral foundations of public policy-making. Moreover, solidarity as a normative foundation of the Greek welfare state has been challenged by the ambivalent judicial stance over reductions in pensions and social benefits amid austerity backlash. This upset Greeks' ... understanding of the welfare state and prevailing conceptions of solidarity as a value and a guiding principle for public policy. Hence, the crisis has raised many questions about solidarity as a moral foundation of public policy and "the institutional responsibility of the whole polity for a certain contribution to the corporeal needs of the individuals" (Tsoukalas, 1998, 1).[64]

Institutional commitment to a unified Europe, bolstered by "Euroenthusiasm," would indicate a broad investment in European solidarity, yet a solidarity between bankers and the financial institutions dedicated to bailing them out seems to be one of the few bonds to survive the Eurogroup's reach. If cynical, such a claim draws on the damage wrought by austerity on cultures founded on solidarity, along with austerity's role in the current

---

64. Mexi, 99. She points also to the way in which individuals and grassroots organizations have stepped in where the state has stepped out: "De Beer's (2005) distinction between 'individual' (micro-level) and 'institutional' (macro-level) solidarity may be informative in this context. Individual solidarity refers to situations in which single persons decide to contribute to the well-being of others; institutional solidarity refers to types of solidarity that have been institutionalized in the form, for instance, of the modern welfare state and social protection systems ... As a result of the State's failure to provide citizens in need with adequate social policies and services, there is evidence—as we have seen—testifying to the (re)-generation of civil society. Emerging solidarity initiatives and grassroots groups mainly, embodying what Harvey (2000) describes as 'new spaces of hope.' These new forms of micro-level solidarity are increasingly functioning as a 'shadow welfare state.' They seem to be filling in historically established 'solidarity gaps' in clientelism-driven social welfare provision that have been further intensified by recent policy choices" (16). Greece's reimagining of micro- and macro-level forms of solidarity in response to shifting economic realities might suggest an organic effectiveness to austerity and a capitalist approach to social welfare. As government exits, individuals enter. Recent anthropological studies suggest, however, that such transitions come at a high cost. Yu's fieldwork in the province of Hainan, China, for example, tells how individuals, already strained by low incomes, familial responsibilities and a culture of increasing materialism, must step into the place vacated by government in order to take on the medical, financial, psychological and educational care of their families and extended families (in-laws). This has led to mass internal immigration in the case of China and, as already noted, staggering increases in sex work and a resulting public health crisis. In other words, what is the cost and who bears this cost in the shift from micro- to macro-solidarity?

legitimation crisis in Europe, as austerity takes precedence over solidarity at the risk of a future democratic Europe.

How, then, do political/financial institutions and the press negotiate the central paradox of neoliberalism, where individuals are at once destroyed and freed? Greece's troubles and how we ought to respond were consistently couched within a framework of traditional moral narratives. When *Der Spiegel* ran headlines such as "Germans Won't Pay for Greece's Vacation from Reality"; "'Pay Your Taxes': Greeks Furious over Harsh Words from IMF and Germany"; and "Reform Hero Takes on Corruption in Thessaloniki," they appealed to stereotypes of laziness and industriousness once popularized in European fables.[65] Such cultural framing positions austerity as a palatable but also necessary—indeed, morally imperative—response to the European debt crisis. Translated here, the good, hardworking people of Germany should not be forced to pay the debts of lazy Greeks and Italians—or the Portuguese or Irish, for that matter. In this telling, the good Greek is the one who admits to this hierarchy and seeks to imitate his good German counterpart: "'Your city is clean, while ours is dirty,' said [Mayor] Yiannis Boutaris, speaking in a deep and gravelly voice. 'What works in your city doesn't work in ours.' He had come to Berlin to learn how to change this deplorable state of affairs. And he wants to do it as quickly as possible."[66]

While appealing in its simplicity, the alternately demoralizing and aggrandizing roles this story foists onto each nation undermines European solidarity as it undermines dignity on one hand and empathy on the other (the inevitable corollary found in Greek papers was that the Germans were behaving like Nazis, looking to create a Fourth Reich by crippling the rest of Europe). More specifically, a narrative of industrious Germany suffering the cost of bailing out profligate Greece foments demands for debt payment at any cost, along with the need to teach Greece a lesson.[67] Of the many complexities the story overlooks, three at least are worth noting: the decade of predatory lending and profit

---

65. Aesop's fable "The Ant and the Grasshopper" being the most common. It appears as no small irony that the author is Greek.

66. Julia Amalia Heyer, "Greece's Model Mayor: Reform Hero Takes on Corruption in Thessaloniki," *Der Spiegel*, February 15, 2012, https://www.spiegel.de/international/europe/greece-s-model-mayor-reform-hero-takes-on-corruption-in-thessaloniki-a-815289.html.

67. john a. powell offers a similar description of American banks during the 2008 financial crisis. powell points specifically to their moralizing tendency: "their rhetoric in this crisis has focused exclusively on blaming the victims of their lending scams—scams yielding enormous profits for those on the inside. How ironic it is that now, after having received staggering infusions of our tax dollars, they turn around and blame the targets and victims of their schemes, for what has happened to all of us—around the world—as a result. Indeed, they frequently throw in a little lecture about the irresponsibility of their targets and victims as well"; *Racing to Justice* (Bloomington: Indiana University Press, 2012), 238.

by German banks; the fact that the loans to Greece came not only from French and German taxpayers but also from the Portuguese, Slovaks and Irish—from taxpayers whose banks had nothing to gain from the bailout, since their banks hadn't suffered the losses; and, not least, the London Debt Agreement of 1953, when Greece along with the other Allied nations forgave German debt by about 50%.[68]

Each point arguably challenges the simple binary roles set out for Greece and Germany. The compulsion to retell the ant and the grasshopper fable, though, in the face of complicating histories and realities, indicates not just the pervasiveness of neoliberal values but also our comfort with neoliberal explanations for what we see, particularly as they involve economic justice. While it has been noted that neoliberals have always been interested in shrinking and publicly marking the demise of the welfare state, the early moral and political foundations for this approach read as particularly draconian. Hayek argued, for example, that the only type of justice that can preserve human dignity and democracy is retributive justice, which considers the crime to the explicit exclusion of the criminal and his future. This line of reasoning has since been described as the "responsibilitarian principle": if individuals are granted the liberty to make their own choices, then they must also fully accept punishment for their bad choices. "Liberty not only means that the individual has the opportunity and the burden of choice; it also means that he must bear the consequences of his actions and will receive praise or blame for them."[69]

Hayek goes on to argue that any judicial system that offers therapy or hospitalization to criminals fails to see everyone as equal before the law and thus fails as a democracy. He sets out this idea under an epigraph by F. D. Wormuth, a largely forgotten political philosopher who argued in his epic *The Origins of Modern Constitutionalism* that the role of justice is to punish the sinner, not to improve him. "Modern penology," Wormuth regrets, "is therapeutic rather than retributive. It denies that *men should all be treated alike*, and that they should be judged on their actions; it argues that potentialities for the future, rather than atonement for the past, should be the guiding considerations" [emphasis added]. The idea is central to Wormuth's argument for a "Rhadamanthine" justice, one that "only records and censures." This is, in actuality, good for the criminal, he writes:

> It attributes a dignity to [him] which is lacking in Plato's scheme [which rules out retribution]. From this point of view the criminal has a right to be punished, for punishment is a vindication of his status as a moral being ... It is doubtful that democracy could survive in a society organized on the principle of therapy

---

68. Varoufakis, 139.
69. Friedrich A. von Hayek, *The Constitution of Liberty* (Chicago: University of Chicago Press, 1960), 64.

rather than judgment, error rather than sin. If men are free and equal, they must be judged rather than hospitalized.[70]

Wormuth's argument for retribution as a fulfillment of democracy and human rights can be said to realize itself in austerity. Not only is it the perfect punishment for a nation that chose to party instead of work, but paying off one's debt also paves the road to self-improvement and moral/financial responsibility.

That neoliberal writers are engaging in such explicit ethical programs complicates a defense that economists have neither the duty nor the right to decide what is moral. Indeed, the foundational histories and arguments of neoliberalism coalesce around a central paradox: the individual must be saved and the individual must be destroyed. The peculiar ethics of this paradox rest in the way the individual comes to be equated with labor, which comes to be equated with capital, even as this is effected for the individual's ultimate freedom. Or the idea that only a punishment blind to context, history, future or family recognizes human rights and fosters dignity. The tragic logic of neoliberalism is, in this sense, strung along narratives of justice and punishment, individualism and freedom, fictions of superior nations and instructive suffering, dramas that pave the way for and continue to justify as they exacerbate the consequences of austerity: disease, unemployment, suicide.

In the year following his speech in Edinburgh, Lamy published *The Geneva Consensus*. In language invoking Enlightenment ideals of self-determination realized through total control of nature and its resources, he affirms in his introduction that the EU has finally "harnessed globalization." The results, he states, have been spectacular: "Trade has been an extremely efficient conveyor belt of globalization. It has been a powerful instrument for promoting growth and development, for reducing poverty and for improving standards of living."[71] On the grounds of this success, he urges readers to further "reduc[e] 'red tape' for the exchange of goods and services across borders" through stronger global governance and better coordination between international institutions.[72] On the cover of the book is a somewhat blurry image: a Mercator projection of the world. In the foreground is a cross-grid and in the background are the continents, in faint pastels, barely visible.[73] This image poses a visual metonym for neoliberalism, from its inception in the writings of Hayek and Mises, through Friedman and up to its contemporary avatars

---

70. Francis D. Wormuth, *The Origins of Modern Constitutionalism* (New York: Harper, 1949), 213.
71. Lamy, *Geneva Consensus*, vii.
72. Lamy, *Geneva Consensus*, vii.
73. Slobodian calls attention to this image in *Globalists*.

in the EMF and IMF. It captures the world from a distance as a shadowy projection.[74] Far beneath the net of a global neoliberal order, one can only guess what lies or lives below.

Figure 7.1. The cover of Pascal Lamy's book *The Geneva Consensus: Making Trade Work for All* (2013).

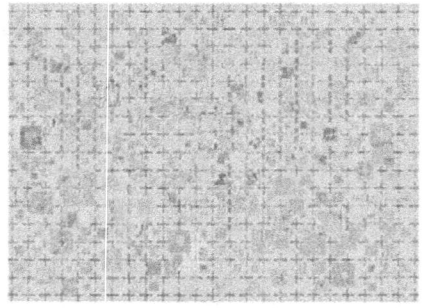

Reproduced by permission from Pascal Lamy, *The Geneva Consensus: Making Trade Work for All* (Cambridge: Cambridge University Press, 2013), cover.

And yet pointing out that people are in fact starving, struggling and dying beneath the pastels means little and does less. There would seem to be, quite simply, communities who justify this suffering as a necessary fact (a fact that might even be applauded) and communities for whom this fact is unjustified. Utilitarian ethics relies on an aggregate approach—whether sacrificial or suffering—to the degree that profit as a positive end achieves itself as it will. As long as suffering remains bounded geographically, financially, its system continues unabated. It is perhaps the greatest fantasy of

---

74. Lamy's choice of a Mercator projection merits attention. Used for navigational purposes, it distorts the size and, by extension, the power of continents, diminishing those at the equator and enlarging those above it. Specifically, Africa appears much smaller than it is, while North America, Europe and Russia appear much larger than they actually are. The result is an argument for the logic of imperial power, with empires appearing greater than they are and the colonized appearing less than they are.

neoliberalism that its repercussions—ecological, social, cultural, psychological and political—can be contained within the confines of the largely postcolonial nations or laboring communities from which it profits. "Contagion" describes the failure of this fantasy. The wildfires are burning. The electrical lines crisscrossing our skies are falling. The ones who seemed unreal become more real than those who we thought most real.

To describe this as contagion, though, is to be trapped in reverberating tragedies. It depends on the illusion that dramatic actions (whether of empire or of neoliberalism) can be delimited. Or that any effects from beyond the delimited borders will be monstrous.[75] How else might we proceed, perceive?

Act 3: The pain of Words

"The image of Greece, faded though it be, endures as an archetype of the miracle wrought by the human spirit."[76]

Might an ethical tradition oriented to particularity focus the macroscopic ethic of neoliberalism? Central to Aristotle's *Nicomachean Ethics* is the idea that no general rule can tell us what it is to be virtuous. Rather, each situation calls on us to act in a different way. Because of this complexity and variability, our best chance for acting justly is to acquire, through a life of practice, the deliberative, emotional and social skills that enable us to put our general understanding of well-being into practice in ways that are suitable to each occasion. And on each occasion, the goal is to find the mean. Aristotle explains his idea of the mean in this way: "The moral virtue is a mean ... between two vices, the one involving excess, the other deficiency. ... Hence also it is no easy task to be good. For in everything it is no easy task to find the middle ...; so too, anyone can get angry— that is easy—or give or spend money; but to do this at the right time, with the right motive, and in the right way, that is not for everyone, nor is it easy."[77]

The radical particularity of Aristotle's ethics necessitates attention to individual cases, individual actions, contexts and histories. Neither an ethics of abstract logic nor a collection of observed facts easily rendered into values, his notion of right judgment is difficult "to determine by reasoning." Instead, "such things depend on particular facts,

---

75. Limited in the sense that it obscures the myriad generative forms of resistance by communities seeking to both reimagine and reclaim identity under duress. Fandango Fronterizo, an annual musical celebration held on both sides of the border wall, as Kabir Sehgal points out, challenges the American narrative of immigrants as thuggish criminals threatening Americans' safety, a contagion to be walled out; Kabir Sehgal, *Fandango at the Wall: Creating Harmony Between the United States and Mexico* (New York: Grand Central, 2018).

76. Henry Miller, *The Colossus of Maroussi* (New York: New Directions, 1941), 74.

77. Aristotle, *Nicomachean Ethics*, trans. David Ross (Oxford: Oxford University Press, 1990), 45.

and the decision [of whether someone has deviated too far from the mean] rests with perception."[78] In his chapter on judgment, Aristotle recognizes the lifelong journey he is setting us upon and so turns us to our elders: "So we ought to attend to the undemonstrated sayings and opinions of experienced and older people or of people of practical wisdom not less than to demonstrations; because experience has given them an eye to see aright."[79] To see with an Aristotelian eye, then, would seem to stand us in better stead in relation to each other. To be virtuous requires that we attend to what is immediately before us, to cull the facts of each situation in its specificity, and then determine what would constitute the mean. Through practice, we improve and are better able to judge the actions of others as well.

Despite their apparent antitheses, Aristotelian and neoliberal ethics share a starting point: the individual as he confronts the world, deciding how to act. Instead of constructing patterns of thought to assess and judge the situations we encounter, though, Hayek turns Aristotle's philosophy on its head, arguing that we are incapable of determining how to act in different situations precisely because each situation is different. In place of increasingly nuanced judgment, he rhetorically throws up his hands and proposes a few golden rules:

> The reliance on abstract rules is a device we have learned to use because our reason is insufficient to master the full detail of complex reality. We all know that, in the pursuit of our individual aims, we are not likely to be successful unless we lay down for ourselves some general rules to which we will adhere without reexamining their justification in every particular instance.[80]

Hayek's is arguably an ethics of inadequacy. But what does he mean by "every particular instance"? It is precisely our encounter with the particular that structures Aristotle's *Ethics*. To surrender judgment in the face of the particular would be to relinquish judgment. Indeed, the limits of our perception, analysis and judgment need not be the limits of our ethical world but rather the beginning of it. Hayek, on the other hand, rejects the Aristotelian concept of an ameliorative life. Adhering through habit to abstract laws, our moral success depends instead on an indifference, if not blindness, to considerations of context, histories, consequences, desires, hopes, beliefs. Aristotle calls this a lack of judgment; Hayek calls it total freedom—"free to sin" and "free to let others sin," we ensure our greatest self-fulfillment.[81] As tempting as it might be to bask in the benevolence

---

78. Aristotle, *Ethics*, 47.
79. Aristotle, *Ethics*, 153.
80. Hayek, Constitution of Liberty, 66.
81. Milton Friedman, *Milton Friedman on Freedom: Selections from the Collected Works of Milton Friedman*, eds. Robert Lesson and Charles G. Palm (Stanford, CA: Hoover Institution Press, 2017), 23, 39, 48, 71. This is Friedman's language as it develops out of Hayek's sociopolitical philosophy.

of Hayek's moral philosophy, it cannot be separated from the retributive judicial system in which we are invited to act, making the idea of letting others sin sound like letting others knot the noose around their neck. Under this net we are all free.

Δέσις and λύσις

In 415 BC Euripides wrote *The Trojan Women*, the third in his trilogy of plays commemorating the Trojan War. The play would have been performed in late March, at dawn, before 15,000 people in the amphitheater on the south side of the Acropolis, high above the lower city or Agora of Athens. Euripides' tragedy is unusual in that it contains little action or plot, instead giving over the stage to the women's lamentation, or *epitaphios logos*—their lamentations for the deaths of husbands and sons, for their lives and their daughters' lives to come as slaves, as concubines, as servants.

The first act is set two days after Troy's capture, before dawn: only silhouettes of shattered buildings against a red glow and rising smoke. Hecuba, the Trojan queen, speaks. She has watched her husband's murder and knows her sons are dead; the city burns behind her. She is about to discover that her daughter Polyxena has been made a living sacrifice at the tomb of Achilles, and that her other daughter, the visionary virgin priestess Cassandra, has been chosen by King Agamemnon for his concubine.

As she describes what she has lost, the Chorus asks: "What words of yours can release pity to match your pain?"[82] In asking this, they seem to be encouraging Hecuba to find such words, words that would bring the Greeks to pity her. Are there any words that would make them stop inflicting pain? And then we might ask, what would it feel like to feel pity equal to her pain? Would it hurt? Would it be painful too? It seems important, though, that the Chorus is not asking for revenge; they are not wishing for the Greeks to suffer the pain that they inflict. They are asking, rather, for words to take shape, words that might change the Greeks from men indifferent to the pain of others to men responsive to it.

The play goes on and Andromache enters. She is the wife of Hecuba's dead son Hector, and she joins the women with her small child. The Chorus tells the Queen: "Hecuba, see! Andromache is coming.... And Hector's son Astyanax is with her. Where are they taking you, sad Andromache, and beside you Hector's sword and armor of bronze, and other spoils of Troy." She replies, "The Achaeans are carrying home their property." Andromache mourns and wonders how she will feign love for a master who has killed her husband. A Greek herald interrupts and informs her that he must take her small child from her. The Greeks are going to kill him by pushing him off the battlements of Troy. The herald continues: "If you call down curses, or struggle or attempt anything unseemly, if you say anything that will make the army angry, no burial for him. If you are quiet, and in a proper

---

82. Euripides, *The Bacchae and Other Plays*, trans. Philip Vellacott (New York: Penguin Classics, 1979), 96.

spirit accept what comes to you, you will not have to leave his body unburied." She relents, silencing her anguish.

What can we learn from this performance two and a half millennia ago? Looking at Euripides' ancient play, we see that as far back as the 5th century BCE, it was accepted at the Dionysia in Athens, at the heart of Western civilization, that what is happening in the play is a tragedy.[83] Enslavement and the forced displacement of people, the deaths of husbands and sons in battle, the separation of children from their mothers and the murder of children is the stuff of tragedy. But what did *tragedy* mean at the time?

Aristotle writes in the *Poetics*, his defense of poetry (contra Plato), that poetry is a valid presentation of the human world, and that the central quality of tragedy is its ability to inspire fear or pity. Tragedy is said to do this when the audience witnesses a *pathos*, a destructive or painful act "such as deaths, paroxysms of pain, woundings." He goes on to say that the audience will feel fear and pity when they see someone fall from good fortune to bad fortune. It is critical, he writes, that this fall is precipitated not by wickedness but by "some mistake of great weight and consequence."[84] If we thread *The Trojan Women* through Aristotle, then, we can say that the women of Troy have fallen from good fortune to bad not because of anything they have done but because of someone else's grave mistake. The Greek army committs just such a mistake in punishing the Trojan women.

One has to wonder, though, if the Athenians would have seen the Greek army's actions as mistaken in this way. At the time *The Trojan Women* was performed, the Athenians had been at war with Sparta for 16 years. As leader of the Delian League, Athens had the allegiance of a collection of 330 city-states and had recently sought additional allegiance from the island of Melos. Melos, an outlier, was a former ally of Sparta and had asked to remain neutral in the war. In response, the Athenians sent 3,400 men to invade. When the Melians still refused to submit the Athenians laid siege to the island, killing all its men and selling the women and children into slavery.

Although *The Trojan Women* is set in Troy and not Melos, the similarity would not have been lost on the Athenians. Euripides was enacting something radical, then; on their day of festal entertainment, he turned the Athenians' eyes back onto themselves, onto an ethics of empire-at-any-cost. Not only does the play expose the tragic error of that ethics, it also makes a radical choice about who is worthy of pity. For all the wisdom of his *Ethics*, Aristotle in the *Poetics* explicitly urges playwrights not to make women and slaves their central characters because, as he explains, "women [are] inferior and the other [i.e., slaves], as a class, worthless."[85] They are the others, the virtual foreigners in the city-state. Although there have been disagreements about Aristotle's acceptance or

---

83. *The Trojan Women* was performed as Euripides' submission for a tragic play in 415 BCE.
84. Aristotle, *Poetics*, trans. Gerald. F. Else (Ann Arbor: University of Michigan Press, 1967), 38.
85. Aristotle, *Poetics*, 43.

problematizing of slavery, it is arguable that his ethics of the particular remains at a theoretical level. There are no stories in the *Ethics* of people, of slaves, of women. Their stories remain untold.

Yet Euripides does tell their story. He chooses as his characters, not men but women— women who are now enslaved. So we have a play whose words ask us to recognize ourselves as the perpetrators of a grave mistake, a play that appeals to us to take pity on those we take to be worthless and inferior, whose drama insists on the breadth of their pain, dignity and desolation.

When the Chorus asks, "What words of yours can release pity to match your pain?" they are speaking not only of what Hecuba might do with her words but also of what Euripides might do with his. And in this sense, Euripides' role as a poet and as playwright collapses into the role of the women and the enslaved as he seeks for the words, trying to release pity to match the pain that has been inflicted. We cannot know what the Athenians felt. We know that playwrights at the time were meant to act as philosophical gadflies, and it is said that Euripides' audiences applauded him and funded 90 performances of his plays. But we know too that he left Athens and remained exiled in Macedonia until his death.

Patterns of sentences and strings of thought might draw 415 BCE into the present, Euripides to austerity. What makes these tragedies tragic is both what is made visible and what is left invisible. Between them are countless tragedies, stories told and untold. To have been in the amphitheater in 415 BCE watching *The Trojan Women*, one had to bear witness to the tragedy unfolding, act by act. But to see is not to have pity. Euripides seems aware of this way we can see and not see. He turns then to words, words that might move us not just to see but to see and have pity—and not a small pity, but a pity to match the pain.

Bibliography

Aristotle. *Nicomachean Ethics*. Translated by David Ross. Oxford: Oxford University Press, 1990.

———. *Poetics.* Translated by Gerald. F. Else. Ann Arbor: University of Michigan Press, 1967.

Carlsen, Laura. "Under NAFTA, Mexico Suffered and the United States Felt Its Pain." *New York Times*, November 23, 2013. https://www.nytimes.com/roomfordebate/2013/11/24/what-weve-learned-from-nafta/under-nafta-mexico-suffered-and-the-united-states-felt-its-pain.

Coates, San, and Marcus Leroux. "Ministers Aim to Build Empire 2.0 with African Commonwealth." *The Times*, March 6, 2017. https://www.thetimes.co.uk/article/ministers-aim-to-build-empire-2-0-with-african-commonwealth-after-brexit-v9bs6f6z9.

Coppola, Frances. "The Terrible Human Costs of Greece's Bailout." *Forbes*, August 31, 2018. https://www.forbes.com/sites/francescoppola/2018/08/31/the-terrible-human-cost-of-greeces-bailouts/?sh=4b5261e44b31.

Crespi, Elena, Silvain Aubry, Mayra Gomez, Bret Thiele and Matthias Sant'ana. *Downgrading Rights: The Cost of Austerity in Greece.* Paris: International Federation for Human Rights/Hellenic League for Human Rights, 2014. https://www.fidh.org/IMG/pdf/downgrading_rights_the_cost_of_austerity_in_greece.pdf.

Crouch, Colin. "Sustainability, Neoliberalism, and the Moral Quality of Capitalism." *Business & Professional Ethics Journal* 31, no. 2 (2012): 363–74. http://www.jstor.org/stable/41705489.

Duménil, Gérard, and Dominique Lévy. *The Crisis of Neoliberalism.* Cambridge, MA: Harvard University Press, 2011.

Euripides. *The Bacchae and Other Plays.* Translated by Philip Vellacott. New York: Penguin Classics, 1979.

"Explaining Greece's Debt Crisis." *New York Times,* June 17, 2016. https://www.nytimes.com/interactive/2016/business/international/greece-debt-crisis-euro.html.

Fallaci, Oriana. *Interview with History.* Translated by John Shepley. Boston: Houghton Mifflin, 1976.

Farnesworth, Kevin, and Zoë Irving. "Austerity: Neoliberal Dreams Come True." *Critical Social Policy* 38, no. 3 (2018): 461–81.

Ferguson, Kathryn, Norma A. Price, Ted Parks, Claudia Aburto Guzmán and John M. Fife. *Crossing with the Virgin: Stories from the Migrant Trail.* Tucson: University of Arizona Press, 2010.

Friedman, Milton. *Capitalism and Freedom.* Chicago: University of Chicago Press, 2002.

———. *Milton Friedman on Freedom: Selections from the Collected Works of Milton Friedman.* Edited by Robert Lesson and Charles G. Palm. Stanford, CA: Hoover Institution Press, 2017.

Giroux, Henry A. *Against the Terror of Neoliberalism: Politics Beyond the Age of Greed.* Boulder, CO: Paradigm, 2008.

———. *Stormy Weather: Katrina and the Politics of Disposability.* Boulder, CO: Paradigm, 2006.

Haberler, Gottfried, Alfred W. Stonier and Frederic Benham. *The Theory of International Trade, with Its Applications to Commercial Policy.* London: W. Dodge, 1936.

Harvey, David. *A Brief History of Neoliberalism.* Oxford: Oxford University Press, 2007.

Hayek, Friedrich A. von. *The Constitution of Liberty.* Chicago: University of Chicago Press, 1960.

———. *The Essence of Hayek.* Edited by Chiaki Nishiyama and Kurt R. Leube. Stanford, CA: Hoover Institution Press, 1984.

———. *Hayek on Hayek: An Autobiographical Dialogue.* Edited by Stephen Kresge and Leif Wenar. Chicago: University of Chicago Press, 1994.

———. *The Road to Serfdom: With the Intellectuals and Socialism.* London: Institute of Economic Affairs, 2005.

Henwood, Doug. Wall Street: How It Works and for Whom. London: Verso, 1997.

Heyer, Julia Amalia. "Greece's Model Mayor: Reform Hero Takes on Corruption in Thessaloniki." *Der Spiegel,* February 15, 2012. https://www.spiegel.de/international/europe/greece-s-model-mayor-reform-hero-takes-on-corruption-in-thessaloniki-a-815289.html.

Hochschild, Adam. *Lessons from a Dark Time.* Oakland: University of California Press, 2018.

Hülsmann, Jörg Guido. *Mises: The Last Knight of Liberalism*. Auburn, AL: Ludwig von Mises Institute, 2007.

Ikonomou, Christos. *Good Will Come from the Sea*. Translated by Karen Emmerich. Brooklyn, NY: Archipelago Books, 2014.

Jackson, Ben. "At the Origins of Neoliberalism: The Free Economy and the Strong State, 1930–1947." *Historical Journal* 53, no. 1 (2010): 129–51.

Kazantzakis, Nikos. *The Fratricides*. London: Faber and Faber, 1967.

Krugman, Paul R. *Arguing with Zombies: Economics, Politics and the Fight for a Better Future*. New York: Norton, 2020.

Lamy, Pascal. "Europe Needs a 'Legitimacy Compact' – Lamy." Speech at awarding of honorary doctorate, University of Edinburgh, June 29, 2012. https://www.wto.org/english/news_e/sppl_e/sppl241_e.htm.

———. *The Geneva Consensus: Making Trade Work for All*. Cambridge: Cambridge University Press, 2013.

———. "Making Trade Work for Development: Time for a Geneva Consensus." Emile Noel Lecture, New York University Law School, October 30, 2006.

Mexi, Maria M. "Greece." In *Solidarity as a Public Virtue? Law and Public Policies in the European Union*, edited by Veronica Federico and Christian Lahusen, 91–108. Baden-Baden: Nomos, 2018.

Mijatovic, Dunja. "Report of the Commissioner for Human Rights Following Her Visit to Greece from 25 to 29 of June, 2018." Strasbourg: Council of Europe, November 6, 2018.

Miller, Henry. *The Colossus of Maroussi*. New York: New Directions, 1941.

Mont Pèlerin Society. "Statement of Aims." https://www.montpelerin.org/statement-of-aims/.

Nevins, Joseph. *Dying to Live: A Story of U.S. Immigration in an Age of Global Apartheid*. San Francisco: City Lights Books, 2008.

Ong, Aihwa. "Neoliberalism as a Mobile Technology." *Transactions of the Institute of British Geographers*, n.s., 32, no. 1 (2007): 3–8. http://www.jstor.org/stable/4639996.

Ostry, Jonathan D., Prakash Loungani and Davide Furceri. "Neoliberalism: Oversold?" *Finance and Development* 53, no 2 (June 2016): 38–41. https://www.imf.org/external/pubs/ft/fandd/2016/06/pdf/ostry.pdf.

Parker, Ian. "The Greek Warrior: How a Radical Finance Minister Took on Europe—and Failed." *New Yorker*, August 3, 2015. https://www.newyorker.com/magazine/2015/08/03/the-greek-warrior.

Perec, George. *W, or the Memory of Childhood*. Translated by David Bellos. Boston: Verba Mundi, 2017.

Pernick, Martin S. "Contagion and Culture." *American Literary History* 14, no. 4 (2002): 858–65. www.jstor.org/stable/3568029.

powell, john a. *Racing to Justice*. Bloomington: Indiana University Press, 2012.

Rachiotis, George, David Stuckler, Martin McKee and Christos Hadjichristodoulou. "What Has Happened to Suicides During the Greek Economic Crisis? Findings from an Ecological Study of Suicides and Their Determinants (2003–2012)." *BMJ Journals* 5, no. 3 (May 10, 2017). doi: 10.1136/bmjopen-2014-007295corr1.

Reich, Robert B. *The Common Good*. New York: Knopf, 2018.

Schulz-Forberg, Hagen. "The Dot-Connector: How the League of Nations Incidentally Gave Birth to Neoliberalism." *The Invention of International Bureaucracy* (blog).

Aarhus University, June 24, 2018. https://projects.au.dk/en/inventingbureaucracy/blog/show/artikel/the-dot-connector-how-the-league-of-nations-incidentally-gave-birth-to-neoliberalism/.

Sehgal, Kabir. *Fandango at the Wall: Creating Harmony Between the United States and Mexico*. New York: Grand Central, 2018.

Slobodian, Quinn. *Globalists: The End of Empire and the Birth of Neoliberalism*. Cambridge, MA: Harvard University Press, 2018.

Thucydides. *The War of the Peloponnesians and the Athenians*. Translated and edited by Jeremy Mynott. Cambridge: Cambridge University Press, 2013.

Tyrovolas, Stefanos, Nicholas J. Kassebaum, Andy Stergachis, Haftom Niguse Abraha, François Alla, Sofia Androudi et al. "The Burden of Disease in Greece, Health Loss, Risk Factors, and Health Financing, 2000–16: An Analysis of the Global Burden of Disease Study 2016." *The Lancet* 3, no. 8 (July 25, 2018): 395–406. https://www.thelancet.com/action/showPdf?pii=S2468-2667%2818%2930130-0.

Usha, K. B. "Social Consequences of Neoliberal Economic Crisis and Austerity Policy in the Baltic States." *International Studies* 51, no. 1–4 (2014): 72–100.

Varoufakis, Yanis. *And the Weak Suffer What They Must? Europe's Crisis and America's Economic Future*. London: Random House, 2016.

Wormuth, Francis D. *The Origins of Modern Constitutionalism*. Harper: New York, 1949.

Yu, Y. J., C. McCarty and J. H. Jones. "Flexible Labor: The Work Strategies of Female Sex Workers in Post-socialist China." *Human Organization* 77, no. 2 (2018): 146–56.

Yu, Y. J., C. McCarty, J. H. Jones and X. Li. "In-Transitivity: Network Patterns of Female Sex Workers in China." *Human Organization* 75, no. 4 (2016): 358–63.

Chapter 8

The Inspirational Role of Greek Traditional Music in the Composition of Modern and Postmodern Guitar Repertoire

Ioannis Andronoglou
University of Western Macedonia, Greece

Abstract

The research challenge addressed in this chapter lies in the relation between Greek guitarist-composers and Greek traditional music, with special attention to the borrowing of certain elements, either directly, in the form of musical themes, rhythms, techniques; or indirectly, as traditional color-schemed works. Furthering the analysis, the original material is placed in the historical and musical/aesthetic frameworks of the time the works were composed, comparing them to contemporary international guitar music events so this musical direction will be fully acknowledged.

Hence, many scientific issues are raised with regards to the music: aesthetic and historical contexts of the Greek guitarists who worked on this musical direction, the effect of international trends on their work, as well as the level of synchronization with international trends in composition for guitar. The main purpose of this essay is to analyse specific works of Greek guitarist-composers by comparing them to several original traditional compositions, to place this musical fact in the history of music in Greece, and to examine the reasons for its topicality today.

Keywords: Greek traditional music, Greek folklore, guitar, Greece, postmodernism, ethnic.

***

Introduction: cultural nationalism and the Greek National Music School

In 1931 the Stefanos Gaitanos music publishing house published its *Guitar Collection*, consisting of 25 issues. Transcripts of folk songs for guitar appeared in all 25 issues of the collection. The songs include "Syrtos Plakiotikos," "Amygdalia Pentozalis," "Dance Kalamatianos," "Haniotikos," "Vasiliki" and others. The transcriptions could be described as simplistic, since the melody is performed with only a bass accompaniment. Nevertheless, these were the first attempts to transcribe Greek folk songs for solo guitar. In contrast, printed editions of guitar music from the Istanbul magazine *Mousiki* of 1910 to 1920, for example, do not include such local material; its transcribed or adapted material for guitar came from Italian operas.[1]

The research question that arises from these observations is why this attention to Greek traditional music was—and still is—occurring as part of the creation of a guitar repertoire in Greece. This chapter will study this musical change historically in order to show how it evolved through various musical styles over the years. More specifically, this compositional change in focus, which evolved into an entire musical direction, began in the context of the National School of Music and continues to this day from a postmodern compositional perspective. Further, I will demonstrate how a musical historical fact has become a current musical necessity.

It is worth noting that, while this question has been investigated by musicologists for modern artistic Greek music creation as a whole, it was not asked with a direct focus on guitar repertoire. Most books and dissertations concerning the guitar in Greece deal with issues such as the overall work of Greek composers for guitar and the technique and teaching of the guitar in Greece. Also, some dissertations are simply biographies of Greek guitarists. Thus the above research question is raised for the first time, and it is worth exploring because of its many extensions beyond separatist music analysis. My doctoral thesis and recently published book, *Greek Traditional Music as a Source of Inspiration in the Composition of Works for Guitar*, directly relate to the historical-cultural-social implications of this issue. This chapter uses the information to frame the historical progression of this musical direction.

In order to understand the beginning of the musical reorientation that took place in 1931, it is useful to look at what was happening a few years earlier. In 1908 a historic concert was given at the Athens Conservatory by the Greek composer Manolis Kalomiris (1883–1962).[2] The concert also marked the beginning of Greece's National School of Music, of which Kalomiris was a prominent member. This development is similar to that of national music schools in other countries, involving, for example, Mikhail Glinka

---

1. Ioannis Andronoglou, "Η εξέλιξη της τεχνικής και της διδασκαλίας της κιθάρας στην Ελλάδα" [The evolution of the technique and instruction of guitar in Greece], PhD diss., National and Kapodistrian University of Athens, 2017, https://pergamos.lib.uoa.gr/uoa/dl/frontend/en/browse, 67–82.

2. For more on Manolis Kalomiris, see Foivos Anogeianakis, "Music in Modern Greece," in Karl Nef, *An Outline of the History of Music*, trans. Foivos Anogeianakis (Athens: Votsis, 1985), 583.

(Russia), Edvard Grieg (Norway), Jean Sibelius (Finland), Bedřich Smetana (Czech), Béla Bártok (Hungary) and Manuel de Falla and Isaac Albéniz (Spain). Kalomiris used Greek traditional music as an inspiration, along with various compositional techniques from Western art music (also called "classical music"), notably techniques from the school of Richard Wagner. In the program for the 1908 concert, which can also be read as a manifesto of the National School of Music, Kalomiris writes about the "National Muse" in combination with the "Foreign Craftswoman."[3] This metaphor vividly expresses the complementary relationship between Greek inspiration and more broadly Western technique.

Kalomiris's introduction to the 1908 concert is ideologically and culturally formulated according to Wagnerian standards of cultural (especially musical) nationalism,[4] for the purpose of developing and appreciating "the culture and traditions of the nation."[5] More generally, Dimitris Tziovas claims that cultural ideology "refers to forms of cultural power, method, and invention, and presupposes the fantastical fabrication of a cultural narrative."[6] Nationalism, according to Markos Tsetsos, "dictates the legitimization of the present and the future, the destination of national music, with reference to its past."[7] Specifically, he mentions that Kalomiris "attempts to link his venture to the music of the nation from antiquity to its time and to restore continuity in the history of Greek music, with reference to the broader context of European music history."[8]

Taking into account Kalomiris's administrative positions as well, it can be said that this period was impregnated by the spirit of his opera *The Masterbuilder* and the "Greek Music Idea," the musical expansion of Hellenism in the East also known as the "Cultural Great Idea."[9] The composer dedicated his opera to the remarkable Greek (Cretan) politician and radical liberal Eleftherios Venizelos, who as prime minister followed the Great Idea with the two Balkan Wars (1912–14). According to George Mavrogordatos,

---

3. Manolis Kalomiris, *Η ζωή μου και η τέχνη μου* [My life and my art] (Athens: Nefeli, 1988), 146.
4. Markos Tsetsos, *Εθνικισμός και λαϊκισμός: Πολιτικές όψεις μιας πολιτισμικής απόκλισης* [Nationalism and populism in modern Greek music: Political aspects of a cultural deviation] (Athens: Sakis Karagiorgas Foundation, 2011), 8.
5. Andrew Heywood, Πολιτικές ιδεολογίες [Political ideologies], ed. Nikos Marantzides, trans. Charidimos Koutris (Athens: Epikentro, 2007), 307.
6. Dimitris Tziovas, *Ο μύθος της γενιάς του τριάντα: Νεωτερικότητα, ελληνικότητα και πολιτισμική ιδεολογία* [The myth of the generation of the thirties: Modernity, Greekness and cultural ideology] (Athens: Polis, 2011), 58.
7. Tsetsos, *Εθνικισμός και λαϊκισμός* [Nationalism and populism], 81.
8. Tsetsos, *Εθνικισμός και λαϊκισμός* [Nationalism and populism], 81.
9. For further information, see Ioannis Andronoglou, *Η ελληνική παραδοσιακή μουσική ως πηγή έμπνευσης στη σύνθεση έργων για κιθάρα* [Greek traditional music as a source of inspiration in the composition of works for guitar] (Heraklion: Aerakis Cretan Musical Workshop & Seistron, 2020), 18–32.

Venizelism is "an unparalleled combination of bourgeois nationalism and bourgeois modernity, in an unbreakable and dialectical unity."[10] Alkis Rigos characterizes this identification as "unobtrusive."[11] It is worth noting, however, that Venizelos also agreed with the specific musical aesthetic conception of the Greek Music Idea; he was a fan of both Western artistic music creation and Greek traditional music.[12]

From 1918 onwards, Kalomiris turned musically to Impressionism, a turn that can be explained politically. The Wagnerian aesthetic of the *Masterbuilder* was connected with the anti-Venizelic party (which was religiously affiliated with the Central Powers), while Impressionism "was the most representative artistic product of French culture, and France was one of the countries of the Entente," as Tsetsos states.[13] Similarly, the political space of Venizelos's liberals was clearly identified with French Impressionism.[14] This turn of Kalomiris was also a meeting point with the generation of the 1930s, an aesthetic movement expressed in modern Greek artistic creation of the time. Representatives of this generation are poets such as Odysseas Elytis and George Seferis, and painters such as Giannis Tsarouchis, Fotis Kontoglou and Nikos Hatzikyriakos-Gikas. The purpose of the Thirties Generation was to create a new Greekness, a reconciliation of the Greek spirit—and especially the Greek folk tradition—with the Western world.[15] It should be noted, however, that Kalomiris did not adopt the Modernist style in his musical creations, as he considered it anti-national and purely internationalist.[16]

As far as guitar music is concerned, the guitarists Dimitris Fampas (1921–96) and Gerasimos Miliaresis (1918–2005) were early proponents in Greece of the guitar as a respected classical instrument, equal in prestige to the violin and piano.[17] Adapting the knowledge they gained from working with the major guitarist of the time, Andrés Segovia (1893–1987), Fampas and Miliaresis also created successful guitar groups that continued the important task of creating a respectable and, ultimately, world-renowned

---

10. Yorgos Mavrogordatos and Christos Hadjiiosif, eds. *Βενιζελισμός και αστικός εκσυγχρονισμός* [Venizelism and bourgeois modernization] (Heraklion: Crete University Press, 1988), 10.

11. Alkis Rigos, *Η β' ελληνική δημοκρατία, 1924–1935* [The second Greek democracy, 1924–1935] (Athens: Themelio, 1999), 175.

12. For further information, see Andronoglou, *Ελληνική παραδοσιακή μουσική* [Greek traditional music], 24–25.

13. Tsetsos, *Εθνικισμός και λαϊκισμός* [Nationalism and populism], 42–43.

14. Tsetsos, *Εθνικισμός και λαϊκισμός* [Nationalism and populism], 42–43.

15. Andronoglou, *Ελληνική παραδοσιακή μουσική* [Greek traditional music], 31.

16. Olympia Frangou-Psychopedi, *Η Εθνική σχολή μουσικής: Προβλήματα ιδεολογίας* [The National School of Music: Issues of ideology] (Athens: Foundation for Mediterranean Studies, 1990), 93.

17. Andronoglou, "Εξέλιξη της τεχνικής" [Evolution of the technique], 2.

Greek guitar school. During his last years as a student at the National Conservatory of Athens, Fampas studied guitar with Manolis Kalomiris. Kalomiris was the founder and leader of the National Music School, as well as the man who in many ways controlled musical taste in Greece. Over the course of his career, he held the following administrative positions: Inspector of Military Musical Bands, Director of the Greek Opera, President of the Union of Greek Composers, and Director of first the Hellenic, then the National Conservatory.[18] Clearly, the musical aesthetic environment around Fampas was conducive to learning about and engaging with tradition. Another important element in Fampas's training was his apprenticeship to the great Spanish guitarist Andrés Segovia at the Chigianna Academy of Siena.

Segovia was a defender of Spanish romantic nationalism[19] in its every musical and political extension, including anti-communist and republican views, as it appears from his letters to Ponce.[20] Clearly, his preference for non-modernist Spanish composers, such as Joaquín Turina, Federico Moreno Torroba and others who used elements from Spanish folklore in their compositions, was not accidental. Segovia had in fact refused to interpret works for guitar such as Arnold Schoenberg's *Serenade* op. 24 (1923) and Frank Martin's *Quatre pièces brèves* (1933); both were participants in the international music avant-garde.[21] The political kinship of Segovia and Kalomiris—they were both conservative liberals—played out also in their common opposition to musical modernism.

Fampas learned from Segovia's example; he was inspired by Greek traditional music and he composed works based on or influenced by it. One of Fampas's most popular works, *Karaguna*, based on the eponymous Thessalian folk dance, was published in 1959 by the Ricordi music house. In this work, Fampas uses the dance's method of processing, quoting the main theme, accompanied by bass, and sometimes chords of impressionistic color (where the third note of the chord is absent to preserve the character of modality). Here is an excerpt:

---

18. On the interconnection of Manolis Kalomiris with Prime Minister Eleftherios Venizelos, see Markos Tsetsos, "Μανώλης Καλομοίρης και Ελευθέριος Βενιζέλος: Ιδεολογικές και αισθητικές όψεις μιας σημαίνουσας σχέσης" [Manolis Kalomiris and Eleftherios Venizelos: Aesthetic and ideological aspects of a significant relationship], in *Ελευθέριος Βενιζέλος και πολιτιστική πολιτική [Eleftherios Venizelos and cultural policy]: Proceedings of Symposium, 21–22 November 2008*, eds. Tasos Sakellaropoulos and Argiro Vatsaki, 270–79 (Athens: Benaki Museum, 2012).

19. Graham Wade and Gerard Garno, *A New Look at Segovia: His Life, His Music*, vol. 2 (Fenton, MO: Mel Bay, 1997), 154. Also see Andronoglou, "Εξέλιξη της τεχνικής" [Evolution of the technique], 85.

20. Miguel Alcázar ed., *The Segovia–Ponce Letters* (Columbus, OH: Orphée, 1989), 167–68.

21. Andronoglou, "Εξέλιξη της τεχνικής" [Evolution of the technique], 84–85 and 88.

Figure 8.1. Dimitris Fampas, *Karaguna*, measures 1–8.

Source: Dimitris Fampas, *Danza Greca no.1: Karaguna* (1959; repr., Milano: G. Ricordi, 1979).

Gerasimos Miliaresis also incorporated Greek traditional music in his transcriptions and arrangements for guitar. It is worthwhile investigating the reasons for this engagement.[22] He received his guitar soloist diploma from the "Hellenic" Conservatory, Athens. The Director of Studies of the Conservatory was Manolis Kalomiris; logically, Miliaresis was not unaffected by Kalomiris's nationalistic views. As mentioned above, he continued his guitar studies with Andrés Segovia. Thus, along with Fampas, Miliaresis became the bearer of those musical and aesthetic ideas, and he adapted them to classical Greek guitar. He was a member of the Union of Greek Composers and also president of the National Council of Music, which by definition means, among other things, the promotion of "home products" in music.

In Miliaresis's work *Danze Greche* (1958), which consists of the parts "Danza di Zalongo" and "Danza di Kalamata," for example, the composer uses the traditional song "Έχε γεια καημένε κόσμε" (Goodbye, poor world). In contrast to the compositional style of Fampas, Miliaresis accomplishes the arrangement of melodies and other elements of traditional guitar music in a more impressionistic way. That is, from the beginning of his engagement with this musical direction, Miliaresis introduces impressionistic chords to accompany the traditional themes, rather than accompanying them with a simple (not contrapuntal) bass line as Fampas did in this style in his first works, and even a year after Miliaresis's *Danze Greche*. Here are such chords in musical notation:

---

22. For more on Miliaresis, see Gerasimos Miliaresis, *Ήχοι και απόηχοι* [Sounds and echoes] (Athens: Kedros, 2002).

Figure 8.2. Gerasimos Miliaresis, "Danza di Zalongo," measures 1–3.

Source: Gerasimos Miliaresis, "Danza di Zalongo," in *2 Danze Greche*, harmonized and transcribed by Gerasimos Miliaresis, 2 (Milano: G. Ricordi, 1958).

The years during which these two works were composed found Greece under the conservative government of Konstantinos Karamanlis. According to Alexander Kitroeff, characteristics of the government of that time were conservatism, communist phobia and anti-intellectualism.[23] These characteristics matched the political positions of Kalomiris and Segovia, and thereby influenced the composition of works for guitar in Greece, such as those of Fampas and Miliaresis. It is not surprising, then, that while the works were composed in the Modernist period, they follow the outdated romantic and impressionist style of Kalomiris's and Segovia's musical tastes.

The Greek musical avant-garde

Traditional music was also a source of inspiration for Greek composers of the musical avant-garde of the time. Nikos Skalkottas (1904–49)[24] was the pioneer of this style in Greece,[25] in works such as *36 Greek Dances* (1934–36) and *The Sea* (1948–49). Costas Tsougras notes that "Skalkottas surpasses the primitivism that was a prerequisite for romantic nationalism,"[26] continuing: "Skalkottas becomes the first perhaps worldwide modern Greek composer who managed to compose universal Greek music, ... because he reached his social quintessence with balance, the sense of proportion and avoidance of excesses of all kinds in his completely personal musical language." Typically, he adds,

---

23. Alexander Kitroeff, "Continuity and Change in Modern Greek Historiography," in *Εθνική ταυτότητα και εθνικισμός στη νεώτερη Ελλάδα* [National identity and nationalism in modern Greece], ed. Thanos Veremis (Athens: National Bank of Greece Cultural Foundation, 2012), 213.

24. For more on Skalkottas, see Anogeianakis, 602.

25. Katy Romanou, "Nikos Skalkottas," in *Serbian and Greek Art Music: A Patch to Western Music History*, ed. Katy Romanou (Chicago: Intellect, 2009), 165.

26. Costas Tsougras, "Η ελληνικότητα της μουσικής του Νίκου Σκαλκώτα: Ένας "εθνικός" ή "παγκόσμιος" συνθέτης" [The Greekness of the music by Nikos Skalkottas: A "national" or "global" composer?], in *Έντεχνη ελληνική μουσική δημιουργία: παράδοση και παγκοσμιοποίηση* [Modern Greek music creation: Tradition and globalization]: *Proceedings of the Musicological Congress*, 24–26 April 2007, ed. Sophia Topouzi (Athens: Union of Greek Composers, 2008), 24.

this language incorporates "elements of Greek folk music in a personal and modernistic manner."[27] In contrast to Kalomiris, as Tsetsos notes,

> responding to the neo-nationalist tendencies of the time, Skalkottas avoids romantic methods of managing folk or popular melodies, incorporating in an abstract way (at the level of manner and rhythm) elements of music within broadening the horizon of his choices. Skalkottas approaches the axiom of "Greekness" either by constructing folk-schemed melodies or by preserving only the tonal element, or, even more abstractly, by preserving a single general rhythmic background.[28]

Adorno identifies the critical mediation between musical nationalism and musical modernity, citing Béla Bartók as an example. Bartók belongs to the neo-national composers, in the spirit of neoclassicism, along with Igor Stravinsky and Leoš Janáček. Their music is distinguished by exoticism, extroverted internationalism and multiculturalism, incorporating the innovations of the early 20th century in harmony and form.[29] According to Tsetsos, a similar example in Greece is Nikos Skalkottas.[30]

The musicologist Yannis G. Papaioannou (1915–2000) distinguishes 13 elements of Greekness in the work of Nikos Skalkottas:

1. use of sounds from the Greek environment;
2. sound proportions with the Greek language;
3. use of micro intervals;
4. use of modal scales;
5. reference to traditional melodic forms;
6. references to traditional rhythmical schemas;
7. elasticity in the metric articulation;
8. elasticity in the large proportions of music;
9. use of the Byzantine drone note—the "ison" compositional technique;
10. gentleness, elasticity, elegance;
11. complex sound units instead of simple;
12. ethos; and
13. themes and titles of works.[31]

---

27. Tsougras, 24–25.
28. Markos Tsetsos, *Νεοελληνική μουσική: Δοκίμια ιδεολογικής και θεσμικής κριτικής* [Greek music: Issues of ideological and institutional critique] (Athens: Papagrigoriou-Nakas, 2013), 81.
29. Tsougras, 19.
30. Tsetsos, *Νεοελληνική μουσική* [Greek music], 34.
31. Tsougras, 20.

Regarding musical characteristics and innovations of musical modernism in general, Katy Romanou notes: "Many of the innovations of modern music are elements of the Greek folk musical tradition (such as micro-intervals, modes, improvisation as a basic component of interpretation, instruments, special techniques and aesthetics of vocal and instrumental performance, etc.)."[32] Thus, for Nikos Skalkottas, who used themes and other musical elements from Greek traditional music, many of those elements—including micro-intervals, modal scales and asymmetric measures—were not foreign; they are common practice in Greek traditional music.[33] Skalkottas collaborated with the head of Greece's Musical Folklore Archives, Melpo Merlie, to write in European musical notation 45 traditional Greek songs and themes from 78 rpm records in Merlie's archive.[34]

In terms of composers on the international avant-garde music scene, a similar case is Béla Bartók, who was involved with Hungarian traditional music. His works include *Piano Concerto no. 2*, Sz. 95 (1930–31), which uses semitoneless pentatonicism, a typical aspect of Hungarian folk music.[35] He uses a semitoneless pentatonic scale for "culmination points" of the concerto; by doing so, Bartók remains a Hungarian composer, as Anthony Damian Ritchie notes.[36] Also, as Ritchie observes, "ethnomusicology was Bartók's chief occupation in life"; furthermore, he writes, "As far as the collection of folk music items was concerned, Bartók was at his happiest."[37]

Technical innovation thrives in all of Western art music, particularly the musical avant-garde. Indicative works in micro-intervals, for example, are the compositions *Three Quarter-Tone Pieces* (1925) by Charles Ives, in which he notes "Piano I to be tuned ¼ tone higher." Arnold Schoenberg's student Nikos Skalkottas transcribes in an innovative way and uses elements from the Greek folk music tradition in his works.

An important example of the guitar works of composers in this style is the *Sonata for Flute and Guitar* (1962) by Yannis A. Papaioannou (1910–89).[38] In this composition, Papaioannou uses the striking rhythms 5/8 (3+2, from the Greek dance "Tsakonikos")

---

32. Katy Romanou, *Ιστορία της έντεχνης νεοελληνικής μουσικής* [History of neohellenic art music] (Athens: Cultura, 2000), 167–68.

33. Anogeianakis, 550.

34. Katy Romanou, "Βιβλιοπαρουσίαση" [Book presentation], *Musicology* 20 (2011), http://musicology-journal.music.uoa.gr/issue020/romanou-dragoumisgr.html.

35. Anthony Damian Ritchie, "The Influence of Folk Music in Three Works by Béla Bártok: Sonata No. 1 for Violin and Piano, Sonata (1926) for Piano, and 'Contrasts' for Violin, Clarinet and Piano," PhD diss., University of Canterbury, 1986, 103–4, https://core.ac.uk/download/pdf/35464018.pdf. https://core.ac.uk/download/pdf/35464018.pdf.

36. Ritchie, 103–4.

37. Ritchie, 22.

38. For further information about Papaioannou, see Romanou, *Ιστορία* [History], 174.

and 9/8 (2+3+2+2, from the Greek Thracian dance "Agrilamas"),[39] as well as ancient Greek modes such as the Aeolian. These elements are an exception to the general philosophy of Modernism, especially in the two decades after the Second World War, because "the motive of the new generation of musicians was total rupture with the past."[40] It is noteworthy that before the war Papaioannou followed the compositional standards of the Greek National School of Music but later "adopts the atonality, the twelve-tone method and more complete methods of serialism."[41]

Figure 8.3. Yannis Papaioannou, *Sonatine for Flute and Guitar*, Allegretto con spirito, measures 1–2.

Source: Yannis Papaioannou, *Sonatine for Flute and Guitar* (Athens: Nakas, 1986).

Figure 8.4. Yannis Papaioannou, *Sonatine for Flute and Guitar*, Finale, measures 1–2.

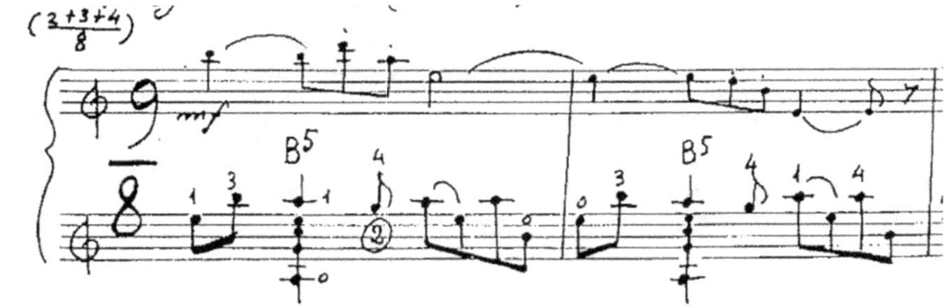

Source: Yannis Papaioannou, *Sonatine for Flute and Guitar* (Athens: Nakas, 1986).

---

39. Serafeim Feggoulis, "Η ρυθμική συγκρότηση της μουσικής της Θράκης" [The rhythmic composition of the music of Thrace], BA thesis, Technological Educational Institute of Epirus, 2011, 28, http://apothetirio.teiep.gr/xmlui/handle/123456789/494.

40. Markos Tsetsos, "Σκέψεις σχετικά με τα αισθητικά αδιέξοδα της σύγχρονης μουσικής δημιουργίας" [Thoughts concerning the aesthetic impasses of contemporary music], in *Ζητήματα αισθητικής και ταυτότητας στη σύγχρονη μουσική δημιουργία* [Issues of aesthetics and identity in contemporary music], ed. Vissilios Kitsos (Lamia: Center of Mediterranean Music, 2004), 91.

41. Romanou, *Ιστορία* [History], 174.

Another prominent figure in modern Greek music is the composer Dimitris Dragatakis (1914–2001),[42] who, according to Romanou, "does not follow a specific method or school but excludes none."[43] In 1969 Dragatakis composed the work *Liz-Va* for two guitars; the title is derived from the names of the guitar duo Evangelos Asimakopoulos and Liza Zoi, to whom he dedicated the work. Dragatakis uses rhythms such as 5/8, 9/8 and 7/8, characteristic of Greek traditional music. It should be noted that in the same year, he composed the work *Concerto for Violin*, in which "one perceives the rugged Epirus character (of nature and people) and the peculiar plurality of folk tradition."[44]

Figure 8.5. Dimitris Dragatakis, *Liz-Va*, Allegro molto, measures 1–6.

Source: Dimitris Dragatakis, *Liz-Va* (Athens: Nakas, 1969).

It is clear that the Greek guitar repertoire was synchronized with the musical avant-garde after the aesthetics of Fampas and Miliaresis, largely through the agency of Kalomiris. Greece in the 1960s—that is, until 1967, when the dictatorship was established—was a nation of rapid development and social liberation following two decades of economic austerity and the restriction of political freedom.[45]

In general, by adapting elements from Greek traditional music, composers who belonged to the Greek musical avant-garde did not contradict the founder of the Second Viennese School, Arnold Schoenberg (1874–1951), because of his contradictions in words and deeds. On one hand, Schoenberg opposed those who used musical themes from traditional music. In his introductory note to the work *Three Satires*, op. 28, he exclaims, "With delight I also strike at folklorists, who may be forced to do so (because their own themes are not at their disposal) or not (because in the end an existing culture and tradition could also sustain even them), who want to apply to the natural, primitive ideas of folk music a technique that only suits a complicated way of thinking."[46]

---

42. For more on Dragatakis, see Institute for Research on Music and Acoustics (IEMA), "Dimitris Dragatakis: Biographical Note," accessed January 24, 2020, http://composers.musicportal.gr/?c=dragatakis.

43. Romanou, *Ιστορία* [History], 175.

44. Romanou, *Ιστορία* [History], 175.

45. Thanos Veremis and Yiannis Koliopoulos, *Ελλάς: Η σύγχρονη συνέχεια, από το 1821 μέχρι σήμερα* [Greece: The modern sequel, from 1821 to the present] (Athens: Kastaniotis, 2006), 430.

46. Réné Leibowitz, *Σένμπεργκ* [Schoenberg], trans. Thomas Sliomis (Athens: Pataki, 2003), 133.

Nonetheless, in his own compositions, he borrowed themes from German folk music, for instance, in his Suite, op. 29. However, this contradiction is legitimized because of its authority. Fredric Jameson defines the paradoxical situation of Schoenberg and other modernist composers: "the contradiction of modernism lay in the way in which that universal value of human production could achieve figuration only by way of the unique and restricted signature of the modernist seer or prophet, thus slowly canceling itself out again for all but the disciples."[47]

A postmodern approach

Since the 1970s, the world's postmodernist aesthetic movement, according to Thomas Sliomis, has been combined with complete de-ideologization while replacing many ideas, many reflections and innovations.[48] As Jameson points out, there is a "new kind of flatness"[49] or "depthlessness," a "new kind of superficiality" that, however, is a morphological feature. We today live in an age of pluralism, when we can use every aesthetic style. Particularly, postmodernism is a mirror of the globalization we are experiencing. Postmodernism seems to be a process of dialectical synthesis using the achievements of Modernism but also elements from the past and tradition.

Since 1970 postmodernism has dominated compositions for guitar. After creating a variety of compositions within the framework of Modernism, using the twelve-tone and serial techniques, nowadays composers use elements of traditional music combined with modern compositional techniques. The top foreign guitar composers have already adopted postmodernism in their works, making it a global trend in guitar composition. Typical examples of such composers are Alberto Ginastera, William Walton,[50] Carlo Domeniconi, Leo Brower and Ronald Dyens. The Italian Carlo Domeniconi (1947–), influenced by Eastern music because he was a professor of guitar at the Istanbul Conservatory, uses various techniques from traditional instruments, in particular the saz, in his works for guitar, as well as melodies from Turkish songs. The Cuban Leo Brower (1939–) uses Cuban rhythms as well as melodies that harmonize with expressionistic harmonies. Tunisian composer Roland Dyens (1955–2016) brings the jazz style of the

---

47. Fredric Jameson, *Το μεταμοντέρνο ή η πολιτισμική λογική του ύστερου καπιταλισμού* [Postmodernism, or the cultural logic of late capitalism], trans. Yorgos Varsos (Athens: Nefeli, 1999), 129.

48. Thomas Sliomis, "Η Δεύτερη Σχολή της Βιέννης, η νέα μουσική αντίληψη και η εξέλιξη της ιστορίας" [The Second Viennese School, the new musical perception and the evolution of history], preface to Leibowitz, 21–22.

49. Jameson, *Μεταμοντέρνο* [Postmodernism], 45.

50. Byde, Michael Geoffrey John, "The Later Orchestral Works of William Walton: A Critical and Analytical Re-evaluation," PhD diss., University of Leeds School of Music, 2008, 265–69, https://core.ac.uk/reader/40056587.

1930s to the guitar. Tsetsos notes that "in the postmodern work, the musical material of the past is 'distorted' through the interventions of an intelligent compositional mind."[51]

On Greek soil, the most important event for the guitar was the presentation of Joaquin Rodrigo's *Concierto de Aranjuez* in 1972 by Costas Cotsiolis and the Athens State Orchestra;[52] Rodrigo "adopt[ed] the postmodernist principles half a century before his time."[53] Thus, as with events that took place on the international guitar scene, such as Walton's *Five Bagatelles*, John Williams's collaboration with Inti Illimani, and Barrios's recordings, the postmodernist texture in compositions for guitar also appeared in Greece.[54]

In 1975, one year after the fall of the dictatorship and the "rebirth of parliamentarism,"[55] the Greek guitarist-composer Kyriakos Tzortzinakis (1950–89)[56] composed *Four Greek Images*, published in 1981 by Nakas. The work consists of four parts highlighting four images, and it is a typical example of postmodernist transformation of Greek folk music elements. *Four Greek Images* uses ancient Greek modes as well as traditional Greek rhythms. The melodies, however, are original to Tzortzinakis. In the first part, "Of the Sea," he uses the Dorian modal scale; in the second part, "Of the Valley," the Ionic; in the third part, "Of the Mountain," the pentatonic; and in the fourth part, "Of the Village," the Aeolian. As for the rhythms, in the second part he uses the mixed rhythm of 7/8, which, as clearly shown by the bass line, divides into 2/8, 2/8 and 3/8, the rhythmic structure of the Thracian dance "Mantilatos."

Figure 8.6. Kiriakos Tzortzinakis, "Of the Valley," measures 1–2.

Source: Kiriakos Tzortzinakis, *Four Greek Images* (Athens: Papagrigoriou-Nakas, 1981).

In the same part, he uses a 4/4 rhythm, with the rhythmic structure of the Cretan dance "Sousta." In the third part, he uses the epic Epirus rhythm "Pogonisio," which has the

---

51. Tsetsos, "Σκέψεις" [Thoughts], 96.
52. Andronoglou, "Εξέλιξη της Τεχνικής" [Evolution of the technique], 201.
53. Matthew Rye, *1001 Classical Recordings You Must Hear Before You Die*, ed. Steven Isserlis (New York: Rizzoli/Universe, 2008), 768.
54. Andronoglou, "Εξέλιξη της Τεχνικής" [Evolution of the technique], 197.
55. Veremis and Koliopoulos, 430.
56. For more on Tzortzinakis, see Ilan, "Κυριάκος Τζωρτζινάκης: Ανήσυχος, δυναμικός, εκρηκτικός, ευαίσθητος" [Kyriakos Tzortzinakis: Anxious, dynamic, explosive, sensitive], *Avgi*, October 28, 2019, https://www.avgi.gr/arheio/328340_kyriakos-tzortzinakis-anisyhos-dynamikos-ekriktikos-eyaisthitos.

characteristic designation *pesante*. In the fourth part he uses the triumphant rhythm "Tsamiko," where the first 16th note is dotted.

Figure 8.7. Kiriakos Tzortzinakis, "Of the Mountain," measures 1–2.

Source: Kiriakos Tzortzinakis, *Four Greek Images* (Athens: Papagrigoriou-Nakas, 1981).

Figure 8.8. Kiriakos Tzortzinakis, "Of the Village," measures 1–2.

Source: Kiriakos Tzortzinakis, *Four Greek Images* (Athens: Papagrigoriou-Nakas, 1981).

Thus the composition of works for guitar is synchronized with the postmodern aesthetics of composition for guitar at an international level. Anthony Giddens has said that this musical development is also a political requirement of our time, as the need for more information gives rise to the need for more democracy.[57] This development is also influenced by the compositional work of composers such as Nikos Mamangakis (1929–2013)[58] and Giannis Markopoulos (1939–).[59] The former even uses the guitar in his works of postmodern texture, such as *To Arkadi*, a suite for voice and seven instruments, and in the ballet suite *Erotokritos*. In the early 1970s, using material from traditional Greek music, Markopoulos released three albums: *Chronicle* (Χρονικό) in 1970, *Rizitika* (Ριζίτικα) in 1971 and *Ithageneia* (Ιθαγένεια) in 1972. He belongs to the leftist music scene, and his vision of "returning to roots" spread to the movement against mismanagement of Greek traditional music by the dictatorship of the Colonels (1967–74). He is part of the Greek postmodernist situation.

The classical or Spanish guitar has also acquired another form in Greece since the 1980s. At this point, the concept of multiculturalism or ethnicity is implicated, according to which, as Augustino Zenakos points out, all cultures of the world "contribute their

---

57. Anthony Giddens, *Sociology*, trans. G. Tsaousis (Athens: Gutenberg, 2002), 460.
58. For more on Nikos Mamangakis, see Giannis Papaioannou, "Nikos Mamangakis: Biographical Note," Musicale, accessed January 30, 2021, http://www.musicale.gr/synthetes/mamagakis_cv_en.html.
59. For more on Giannis Markopoulos, see Hellenica World, "Giannis Markopoulos," accessed January 30, 2021, http://www.hellenicaworld.com/Greece/Person/gr/GiannisMarkopoulos.html.

own" to the extent that they are represented in the "crucibles."⁶⁰ A good example and a pioneer of this genre is the musical group Νότιος Ήχος (Southern Sound), created in 1994 by Achilleas Persidis on Spanish guitar, Panagiotis Katsikiotis and Taki Canello on percussion and Elias Tsagaris on bass.⁶¹ In this musical project, the Spanish guitar plays a leading role and collaborates with musical instruments belonging to the Greek folk music tradition—Cretan lyre (Ross Daly), Cretan lute (George Xylouris "Psarogiorgis"), stamnes or udu drums (Panagiotis Katsikiotis), and kaval and zournas (Manos Achalinotopoulos)—along with Western instruments such as the piano (Panos Gekas). After all, as Samuel Baud-Bovy notes, "there is no traditional hatred in music."⁶²

Figure 8.9. I. Andronoglou, "Fantasia on a Thracian Folksong," measures 42–46.

Source: Ioannis Andronoglou, "Fantasia on a Thracian Folksong" (Heraklion: Aerakis Cretan Musical Workshop & Seistron, 2016).

This project gained a special dynamic from 2010 onwards, as young guitarists created music using interactions among instruments identified with different nations. The beginning of this movement was the release of my album *Travelling*.⁶³ In the album's compositions, I adapted themes from the Greek—especially the Thracian—folk music tradition and used elements from the Greek folk tradition. For instance, "Fantasia on a Thracian Folksong," included on the album, is based mainly on a traditional song from Evros in West Thrace, "Δω στα λυανοχορταρούδια" (Here upon the grassy meadow).⁶⁴

The dance accompanying "Fantasia on a Thracian Folksong" is called "Zonaradikos"; it was brought to western Thrace by Greek refugees from eastern Romylia (northern

---

60. Augustinos Zenakos, "Η μόδα και η κουλτούρα" [Fashion and culture], *To Vima*, April 21, 2002, https://www.tovima.gr/2008/11/24/culture/i-moda-kai-i-koyltoyra/.
61. Ilan, "Αχιλλέας Περσίδης: Ήχος νότιος ζεστός, στη σκιά της θάλασσας" [Achilleas Persidis: Sound warm south, in the shadow of the sea], *Avgi*, April 13, 2020, https://www.avgi.gr/tehnes/348930_ahilleas-persidis-ihos-notios-zestos-sti-skia-tis-thalassas.
62. Samuel Baud-Bovy, *Δοκίμιο για το ελληνικό δημοτικό τραγούδι* [Essay on the Greek folk song] (Nafplio: Peloponnese Folklore Foundation, 1996), 41.
63. Ioannis Andronoglou, *Travelling*, with Yiannis (Ioannis) Andronoglou (classical guitar), Legend Classics 2201159993, 2010; reissue, Aerakis Cretan Musical Workshop AMA 356, 2014, compact disc.
64. "Fantasia" is also available online: "ΓΙΑΝΝΗΣ ΑΝΔΡΟΝΟΓΛΟΥ - FANTASIA ON A THRACIAN FOLK SONG (ZONARADIKOS)," 2014, YouTube video, 7:11 min., https://www.youtube.com/watch?v=KtpSqlLLyLk&list=PLQ2WhmkOXlTldKg3rjCMdQEzMoX0Js6cV.

Thrace).⁶⁵ As far as musical elements are concerned, the rhythm is 6/8, so the song is based on the Aeolian scale. The treatment of the theme in a contemporary musical style classifies this work as postmodernist, as well as being a work of art that forges coherence among different ethno-cultural communities. A special feature of this artistic effort is the direct reference to Greek musical elements and the adoption of techniques used by traditional Greek (folk) instrumentalists, all with the intention of changing the character of the instruments from Western to "Grecized."

The term *Grecization* refers not only to the repertoire and the techniques used, but also to acceptance of listening to the guitar (as a solo musical instrument) by the Greek people as a whole. I have described the change this way: "The guitar is transformed into a solo instrument that enters the culture of the Greek people and leaves the isolated excellence of western art music creation."⁶⁶ It should also be observed that 2010 was the beginning of the 10-year economic crisis in Greece, resulting in a shift of Greek cultural creation to indigenous cultural elements.

Concluding thoughts

The final question that I want to consider here is whether postmodernism is a functional mechanism for the promotion of Greek music, and of Greek folklore, though not in the sense of attractions for tourists such as the bouzouki, moussaka and tzatziki, the sea and the islands, sirtaki dancing and, in some cases, the Parthenon—all features of the promotion of Greece as a tourist destination since the 1960s. Veremis and Koliopoulos state about that decade that "the dominant elements of the philosophical carelessness that our country taught to the 'loopy' westerners at that time were 'Τα παιδιά του Πειραιά' [the children of Piraeus], Zorba and Melina Mercouri."⁶⁷ They conclude that it is the duty of the Greeks to promote the achievements of modern Greek culture so that foreigners will know better "why they appreciate modern Greece."⁶⁸

With regard to the above question, is it true what Michael Meraclis says about customs? He claims that "to a certain extent, this century seems not to create new customs but is fed by the reheated old customs,"⁶⁹ and "it also seems that the bourgeoisie prefers peasant bread, while the peasant wants nothing more than to become a bourgeois."⁷⁰ In the same context, Jameson states that "nature is abolished along with the traditional countryside

---

65. Petroula Sini, "Ζωναράδικος" [Zonaradikos], Λαογραφία [Folklore] (blog), April 29, 2014, https://laografiaparadosi.blogspot.com/2014/04/blog-post_96.html.
66. Andronoglou, *Ελληνική παραδοσιακή μουσική* [Greek traditional music], 74.
67. Veremis and Koliopoulos, 552.
68. Veremis and Koliopoulos, 553.
69. Michael Meraclis, *Ελληνική λαογραφία* [Greek folklore], 3rd ed. (Athens: Kardamitsa, 2011), 140.
70. Meraclis, *Ελληνική λαογραφία* [Greek folklore], 441.

and traditional agriculture; even the surviving historical monuments, now all cleaned up, become glittering simulacra of the past, and not its survival. Now everything is new, but by the same token, the very category of the new then loses its meaning and becomes itself something of a modernist survival."[71] In the context of postmodernism, Jameson characterizes the past as a matter of idle curiosity that comes to look a little like an in-group hobby or adoptive tourism.[72]

The positive signification of the bourgeois/peasant, or peasant-dipole, schema may also be recognized in this issue. The positive element of this schema is emphasized by Meraclis: "I think that this contradictory twin—farmer-bourgeois—that exists in almost every Greek, more than divides it, suspends its complete urbanization. And this is something positive, not negative versus the threatened global leveling simulation."[73] In the same context, Jameson claims that "postmodernism is to be seen as the production of postmodern people capable of functioning in a very peculiar socioeconomic world."[74]

The foregoing argument is meant to promote not a sovereign ideology but a point of view in what musicologist Anastasia Siopsi calls a "multicultural reality."[75] On this issue, Siopsi argues,

> composers who refer to elements of Greek traditional music, both ancient and new, can reinforce the linkage of the past with the present so that the distinctive artistic entity of musical works in a complex and multicultural present brings forth its maximum values in the context of 'globalization': the peaceful coexistence of different cultural values and tolerance of the different.[76]

After all, according to Christos Yannaras, the Greek proposition remains timely "for the meaning of existence, of the world and of history."[77] Yannaras also believes that only

---

71. Jameson, Μεταμοντέρνο [Postmodernism], 121.
72. Jameson, Μεταμοντέρνο [Postmodernism], 188.
73. Meraclis, Ελληνική λαογραφία [Greek folklore], 10.
74. Jameson, Μεταμοντέρνο [Postmodernism], 19.
75. Anastasia Siopsi, "Η έννοια του 'εθνικού' ή η 'ελληνικότητα' με άλλη σημασία και το φαινόμενο της παγκοσμιοποίησης στη μουσική ζωή της σύγχρονης ελληνικής κοινωνίας" [The notion of "national" or "Greek," with another significance and the phenomenon of globalization in the musical life of contemporary Greek society], in Έντεχνη ελληνική μουσική δημιουργία: Παράδοση και παγκοσμιοποίηση [Modern Greek music creation: Tradition and globalization]: *Proceedings of the Musicological Congress, 24–26 April 2007*, ed. Sophia Topouzi (Athens: Union of Greek Composers, 2008), 12.
76. Siopsi, "Έννοια του 'εθνικού'" [Notion of "national"], 13.
77. Christos Yannaras, Αφελληνισμού παρεπόμενα [Consequences of de-hellenizing] (Athens: Kaktos, 2005), 32.

if "the Greek again represents a cultural proposition, this small country could historically survive."[78]

Based on my research and study of the theoretical field,[79] I believe that combining elements of traditional Greek music with modern compositional techniques and styles in the composition of works for guitar not only furthers the international spread of Greek traditional music but also has become a truly Greek postmodern musical innovation, comparable to world music such as flamenco and the blues. Along with the wide diffusion of Greek traditional music through postmodernist transformation, this change is also significant when seen from the perspective of the guitar. Regarding the guitar not simply as an accompanying or solo musical instrument belonging exclusively to Western art music, instead seeing it as integral to the musical tradition and creativity of the Greeks, transforms the solo classical guitar into an instrument capable of contributing to the development of the contemporary musical culture of Greece.[80]

Bibliography

Alcázar, Miguel, ed. *The Segovia-Ponce Letters*. Columbus, OH: Orphée, 1989.

Andronoglou, Ioannis. "Η εξέλιξη της τεχνικής και της διδασκαλίας της κιθάρας στην Ελλάδα (με αναφορά στις μεθόδους και στις μουσικές συνθέσεις)" [The evolution of the technique and instruction of guitar in Greece (by reference to the methods and the musical compositions)]. PhD diss., National and Kapodistrian University of Athens, 2017. https://pergamos.lib.uoa.gr/uoa/dl/frontend/en/browse.

———. *Η ελληνική παραδοσιακή μουσική ως πηγή έμπνευσης στη σύνθεση έργων για κιθάρα* [Greek traditional music as a source of inspiration in the composition of works for guitar]. Heraklion: Aerakis Cretan Musical Workshop & Seistron, 2020.

Anogeianakis, Foivos. "Music in Modern Greece." In Karl Nef, *An Outline of the History of Music*, 546–611. Translated by Foivos Anogeianakis. Athens: Votsis, 1985.

Baud-Bovy, Samuel. *Δοκίμιο για το ελληνικό δημοτικό τραγούδι* [Essay on the Greek folk song]. Nafplio: Peloponnese Folklore Foundation, 1996.

Byde, Michael Geoffrey John. "The Later Orchestral Works of William Walton: A Critical and Analytical Re-evaluation." PhD diss., University of Leeds School of Music, 2008. https://core.ac.uk/reader/40056587.

Feggoulis, Serafeim. "Η ρυθμική συγκρότηση της μουσικής της Θράκης" [The rhythmic composition of the music of Thrace]. BA thesis, Technological Educational Institute of Epirus, 2011. http://apothetirio.teiep.gr/xmlui/handle/123456789/494.

Frangou-Psychopedi, Olympia. *Η Εθνική σχολή μουσικής: Προβλήματα ιδεολογίας* [The National School of Music: Issues of ideology]. Athens: Foundation for Mediterranean Studies, 1990.

Giddens, Anthony. *Sociology*. Translated by G. Tsaousis. Athens: Gutenberg, 2002.

---

78. Yannaras, *Αφελληνισμού* [De-hellenizing], 57.

79. For further analysis, see Andronoglou, *Ελληνική παραδοσιακή μουσική* [Greek traditional music], 90–103.

80. Andronoglou, *Ελληνική παραδοσιακή μουσική* [Greek traditional music], 103.

Hellenica World. "Giannis Markopoulos." Accessed January 30, 2021. http://www.hellenicaworld.com/Greece/Person/gr/GiannisMarkopoulos.html.
Heywood, Andrew. Πολιτικές ιδεολογίες [Political ideologies] (1992). Edited by Nikos Marantzides. Translated by Charidimos Koutris. Athens: Epikentro, 2007.
Ilan. "Αχιλλέας Περσίδης: Ήχος νότιος ζεστός, στη σκιά της θάλασσας" [Achilles Persidis: Sound warm south, in the shadow of the sea]. *Avgi,* April 13, 2020. https://www.avgi.gr/tehnes/348930_ahilleas-persidis-ihos-notios-zestos-sti-skia-tis-thalassas.
———. "Κυριάκος Τζωρτζινάκης: Ανήσυχος, δυναμικός, εκρηκτικός, ευαίσθητος" [Kyriakos Tzortzinakis: Anxious, dynamic, explosive, sensitive]. *Avgi,* October 28, 2019. https://www.avgi.gr/arheio/328340_kyriakos-tzortzinakis-anisyhos-dynamikos-ekriktikos-eyaisthitos.
Institute for Research on Music and Acoustics (IEMA). "Dimitris Dragatakis: Biographical Note." Accessed January 24, 2020. http://composers.musicportal.gr/?c=dragatakis.
Jameson, Fredric. *Το μεταμοντέρνο ή η πολιτισμική λογική του ύστερου καπιταλισμού* [Postmodernism, or, the cultural logic of late capitalism]. Translated by Yorgos Varsos. Athens: Nefeli, 1999.
———. *Μια μοναδική νεωτερικότητα: Δοκίμιο για την οντολογία του παρόντος* [A singular modernity: Essay on the ontology of the present]. Translated by Spiros Marketos. Athens: Alexandria, 2007.
Kalomiris, Manolis. *Η ζωή μου και η τέχνη μου* [My life and my art]. Athens: Nefeli, 1988.
Kitroeff, Alexander. "Continuity and Change in Modern Greek Historiography." In *Εθνική ταυτότητα και εθνικισμός στη νεώτερη Ελλάδα* [National identity and nationalism in modern Greece], edited by Thanos Veremis, 271–322. Athens: National Bank of Greece Cultural Foundation, 2012.
Leibowitz, René. *Σένμπεργκ* [Schoenberg]. Translated by Thomas Sliomis. Athens: Pataki, 2003.
Mavrogordatos, Yorgos, and Christos Hadjiiosif, eds. *Βενιζελισμός και αστικός εκσυγχρονισμός* [Veniselism and bourgeois modernization]. Heraklion: Crete University Press, 1988.
Meraclis, Michael. *Ελληνική λαογραφία* [Greek folklore]. 3rd ed. Athens: Kardamitsa, 2011.
Miliaresis, Gerasimos. *Ήχοι και απόηχοι* [Sounds and echoes]. Athens: Kedros, 2002.
Papaioannou, Giannis. "Nikos Mamangakis: Biographical Note." *Musicale.* Accessed January 30, 2021. http://www.musicale.gr/synthetes/mamagakis_cv_en.html.
Rigos, Alkis. *Η β' ελληνική δημοκρατία, 1924–1935* [The second Greek democracy, 1924–1935]. Athens: Themelio, 1999.
Ritchie, Anthony Damian. "The Influence of Folk Music in Three Works by Béla Bártok: Sonata No. 1 for Violin and Piano, Sonata (1926) for Piano, and 'Contrasts' for Violin, Clarinet and Piano." PhD diss., University of Canterbury, 1986. https://core.ac.uk/download/pdf/35464018.pdf.
Romanou, Katy. "Βιβλιοπαρουσίαση" [Book presentation]. *Musicology* 20 (2011). http://musicology-journal.music.uoa.gr/issue020/romanou-dragoumisgr.html
———. *Ιστορία της έντεχνης νεοελληνικής μουσικής* [History of neohellenic art music]. Athens: Cultura, 2000.
———. "Nikos Skalkottas." In *Serbian and Greek Art Music: A Patch to Western Music History,* edited by Katy Romanou, 163–87. Chicago: Intellect, 2009.
Rye, Matthew. *1001 Classical Recordings You Must Hear Before You Die.* Edited by Steven Isserlis. New York: Rizzoli/Universe, 2008.

Sini, Petroula. "Ζωναράδικος" [Zonaradikos]. Λαογραφία [Folklore] (blog), April 29, 2014. https://laografiaparadosi.blogspot.com/2014/04/blog-post_96.html.

Siopsi, Anastasia. "Η έννοια του «εθνικού» ή η «ελληνικότητα», με άλλη σημασία, και το φαινόμενο της παγκοσμιοποίησης στη μουσική ζωή της σύγχρονης ελληνικής κοινωνίας" [The notion of "national" or "Greek," with another significance, and the phenomenon of globalization in the musical life of contemporary Greek society]. In *Έντεχνη ελληνική μουσική δημιουργία: Παράδοση και παγκοσμιοποίηση* [Modern Greek music creation: Tradition and globalization]: *Proceedings of the Musicological Congress, 24–26 April 2007*, edited by Sophia Topouzi, 10–13. Athens: Union of Greek Composers, 2008.

Sliomis, Thomas. Preface: "Η Δεύτερη Σχολή της Βιέννης, η νέα μουσική αντίληψη και η εξέλιξη της ιστορίας" [The Second Viennese School, the new musical perception and the evolution of history]. In Leibowitz, *Σένμπεργκ* [Schoenberg], 9–23. Athens: Pataki, 2003.

Tsetsos, Markos. *Εθνικισμός και λαϊκισμός στη νεοελληνική μουσική: Πολιτικές όψεις μιας πολιτισμικής απόκλισης* [Nationalism and populism in modern Greek music: Political aspects of a cultural deviation]. Athens: Sakis Karagiorgas Foundation, 2011.

———. "Μανώλης Καλομοίρης και Ελευθέριος Βενιζέλος: Ιδεολογικές και αισθητικές όψεις μιας σημαίνουσας σχέσης" [Manolis Kalomiris and Eleftherios Venizelos: Aesthetic and ideological aspects of a significant relationship]. In *Ελευθέριος Βενιζέλος και πολιτιστική πολιτική* [Eleftherios Venizelos and cultural policy]: *Proceedings of Symposium, 21–22 November 2008*, edited by Tasos Sakellaropoulos and Argiro Vatsaki, 270–79. Athens: Benaki Museum, 2012.

———. *Νεοελληνική μουσική: Δοκίμια ιδεολογικής και θεσμικής κριτικής* [Greek music: Issues of ideological and institutional critique]. Athens: Papagrigoriou-Nakas, 2013.

———. "Σκέψεις σχετικά με τα αισθητικά αδιέξοδα της σύγχρονης μουσικής δημιουργίας" [Thoughts concerning the aesthetic impasses of contemporary music]. In *Ζητήματα αισθητικής και ταυτότητας στη σύγχρονη μουσική δημιουργία* [Issues of aesthetics and identity in contemporary music], edited by Vissilios Kitsos, 91–98. Lamia: Center of Mediterranean Music, 2004.

Tsougras, Costas. "Η ελληνικότητα της μουσικής του Νίκου Σκαλκώτα: Ένας «εθνικός» ή «παγκόσμιος» συνθέτης;" [The Greekness of the music by Nikos Skalkottas: A "national" or "global" composer?] In *Έντεχνη ελληνική μουσική δημιουργία: Παράδοση και παγκοσμιοποίηση* [Modern Greek music creation: Tradition and globalization]: *Proceedings of the Musicological Congress, 24–26 April 2007*, edited by Sophia Topouzi, 19–25. Athens: Union of Greek Composers, 2008.

Tziovas, Dimitris. *Ο μύθος της γενιάς του τριάντα: Νεωτερικότητα, Ελληνικότητα και πολιτισμική ιδεολογία* [The myth of the generation of the thirties: Modernity, Greekness and cultural ideology]. Athens: Polis, 2011.

Veremis, Thanos, and Yiannis Koliopoulos. *Ελλάς: Η σύγχρονη συνέχεια, από το 1821 μέχρι σήμερα* [Greece: The modern sequel, from 1821 to the present]. Athens: Kastaniotis, 2006.

Wade, Graham, and Gerard Garno. *A New Look at Segovia: His Life, His Music*. 2 vols. Fenton, MO: Mel Bay, 1997.

Yannaras, Christos. *Αφελληνισμού παρεπόμενα* [Consequences of de-hellenizing]. Athens: Kaktos, 2005.

Zenakos, Augustinos. "Η μόδα και η κουλτούρα" [Fashion and culture]. *To Vima*, April 21, 2002. https://www.tovima.gr/2008/11/24/culture/i-moda-kai-i-koyltoyra/.

Musical Works

Andronoglou, Ioannis. "Fantasia on a Thracian Folksong." In *Fantasia on a Thracian Folksong: Mandilatos Impressions*, 2–7. Heraklion: Aerakis Cretan Musical Workshop, 2016. https://www.youtube.com/watch?v=KtpSqlLLyLk&list=PLQ2Whm kOXlTldKg3rjCMdQEzMoX0Js6cV.

———. *Travelling*. Legend Classics 2201159993, 2010. Reissue, Aerakis Cretan Musical Workshop A.M.A. 356, 2014. Compact disc.

Dragatakis, Dimitris. *Liz-Va*. Athens: Nakas, 1969.

Fampas, Dimitris. *Danza Greca no.1: Karaguna*. 1959. Repr., Milano: G. Ricordi, 1979.

Miliaresis, Gerasimos. "Danza di Zalongo." In *2 Danze Greche*, harmonized and transcribed by Gerasimos Miliaresis, 2. Milano: G. Ricordi, 1958.

Papaioannou, Yannis. *Sonatine for Flute and Guitar*. Athens: Nakas, 1986.

Tzortzinakis, Kiriakos. *Four Greek Images*. Athens: Papagrigoriou-Nakas, 1981.

Chapter 9

The Legacy of Talos: From Antiquity until Now

Hélène Jeannin

Orange Innovation, France

Ioannis Kostopoulos

Independent Researcher

Abstract

We have become accustomed to exoskeletons through images diffused among the general public by American blockbuster movies; these specific armors graft themselves to the body, permitting superior strength. They are considered as innovations that laid the foundation and served as an incentive for warriors' performance. Talos, also nicknamed "Iron Man," is considered as a technological breakthrough helping the United States to maintain overwhelming preponderance in the military sphere.

The contemporary name TALOS (Tactical Assault Light Operator Suit) pays tribute to the first exoskeleton or robot ever recorded as a means for defense. Hephaistos (Vulcan) created Talos in his forge. This giant would circumnavigate the Greek island of Crete several times each day at high speed, thus guaranteeing territorial security. Researchers have derived knowledge and inspiration for conceiving revamped weaponry from Talos in an attempt to improve effectiveness, but also to open up new markets and application fields. Talos also inspired a video game, as well as super heroes by Marvel comics, among others. Through a review of Talos's lineage the present essay focuses on the links among technologies in Antiquity and their impact on today's culture.

Keywords: Talos, Ancient Greek Technology, Antique Myth, Ancient Tale, Hellenic Heritage, scientific imagination, minister of justice, artificial man, robot border security, exoskeleton, humanoid robot.

***

Introduction

The influence of ancient Greece on Western culture is well-known. We are most familiar with its influence on the arts, literature, science, medicine and, of course, politics; we are accustomed to hearing about it and seeing it with our own eyes in architecture, sculpture, paintings and so on. Less well-known is the impact of ancient Greece on today's technology. Antiquity is so embedded in our culture that it is constantly being reworked in new and most unexpected places; perhaps surprisingly, technology is one of them.

We are indebted to the past. Nothing is invented from scratch: from the past we inherit knowledge, mistakes and errors, stereotypes and stories. Over time, some of those stories, however old, persist. They are so intriguing, so wonderful and extraordinary that they remain vivid in people's minds. However, sometimes they are also so unbelievable and formidable that they are transformed and adapted to the times, which is why we have several versions of a particular extraordinary event.

The story of Talos fits this description. It confirms that antiquity's importance today is as strong as ever. Robotics and computing, for instance, existed during antiquity. We know because traces have been found, including the Antikythera mechanism.[1] Especially interesting are an ancient super-robot, Talos, and the legends about him. Talos was—and still is—connected with advances in the mechanical arts and the military field. Talos reveals that men have long aspired to create armor that will prevent them from being killed or even wounded.

Who or what was Talos?

Several ancient sources refer explicitly to Talos. He was first described by the poets Hesiod (c. 700 BCE) and Simonides (c. 556–468 BCE). From Hesiod's *Works and Days*:

> And Zeus the father made a race of bronze,
>
> Sprung from the ash tree, worse than the silver race,
>
> But strange and full of power. And they loved
>
> The Groans and violence of war; they ate
>
> No bread; their hearts were flinty-hard; they were
>
> Terrible men; their strength was great, their arms
>
> And shoulders and their limbs invincible.[2]

---

1. Jo Marchant, "Decoding the Antikythera Mechanism, the First Computer," *Smithsonian Magazine*, February 2015, https://www.smithsonianmag.com/history/decoding-antikythera-mechanism-first-computer-180953979/.

2. Hesiod, *Theogony and Works and Days*, trans. Dorothea Wender (Harmondsworth, UK: Penguin, 1973), 63.

Plato (c. 427 BCE) writes in "Minos:"

> For Minos used him [Rhadamanthus] as guardian of the law in the city, and Talos as the same for the rest of Crete. For Talos thrice a year made a round of the villages, guarding the laws in them, by holding their laws inscribed on brazen tablets, which gave him his name of brazen.[3]

According to book 4 of the *Argonautica*, an epic poem by Apollonius of Rhodes (born c. 295 BCE), Talos was "a man of bronze" who,

> as he broke off rocks from the hard cliff, stayed them from fastening hawsers to the shore, when they came to the road-stead of Dicte's haven. He was of the stock of bronze, of the men sprung from ash-trees, the last left among the sons of the gods; and the son of Cronos gave him to Europa to be the warder of Crete and to stride round the island thrice a day with his feet of bronze. Now in all the rest of his body and limbs was he fashioned of bronze and invulnerable; but beneath the sinew by his ankle was a blood-red vein; and this, with its issues of life and death, was covered by a thin skin.[4]

"Appolodorus" (c. 100–200 BCE), in *The Library*, reflects the ambiguity regarding his provenance:

> Some say that he was a man of the Brazen Race, others that he was given to Minos by Hephaestus; he was a brazen man, but some say that he was a bull. He had a single vein extending from his neck to his ankles, and a bronze nail was rammed home at the end of the vein. This Talos kept guard, running round the island thrice every day; wherefore, when he saw the Argo standing inshore, he pelted it as usual with stones.[5]

To sum up, uncertainty about Talos's origins led to variations in the accounts. Most sources suggest that Talos was built of bronze by Hephaestus, the smith god, who made it as a gift to King Minos of Crete. In short, Talos was either given to King Minos by the god of handcraft, Hephaestus, or, in other versions, to Europe by Cronos's son Zeus.[6]

---

3. Plato, "Minos," in *Plato in Twelve Volumes*, vol. 12, trans. W. R. M. Lamb (Cambridge, MA: Harvard University Press, 1925), 320c.

4. Apollonius of Rhodes, *Argonautica*, bk. 4, trans. Richard Hunter (Cambridge: Cambridge University Press, 2015), 407.

5. Apollodorus, *The Library*, trans. James George Frazer (London: Heinemann, 1921), 1.9.26, 119.

6. John Papadopoulos, "Talos," in *Lexicon iconographicum mythologiae classicae* (Zurich: Artemis & Winkler, 1994), 834.

Thus "the creation of Life itself depends on divine impetus."[7] As Bruce J. Douglas remarks, usually Talos is a brass giant manufactured by Hephaestus and given by him to Minos to guard Crete.[8] Only Apollodorus states differently, apparently having Hesiod's passage in mind, but he uses the adjective in a literal sense, considering the men of the Brazen Age as really made of brass.

The Bronze Age marked the first time human beings started to work with metal. Bronze tools and weapons replaced earlier stone versions and became of the utmost value and importance. Different human societies entered the Bronze Age at different times. In Greece, the era dates to before 3000 BC, with the Cycladic and Minoan civilizations, the first such advanced cultures in Europe.[9]

Talos's missions were threefold. First of all, he was invented mainly to guard the island of Crete from pirates and invaders. To fulfill his duty to guarantee territorial security and the safety of Europa or Minos, he would circumnavigate the island's shores three times a day, at an average speed of about 155 miles per hour. That is very fast even now, so imagine how great the performance was at that time. This speediness began to build his reputation.

He would not only circle the island three times a day to check if an enemy was approaching, he would also deter any trespassers from setting foot on the island, in a highly effective manner. In particular, he would hurl enormous boulders at approaching enemy vessels in order to sink them and thus prevent them from landing on the island. If they got through this initial bombardment and succeeded in reaching the coast anyway, the giant captured them and then heated up his bronze body. He would clasp the strangers in his burning embrace, which made them perish in flames. So Talos was polyvalent, reacting and adapting to multiple situations of danger and brave in all circumstances.

Above all, Talos was also an upholder of justice, having the duty to protect Crete and Europa/King Minos not only from enemies but also from all sorts of lawbreaking. He would go around to all the villages of the island three times a year, according to Plato, carrying on his back bronze tablets that were inscribed with the laws. He was merely a strict minister of justice and was called "brazen" because he was bearing laws engraved on brass. By ensuring that the laws were respected and applied, and by resolving disputes, Talos acted as a judge. This detail is highly important, because it reveals the existence of

---

7. Christian Fron and Oliver Korn, "A Short History of the Perception of Robots and Automata from Antiquity to Modern Times," in *Social Robots: Technological, Societal and Ethical Aspects of Human–Robot Interaction* (Cham, Switzerland: Springer International, 2019), 3.

8. James Douglas Bruce, "Human Automata in Classical Tradition and Mediaeval Romance," *Modern Philology* 10 (1913): 4.

9. History.com, "Bronze Age," last updated August 24, 2021, https://www.history.com/topics/prehistory/bronze-age.

writing and legal systems, with all that is involved as part of working toward an organized society with its own rules and knowledge.

Talos was exceptionally agile, reaching all parts of the island faster than the wind. This explains why he is sometimes depicted with wings, for instance, on coins discovered in the Minoan palace of Phaistos on the island of Crete (fig. 9.1). Talos was featured in Athenian plays and appeared in paintings on walls and vases of the 5th century BCE, such as the so-called Talos Vase in the National Archaeological Museum Jatta in Ruvo di Puglia, Italy (fig. 99.2). There is also a virtually identical fragment in Ferrara, at the Museo Archeologico Nazionale.[10]

Figure 9.1. The giant Talos armed with a stone. Silver didrachm from Phaistos, Crete, c. 300 or 280–70 BCE, obverse.

Source: Wikimedia Commons,
https://commons.wikimedia.org/wiki/File:Didrachm_Phaistos_obverse_CdM.jpg.

Talos had a single vein of molten metal running from his neck to his ankle, a sort of blood vein. A bronze peg in his ankle prevented this life-giving fluid from pouring out. The fluid was called ichor, which was the blood of gods and immortals.[11] This liquid

---

10. Tatiana Bur, "Mechanical Miracles: Automata in Ancient Greek Religion," PhD diss., University of Sydney, 2016, 53.

11. S. Vasileiadou, D. Kalligeropoulos and N. Karcanias, "Systems, Modelling and Control in Ancient Greece; Part 1: Mythical Automata," *Measurement and Control* 36, no. 3 (2003): 78.

resembled what we now know as mercury, beneficial to gods but poisonous to humans. Also, his head looked like that of a bull. Unfortunately, Talos was flawed: his ankle was a unique point of weakness where his single vein could be attacked, and the bronze nail could be removed so that the liquid in the vein—the divine liquid that allowed his metal limbs to move—leaked out. And that is how he died or was killed (depending on the version).

Figure 9.2. The death of Talos, depicted on the 5th-century BCE krater known as the Talos Vase. Collection of the Jatta National Archaeological Museum, Ruvo di Puglia, Italy.

Source: Wikimedia Commons,
https://commons.wikimedia.org/wiki/File:Vaso_di_Talos_particolare.JPG.

Hephaestus, said in most sources to be the creator of Talos, is famous for his technical prowess, remarkable ingenuity and cleverness, which allowed him to transgress the limits of artisanal creation. He is often depicted with blacksmith's attributes such as a sword, a hammer or pliers. Hephaestus forged Achilles' glorious armor. He also created machines resembling living beings, endowed with a soul, strength and human abilities, including tripods, automatic doors or golden servants capable of moving and speaking like real humans.[12] However, Homer never says this was magic or sorcery; he only vividly celebrates his genius (particularly in book 18).

Talos appears to have been the greatest achievement of Hephaestus. Christopher Faraone's analysis of guardian statuary in the classical period and the brazen man of Greek myth claims that Talos outperforms other automata, such as the bronze lion and

---

12. Homer, *The Iliad*, trans. Robert Fagles (London: Penguin Classics, 1999).

the gold and silver dogs of Alcinous, that also served the purpose of protection. For none of those, despite being able to move limbs or utter words, were capable of achieving Talos's level of ambulatory and motor skill.[13] Unlike Talos, those mechanisms bore little resemblance to people.

Talos's legacies: fictions and narratives

Talos's legacy is perennial because of ancient narratives. Fiction and stories have played a major part in spreading his long-lasting legend. Over the centuries, literature is filled with references to this wonderful creature and casts light on his creator's resourcefulness. These references explain why Talos's deeds are "among the most enduring Greek legends about artificial men,"[14] resurfacing in many later tales. For instance, Edmund Spenser's 16th-century English epic *The Faerie Queene* includes Artegall, a knight who is the embodiment and champion of justice. Artegall is assisted in his task by Talus, a metal man who never sleeps or tires. Talus obeys Artegall's commands and dispenses justice without mercy, just like the ancient bronze Talos.[15] According to Lindsey McCulloch, Spenser's Talus is positioned as both subhuman and superhuman, war machine and wondrous spectacle, the poet's application of technology to both military and judicial contexts.[16]

Since its inception five centuries ago, Spenser's Renaissance appropriation has been scrutinized by scholars and has become popular in its many adaptations for children, especially in the 19th and 20th centuries. In England and the United States, for instance, Talos appears in Thomas Bulfinch's 1855 *Stories of Gods and Heroes* (fig. 9.3) and in Herman Merville's "The Bell Tower," from the same year. Nowadays, this character is still significant. Richard K. Simon sees extensive parallels between George Lucas's *Star Wars* films and Spenser's work. He states: "Almost everything of importance that we see in the *Star Wars* movie has its origin in *The Faerie Queene*, from small details of weaponry and dress to large issues of chivalry and spirituality."[17]

---

13. Christopher A. Faraone, "Hephaestus the Magician and Near Eastern Parallels for Alcinous' Watchdogs," *Greek, Roman and Byzantine Studies* 28, no. 3 (1987): 263.

14. Kevin LaGrandeur, "Robots, Moving Statues, and Automata in Ancient Tales and History," in *Critical Insights: Technology and Humanity*, ed. Carol Colatrella (New York: Salem, 2012), 102.

15. Edmund Spenser, *The Faerie Queene*, bk. 5 (London: William Ponsonbie, 1596), https://scholarsbank.uoregon.edu/xmlui/bitstream/handle/1794/784/faeriequeene.pdf.

16. Lindsey McCulloch, "Antique Myth, Early Modern Mechanism, The Secret History of Spenser's Iron Man," in *The Automaton in English Renaissance Literature*, ed. Wendy Beth Hyman (Farnham, UK: Routledge, 2011), 96, 99.

17. Richard K. Simon, "Star Wars and the Faerie Queene," in *Trash Culture: Popular Culture and the Great Tradition* (Berkeley: University of California Press, 1999), 33.

Figure 9.3. "Medeia and Talos." Illustration by Sybil Tawse (1886–1971), in Thomas Bulfinch, *Stories of Gods and Heroes* (Thomas Y. Crowell, c. 1919).

Source: Public domain. Reproduced in Oliver Korn, Gerald Bieber and Christian Fron, "Perspectives on Social Robots. From the Historic Background to an Experts' View on Future Developments," in *Proceedings of the 11th Pervasive Technologies Related to Assistive Environments Conference (PETRA '18)*, 186–93 (New York: Association for Computing Machinery, 2018), doi:https://doi.org/10.1145/3197768.3197774.

Plenty of stories about this incredible creature circulated through the centuries. What Talos accomplished was so extraordinary that in times such as the Middle Ages it was very difficult to account for it. Let's not forget also that the Great Library of Alexandria, the most illustrious center of arts and sciences of its time, was burned and all its treasures destroyed. Many valuable texts that could have enlightened us have vanished. The know-how having been lost, incomprehension led to applying the term *magic* for what could not be explained. So throughout the ages, a certain perplexity may have surrounded Talos's feats. One thing is for sure: he captured people's imaginations. He was created to perform specific tasks with such perfection as to become closer to the divine powers.

Through the metal that composed him, he also had particularly remarkable immortality and resistance, bronze being the ultimate material of the time.

Antiquity serves as inspiration in mass culture,[18] and science fiction in particular.[19] It was not Hephaestus himself but his "famed automatons, or self-operating machines that became a staple of the fantasy variant of the peplum genre."[20] Talos's image became widespread in popular culture, not only in books but also in Marvel comics and subsequent Hollywood movies such as *Jason and the Argonauts*,[21] as well as the superhero Iron Man. Talos also appears in *Star Wars* as a soldier. In the television series *Star Trek*, Talos is a planet where the Talosians live; they were initially warriors but became a telepathic humanoid species.

Talos's legacies: a scientific basis for robotics and artificial intelligence

In early accounts, Talos is described as a technological production, an animated metal machine in the form of a man, programmed to carry out complex human-like actions. He was envisaged either as an android (a human-resembling robot with its vein located under artificial skin) or as a member of a living species from a past era, more than just a giant automaton made of bronze. An automaton is a self-moving or self-operating machine; in historical and literary studies, it designates such machines that were created before the 20th century.[22]

Innovative engineers from the Higher Technical School in Alexandria, who flourished in the library of Alexandria, worked to marry the sciences of machines and mathematics. Prominent scientists included Heron of Alexandria (also called Hero), Apollonius of Perga, Aristarchus, Conon, Hipparchus, Ctesebius and Philon of Byzantium, as well as many others. They described how to build a large number of automata powered by hydraulics, pneumatics or gravity. Their writings preserved for posterity a knowledge of mathematics and engineering gathered from a variety of sources. A large number of Heron's works have survived, although the authorship of some is disputed. *Automata, Pneumatica* (which studies mechanical devices worked by air, steam or water pressure)

---

18. See Dunstan Lowe and Kim Shahabudin, *Classics for All: Reworking Antiquity in Mass Culture* (Newcastle-upon-Tyne, UK: Cambridge Scholars, 2009).

19. See Brett M. Rogers and Benjamin Eldon Stevens, *Classical Traditions in Science Fiction* (Oxford: Oxford University Press, 2015).

20. Vito Adriaensens, "From Hephaistos to the Silver Screen: Living Statues, Antiquity and Cinema," *CineAction* 91 (2013): 46, https://www.thefreelibrary.com/From+Hephaistos+to+the+silver+screen%3a+living+statues%2c+antiquity+and...-a0346142604.

21. Don Chaffey, dir., *Jason and the Argonauts* (Culver City, CA: Columbia Pictures, 1963), film, 104 min.

22. Clara Bosak-Schroeder, "The Religious Life of Greek Automata," *Archiv für Religionsgeschichte* 17, no. 1 (2016): 123, https://doi.org/10.1515/arege-2015-0007.

and *Mechanica* provided the first documentation on workable robots and paved the way for development of today's automatic machines.

Rossi considers that automatic devices were first designed by the scientists and engineers of the Hellenistic age, which encompasses the Mediterranean area and a specific time period between 323 BCE and 31 BCE but from a cultural point of view ranges between the 3rd century BCE and the 2nd century CE.[23] In Rossi's view, our predecessors about 2,000 years ago were so advanced in almost every field of culture, as well as in terms of technology and engineering, that we owe to them the foundations of today's society. We must pay tribute to them for the knowledge that led to making our lives easier. It was not until the 18th century at the earliest that their inventions were surpassed.[24] Pierre-Jacquet Droz (1721–90) and Jacques de Vaucanson (1709–82), for example, who designed automatons reproducing the main vital functions of the human body (digestion, blood circulation and breathing), are among the ancient technologists' famous heirs.[25]

As summarized by Sawday, we are "the heirs to the mechanical culture of the Renaissance," which was itself inherited from the mechanical culture of the medieval and classical periods.[26] A typical example of ancient Greek high technology is the Antikythera mechanism, so called because it was discovered in an ancient shipwreck off Antikythera island in 1901.[27] It is the oldest known scientific computer,[28] a cultural treasure that continues to engross scholars across many disciplines.[29]

Is Talos closer to a living being than a machine? As Tatiana Bur points out, at no time is he described as an automaton, nor is the vocabulary of automation ever applied to him. His internal system, as detailed in the *Argonautica,* is the source of his power, animation and intelligent behavior. He is kept alive thanks to a blood-red vein that runs down to his

---

23. Cesare Rossi, "The Beginning of the Automation: A Brief Review on the Automatic Devices in the Hellenistic Age," in Advances in Robot Design and Intelligent Control: Proceedings of the 24th International Conference on Robotics in Alpe-Adria-Danube Region (RAAD), ed. Theodor Borangiu (Cham: Springer International, 2016), 60, https://doi.org/10.1007/978-3-319-21290-6_6.

24. Rossi, 66. See also Cesare Rossi, Flavio Russo and Ferruccio Russo, "Automata (Towards Automation and Robots)," in *Ancient Engineers' Inventions: Precursors of the Present*, 269–302 (Cham: Springer International, 2017).

25. Alfred Chapuis and Edmond Droz, *Automata: A Historical and Technological Study* (Neufchatel: Griffon, 1958).

26. Jonathan Sawday, *Engines of the Imagination*: Renaissance Culture and the Rise of the Machine (New York: Routledge, 2007), 70.

27. François Charette, "High Tech from Ancient Greece," *Nature* 444 (2006): 551.

28. Marchant.

29. Tony Freeth et al., "A Model of the Cosmos in the Ancient Greek Antikythera Mechanism," *Scientific Reports* 11, no. 5821 (2021): 1, https://doi.org/10.1038/s41598-021-84310-w.

ankle and is held in place by a bronze nail. Apart from this detail, Talos has quite a number of human attributes. The iconographic tradition lends him many human features. On the Talos Vase, he is distinguished by his bright white color, but there is nothing technological about his presentation. Having a nail in his ankle may suggest something slightly mechanical about him, but Bur prefers not to make a firm statement. When discussing such a complex and diverse culture, it is acceptable to stick to vague and overlapping categories.[30]

Some authors, however, do take a stand. Christos Iavazzo and his co-authors consider that Talos's functions are similar to those of current sophisticated robots that carry out heavy manufacturing processes, transportation and management of objects, transferring orders and decision-making by searching rules through databases, for example.[31] Like a social robot, Talos represents "the universal longing to create a model of humans to match personal desires and necessities."[32] *Robot* was a term coined by Karel Čapek in his 1921 play *R.U.R.*,[33] around the time when Talos was envisioned as such by the illustrator Sybil Tawse (fig. 9.3).

Adrienne Mayor, in *Gods and Robots,* states that Talos is part machine, part human. She considers that the basic conditions for being a robot are met: "a self-moving android with a power source that provides energy, '*programmed*' to '*sense*' its surroundings and possessing a kind of '*intelligence*' or way of processing data to '*decide*' to interact with the environment to perform actions or tasks." She adds: "ancient writers and artists represented Talos as an automaton, a 'self-mover,' a bronze statue animated by 'an internal mechanism,' in this case the single tube or vessel containing a special fluid, a system that has been described in biological, medical, and machine-like terms."[34] John Cohen claims that Talos inaugurated the modern technicist era.[35] More generally, Marta Perez Garcia, Sarita Saffon Lopez and Hector Donis argue that Talos's story illustrates

---

30. Bur, 54.
31. Christos Iavazzo et al., "Evolution of Robots Throughout History from Hephaestus to Da Vinci Robot," *Acta Medico-historica Adriatica* 12, no. 2 (2014): 250, http://www.amha-journal.com/index.php/AMHA/article/view/462.
32. Oliver Korn, Gerald Bieber and Christian Fron, "Perspectives on Social Robots: From the Historic Background to an Expert's View on Future Developments," in *Proceedings of the 11th Pervasive Technologies Related to Assistive Environments Conference (PETRA '18)* (New York: Association for Computing Machinery, 2018), 187, doi:https://doi.org/10.1145/3197768.3197774.
33. R.U.R. is an abbreviation for *Rossumovi univerzální roboti* (Rossum's Universal Robots).
34. Adrienne Mayor, *Gods and Robots: Myths, Machines and Ancient Dreams of Technology* (Princeton, NJ: Princeton University Press, 2018), 22.
35. John Cohen, *Human Robots in Myth and Science* (London: Allen & Unwin, 1966), 18, 25.

"humans' interest in building a machine that is able to perform some kind of reasoning"[36] and is an endless source of inspiration for today's engineers and scientists.

As Jean-Pierre Merlet writes, "Recent robotics is the result of a large historical tradition dating back from Antiquity and based on still older religious beliefs."[37] Roboticists' "desire and fascination with intelligent machines dates back to antiquity's mythical *automaton* Talos."[38] They reckon that the idea of and imagining programmable machines and automata go back to ancient myths, and that both robotics and artificial intelligence (AI) make their first appearance in the ancient Greek form of Talos. He testifies to the human desire for an artificial helper to assume the burden of unpleasant or hard labor. Therefore he is often cited in scientific papers as the first, the ancestor of a long lineage: "Historically, the first automatic (the term coming from the Greek word automatos—"moving on its own") mechanical humanoid system can be considered the legendary Talos. This one, described in several texts from antiquity, had a human-like mechanical structure and it was driven by a special liquid."[39]

Artificial intelligence was not described as existing without embodiment. Researchers in the field have stated that AI "history is far longer ... with ancient Greeks describing the artificially intelligent automaton Talos."[40] Others add that "AI is preceded by the ancient legend of the bronze giant Talos, the mechanical guardian of Crete; his prodigies are dreamt of by many medieval myths, from the automatic soldiers protecting the relics of Buddha evoked by the Indian Lokapannatti to the famous Golem."[41]

Europe's borders

It is interesting to note that Talos is still referred to in both Europe and the United States, where he often appears in various forms. What matters is what he does, which actions he performs. Because of cultural sensitivities, as well as various needs and priorities, each

---

36. Marta Perez Garcia, Sarita Saffon Lopez and Hector Donis, "Everybody Is Talking about Virtual Assistants, But How Are People Really Using Them?" in *Proceedings of the 32nd International BCS Human Computer Interaction Conference (HCI)* (Belfast: BCS Learning and Development, 2018), 1.

37. Jean-Pierre Merlet, "A Historical Perspective of Robotics," in *International Symposium on History of Machines and Mechanisms: Proceedings*, ed. Marco Ceccarelli (Cassino: Kluwer Academic, 2000), 379.

38. Nima Dehghani, "Design of the Artificial: Lessons from the Biological Roots of General Intelligence," arXiv, Cornell University March 8, 2017, 1, https://arxiv.org/pdf/1703.02245.pdf.

39. Ionel Staretu, "Main Stages of Evolution from Mechanical Automatic Systems to Humanoid Robot," *Journal of Mechanics Engineering and Automation* 5 (2015): 309.

40. Tobias Eljasik-Swoboda, Christian Rathgeber and Rainer Hasenauer, "Artificial Intelligence for Innovation Readiness Assessment," in *International Symposium on Innovation and Entrepreneurship (TEMS-ISIE)* (New York: IEEE, 2019), 2, https://doi.org/10.1109/TEMS-ISIE46312.2019.9074291.

41. Alexandre Gefen, Léa Saint-Raymond and Tommaso Venturini, "AI for Digital Humanities and Computational Social Sciences," in *Reflections on AI for Humanity*, eds. Bertrand Braunschweig and Malik Ghallab (Berlin: Springer, 2021), 192.

country or continent has taken from the story what is most flattering or most beneficial to it. In Europe, for instance, he gave his name to a project intended to protect Europe's borders. Its acronym, TALOS, stood for "Transportable and Autonomous Land Border Surveillance system."

The overall goal of the TALOS project was to demonstrate the concept of a surveillance system that would offer a novel and innovative approach to land-border protection, based on autonomous ground and air vehicles. Conventional border-protection systems are too costly in terms of the manpower and apparatus required. Patrolling Europe's vast borders is a huge challenge. With new members and many more to come, the European Union's border is extending drastically, exposing it to illicit trafficking, smuggling and illegal immigration.

The systems FRONTEX and EUROSUR (European Surveillance System for Borders) had proved insufficient. TALOS was a robotic system that addressed the issue. Two TALOS prototypes for protecting and securing Europe's borders were tested between June 1, 2008, and May 31, 2012. The prototypes looked like small military tanks with a beige platform with a green top and two cameras in the front that resembled eyes. The system was developed by experts working at 14 different institutions in eight European member states (Belgium, Estonia, Finland, France, Greece, Poland, Romania and Spain) as well as two associate countries (Turkey and Israel). The consortium was made up of industrial companies, research institutions, small and medium enterprises (SMEs) and a technical university. The project budget came to nearly 20 million euros, 13 million of which were granted by the European Community.

The TALOS project influenced European research by contributing to exploration in the fields of robotic perception and multi-robot command and control, as well as mobile communication. It also promoted research in other fields: mapping and localization, artificial intelligence, low-level vehicle control and robotic navigation.[42] It was tasked with securing Europe's border, just like the ancient Talos. What Europe wanted to retain was Talos's role as a warden, a security guard.

In 2016 the European TALOS project inspired a two-year artistic research initiative by the choreographer Arkadi Zaides and his team of collaborators. Their performance demonstrated that the military's robot was a cartoonish failure and that terminating funding for the TALOS project (in 2012) had been the right move.[43]

---

42. European Commission, "Transportable Autonomous Patrol for Land bOrder Surveillance," last updated May 30, 2017, https://cordis.europa.eu/project/id/218081.

43. *Talos*, chor. Arkadi Zaides et al., 2016–18 (first performed at Hebbel am Ufer, Berlin, August 30, 2017), arkadizaides.com.

Nevertheless, a cultural insight emerges from reflecting on the TALOS project. The idea of robotic border security partakes of the European longing for connection with ancient Greece; with TALOS, Europe could return to its roots and reclaim its Hellenic heritage. Rutgeerts and Scholts argue, however, that there is a sinister aspect to this seemingly benign nostalgia: the normalizing of this connection could be "a powerful means to employ the mythical figure to shape our vision on the future."[44]

Talos: the ultimate enhanced soldier, a warrior augmented with advanced technology

The search for power extends to anxieties concerning national defense, including naval warfare. Talos is considered by some as "an early version of a technological weapon."[45] Once captured in his brass grasp, ships were held to his heated metal chest until they ignited. He fulfills the hope of many countries to attain military might without the cost of human lives and damage to frail human bodies, its current consequence being remote drone warfare.[46]

As Adrienne Mayor recalls, the U.S. military showed an early fascination with Talos. In 1947, when the development of the largest surface-to-air guided missile began (it became operational 11 years later), it sought an "appropriate name" and found it in Thomas Bulfinch's popular *Stories of Gods and Heroes*. According to the official history of the missile, Talos

> watched over and guarded the island of Crete. He was made of brass and was reputed to fly through the air at such terrific speed that he became red hot. His method of dealing with his enemies was to clasp them tightly to his breast, turning them to cinders at once. Talos was approved as the name for the new ramjet missile by the US Bureau of Ordnance and by the Guided Missiles Subcommittee of the Aeronautical Board on January 5, 1948.[47]

In this modern telling, Talos was airborne, recalling the winged images of him on the coins of Phaistos (fig. 9.1), and heated by intense friction. Paralleling the duties of Crete's

---

44. Jonas Rutgeerts and Nienke Scholts, "TALOS/Talos: What Sort of Future Do We Want to See Performed?" *FORUM* 25, no. 2 (2018): 8, http://www.forum-online.be/nummers/zomer-2018/what-sort-of-future-do-we-want-to-see-performed.

45. Daniel Dinello, *Technophobia! Science-Fiction Visions of Posthuman Technology* (Austin: University of Texas Press, 2005), 37.

46. Krista Kennedy, "The Anxiety of Automation: Attending to the Deep History of Automated Entities," *Writing Studies, Rhetoric, and Composition* 18 (2017): 4–5, https://surface.syr.edu/wp/18.

47. William Garten Jr. and Frank A. Dean, "Evolution of the Talos Missile," *Johns Hopkins APL Technical Digest* 3, no. 2 (1983): 118, https://www.jhuapl.edu/Content/techdigest/pdf/V03-N02/03-02-Garten.pdf.

mythical bronze giant, the Talos missiles served as a frontline defense and were extremely fast. They were automatically directed but became partly autonomous at closer range. This is a good showcase for how military planners were inspired by the Greek myth.

Dr. Derek J. Smith, a former cognitive scientist with Cardiff Metropolitan University, offers another approach.[48] He says that the legendary Talos can be considered as either the first robot or the first "robot-like" creature in history. Talos was "robotic in shape, but probably consisted of a person in a suit."[49] So to him the boundary is blurred between these two categories, which is in line with Bur's point of view, quoted above. A person in a suit is nowadays said to be wearing an exoskeleton. *Exoskeleton* is a word inspired by the external skeleton of a beetle or a crustacean. It means a sort of armor that enables extra movement or strength. One example of its use would be for soldiers. Exoskeletons are specific armors that graft themselves to the body, permitting superior abilities and skills. Armor is considered the innovation that laid the foundation for and served as an incentive for warriors' performance.

To stay in the race, military powers need to develop new kinds of weaponry. The modern battlespace requires agile, dynamic forces able to act with speed and precision. The concept of network-centric warfare, pioneered by the U.S. Defense Department since the 1990s, corresponds to a military doctrine that has been widely adopted by other countries. This doctrine stipulates that modern military environments are far too complex for human comprehension, and thus must rely on extra information. Information sharing is becoming the key to success, and mission effectiveness relies on specific types of equipment and data exchange. All forces need to be integrated and synchronized. The soldiers of the future and the wars they fight will become more and more mechanically mediated and networked than ever before.

In this context, the soldier is considered the weak link. But ground forces are necessary on a battlefield. In the 1990s, the Defense Advanced Research Projects Agency (DARPA) in the United States, whose aim is to make significant technological breakthroughs and ensure America's supremacy, proclaimed that the situation had to be corrected. It therefore initiated research programs to modify the human body with biology and technology and to develop new capabilities and combat skills; this has been documented in unclassified reports. It was taking place at the same time as the rise of transhumanism— the belief that advanced technology can enhance human physiology, psychology and intelligence. Because of the secrecy of the military-industrial complex and the entanglement of projects, it is difficult to know exactly how much money has been spent on efforts to

---

48. Derek J. Smith, "A Brief History of Automata," last updated July 8, 2018, http://www.smithsrisca.co.uk/automata-history.html.

49. See his interview at 8:15 min. of "Ancient Robots 15," episode 9, season 3 of *Ancient Discoveries*, History Channel, https://www.dailymotion.com/video/x2nz3ok.

create the enhanced soldier, but it is estimated that in 2017 DARPA had a budget of nearly $3 billion for the project.[50]

In 2000, DARPA funded the BLEEX (Berkeley Lower Extremity Exoskeleton) project at the University of California, Berkeley, robotics and engineering department, which resulted in an experimental exoskeleton prototype. A year later, the agency initiated the development of exoskeletons in a five-year Exoskeletons for Human Performance Augmentation program, through which several generations of exoskeletons came to be.[51] After 2013 the U.S. Department of Defense decided that the protection of ground personnel needed an upgrade. The death of a special operator became the primary reason for SOCOM (Special Operations Command) to partner with DARPA in order to begin the development of the innovative futuristic TALOS. In February 2014, President Barack Obama announced, "We are building Iron Man."[52]

In 2018 a leap forward was made with the arrival of TALOS. TALOS stands for "Tactical Assault Light Operator Suit," but more casually, it is called the "Iron Man suit." According to a scientific press article, TALOS's name "pays homage to a metal giant of Greek mythology who guarded the island of Crete, effortlessly circling it three times a day."[53] It is designed to "provide operators lighter, more efficient full-body ballistics protection and super-human strength. Antennas and computers embedded into the suit will increase the wearer's situational awareness by providing user-friendly and real-time battlefield information."[54] In effect, TALOS is a powered set of armor. It incorporates specialized lightweight armor with a robotic exoskeleton and 3D augmented-reality displays.[55]

Military leaders seeking to give soldiers more strength, stamina and protection have long dreamed of something similar to Marvel Comics' Iron Man, whose powers come from a robotic suit. In the late 1960s, the U.S. Office of Naval Research funded the development of "Hardiman," a massive exoskeleton. Hardiman was abandoned, but the idea did not die.[56]

---

50. Ioana Puscas, "La quête du soldat augmenté," *Le monde diplomatique* 762 (September 2017), 3.

51. B. S. Richardson, ed., *Phase I Report: DARPA Exoskeleton Program* (Oak Ridge, TN: Oak Ridge National Laboratory, 2004), 1, https://info.ornl.gov/sites/publications/Files/Pub57312.pdf.

52. Jesus Diaz, "Obama Says US Army Is Building a Real Iron Man and No, He Is Not Joking," *Gizmodo*, March 27, 2014, https://gizmodo.com/obama-says-us-army-is-building-real-iron-man-and-no-he-1532582334.

53. Warren Cornwall, "In Pursuit of the Perfect Power Suit," *Science* 350, no. 6258 (October 16, 2015): 270, doi: 10.1126/science.350.6258.270.

54. Donna Miles, "Iron Man," *Army Technology* 2, no. 3 (May/June 2014): 10.

55. Tim Lenoir and Luke Caldwell, *The Military-Entertainment Complex* (Cambridge, MA: Harvard University Press, 2018), 42.

56. Cornwall, 271.

With TALOS, the military is really going big. TALOS is considered a technological breakthrough that will allow the United States to maintain its overwhelming hegemony in the military sphere. The suit also features multiple "eyes" like Argus's. Soldiers of the future will ideally have their ordinary human performance increased threefold in terms of abilities, memory and foregoing sleep. From the start, TALOS has had a touch of Hollywood. Legacy Effects, a California company that builds suits for the Iron Man movies, has also worked for the military. Former navy admiral Bill McRaven, who until 2014 led the Pentagon's SOCOM, says, "Science fiction can drive science. We may never get something that looks just like Iron Man, but that's what we're aiming for."[57]

A video game that reflects an armament culture

In *The Military-Entertainment Complex,* Tim Lenoir and Luke Caldwell describe the close links between the military and entertainment industries. Video games inscribe in our imagination a new American way of conducting war.[58] The emergence of an armament culture occurred simultaneously, and the characteristics of the soldier—equipment, garments, size and weight of protection systems—form an integral part of representations of masculinity in many spheres.[59]

Some of the questions raised by the Talos tale have not escaped modern video-game makers. From 2014 onwards, Talos inspired a video game with a deluxe edition, *The Talos Principle*. It is a narrative-based puzzle game played from a first- or third-person perspective. The player takes the role of an AI robot with a human-like consciousness and autonomy. He explores a number of environments that include more than 120 puzzles. With futuristic technology, these environments interlock greenery, desert and stone ruins. Progressing through a complex world littered with classical ruins and relics of a lost modern dystopia, the player reacts to obstacles, clues and choices in order to solve metaphysical dilemmas. The game combines artificial intelligence, free will and transhumanism.

Time magazine featured *The Talos Principle* as the "favorite hidden gem" of the 2014 Electronic Entertainment Expo (E3), where it received broad acclaim. Reviewers warmly praised both the challenges of the puzzles and the elements of philosophy built into the game's narrative.[60]

---

57. Cornwall, 271.
58. Lenoir and Caldwell, 34.
59. Michael Salter, "Toys for the Boys? Drones, Pleasure and Popular Culture in the Militarisation of Policing," *Critical Criminology* 22 (2014): 164–67.
60. Jared Newman and Matt Peckham, "E3 Hidden Gems: Our Sleeper Picks for 2014," *Time*, June 16, 2014, https://time.com/2873244/e3-best-indie-games/.

Other legacies of Talos

Generally speaking, because of the tasks he performed with such great efficiency, Talos has become associated with many positive attributes. He is the basis of a marvelous and fascinating story that paved the way for the fantasy and imagination of future superheroes such as those we find in Marvel Comics. Other associations and qualities of Talos include

- law enforcement
- technical breakthrough and innovation
- automation
- advanced mechanical devices such as robots and exoskeletons
- exceptional warriors with superior strength, power and speed
- military superiority and predominance
- a warden who guarantees defense and protection
- enhancement of defensive strength, with increased agility and great mobility of action
- efficient body armor
- invulnerability, reliability and resilience, and ...
- indestructibility.

There are many other references to Talos in today's culture. The acronym TALOS has proven to be convenient and frequently used for several purposes. Similarities to the actions of the ancient Talos are striking, but what matters is what "Talos" can evoke or refer to. Some of these uses include

- a dancing robot in the French dance company Matos's 1988 production *Talos and Koïné*, choreographed to highlight how much technology is transforming human gesture;[61]
- a bipedal humanoid robot as tall as a person, designed for research in complex industrial environments;[62]
- an application for neutralizing vulnerabilities in software, information systems and smart electronics;[63]
- a law firm specializing in consumer protection and criminal defense;

---

61. Joanna Pomian, "Portrait de groupe avec robot," *Terminal* 37 (1988): 14.
62. Pal Robotics, "Talos," 2020, https://pal-robotics.com/robots/talos/.
63. Zhen Huang et al., "Talos: Neutralizing Vulnerabilities with Security Workarounds for Rapid Response," *2016 IEEE Symposium on Security and Privacy* (New York: IEEE, 2016), 618, doi: 10.1109/SP.2016.43.

- a custom art company that uses state-of-the-art technology to design metal jewelry and figurines;[64]
- and a research project of the National Observatory of Athens, the "Thunder And Lightning Observing System."[65] What place could have more legitimacy than Greece for using it?

Antiquity still fascinates us, and Talos provides a clear demonstration of this continuing enthusiasm. According to ancient Greek mythology, Hephaistos laid the groundwork for robotic machines, and most of the mechanical principles we know today were known in that era. The ancients clearly understood the concept of robotics. Talos was not the only robot in the ancient world; there are many other examples that prove the existence of ancient androids and computers.

The Talos story continues to provide inspiration. Numerous Hollywood directors, children's authors, politicians, computer game developers and broadcasters have cast the ancient creation into new forms. Researchers and engineers derive knowledge and inspiration for building new weaponry, as well as for opening new markets and fields of application.[66] Analysis of the Talos story can help us to understand the multiple ways in which mythical narratives about technology can be inspiring even today.

Bibliography

Adriaensens, Vito. "From Hephaistos to the Silver Screen: Living Statues, Antiquity and Cinema." *CineAction* 91 (2013): 41–49. https://www.thefreelibrary.com/From+Hephaistos+to+the+silver+screen%3a+living+statues%2c+antiquity+and...-a0346142604.

Apollodorus. *The Library.* Translated by James George Frazer. Bk. 1, 4, 6, 9 and 26. London: Heinemann, 1921.

Apollonius of Rhodes. *Argonautica.* Translated by Richard Hunter. Bk. 4. Cambridge: Cambridge University Press, 2015.

Bruce, James Douglas. "Human Automata in Classical Tradition and Mediaeval Romance." *Modern Philology* 10 (1913): 511–26.

Bulfinch, Thomas. *Bulfinch's Mythology: Stories of Gods and Heroes.* 1855. Rpt., San Diego, CA: Canterbury Classics, 2015.

---

64. Voudas, "Who Is Talos" (blog post), August 18, 2019, Talos Crafts, https://taloscrafts.com/who-is-talos/.

65. National Observatory of Athens, "The TALOS Project," 2020, https://www.meteo.gr/talos/en/.

66. In 2018 a European Research Council program assessed the influence of classical antiquity on modern youth cultures. In summer 2019 an exhibition at the Louvre-Lens Museum explored Homer's impact in France, and from September 30, 2021, to February 7, 2022, the Louvre in Paris presented *Paris–Athens: The Birth of Modern Greece, 1675–1919,* an exhibition that both traced the cultural, diplomatic and artistic ties that have bonded France and Greece since the 19th century and showed how rediscovery of the splendor of Greek antiquity changed perceptions of Greece in Europe.

Bur, Tatiana. "Mechanical Miracles: Automata in Ancient Greek Religion." PhD diss., University of Sydney, 2016.

Chaffey, Don, dir. *Jason and the Argonauts*. Culver City, CA: Columbia Pictures, 1963. Film. 104 min.

Chapuis, Alfred, and Edmond Droz. *Automata: A Historical and Technological Study*. Neufchatel: Griffon, 1958.

Charette, François. "High Tech from Ancient Greece." *Nature* 444 (2006): 551–52.

Cohen, John. *Human Robots in Myth and Science*. London: Allen & Unwin, 1966.

Cornwall, Warren. "In Pursuit of the Perfect Power Suit." *Science* 350, no. 6258 (October 16, 2015): 270–73. doi: 10.1126/science.350.6258.270.

Dehghani, Nima. "Design of the Artificial: Lessons from the Biological Roots of General Intelligence." ArXiv, Cornell University, March 8, 2017. https://arxiv.org/pdf/1703.02245.pdf.

Diaz, Jesus. "Obama Says US Army Is Building a Real Iron Man and No, He Is Not Joking." Gizmodo, March 27, 2014. https://gizmodo.com/obama-says-us-army-is-building-real-iron-man-and-no-he-1532582334.

Dinello, Daniel. *Technophobia!: Science-Fiction Visions of Posthuman Technology*. Austin: University of Texas Press, 2005.

Eljasik-Swoboda, Tobias, Christian Rathgeber and Rainer Hasenauer. "Artificial Intelligence for Innovation Readiness Assessment." In *International Symposium on Innovation and Entrepreneurship (TEMS-ISIE)*. New York: IEEE, 2019. https://doi.org/10.1109/TEMS-ISIE46312.2019.9074291.

European Commission. "Transportable Autonomous patrol for Land bOrder Surveillance." Last updated May 30, 2017. https://cordis.europa.eu/project/id/218081.

Faraone, Christopher A. "Hephaestus the Magician and Near Eastern Parallels for Alcinous' Watchdogs." *Greek, Roman and Byzantine Studies* 28, no. 3 (1987): 257–80.

Freeth, Tony, David Higgon, Aris Dacanalis, Lindsay MacDonald, Myrto Georgakopoulou and Adam Wojcik. "A Model of the Cosmos in the Ancient Greek Antikythera Mechanism." *Scientific Reports* 11, no. 5821 (2021). https://doi.org/10.1038/s41598-021-84310-w.

Fron, Christian, and Oliver Korn. "A Short History of the Perception of Robots and Automata from Antiquity to Modern Times." In *Social Robots: Technological, Societal and Ethical Aspects of Human-Robot Interaction*, 1–12. Cham: Springer International, 2019.

Garten, William, Jr., and Frank A. Dean. "Evolution of the Talos Missile." *Johns Hopkins APL Technical Digest* 3, no. 2 (1983): 117–22. https://www.jhuapl.edu/Content/techdigest/pdf/V03-N02/03-02-Garten.pdf.

Gefen, Alexandre, Léa Saint-Raymond and Tommaso Venturini. "AI for Digital Humanities and Computational Social Sciences." In *Reflections on AI for Humanity*, edited by Bertrand Braunschweig and Malik Ghallab, 191–202. Berlin: Springer, 2021.

Hesiod. *Theogony and Works and Days*. Translated by Dorothea Wender. Harmondsworth, UK: Penguin, 1973.

History Channel. "Ancient Robots 15." Episode 9 of *Ancient Discoveries*, season 3. https://www.dailymotion.com/video/x2nz3ok.

History.com. "Bronze Age." Last updated August 24, 2021. https://www.history.com/topics/pre-history/bronze-age.

Homer. *The Iliad*. Translated by Robert Fagles. London: Penguin Classics, 1999.

Huang, Zhen, Mariana D'Angelo, Dhaval Miyani and David Lie. "Talos: Neutralizing Vulnerabilities with Security Workarounds for Rapid Response." In *2016 IEEE Symposium on Security and Privacy*, 618–35. New York: IEEE, 2016. doi: 10.1109/SP.2016.43.

Iavazzo, Christos, Xanthi-Ekaterini D. Gkegke, Paraskevi-Evangelia Iavazzo and Ioannis D. Gkegkes. "Evolution of Robots Throughout History from Hephaestus to Da Vinci Robot." *Acta Medico-Historica Adriatica* 12, no. 2 (2014): 247–58. http://www.amha-journal.com/index.php/AMHA/article/view/462.

Kennedy, Krista, "The Anxiety of Automation: Attending to the Deep History of Automated Entities." *Writing Studies, Rhetoric, and Composition* 18 (2017). https://surface.syr.edu/wp/18.

Korn, Oliver, Gerald Bieber and Christian Fron. "Perspectives on Social Robots: From the Historic Background to an Expert's View on Future Developments." In *Proceedings of the 11th Pervasive Technologies Related to Assistive Environments Conference (PETRA '18)*, 186–93. New York: Association for Computing Machinery, 2018. doi:https://doi.org/10.1145/3197768.3197774.

LaGrandeur, Kevin. "Robots, Moving Statues, and Automata in Ancient Tales and History." In *Critical Insights: Technology and Humanity*, edited by Carol Colatrella, 99–111. New York: Salem, 2012.

Lenoir, Tim, and Luke Caldwell. *The Military-Entertainment Complex*. Cambridge, MA: Harvard University Press, 2018.

Lowe, Dunstan, and Kim Shahabudin. *Classics for All: Reworking Antiquity in Mass Culture*. Newcastle-upon-Tyne: Cambridge Scholars, 2009.

Marchant, Jo. "Decoding the Antikythera Mechanism, the First Computer." *Smithsonian Magazine*, 2015. https://www.smithsonianmag.com/history/decoding-antikythera-mechanism-first-computer-180953979/.

Mayor, Adrienne. *Gods and Robots: Myths, Machines and Ancient Dreams of Technology*. Princeton, NJ: Princeton University Press, 2018.

McCulloch, Lindsey. "Antique Myth, Early Modern Mechanism: The Secret History of Spenser's Iron Man." In *The Automaton in English Renaissance Literature*, edited by Wendy Beth Hyman, 95–122. Farnham, UK: Routledge, 2011.

Merlet, Jean-Pierre. "A Historical Perspective of Robotics." In *International Symposium on History of Machines and Mechanisms: Proceedings*, edited by Marco Ceccarelli, 379–86. Cassino: Kluwer Academic, 2000.

Miles, Donna. "Iron Man." *Army Technology* 2, no. 3 (May/June 2014): 10–11.

Newman, Jared, and Matt Peckham. "E3 Hidden Gems: Our Sleeper Picks for 2014." *Time*, June 16, 2014. https://time.com/2873244/e3-best-indie-games/.

Pal Robotics. "Talos." 2020. https://pal-robotics.com/robots/talos/.

Papadopoulos, John. "Talos." In *Lexicon iconographicum mythologiae classicae*, 834–37. Zurich: Artemis & Winkler, 1994.

Perez Garcia, Marta, Sarita Saffon Lopez and Hector Donis. "Everybody Is Talking about Virtual Assistants, But How Are People Really Using Them?" In *Proceedings of the 32nd International BCS Human Computer Interaction Conference (HCI)*, 1–5. Belfast: BCS Learning and Development, 2018.

Plato. "Minos." In *Plato in Twelve Volumes*. Vol. 12, edited by W. R. M. Lamb. Cambridge, MA: Harvard University Press, 1925.

Pomian, Joanna. "Portrait de groupe avec robot." *Terminal* 37 (1988): 13–14.

Richardson, B. S., ed. *Phase I Report: DARPA Exoskeleton Program*. Oak Ridge, TN: Oak Ridge National Laboratory, 2004. https://info.ornl.gov/sites/publications/Files/Pub57312.pdf.

Rogers, Brett M., and Benjamin Eldon Stevens, eds. *Classical Traditions in Science Fiction*. Oxford: Oxford University Press, 2015.

Rossi, Cesare. "The Beginning of the Automation: A Brief Review on the Automatic Devices in the Hellenistic Age." In *Advances in Robot Design and Intelligent Control: Proceedings of the 24th International Conference on Robotics in Alpe-Adria-Danube Region (RAAD)*, edited by Theodor Borangiu, 59–67. Cham: Springer International, 2016. https://doi.org/10.1007/978-3-319-21290-6_6.

Rossi, Cesare, Flavio Russo and Ferruccio Russo. "Automata (Towards Automation and Robots)." In *Ancient Engineers' Inventions: Precursors of the Present*, 269–302. (Cham: Springer International, 2017).

Rutgeerts, Jonas, and Nienke Scholts. "TALOS/Talos: What Sort of Future Do We Want to See Performed?" *FORUM* 25, no. 2 (2018): 3–14. http://www.forum-online.be/nummers/zomer-2018/what-sort-of-future-do-we-want-to-see-performed.

Salter, Michael. "Toys for the Boys? Drones, Pleasure and Popular Culture in the Militarisation of Policing." *Critical Criminology* 22 (2014): 163–77.

Sawday, Jonathan. *Engines of the Imagination: Renaissance Culture and the Rise of the Machine*. New York: Routledge, 2007.

Simon, Richard K. "*Star Wars* and *The Faerie Queene*." In *Trash Culture: Popular Culture and the Great Tradition*, 29–37. Berkeley: University of California Press, 1999.

Spenser, Edmund. *The Faerie Queene*. Bk. 5. London: William Ponsonbie, 1596. https://scholarsbank.uoregon.edu/xmlui/bitstream/handle/1794/784/faeriequeene.pdf.

Staretu, Ionel. "Main Stages of Evolution from Mechanical Automatic Systems to Humanoid Robot." *Journal of Mechanics Engineering and Automation* (2015): 309–16.

Vasileiadou, S., D. Kalligeropoulos and N. Karcanias. "Systems, Modelling and Control in Ancient Greece. Part 1: Mythical Automata." *Measurement and Control* 36, no. 3 (2003): 76–79.

Voudas. "Who Is Talos." Blog post, August 18, 2019. Talos Crafts. https://taloscrafts.com/who-is-talos/.

Zaides, Arkadi, et al., chor. *Talos*. 2016–18. First performed at Hebbel am Ufer, Berlin, August 30, 2017.

Index

A

Achalinotopoulos, Manos, 249
activism
    against climate change, 159–60, 161, 162, 172–73
    against racism, 146, 159
Adler, Cyrus, 36
Adorno, Teodor, 242
Agamben, Giorgio, 125–26
Alaskan Native Heritage Center, 165
Albéniz, Isaac, 236–37
Albert, Gerrard, 161
Albrecht, Glenn, 141
Alexander the Great, 145
Alexandria, Great Library of, 265, 266
Alps (dir. Lanthimos), 103
Alvanos, Raymondos, 11
Amazonia (Brazil), 161–62
American School of Classical Studies (Athens), 41, 43, 47, 48, 54
Amnesty International, 16, 152
Anaya, James, 157–58
Andreas, Heri, 148
Andronoglou, Ioannis, 236, 249–50
And the Weak Suffer What They Must? (Varoufakis), 214–15, 219
Angel, John Lawrence, 44, 47–48, 51
Angelopoulos, Theo(dor), 84–85, 114, 123–24
Anthropocene, 139–40
Antikythera mechanism, 266
antiquarianism, 23–24
antiquities
    collections of, 31, 34, 36, 41, 44
    exhibits of, 25, 42, 53–54
    protection of, 36n32, 51–52
    trade in, 26, 27, 32, 54

Apollo, 182, 184, 193. *See also* Delphi oracle
Apollodorus, 259, 260
Apollonius of Perga, 265
Apollonius of Rhodes, 259, 266–67
Archaeological Institute of America, 40, 49
Argonautica (Apollonius of Rhodes), 259, 266–67
Argyropoulos, Pericles, 31
Aristarchus, 265
Aristotle, 188, 225–26, 228–29
armor, 270–71, 272–73
artificial intelligence (AI), 267–68
Athena, 184
Athens, 107, 108, 109, 228
Attenberg (dir. Tsangari), 103, 106
austerity politics. *See also* Greece: financial crisis; neoliberalism
    effects on population, 202–3, 219
    films as reflection of, 82–83, 85, 96, 104–5
    neoliberalism and, 111, 112, 121, 124
    as retribution, 203–4, 222–23
    as tragedy, 227–29
    and welfare state, 219–20, 222
Australia
    Greek immigrants in, 1, 4–6, 8–15
    Macedonian identity in, 9, 10–11, 15
    and multiculturalism, 2, 5–6
Austria, 216–17
auto-ethnography, 2–3
automata, 265–66. *See also* Talos
Avdela, Ephe, 8
Avranas, Alexandros, 96. *See also Miss Violence*

B

Bakalaki, Alexandra, 8
Bakhshi, Massoud. *See Tehran Has No More Pomegranates*
Balkan Wars (1912–14), 236–37
"bankruptocracy", 92
Barrios, Agustín, 247
Bártok, Béla, 236–37, 242, 243
Bassot, Barbara, 2, 17
Baud-Bovy, Samuel, 249
Beaton, Roderick, 8
Benaki Museum (Athens), 42
Beneath the 12-Mile Reef (dir. Webb), 73–74
Bennett, Carolyn, 158
Berglund, Axel-Ivar, 187
Berlant, Lauren, 120–21
Beyzai, Bahram, 96. *See also Killing Mad Dogs*
Binding, Karl, 91
The Birth of Democracy (museum exhibit), 54
BLEEX project (U.S.), 272
Boeschoten, Riki van, 11–12
Bolsonaro, Jair, 162, 164
Borrows, John, 143, 165–66
Bosnia-Herzegovina, 9
Botsaris, Andreas, 4–5
Boutaris, Yiannis, 221
Brazil, 161–62
Brecht, Bertolt, 116
Brenner, Neil, 94
Bribri people (Costa Rica), 163
Bridges, Lloyd, 72, 74
Brock, Gillian, 164
Broneer, Oscar, 47
Bronze Age, 49, 184, 260
Brower, Leo, 246
Brumidi, Constantino, 27
Buitron-Oliver, Diane, 25
Bulfinch, Thomas, 263, 270–71

Bulgaria, 9
Bur, Tatiana, 266–67
Bush, George H. W., 54
Bush, George W., 54
Byron, George Gordon, Lord, 8

C

Caldwell, Luke, 273
Camp, John McK., II, 54
Camps, Oscar, 155
Canada
    climate change in, 138–39, 166
    Indigenous peoples in, 143, 157–60, 162
    Truth and Reconciliation Commission, 149, 158, 171
    universities in, 148–49
Canada's Indigenous Constitution (Borrows), 165–66
Canadian Political Science Association, 171
Canello, Taki, 249
Čapek, Karel, 267
capitalism, 91, 113. *See also* neoliberalism
    threats to, 200, 204–5
Capitalism and Freedom (Friedman), 219
Carusi's Saloon (Washington), 26
Casanowicz, Immanuel, 36, 40
Caskey, John, 47
Cass, Lewis, 31
Cattaneo, Christina, 156
censorship, 84, 85, 96
Center for Hellenic Studies (Washington), 42, 51
Central America, 163
Cesnola, Luigi Palma di, 34
Chandler, Tanis, 72
Chaney, Lon, Jr., 69, 70, 72
Chang, Heewon, 2–3

Chaniadaki, Senti (Stamatia), xvii
Chartrand, Paul, 158
Cheyney, John, 66
Chicago (IL), 107–8
"Chicago" (Sandburg), 107
China, 215–16
Chrysippus, 145
cities, 106–7
  neoliberalism and, 94–95, 107–10,
    111–12
"Classical Bouquet"/*Klassiki
  anthodesmi* (Contaxaki), 28–29, 31
Cleland, Andrea, 15, 17–18
Clement, Paul, 47
climate change, 138–42, 148
  activism against, 159–60, 161, 162,
    172–73
  in Canada, 138–39, 166
  as global crisis, 140–41, 143, 153
  and human rights, 150–51, 153–54,
    164
  and Indigenous peoples, 139, 140,
    142–43, 171–72, 186–87
  in Mediterranean, 139, 142, 150–
    54
  refugees from, 139, 153, 154, 155–
    56, 215–16
Climate Clock, 141–42
Climate Emergency Declaration
  (2016), 142
Clinton, Hillary Rodham, 52
Clogg, Richard, 8
The Cloud (dir. Demetrius), 85, 112
Cocoris, John, 66
Cohen, John, 267
Columbian Institute for the Promotion
  of Arts and Sciences (Washington),
  24
Communist Party (Greece), 12, 13, 83
compassion fatigue, 148, 155–56
Conon of Samos, 265
Constantine II, King of Greece, 51

Constantou, Petros, 151–52
Constantoulis, Nestor, 47
constructivism, 10
Contaxaki, Elisavet, 25, 28–31
Corcoran, William Wilson, 32–33
Corcoran Gallery of Art (Washington),
  32–33, 49
cosmopolitanism, 164
  Eurocentric, 144–46, 160
  Indigenous, 157, 165–66, 171, 172,
    173
  and migrants, 155–57
  and neo-colonialism, 144–45
  as racist, 146, 160–61
Cotsiolis, Costas, 247
Countdown 2°C Clock, 141–42
The Cow (dir. Mehrjui), 97, 98–99
Cramer, Wolfgang, 150
Crete, 30, 31, 259–60
Croatia, 9
Ctesebius, 265
culture, 81
  austerity politics and, 219–20
  Hellenism and, 6–7, 8, 237–38,
    240, 251–52
  nationalist approach to, 236–37
Cutbush, Edward, 24
The Cycle (dir. Mehrjui), 122–23
Cynics. *See* Diogenes
Cyprus, 51

D

Daddy's War (Kacandes), 13–14
Daly, Ross, 249
Damianos, Alexis, 84–85
Damousi, Joy, 13, 14, 18
Danforth, Loring, 9–10, 12
Danze Greche (Miliaresis), 240–41
Dardenne, Luc and Jean-Pierre, 120
DARPA (Defense Advanced Research
  Projects Agency), 271–72

Debord, Guy, 126
debt, 88–90. *See also* Greece: financial crisis
decolonization, 144, 171, 173
de Falla, Manuel, 236–37
deforestation, 161–62
Deilaki, Evangelia Protonotariou, 47
Delian League, 228
Delphi oracle, 182, 183, 184, 185, 193
Demetrius, Michael. *See The Cloud*
Deng Xiaoping, 205
Diamantides, Petros, 42
diaspora (Greek)
　in Australia, 2, 3, 4–6
　identity formation in, 5–7, 17–18
　in United States, 66–68, 72
Diogenes, 138, 140, 145, 146
Dogtooth (dir. Lanthimos), 103–4, 121
Domeniconi, Carlo, 246
Donis, Hector, 267–68
Douglas, Bruce J., 260
Dragatakis, Dimitris, 245
Droz, Pierre-Jacquet, 266
Duris kylix, 34, 35
Dyens, Ronald, 246–47
Dyson, Stephen, 51

E

Earth. *See also* climate change; globalization; nature
　population distribution, 146–48
economies. *See also* "bankruptocracy"
　as contagious, 209–11, 225
　and culture, 81
　policing of, 91, 93
education
　as enculturation, 6–7, 8
　and Indigenous peoples, 148–49, 171
Egypt (ancient), 36, 192
Ehrlich, P. R., 141

Eliot, Alexander, 186
Elsipogtog First Nation (Canada), 162
Elytis, Odysseas, 238
Entezami, Ezzatollah. *See The Cow*
entrepreneurialism
　in films, 98, 121–24
　under neoliberalism, 86, 95, 106, 109, 112, 219
environment. *See* climate change
Espinosa Garcés, María Fernanda, 166
Euripides, 227–28, 229
Eurocentrism, 146, 154
Euromed Rights, 153–54
European Central Bank, 201, 203, 207
European Commission, 11–12, 201
European Union
　and climate refugees, 154–55
　defensive systems, 269–70
　and Greek financial crisis, 79, 85, 86, 201–2, 209–11, 220–22
　and neoliberalism, 205–6
Evans, Robert, 43

F

The Faerie Queene (Spenser), 263
Fallaci, Oriana, 213–14
Fampas, Dimitris, 238–40
"Fantasia on a Thracian Folksong" (Andronoglou), 249–50
Faraone, Christopher, 262–63
fascism, 205, 218–19
Fatolitis, Philip, 73
Feldary, Eric, 72
Felton, Cornelius Conway, 27
Fields of Wheat, Hills of Blood (Karakasidou), 16–17
films. *See also specific films, actors, and directors*
　approach to viewing, 81–82, 126–27

austerity politics in, 82–83, 85, 96, 104–5
censorship of, 84, 85, 96
delusion in, 98–99, 101
as discourse medium, 79–80
entrepreneurialism in, 98, 112–24
Greek, 79, 84–85, 96, 104–5
"Greeks" in, 65–66, 68–69, 72, 73, 74–75
Iranian, 79, 84, 85, 96–102, 117–18
  as narrative, 80–81, 124–26
  neoliberalism and, 87, 96
  neoliberalism in, 96–102, 122–23
  and politics, 84–85, 97–99, 123, 124, 127
  as reflection of reality, 82–83, 124
  revolution in, 116–17, 119–20
  vengeance narratives in, 116–20
Fiske, John, 81
Flores Silva, Fabián, 165
Flouda, Georgia, 36
folk music, 235–36
  influence of, 237, 239–41, 243, 245–47, 249–50
Forbes, Edward W., 40
Forte, Maximilian C., 146
Four Greek Images (Tzortzinakis), 247–48
Four Wives – One Man (dir. Persson Sarvestani), 99–100, 102, 121
France, 205
Frantz, Alison, 47
freedom. *See* neoliberalism
Freer, Charles Lang, 40
Friedman, Milton, 87, 92, 219
Fritzl, Josef, 104
Frosh, Paul, 17
Furtwängler, Adolf, 36

G

Gaddafi, Muammar, 154
Galanakis, Yannis, 32
Gathii, James T., 171–72
Gaye, Lisa, 75
Gekas, Panos, 249
The Genealogy of Morals (Nietzsche), 113–14
The Geneva Consensus (Lamy), 215, 223–24
Geneva School, 205. *See also* neoliberalism; *individual members*
George, Anthony, 75
Germany, 201, 222
Giddens, Anthony, 248
Gidley, Ben, 3
Ginastera, Alberto, 246
Gleason, Regina, 74, 75
Glinka, Mikhail, 236–37
Globalists (Slobodian), 208, 218
globalization, 172–73
  and music, 246, 251
  in neoliberal agenda, 215, 218, 223–24
global warming. *See* climate change
Gods and Robots (Mayor), 267, 270
Golden Dawn, 105, 151
Gonatos, John, 72
Gonatos, Michael, 72
Good Will Come from the Sea (Ikonomou), 198–200, 214
Grace, Virginia, 47
Graham, Helen, 189, 190
Graves, Peter, 73
"Grecomans", 12–13
Greco-Turkish War (1919–22), 4
Greece, ancient. *See also* Greece, modern
  Bronze Age in, 49, 184, 260
  practices/beliefs, 183–84, 187, 189
  technology, 258, 265–66

Greece, modern. *See also* Greece: financial crisis *(below)*
   Civil War (1946–49), 2, 12, 13, 15–16, 200n11
   climate change and, 150
   under the Colonels, 51, 103, 104–5, 116, 248
   compared with Iran, 83–85
   and environmental refugees, 151–52
   films from, 79, 84–85, 102–5
   Germany and, 201, 222
   as idea, 6–9
   immigrants from, 1, 4–6, 8, 12–14, 65–67, 104
   and minorities, 6, 11, 15, 16–17
   politics of, 83–84, 109, 237–38, 241, 245
Greece: financial crisis, 78, 92, 201–3. *See also* austerity politics; neoliberalism
   as contagion, 209–11, 225
   effects, 202–3, 219–20
   European bailout, 79, 85, 92, 201–2, 222
   global reach, 82, 93
Greece Through the Stereoscope (Richardson), 53
Greek-Americans, 65–67. *See also* United States
   as stereotypes, 65–66, 68–69, 72, 73, 74–75
Greek Costumes and Embroideries (museum exhibit), 42
The Greek Miracle (museum exhibit), 53–54
Greek Orthodox Church, 183
   in Australia, 1, 4–6
   in the United States, 67–68, 72
Grieg, Edvard, 236–37
guitar music, 235–36, 238–39, 246–47, 252

H

Haberler, Gottfried, 217–18
Hagman, Larry, 74, 75
Hamilakis, Yannis, 55
Hansen, Christian, 27
harmony, 185–87
Hartley, John, 81
Hatzikyriakos-Gikas, Nikos, 238
Haupt, Paul, 36
Hayek, Friedrich von, 87, 218–19, 222, 226–27
healing
   breath and, 183, 187, 188, 190–92
   divine, 182, 184–85, 187–89
   energy-based, 189–93
   holistic, 182, 188
   nature and, 190, 192
   in Zululand, 181–82, 185, 187, 190–92, 193
health
   austerity politics and, 202–3
   beliefs about, 185, 187, 189
HeartMath Institute, 192–93
Hedrick, Charles, 54
Hellenic League for Human Rights, 207–8
Hellenism
   cultural, 237–38, 240, 251–52
   diasporic, 5–7, 8
   musical, 237–38, 240–41, 242, 250–52
Hellenization, 6–9, 12–13, 16
Henry, Joseph, 26–27, 32
Henry, Mary, 27
Hephaestus, 259, 262
Hero(n) of Alexandria, 265–66
Hesiod, 258
Hestia, 189
Higher Technical School (Alexandria), 266
Hill, John Henry, 30

Hipparchus, 265
Hirshhorn, Joseph, 44
history, 8, 95–96. *See also* antiquities
History of the Peloponnesian War (Thucydides), 215
Hoche, Alfred, 91
Homer, 183, 262
Howland, Richard Hubbard, 42, 44, 48–49, 51
human rights
  climate change and, 150–51, 153–54, 164
  neoliberalism and, 206–8, 210, 211–12, 215–16
  United Nations committee on, 150–51
Human Rights Watch, 16, 152

I

Iavazzo, Christos, 267
ichor, 261–62
identity formation, 9–10
  archaeology and, 36
  in diaspora, 5–7, 17–18
  Greek/Hellenic, 5–9, 12–14, 52
  Macedonian vs. Greek, 9, 10–11, 12–13, 15
Ikonomou, Christos, 198–200, 214
Illimani, Inti, 247
illness, 185, 187, 189. *See also* healing; health
immigrants (Greek), 104. *See also* migrants
  in Australia, 1, 4–6, 8–15
  in United States, 65–67
Impressionism (in music), 238, 241
Indigenous peoples, 139. *See also specific groups*
  as activists, 159–60, 161, 162
  in Canada, 143, 157–60, 162
  climate change and, 139, 140, 142–43, 171–72, 186–87
  as cosmopolitan, 157, 165–66, 171, 172, 173
  education and, 148–49, 171
  healing practices, 181–82
  knowledge systems, 183
  and the land, 161, 162–66
  and nature, 143–44, 157
  neo-colonialism and, 139, 140, 149, 171
  racism against, 157–59
  resurgence of, 157, 159–60, 161–62
individualism. *See* cosmopolitanism
Indonesia, 148
Intergovernmental Panel on Climate Change (IPCC), 142, 162–63
International Circumpolar Council (ICC), 172
International Federation of Human Rights, 207–8
International Monetary Fund (IMF), 201–2
Inuit, 139, 166–69. *See also* Nunavut
Inuit Qaujimajatuqangit (IQ), 166, 167–68, 169, 170
Iran
  compared with Greece, 83–85
  films from, 79, 84, 85, 96–102, 117–18
  land reform in, 97–98
  neoliberalism in, 96–98, 113
  under Pahlavi regime, 97–98, 109, 122
  politics of, 78, 83–84, 96–97, 109
  urban life in, 108–9
Irniq, Piita (Peter), 168, 169, 170
Iron Man, 265, 272–73
*isangoma*s (Zulu healers), 181–82, 184, 190
Isfahan (Iran), 108

Italy, 154–55
Ives, Charles, 243

J

Jakarta (Indonesia), 148
Jameson, Fredric, 246, 250–51
Janáček, Leoš, 242
Jason and the Argonauts (dir. Chaffey), 265
Johnston, Alan, 183
judgment, 225–27

K

Kacandes, Irene, 13–14
Kalomiris, Manolis, 236–37, 239, 240, 245
Kant, Immanuel, 146
Karaguna (Fampas), 239–40
Karakasidou, Anastasia, 16–17
Karamanlis, Konstantinos, 241
Karimi, Keywan, 110. *See also Writing on the City*
Karzai, Anas, xvii
Katsikiotis, Panagiotis, 249
Kermode, Mark, 119
Kerpius, Pamela, 156
Kesler-D'Amours, Jillian, 157
Killing Mad Dogs (dir. Beyzai), 117–18
The Killing of a Sacred Deer (dir. Lanthimos), 117, 118–20, 126
Kimiayi, Masoud, 117
Kitroeff, Alexander, 241
Koeppen, Adolph Ludvig, 26–27
Koliopoulos, Yiannis, 250
Kolokotronis, Theodoros, 8
Kontoglou, Fotis, 238
Koperqualuk, Lisa, 172
Kotsko, Adam, 87, 89
Koumaris, John, 47–48

L

labor, 215–18
Lambrinidis, Stavros, 52
Lamy, Pascal, 208–11, 215, 223–24
Langley, Samuel P., 38
Lanthimos, Yorgos, 96, 103. *See also specific films*
League of Nations, 205
leftists. *See* Communist Party
Leith, Denise, 2, 17
Leitner, Helga (et al.), 88–89, 91–92
Lemos (Greece), 3
Lenin, Vladimir Ilyich, 120
Lenoir, Tim, 273
Lheidli T'enneh First Nation (Canada), 159
Library of Alexandria, 265, 266
Libya, 154
Lines (dir. Mazomenos), 85
Little England (dir. Voulgaris), 124
Liz-Va (Dragatakis), 245
London Debt Agreement (1953), 222
Luce, Clare Boothe, 79

M

Macedonia, Republic of (Yugoslavia), 9
Macedonians (Greek), 9–11, 17–18
  as immigrants, 4, 10–11, 12
Makovenyi, Steven, 42
Malabou, Catherine, 113–16, 120
Mamangakis, Nikos, 248
Mammelis, Christos, 43
Māori (New Zealand), 161
Marcy, William, 31
Marinatos, Spyridon, 47
Markezinis, Spyros, 42
Markopoulos, Giannis, 248
Martin, Frank, 239
Maryland Historical Society, 25

Mashhad (Iran), 108
Mason, Otis, 36
The Masterbuilder (Kalomiris), 237, 238
Mathews, Damon, 141–42
Mati (child from Mali), 156
Mattox (cartoonist), 155–56
Mavrogordatos, George, 238
Mayor, Adrienne, 267, 270
McCown, Theodore, 47
McCulloch, Lindsey, 263
McLachlin, Beverley, 157
McRaven, Bill, 273
Meany, Paul, 145
meditation, 192. *See also* healing, energy-based
Mediterranean Institute for Biodiversity and Ecology, 150
Meggers, Betty, 44
Mehrjui, Dariush. *See The Cow*; *The Cycle*
Melentis, John, 47
Melos (island), 215, 228
Melville, Herman, 263
Menton, Mary, 164
Meraclis, Michael, 250, 251
Mercouri, Melina, 51, 250
Merlet, Jean-Pierre, 268
Merlie, Melpo, 243
Merrit, Benjamin D., 47
Mesoamerican Alliance of Peoples and Forests (AMPB), 163
Metaxas, Ioannis, 6, 11, 12
Mexi, Maria, 219
Mexico, 207
migrants. *See also* immigrants
  in China, 215–16
  cosmopolitanism and, 155–57
  dehumanization of, 139, 153, 154, 155–56
Migrants of the Mediterranean, 156–57

Miliaresis, Gerasimos, 238–39, 240–41
The Military-Entertainment Complex (Lenoir and Caldwell), 273
Millennium Development Goals, 143
Mining the Museum (museum exhibit), 25
minorities, 6, 11–12, 15, 16–17
Mises, Ludwig von, 216, 217, 218. *See also* Geneva School
Miss Violence (dir. Avranas), 85, 102–3
Mitsotakis, Kyriakos, 68
modernism. *See also* postmodernism
  in Iran, 108–9
  in music, 238, 241–42, 243–44, 246
Montenegro, 9
Moore, Terry, 73
Mordecai, Erin, 163–64
Moreno Torroba, Federico, 239
Mousiki (magazine), 236
museums. *See specific museums and exhibits*
music. *See also specific artists and pieces*
  avant-garde/modernist, 239, 241–46
  folk, 235–36
  folk influences in, 237, 239–41, 243, 245–47, 249–50
  globalization and, 246, 251
  for guitar, 235–36, 238–39, 246–47, 252
  Hellenism in, 237–38, 240–41, 242, 250–52
  Impressionist, 238
  multicultural, 248–49, 251
  nationalist approach to, 236–41, 242, 250–51
  and politics, 248
  postmodern, 246–50, 251, 252

Mussolini, Benito, 6
Mutwa, Credo, 191–92
Mycenae, 42
Mylonas, George, 42, 47

N

Naderi, Amir. *See Tangsir*
narratives
   films as, 80–81, 124–26
   of vengeance, 116–20
National Council of Music (Greece), 240
National Gallery of Art (Washington), 53–54
National Institution for the Promotion of Science (Washington), 24
National Inuit Climate Change Strategy, 168–69
nationalism (cultural), 236–41, 242, 250–51
National Museum of Natural History (Washington), 34, 35, 40, 41, 42, 44, 50
National Observatory of Athens, 275
National School of Music (Greece), 236–37, 244
nature
   harmony with, 186–87
   and healing, 190, 192
   Indigenous peoples and, 143–44, 157
   personhood of, 157, 161
   as unifying force, 173
Naufraghi senza volto (Cattaneo), 156
neo-colonialism, 139–40
   cosmopolitanism and, 144–45
   and Indigenous peoples, 139, 140, 149, 171
neoliberalism. *See also* austerity politics; capitalism
   agency under, 113, 118, 119, 121
   application of, 87–88, 89, 92, 93–94
   and austerity, 111, 112, 121, 124
   and cities, 94–95, 107–10, 111–12
   defining, 85–87, 89–90, 219
   entrepreneurship under, 86, 95, 106, 109, 112, 121–24, 219
   ethics of, 225–26
   in Europe, 205–6
   and film, 87, 96
   in film, 96–102, 122–23
   and globalization, 215, 218, 223–24
   global reach of, 91, 92–93, 206–8, 218–19, 223–24
   and history, 95–96
   and human rights, 206–8, 210, 211–12, 215–16
   ideas behind, 87–88, 113, 204–5
   and the individual, 90, 219–20, 221
   in Iran, 96–98, 113
   and labor, 215–18
   moral logic of, 89–91, 93, 121, 124, 208–10, 215, 221–23
   patriarchy as, 99–100
   resistance to, 95, 113, 214
   and selective permission, 111–12
   Varoufakis on, 85–87
   victim-blaming under, 90–91, 97–98, 102
   and welfare state, 219–20, 222
New Zealand/Aotearoa, 161
Ngubane, Harriet, 189
Nicomachean Ethics (Aristotle), 225–26, 228–29
Nietzsche, Friedrich, 113–15
Nomkhubulwana (Zulu god), 184
North American Free Trade Agreement (1994), 207
Norton, Charles Eliot, 40, 41
Norton, Richard, 40
Νότιος Ἦχος (Southern Sound), 249

Noys, Benjamin, 125–26
Nunavut (Canada), 143, 166–67, 168, 170. *See also* Inuit

O

Obama, Barack, 272
Obed, Natan, 168–69
Ober, Josiah, 54
Ohi (όχι) Day, 6
O'Neill, Sally, 68–69
The Origins of Modern Constitutionalism (Wormuth), 222–23
Ottoman Empire, 31

P

Pahlavi family (Iran), 97–98, 109, 122
Panourgia, Neni, 14–15, 17
Papadopoulou, Alexandra, 25
Papaioannou, Yannis G., 242, 243–44
Papandreou, George, 201
Parthenon, 184, 250
   museums and, 31, 32, 33, 38, 41, 42–43, 54
patriarchy
   in films, 99–100, 101–3, 118
   in Iran, 106
Paul, King of Greece, 42
Paul, Monica, 159
Pavsek, Christopher, 116
Peltier, Autumn, 159–60
PEN International, 16
Perec, George, 212–13, 214
Perez Garcia, Marta, 267–68
Pericles, 184
Persidis, Achilleas, 249
Persson Sarvestani, Nahid, 96. *See also Four Wives – One Man*
Petrie, Flinders, 36
philhellenes, 8, 26, 31, 47n49

Philon of Byzantium, 265
Plato, 259
Podesta, John, 150, 151
Poetics (Aristotle), 228–29
Poinsett, Joel, 24
Polanyi, Karl, 97
politics. *See also* austerity politics
   films and, 84–85, 97–99, 123, 124, 127
   of Greece, 83–84, 109, 237–38, 241, 245
   of Iran, 78, 83–84, 96–97, 109
   music and, 248
Pope, Annemarie, 42
Port Adelaide (Australia), 4–6
postmodernism (in music), 246
Poulianos, Aris, 47
power, 114, 213–14
Prespa Agreement (2018), 11
primordialism, 9–10
Pritchett, William K., 42
La Promesse (dir. L. and J.-P. Dardenne), 120–21
psyche (breath/soul), 183, 187, 188

Q

Quinn, Anthony, 66

R

racism
   activism against, 146, 159
   cosmopolitanism and, 146, 160–61
   effects of, 153, 157–58
   and environment, 164
   against Indigenous peoples, 157–59
Rackete, Carola, 154–55
Radin, Michael, 15
Rangavis, Alexandros Rizos, 32
Rashidi, Rouzbeh, 115

Rau, Charles, 33
Reagan, Ronald, 205
refugees (environmental), 142, 150–57. *See also* migrants
Regas, George, 69
Renwick, James, Jr., 26
repetition, 113–16, 117, 120, 123, 126
representation, 124–25
"residence time", 153, 158–59
resistance. *See also* activism; revolution
  to capitalism, 200
  to Eurocentrism, 146, 154
  to neoliberalism, 95, 113, 214
revenge, 116–20, 222–23
revolution, 113, 114, 115, 120, 124
  in films, 116–17, 119–20
Richardson, Rufus B., 53
Rigos, Alkis, 238
Ripley, Dillon, 51
Ritchie, Anthony Damian, 243
The Road to Serfdom (Hayek), 218–19
Robinson, David, 47
robots, 267–68, 271
Rodrigo, Joaquin, 247
Roebling, John A., II, 41
Roebling, Washington, 41
Roland, Gilbert, 73
Romanou, Katy, 243, 245
Rosetta (dir. L. and J.-P. Dardenne), 120–21
Ross, Ludwig, 27
Rossi, Cesare, 266
Roudometof, Victor, 3–4
Royal Canadian Mounted Police (RCMP), 162
R.U.R. (Čapek), 267
Rutgeerts, Jonas, 270

S

Saffon Lopez, Sarita, 267–68

Saljoughi, Sara, 97
Salvini, Matteo, 154, 155
Sampson, Alden, 40–41
Samson, George W., 33
Sandburg, Carl, 107
San people (southern Africa), 190
Santos, Juan Manuel, 140–41
Sawday, Jonathan, 266
Schliemann, Heinrich, 36
Schliemann, Sophia, 36
Schoenberg, Arnold, 239, 243, 245–46
Scholts, Nienke, 270
Sea Hunt (TV series), 72, 74–75
Second World War, 6
Seferis, George, 238
Segovia, Andrés, 239
Serbia, 9
Shahid-Saless, Sohrab, 96. *See also Utopia*
Shear, Theodore Leslie, 47
Shoe, Lucy, 47
Sibelius, Jean, 236–37
Silver Springs (FL), 74, 75
Simon, Mary, 139–40
Simon, Richard K., 263
Simonides, 258
Simpsi, Aspasia, 6, 7
Sinclair, Murray, 149, 158
Siopsi, Anastasia, 251
16 Fathoms Deep (dir. Schaeffer), 68–70
16 Fathoms Under (dir. Allen), 70–73
Skalkottas, Nikos, 241–42
slavery, 23–24, 25, 228–29
Slavs, 11, 12–13
Slimani, Leïla, 152
Sliomis, Thomas, 246
Slobodian, Quinn, 208, 218
Slovenia, 9
Smetana, Bedřich, 236–37
Smith, Adam, 89
Smith, Derek J., 270

Smithson, James, 26
Smithsonian Institution. *See also individual branches and staff members*
   collections, 27, 32–36, 39–41, 49–50
   exhibits, 25, 27, 38, 42–43, 53–54, 55
   and Greek heritage, 26–27, 52
   seminars and lectures, 49, 54–55
snakes, 182, 192
Society for the Preservation of Greek Heritage (Washington), 49, 54
solastalgia, 141
solidarity, 166
   human, 152, 210
   Indigenous, 146, 162
   neoliberalism and, 199, 210, 219–21
Sonata for Flute and Guitar (Papaioannou), 243–44
Southeast Asia, 148
Southern Sound (Νότιος Ἦχος), 249
Soviet Union, 13, 205, 206
Spence, Carroll, 28
Spenser, Edmund, 263
sponge diving, 66–68
Stalin, Joseph, 13
Stamm, Richard, 38
Stanley, Fiona, 142
Star Trek (TV series), 265
Star Wars (dir. Lucas), 263, 265
Stevens, Gorham Phillip, 43
Stoics, 145
Stories of Gods and Heroes (Bulfinch), 263, 270–71
Stravinsky, Igor, 242
Sucre Romero, Levi, 163, 164
supernatural, 185, 187
Symposium on the Greeks (2019), xvii, 82
Syria, 151, 154

Syriza party, 92. *See also* Varoufakis, Yanis

T

Tait, Karla, 162
Talos, 257–75
   in ancient accounts, 258–63
   in art, 261, 267, 275
   as automaton, 265–67
   in dance, 269, 274
   as inspiration, 268–74
   as robot, 267–68, 271
   as science fiction, 265, 273
TALOS (Tactical Assault Light Operator Suit), 272–73
Talos missiles (U.S.), 271
The Talos Principle (video game), 273
TALOS project (Europe), 269–70
Tamis, Anastasios, 10–11
Tangsir (dir. Naderi), 117, 120
Tarbell, Frank, 34–35
Tarpon Springs (FL), 66–68, 72
   as movie setting, 70–71, 73, 74, 75
Tawse, Sybil, 267
Te Awa Tupua (New Zealand), 161
Tehran, 108–9
Tehran Has No More Pomegranates (dir. Bakhshi), 109–10
television, 81. *See also specific programs*
   "Greeks" portrayed on, 72, 74–75
Tester, Frank, 170
Thatcher, Margaret, 205
Theodore, Nik, 94
Thompson, Dorothy B. and Homer, 47
Thucydides, 215
Tito, Josip Broz, 9
Todd, Zoe, 153, 159, 160–61
To Those Born After (dir. Pavsek), 116
tragedy, 227–28, 229
Tramountanas, George (North), 4

Tramountanis, Angelo, 152
Travelling (Andronoglou), 249–50
Travlos, John, 43
The Trojan Women (Euripides), 227–28, 229
Trump, Donald, 90
Tsagaris, Elias, 249
Tsangari, Athina Rachel. *See Attenberg*
Tsarouchis, Giannis, 238
Tsetsos, Markos, 237, 238, 242, 247
Tsougras, Costas, 241–42
Turina, Joaquín, 239
Tyquiengco, Marina, 165
Tziovas, Dimitris, 237
Tzortzinakis, Kyriakos, 247–48

U

Uganda, 188
Ulyanov, Aleksandr Ilyich, 120
Ulysses' Gaze (dir. Angelopoulos), 123–24
Union of Greek Composers, 240
United Nations
    High Commissioner for Refugees (UNHCR), 142
    Human Rights Committee, 150–51
    Intergovernmental Panel on Climate Change (IPCC), 142, 162–63
    International Day of the World's Indigenous Peoples, 144
    International Organization for Migration, 154
United States. *See also* Greek-Americans
    Civil War, 32
    and climate change, 172–73
    Defense Department, 270–72
    and European cultural heritage, 24–25
    and Greece, 51–52, 54
    NAFTA and, 207
    slavery in, 23–24, 25
uNkhulunkulu (Zulu god), 184
Usha, K. B., 216
Usher, David, 141–42
Utopia (dir. Shahid-Saless), 100–102, 121

V

Van Beek, Gus, 42–44, 49
Vanderpool, Eugene, 43
Vaneigem, Raoul, 111
Vardalos, Marianne, xvii
Varoufakis, Yanis, 78, 79
    on capitalism, 91, 113
    on Greek financial crisis, 85, 86–87, 92–93, 201
    on neoliberalism, 85–87, 214–15
Vatsikopoulos, Helen, 2, 9, 17
    childhood, 4, 12–13, 14
Vaucanson, Jacques de, 266
Vega Cardenas, Yenny, 164
Veland, Siri, 169–70
Venizelos, Eleftherios, 237–38
Veremis, Thanos, 250
video games, 127, 273
Vivlios, Dimitrios, 6
Voulgaris, Pantelis, 84–85, 96, 124

W

W, or the Memory of Childhood (Perec), 212–13, 214
Wagner, Robert, 73
Walton, William, 246, 247
Ward, Shelby, 139–40
Washington (DC), 23–24, 25. *See also specific institutions*
Washington, Hayden, 141
Watt-Cloutier, Sheila, 169

Webster Smith, Franklin, 38
The Weeping Meadow (dir. Angelopoulos), 123
welfare state, 219–20, 222
Western Civilization: Origins and Traditions (museum exhibit), 42
Wet'suwet'en First Nation (Canada), 162
Whanganui people (New Zealand), 161
Wikwemikong First Nation (Canada), 159
Williams, John (guitarist), 247
Williams, Raymond, 124
Wilson, Fred, 25
Wilson, James Frank, 36
Wilson, Thomas, 33–34, 36
women
    in China, 215–16
    in Iran, 99–102, 106
workers, 215–18
World Bank, 143, 207
World Health Organization (WHO), 190
World Trade Organization (WTO), 207. *See also* Lamy, Pascal
Wormuth, F. D., 222–23
Writing on the City (dir. Karimi), 110–11
Wynter, Sylvia, 160

X

Xylouris, George "Psarogiorgis", 249

Y

Yannaras, Christos, 251–52
Yu, Yeon Jung, 215–16
Yugoslavia, 9

Z

Zaides, Arkadi, 269
Zenakos, Augustino, 248–49
Zeno of Citium, 145
Zerefos, Christos, 142
Zeus, 184, 189, 258, 259
Zorba the Greek (dir. Cacoyannis), 66, 250
Zululand
    ancestor reverence in, 182, 185, 188, 189, 190–91
    healers in, 181–82, 185, 187, 190–92, 193
    spiritual/cosmological beliefs, 184, 185, 186–87, 189